# Caché

# ObjectScript

# and MUMPS

# Technical Learning Manual

This book serves as an explanation of Caché ObjectScript and the MUMPS programming language. It is designed as both a comprehensive learning guide and a technical reference manual. This is useful to programmers of any level, whether you are new to the language or an experienced developer looking for more information on Caché Objects, containing hundreds of code examples . . . the perfect desk top reference.

Printed and Distributed by CreateSpace.

ISBN-13: 978-1466499089
ISBN-10: 1466499087

# Forward

This book is written for all those who want a *Caché ObjectScript/Caché Objects and MUMPS* book for the beginner.  Although it starts from the very basic commands, it does progress to the point that even the most experienced programmer will learn.  It is not an exhaustive treatment of the subjects covered. It serves as a desktop reference with many examples, the concepts are taught (as far as possible) through examples. It is very much an example driven book.

The book has been a 12 year labor of love for me, howbeit infuriating  at times. I hope you enjoy working through it as much as I did writing it. I invite your comments and suggestions and will make every attempt to respond.

Paul "Mike" Kadow 2012 – mike@cosmumps.org

www.cosmumps.org

# Ackowledgements

I wish to acknowledge the follow people (and company) who have contributed to this book:

Peter Armstrong, Paul Bradney, Ed de Moel, Deborah Graham, John Kadow,

Bill Losey, Dick Martel, Anil Mathew, John Mitchell, John Reid, Gene Scheffler,

Andy Shaw, Bob Shetler, Arthur B. Smith, Jack Snyder, Mark Sires, Karl Thiebolt,

Rob Tweed, Richard F. Walters, and the InterSystems Corporation.

# Special Thanks

Special thanks goes to Paul Bradney for his meticulous (and often pedantic!) attention to detail in his editing.

# Dedication

This book is dedicated to my lovely wife of 36 years; true beauty comes from the inside.

# What others are saying about *Caché ObjectScript and MUMPS*

"I've been a programmer for almost 30 years now and I'm finding your book very intuitive in learning about Caché, in both the new stuff which I'm a bumbling amateur at and even learning features about stuff I thought I already knew. "

– Paul Bradney (Futurecode Ltd.)

"In short, with the little I have read so far, I would recommend this book for both new students of the language, and for people who are moving from a non-Caché implementation to Caché, as well as for people who are starting to use the object extensions in Caché."

- Ed de Moel (Author 'M[UMPS] by Example')

"This book is aimed at users of Intersystems Caché, with many useful tips as to its effective use. I highly recommend it for Caché users."

– Richard F. Walters (Author 'M Programming, A comprehensive Guide')

"...So far there has been an acute shortage of books for developers of MUMPS/COS. This book is a great guide those who are new to the COS (Caché Object Script) as well as a great refresher for those who have been programming using MUMPS. This to my knowledge is the first book on MUMPS/Caché with a progressive learning curve for developers . . . The language is simple and there are lots of examples making it very easy to understand. This will be a great hand book for those who are starting with Caché and will really help them to realize the potential of this very efficient database to its full extent."

– Anil Mathew (Software Support & Implementation Manager for a Software Publishing Company called Fayafi Infomatic Co LLc. based on Dubai. )

"This book is a rollicking ride through the wild new territory of Caché & MUMPS, where we are all bound to be battling scorpions for years. It takes you through basic concepts so you understand the purposes of the Caché & MUMPS design, and then into each area so you know your way around. Like all amazing and great tech books, it replaces dry recitation with lively, memorable, fact-laden bursts of information. . ."

- Nikesh Gogia (Siemens Information Systems Ltd Bangalore India)

"This book is most timely. MUMPS, for many years the ugly-duckling of the database world, is having something of a renaissance, driven by several factors:

- the NoSQL movement that has brought non-relational databases back into vogue;

- the rise of web applications, for which a number of characteristics of MUMPS fortuitously seem tailor-made;

- the rise of Open Source software, particularly within the sector where MUMPS has always reigned supreme: healthcare;

- the cripplingly-expensive and embarrassingly high-profile failed conversions of MUMPS healthcare applications to "mainstream" languages and databases.

There are a lot of MUMPS applications in the commercial world, quietly performing their day-to-day responsibilities in a reliable and scalable way, and the above factors mean they aren't going away soon. On the contrary, enlightened developers are realising that there are new and exciting ways now available for extending the capabilities and reach of these "legacy" applications. Modern, web-based MUMPS applications are capable of being at the very leading edge in terms of their functionality, UI design, performance and scalability: it's a very exciting time to be a MUMPS developer.

All this means two things:

- we urgently need a new generation of MUMPS developers to take over the support, maintenance and extension of those applications;

- there's a lot of work available for young developers who are willing to learn about MUMPS.

Mike's book is a new and modern guide for anyone wanting to find out about this fascinating language and database to which I've been hopelessly addicted since the early 1980s and for which I've been an unrelenting advocate. It gently guides the student through the basics and provides a comprehensive coverage of the advanced aspects of the language. Importantly, it also covers the extensions of the technology that is specific to Caché.

I thoroughly recommend this book to anyone wanting to learn MUMPS, or anyone wishing to provide guidance to new staff who need to get up to speed with MUMPS. "

- Rob Tweed (M/Gateway Developments Ltd.)


"This is the book we MUMPS programmers have been waiting for. It's a great resource to help us learn and use the "new" Caché ObjectScript (COS) tools as well as being an excellent desktop reference when we are coding. The examples make the concepts very clear and enable the reader to immediately use the commands and structures of COS. At the same time, it also serves as a refresher and reference when using the older MUMPS commands and structures. The perfect tool for the MUMPS programmers who want to reinvent themselves with the latest technology."

– John Mitchell

"As an experienced MUMPS programmer, I did not know what to expect when asked to review this book. I had experience coding MUMPS in the Caché environment but no experience with Caché Object Script (COS). My first pass was to visit the COS chapters as this was all new to me. This provided me with a great overview of COS and I found myself coding tools for myself in a very short time. Next I went back to skim the first part of the book which provides a thorough foundation in MUMPS coding. The examples provided in this book are the better than any I have seen in tutorials and other MUMPS publications. The author has created an exceptional MUMPS and COS reference which will be a much needed resource for today's MUMPS and COS programmers."

– Bill Losey

"This book is a good start, middle, and end (if programmers ever consider themselves at the end of learning a language). There are topics that will take you from a newbie to a guru and provide new information at every level. Topics I thought I knew well were delivered in an interesting way. Topics I haven't used were easy to grasp and apply in practice. This book will be referred to a lot every day as I create the routines we use for the reports users require. It's good to work in a language that is so easy to learn and so powerful that it gives the users the data they need. Thank you for a book that helps me look really, really good at what I do!"

- Deborah Graham (Senior Programmer, UMass Memorial Health Care)

I am grateful for all the reviewers who took time out of their lives to review this book. I am also very thankful for their gracious words.

– Paul "Mike" Kadow

# Table of Contents

# *Chapter 1 Basic Concepts I*

The first two chapters explain **Basic Concepts** of Caché ObjectScript (COS). They give definitions, basic commands, structure and flow of COS Programs.

## *What is MUMPS?*

**MUMPS** is short for *Massachusetts General Hospital Utility Multi-Programming System*. Some refer to it as just "M". *MUMPS* was developed at Massachusetts General Hospital in the 1960s for use in the Healthcare Industry. MUMPS is a fast and efficient database system and a flexible programming interface language.

## *What is M?*

**M** was thought of as a shorter, perhaps more elegant name for MUMPS. It was short lived.

## *What is Caché?*

**Caché** is a product offered by InterSystems Corporation, *www.intersystems.com*. InterSystems Corporation (creators of Caché) is a privately held software company based in Cambridge, Massachusetts. It was founded in 1978 and was one of the original vendors of M-technology (aka MUMPS), with a product called ISM.

Over the years, InterSystems acquired several other MUMPS implementations: DTM from Data Tree; DSM from Digital Equipment Corporation; and MSM from Micronetics. InterSystems started combining features from these implementations into one they called OpenM and later called Caché.

One of the genuine strengths of the Caché Multi-Dimensional Data Engine and MUMPS database is its ability to process large amounts of data, (up to the terabyte range) with excellent performance.

## *Caché ObjectScript (COS)*

**Caché ObjectScript** or "COS" is one of the programming languages for Caché, similar to the *MUMPS Programming Language*.

---

### *A word about the Lexicon*

MUMPS is an acronym and as such should be written in all capital letter.

Caché should have the accent above the "e", without the accent the word means temporary storage.

---

## Advantages of Caché

> It has excellent string handling capabilities

> It makes use of sparse arrays

> Programming is easy and fast

> It processes large amounts of data quickly

> It has the capability of using alphabetic as well as numeric subscripts in arrays

> It makes use of dynamic code generation

## Disadvantages and Criticisms of Caché

> The ability for "fast and easy coding" may promote cryptic routines

> Dangerous Kill (delete) command with no "undelete"

> Naked database indicators or naked references may make program maintenance troublesome; (Naked references are shortcut methods to access data on disk)

## Quote by Arthur B. Smith on Databases

"Databases that have a lot of many-to-many relations, and/or a lot of sparse information (fields that are more often empty than filled in) do not fit the relational model well. While a relational database can represent this data, it does it with great complexity or inefficiency. The sparse hierarchical array structure assumed by M is a much more natural fit for this type of data."

-Arthur B. Smith
From M Technology and MUMPS Language FAQ,
used with permission.

## Variable Manipulation and Interrogation

Like other computer programming languages, COS uses **Variables** and the values they represent to control programming. *Variables* are elements that represent data values. Manipulating and interrogating variables is at the root of programming. *Variable* names are case-sensitive.

### Set command

The **Set** command is the primary method of assigning values to variables. A variable consists of the variable name and the value that the variable represents.

**Example 1-1 Setting variable X to a value with the Set command**

```
Set X=12
Set X="ABC"
```

In Example 1-1, variable X is first set to 12 and then to "ABC" using the *Set* command. Notice that when setting a variable to a numeric value, no quotation marks are necessary. However, when setting a variable to an alphanumeric value, double quotation marks are required.

## Write command

### Write command displays the value of variables

**Example 1-2 Write command displays the value of variables**

```
Set X=12
Write X
12

Set X="ABC"
Write X
ABC
```

In Example 1-2, the *Write* command displays the value of variable X. When variable X is set to 12, the *Write* command displays 12, and when the variable is set to "ABC" (using quotes of course), ABC is displayed.

### Write command with carriage return line feed

When the exclamation point "!" is inserted after a *Write* command, a carriage return and line feed combination is produced. Note in Example 1-3, that a comma separates the exclamation point from the variable "X".

**Example 1-3 Write command with carriage return line feed**

```
Set X=12
Write !,X
                    ;carriage return and line feed inserted here
12
```

Example 1-3 demonstrates the *Write* command with the exclamation point producing a carriage return line feed. A semi-colon is a way of including a comment line, more on comment lines in Chapter 2.

### Write command displays all variables

To display all variables - use the *Write* command with no parameters.

**Example 1-4 Write command displays all variables**

```
Set X=12
Set Y=13
Set Z=14
W                       ;Write command with no parameters
X=12
Y=13
Z=14
```

In Example 1-4, the *Write* command with no parameters displays all variables.

## Multiple commands

**Example 1-5 Multiple commands**

```
Set X=12,Y=13,Z=14 ;single Set command with variables separated by commas

Write !,X,!,Y,!,Z          ;single Write command with variables
                           ;separated by commas

12
13
14
```

Example 1-5 demonstrates how to combine *Set* commands and *Write* commands separated by commas.

# If command

## If command with numeric operands

As in other computer programming languages, the **If** command is the primary decision maker.

**Example 1-6 If command with numeric operands**

```
Set X=12
If X=12 Set X=13
Write X
13
```

Example 1-6 sets the variable X to the value of 12. Then the *If* command determines whether X is equal to 12 and because it is, it sets X to 13. The *Write* command then displays the value of X, which is 13.

## If command with alphanumeric operands

**Example 1-7 If command with alphanumeric operands**

```
Set X="ABC"
If X="ABC" Set X="XYZ"
Write X
XYZ
```

Example 1-7 is the same as Example 1-6, except that it uses alphanumeric data. Whenever alphanumeric data is being referenced, quotation marks are required.

## Structured Code with If command

Caché ObjectScript (COS) allows for a more contemporary style of programming, called *Structured Code*.

## Structured Code with If command

**Example 1-8 Structured Code with If command**

```
Set X=12
If (X=12) {Set X=13}
Write X
13
```

In Example 1-8, notice the placement of the parentheses () and curly brackets {}. The format of *Structured Code* using the *If* command is:

➢ If (decision code) {action code}

The decision code is inside of the parentheses, and the action code is inside of the curly brackets. If the *decision code* is true, the *action code* is executed. Using *Structured Code*, the curly brackets may occur on any line and may include multiple lines of code. *Structured Code* enhances readability.

# Plus sign (+) operator

Typically, the Plus sign (+) adds two numbers together. This is true in COS, but COS uses it in other ways as well.

## Plus sign, set the variable X to a value of +12

**Example 1-9 Plus sign, set the variable X to a value of +12**

```
Set X=+12
Write X
12
```

In Example 1-9, the variable X is set to plus 12. Since 12 is already numeric and is assumed to be positive, nothing changes.

## Plus sign, set the variable X to a value of +"ABC"

**Example 1-10 Plus sign, set the variable X to a value of +"ABC"**

```
Set X=+"ABC"
Write X
0
```

In Example 1-10, the *Set* command sets the variable X to +"ABC". Since X is not numeric, the plus sign forces X to be numeric.

**Example 1-11 Plus sign, set the variable X to "ABC" and write +X**

```
Set X="ABC"
Write +X
0
Write X
ABC
```

In Example 1-11, the variable X is set to "ABC". However, +X is written, so the numeric value zero is written. The value of X is not changed when used this way. The variable X still contains "ABC."

**Example 1-12 Set the variable X to "ABC", if +X equals 0, write X**

```
Set X="ABC"
If +X=0 Write X
ABC
```

In Example 1-12, the variable X is set to "ABC". If +X equals zero, then Write X, outputs "ABC", because the value of X is not changed by the (+).

COS programmers use the *Plus Sign* often, so become familiar with it.

## Kill command

Thus far, we have learned how to set a variable to a value with the *Set* command; display that value using the *Write* command; and using the *If* command, conditionally set a variable to another value. Now we will completely delete the variable and its value.

## Kill a variable

**Example 1-13 Kill a variable**

```
Set X="ABC"
Kill X
Write X
<UNDEFINED>
```

In Example 1-13, the *Kill* command completely deletes the variable and any value that it contains. After killing the variable X, any attempt to access X results in an <UNDEFINED> error. Notice that the *Kill* command not only removes the value a variable holds, but completely removes or deletes the variable as well.

## Kill all variables

The *Kill* command used with no parameters or variables, removes all variables defined thus far.

**Example 1-14 Kill all variables**

```
Set X=12,Y=13,Z=14        ;set variables
W                         ;write all variables
X=12
Y=13
Z=14
```

```
K                          ;kill all variables

W                          ;write all variables, but none exist
<>
```

Example 1-14 shows the *Kill* command with no variables, a *Write* command with no variable produces no output because no variables exists.

You will notice the semi-colon in this example, a semi-colon means a comment and anything after it is deemed a comment. More on comments in Chapter 2.

## *Your own copy of Caché*

As I mentioned in the forward to the book, you will benefit from obtaining your own copy of a Caché system and replicating the sample code shown in this book. InterSystems Inc. allows you to download a single copy of Caché to your personal computer at no cost. This is available from www.intersystems.com.

Follow the instructions when you install Caché. After it is installed you will see a small blue cube in your system tray. Clicking on the Cube will produce a menu of options to help get you started in Caché. The menu options are:

- ➢ Getting Started
- ➢ Start Caché
- ➢ Stop Caché
- ➢ Studio
- ➢ Terminal
- ➢ System Management Portal
- ➢ Documentation
- ➢ DeepSee
- ➢ Remote System Access
- ➢ Preferred Server
- ➢ About
- ➢ Exit

I suggest for the new user looking at *Getting Started* and searching for *Tutorials* in the

*Documentation* menu entry.

## Exercises on Set, Write, If, Plus and Kill commands

Write a line of COS code that will accomplish each of the following:

> ➢ Set the variable X to the value of "ABC".
>
> ➢ Set the variable X to the value of 12.
>
> ➢ Display the value of X.
>
> ➢ Set the value of X to 13 if the current value of X is 12.
>
> ➢ Set the value of X back to 12 if the current value of plus-X is 13.
>
> ➢ Delete the X variable.

## Answers to exercises on Set, Write, If, Plus and Kill commands

**Example 1-15 Answers to Exercises**

```
Set the variable X to the value of "ABC"
Set X="ABC"

Set the variable X to the value of 12
Set X=12

Display the value of X
Write X

Set the value of X to 13 if the current value of X is 12
If X=12 Set X=13

Set the value of X back to 12 if the current value of plus-X is 13
If +X=13 Set X=12

Delete the X variable
Kill X
```

Example 1-15 shows the answers to the exercise on *Set, Write, If, Plus* and *Kill*.

## Concatenation - the underscore character

## Concatenating two Variables

To connect the value of two variables together, use the concatenate character "_" or underscore.

**Example 1-16 Concatenating two Variables**

```
Set X="My dog's name is"
Set Y="Teddy."
Set DOG=X_" "_Y
Write DOG
My dog's name is Teddy.
```

Example 1-16 demonstrates the concatenation "_" or underscore character. The variable X is "My dog's name is" and the variable Y is "Teddy". The DOG variable is set to X joined with a literal space and the variable Y. The result of setting the DOG variable is "My dog's name is Teddy."

## Concatenate versus the plus sign

The programmer needs to be careful when deciding when to use the concatenation character and when to use the plus sign.

**Example 1-17 Concatenate versus the plus sign**

```
Write "My dog's name is "_"Teddy."        ;concatenation used properly
My dog's name is Teddy

Write "My dog's name is "+"Teddy."        ;plus sign used improperly
0

Write 1_1                                 ;concatenation used improperly
11

Write 1+1                                 ;plus sign used properly
2
```

Example 1-17 shows two uses of the concatenate character and the plus sign. Generally, the concatenate character pertains to alphanumeric variables, and the plus sign pertains to numeric variables.

## Operator Precedence

*Operator Precedence* means the order in which mathematical operators are executed. In a Mathematical expression, you may have Multiplication, Addition, Subtraction, and Division. Which of these should be executed first, second, third, etc.?

The basic *Operator Precedence* of mathematics is:

**Multiplication and Division has precedence over Addition and Subtraction**

In normal mathematics when you encounter an expression like 5+7*10, the multiplication and division is executed first, and then addition and subtraction, so 5+7*10 is 75 (7*10=70+5=75). However, in Caché the *Operator Precedence* is strictly left to right, so 5+7*10=120, (5+7=12*10=120).

**Example 1-18 Operator Precedence Comparison**

```
Write 5*7+6        ;Operator Precedence in Caché same as in Mathematics
41

Write 4+6*10/5     ;Caché Operator Precedence 4+6=10, 10*10=100, 100/5=20
20

Write 4+(6*10/5)   ;Mathematical Operator Precedence: 4+(60/5)
16
```

In Example 1-18, we see examples of how Caché computes numbers compared to the mathematical *Operator Precedence*. If you want your expressions interpreted a specific way, you must use parenthesis around the expressions you want evaluated first. Although this concept seems simple enough, I would dare say there is not a Caché/MUMPs programmer alive that has not been bitten by *Operator Precedence,* keep an eye on this one.

# For Loop command

One of the most powerful and useful commands in COS is the *For* command, or the *For Loop* command. The *For Loop* command continually executes until the end condition is met. It has several formats.

## For Loop command, First Format

For variable=startvalue:incrementvalue:endvalue

In this first format, there are four elements to consider:

> ➢ Variable – the variable is the data item that is incremented throughout the process

> ➢ Startvalue – the starting value for the variable

> ➢ Incrementvalue – the increment value for the variable, typically a 1

> ➢ Endvalue – the ending value for the variable

When COS starts the loop, it sets the variable to the start value. Next, it compares the variable to the end value. If the variable is less than or equal to the end value, process the code. Then the variable is incremented. Execution of the loop continues until variable would exceed the end value.

**Example 1-19 For Loop command**

```
FOR VARIABLE=STARTVALUE:INCREMENTALVALUE:ENDVALUE CODE
```

Example 1-20 (in English) interprets the *For Loop* format from Example 1-19.

**Example 1-20 For Loop command, English interpretation**

```
Step 1: Set the VARIABLE to the STARTVALUE,
Step 2: If VARIABLE is not more than the ENDVALUE,
        Write again, otherwise stop
Step 3: Increment the VARIABLE by the INCREMENTALVALUE
Step 4: Go to Step 2
```

The next few examples expand and further illustrate the *For Loop* command.

**Example 1-21 For Loop command continued**

```
For I=1:1:3 Write I
```

Example 1-22 (in English) interprets The *For Loop* command in Example 1-21.

**Example 1-22 For Loop command interprets - "For I=1:1:3 Write I"**

```
Set variable I to 1,
Variable I is not more than the end value (3), so Write I,
Increment variable I by 1, it is now 2,
Variable I is not more than the end value (3),
    so Write I again,
Increment variable I by 1, it is now 3,
Variable I is not more than the end value (3),
    so Write I again,
At this point the loop will stop because attempting
    to incrementing variable I
    will cause it to exceed the end value of 3,
End of For loop command.
```

**Example 1-23 For Loop command output**

```
For I=1:1:3 Write I,!
1
2
3
```

Example 1-23 demonstrates the *For Loop* command and its output from Example 1-22.

Following are several more examples of the first format of the *For* command.

**Example 1-24 For Loop command example**

```
For I=4:1:7 Write I,!
4
5
6
7
```

In Example 1-24, the variable I starts at 4 and ends at 7.

**Example 1-25 For Loop command example**

```
For I=2:2:8 Write I,!
2
4
6
8
```

In Example 1-25, variable I starts at 2, is incremented by 2 and ends at 8.

**Example 1-26 For Loop command example**

```
For I=7:-1:4 Write I,!
7
6
5
4
```

In Example 1-26, variable I starts at 7, is incremented by -1 and ends at 4.

## For Loop command, Second Format

**Example 1-27 For Loop command, Second Format**

```
FOR VARIABLE="VALUE1","VALUE2","VALUE3" Write !,VARIABLE
```

Example 1-27 demonstrates the second format of the *For Loop* command. This command assigns multiple values to a variable.

**Example 1-28 Output from Example 1-27**

```
FOR VARIABLE="VALUE1","VALUE2","VALUE3" Write !,VARIABLE
VALUE1
VALUE2
VALUE3
```

As shown in Example 1-28, the second format of the *For Loop* command allows the programmer to assign multiple values to a variable and then write the variable.

## For Loop command, Third Format

**Example 1-29 For Loop command, Third Format**

```
FOR   Read VARIABLE WRITE !,VARIABLE If VARIABLE="END" QUIT
                    ;notice the two spaces after the "FOR"
```

Example 1-29 shows the third format of the *For Loop* command, also known as a *Forever Loop* command. This command will literally process forever or until the Quit condition is met. Note the two spaces after the "For". The *Forever Loop* command in Example 1-29 will read and write a variable forever until the variable equals "END".

Now suppose we ran the *For* command in Example 1-29 feeding the read command "First", "Second", "Third", and "END". The output would look like Example 1-30

**Example 1-30 For Loop command, Third Format, output**

```
FOR   Read VARIABLE WRITE !,VARIABLE If VARIABLE="END" QUIT
First
Second
Third
END
```

Example 1-30 shows the output from running the code in Example 1-29. Note that the *For* command will continue indefinitely until it receives the value "END" in the VARIABLE.

Throughout this book, we will see other *For* and *For Loop* commands demonstrated.

## Halt command

Now to exit Caché use the **Halt** command or just "H."

**Example 1-31 Halt command**

```
Halt
```

## Chapter 1 Summary

The first two chapters explain basic concepts of Caché ObjectScript (COS). This chapter covered the definitions of Caché and MUMPS and explained some basic commands and concepts, specifically: *1) Set command, 2) Write command, 3) If command, 4) Structured Code, 5) Plus sign, 6) Kill command, 7) Your own copy of Caché, 8) Exercises on Set, Write, If, Plus and Kill commands, 9) The Concatenate character, 10) Operator Precedence*, and *11) For Loop* command.

*"It is not how much you know, but how well you communicate it to others."*

# *Chapter 2 Basic Concepts II*

The first two chapters explain **Basic Concepts** of Caché ObjectScript (COS). They give definitions, basic commands, structure and flow of COS Programs.

## *Routine Definition*

A **Routine** the name that COS calls computer programs. A *Routine* consists of a number of lines of instructions to the computer. The execution of the lines of code normally flows from the top of a routine to the bottom.

## *Routine Line Types*

### *Labels and Executable code lines*

**Executable Code Lines** start in column two, whereas **Labels** start in column one. *Labels* are the targets of the *Do* and *Goto* commands.

**Example 2-1 Labels and Executable code lines**

```
START                   ;Label
   Set X=5              ;Executable Code line
```

In Example 2-1, the first line containing the word *START* is an example of a *Label line.* The line containing the string "Set X=5" is an example of an *Executable code line.* It is possible to have a *Label* and *Executable code* on the same line.

**Example 2-2 Label and Executable code on the same line**

```
START     Set X=5
```

Example 2-2 demonstrates how one line can have both a *Label* and *Executable code.* At least one space or tab separates the *Label* from the *Executable code.*

### *Routine Header line*

All routines should start with the routine name on the first line in the first column.

**Example 2-3 Routine Header Line**

```
ROUTINEA                ;name of the routine on the first line
Start                   ;Label
   Set X=1              ;Code
   .
   .
```

```
Quit
```

Example 2-3 shows the *Routine Header Line*, the first line of a routine. The *Routine Header Line* should contain the *Routine Name*.

---

### *Save Routines with a .MAC Extension*

When saving your routines, be sure to specify a .MAC file extension and not a .INT extension. .INT routines are intermediate routines.

---

## Comment Lines

The best-written code is seldom self-evident as to its intended purpose. Therefore, clearly stated, concise comments are necessary.

There are several ways to indicate a comment in COS.

**Example 2-4 Comment Lines**

```
PROC       ;comments may follow a label
  ;
  ; Everything that follows the ";" is a comment
  ;
  Set X=1                     ; comments may follow code


PROC2     //comments may follow a label
  //
  // Everything that follows the "//" is a comment
  //
  Set X=1                     // comments may follow code


  /*      starts a multi line comment
  more comments
  more comments
  */      end a multi-line comment
```

Example 2-4 demonstrates comments lines. Comments may follow ";" and "//".

Also, "/*" starts a multi-line comment and "*/" ends it.

# Controlling Process Flow

**Controlling Process Flow** means controlling the execution path of code. The execution of code flows from the top to the bottom in a routine, except for the following:

➢ Do and Quit commands

➢ Goto command

➢ Inline DO command

➢ Structured Code

## Do and Quit commands

A **Do** command and some form of **Quit** command should always be paired. The *Do* command transfers code execution to a *Label*. Code execution continues until it encounters a *Quit* command. The *Quit* may be explicit or implied.

**Example 2-5 Do and Quit commands**

```
To run this code you must put the code in a routine, save the routine, and then
run the routine from the terminal.

START
  Write !,"At Start label"
  Do PROC                        ;Do command
  Write !,"At Start:Quit"
  Quit                           ;Quit command
PROC
  Write !,"At Proc label"
  Set X=5
  Write !,"At Proc:Quit"
  Quit                           ;Quit command
```

Example 2-5 demonstrates the *Do* and *Quit* commands. Code execution begins at the START Label. Upon encountering the "Do PROC" line, execution jumps to the PROC Label. When the *Quit* is encountered under the PROC Label, execution jumps back to the line immediately after "Do PROC". Execution continues from that point with the writing of "At Start:Quit" and then it quits.

**Example 2-6 Output from Example 2-5**

```
At Start label
At Proc label
At Proc:Quit
At Start:Quit
```

Example 2-6 shows the output from running the code in Example 2-5.

For every *Do* command, there must be some form of *Quit* command. The *Quit* may be explicit, but also may be implicit or implied. You will see the *Implied Quit* in Example 2-9.

**Orphan Quits** (Quits with no associated Do) can cause havoc. Unlike other programming languages, there is no enforcement of *Do* and *Quit* pairs in COS. *Orphan Quits* are really a misuse of the *Quit* command and should be avoided.

## *Goto command*

The **Goto** command transfers control to a Line Label. Unlike the *Do* command, the *Goto* command does not have an associated *Quit* command.

**Example 2-7 Goto command**

```
To run this code you must put the code in a routine, save the routine, and then
run the routine from the terminal.

START
   Write !,"At Start label"
   Goto PROC
   Write !,"At Start:Quit"
   Quit
PROC
   Write !,"At Proc label"
   Set X=5
   Write !,"At Proc:Quit"
   Quit
```

Example 2-7 demonstrates the *Goto* command. Code execution begins at the START Label. Upon encountering the "Goto PROC" line, execution jumps to the PROC Label. When the *Quit* command is encountered under PROC, execution stops. The *Quit* command under the START Label is never executed.

**Example 2-8 Output from Example 2-7**

```
At Start label
At Proc label
At Proc:Quit
```

Example 2-8 shows the output from running the code in Example 2-7.

It is a good idea to try to limit the number of *Goto* commands. There are times when it is unavoidable, especially in some error conditions.

## *Inline Do*

The **Inline Do** gives COS enhanced capability and readability, especially when combined with the *For Loop* command.

**Example 2-9 Inline Do**

```
To run this code you must put the code in a routine, save the routine, and then
run the routine from the terminal.

For I=1:1:3 Do
. Write !,I
. Write !,I+10
Write !,"End of For Loop"
```

In Example 2-9, the *Do* command refers to the inline code that follows the *Do*. The dots, or periods, that follow are part of the *Do*. When the dots or periods cease, the *Do* is over; a *Quit* command is unnecessary. This is an *Implied Quit*.

**Example 2-10 Inline Do output from Example 2-9**

```
1
11
2
12
3
13
End of For Loop
```

Example 2-10 shows the output from the code in Example 2-9. The *Inline Do* is used widely in COS systems.

## Nested Inline Do command

*Inline Do* commands may be nested. Each nested level requires an additional dot or period. Nesting of the *Inline Do* command may continue for many layers. Too many layers may become difficult to read. Some programmers feel that inserting a space between the dots enhances readability. An extra space between the dots does not affect the execution of the code.

**Example 2-11 Nested Inline Do commands**

```
To run this code you must put the code in a routine, save the routine, and then
run the routine from the terminal.

 For I=1:1:3 Do
 . Write !,"First Level: ",I
 . For II=1:1:3 Do
 . . Write !,"  Second Level: ",I+II
 Write !,"End of For Loop"
```

Example 2-11 shows a *Nested Inline Do* command. The *Inline Do* may be nested many times, each one with an additional dot or period. Note that when the inner loop stops the outer loop does not stop, but continues.

**Example 2-12 Output of Example 2-11**

```
First Level: 1
   Second Level: 2
   Second Level: 3
   Second Level: 4
First Level: 2
   Second Level: 3
   Second Level: 4
   Second Level: 5
First Level: 3
   Second Level: 4
   Second Level: 5
   Second Level: 6
End of For Loop
```

Example 2-12 shows the output from the code in Example 2-11. Notice how the output is incremented as the variables I and II are added together.

## Structured Code with Inline Do and For Loop

Example 2-13 is the same as Example 2-11 but uses *Structured Code*.

**Example 2-13 Inline Do and For Loop commands with Structured Code**

```
To run this code you must put the code in a routine, save the routine, and then
run the routine from the terminal.

 For I=1:1:3 {
   Write !,"First Level: ",I
   For II=1:1:3 {
     Write !,"  Second Level: ",I+II
   }
 }
 Write !,"End of For Loop"
```

In Example 2-13, note the placement of the curly brackets, {}. They define the start and end of each section of repeating code.

# Routines and Labels

**Routines** are computer programs with a number of executable code lines. **Labels** are tags or starting points in a routine. **Variables** are elements that represent data values. **Parameters** are a formalized list of data passed between routines.

## Routines, Subroutines/Modules and Functions

➢ Routines are the name that COS calls computer programs

➢ Subroutines and Modules are subsections within a Routine that start with a Label Line and end with a Quit command

➢ Functions are the same as Subroutines but Functions always return a value

## Executing Routines

**Example 2-14 Executing a routine**

```
ROUTINEA              ;name of the routine on the first line
  Do ^ROUTINEB        ;execution jumps to ^ROUTINEB
  Quit
```

Example 2-14 shows ROUTINEA, identified by the routine name on the first line. When the *Do* command "Do ^ROUTINEB" is encountered, execution jumps to ROUTINEB. The Caret (^) before ROUTINEB signifies that ROUTINEB is a separate routine. If no Caret (^) is found on the *Do* command, execution jumps to a Label inside the current routine.

## Executing a Label in a Routine

**Example 2-15 Executing a LABEL in a routine**

```
To run this code you must put the code in a routine, save the routine, and then
run the routine from the terminal.

ROUTINEA
  ;
  Do PROC          ;execution jumps to PROC
  ; code
  ; code
  Quit
PROC      ;
  ; code
  ; code
  Quit             ;execution jumps back to the line following "Do PROC"
```

Example 2-15 shows ROUTINEA. When the line "Do PROC" is encountered, execution jumps to the PROC *Label* and continues until it reaches the *Quit* command. At the *Quit*, execution jumps back to the line following "Do PROC".

## Executing a Label in another Routine

**Example 2-16 Executing a LABEL in another routine**

```
To run this code you must put the code in a routine, save the routine, and then
run the routine from the terminal. ROUTINEA and ROUTINEB need to be in separate
routines.

ROUTINEA
  ;
  Do PROC^ROUTINEB      ;execution jumps to PROC in ^ROUTINEB
  ; code
  ; code
  Quit

  = = = = = = = = = = = = = = = = = = = = = = = = = = = = = =

ROUTINEB
  ;
PROC
  ; code
  ; code
  Quit   ;execution jumps to the line following PROC in ^ROUTINEA
```

Example 2-16 shows two separate routines, ROUTINEA and ROUTINEB. In ROUTINEA, when the line "Do PROC^ROUTINEB" is encountered, execution jumps to the PROC label inside ROUTINEB. When the *Quit* command under PROC^ROUTINEB is reached, execution jumps to the line following "Do PROC^ROUTINEB" in ROUTINEA

## *Routines and Variables*

A routine has access to all the variables it creates. When ROUTINEA calls ROUTINEB and ROUTINEB calls ROUTINEC, and so forth, this is known as a **Call Stack**. All routines in the *Call Stack* may modify any variable created by any other routine in the *Call Stack*. All the routines have access to the **Variable Pool,** A group of variables shared by all routines in the *Call Stack*, with the following two exceptions:

➢ **The New** command, covered in Chapter 9

➢ **Private Variables,** covered in Chapter 15

**Example 2-17 Routines and Variables**

To run this code you must put the code in a routine, save the routine, and then run the routine from the terminal. ROUTINEA, ROUTINEB, and ROUTINEC need to be in separate routines.

```
ROUTINEA
    Set X="A",Y="A",Z="A"          ;X,Y and Z all set to "A"
    Write !,"ROUTINEA - X: ",X
    Write !,"ROUTINEA - Y: ",Y
    Write !,"ROUTINEA - Z: ",Z
    Do ^ROUTINEB
    Write !!,"ROUTINEA - X: ",X
    Write !,"ROUTINEA - Y: ",Y
    Write !,"ROUTINEA - Z: ",Z
    Quit


    = = = = = = = = = = = = = = = = = = = = = = = = = = = = = = =


ROUTINEB
    Set Y="B",Z="B"                ;Y and Z set to "B"
    Write !!,"ROUTINEB - X: ",X
    Write !,"ROUTINEB - Y: ",Y
    Write !,"ROUTINEB - Z: ",Z
    Do ^ROUTINEC
    Write !!,"ROUTINEB - X: ",X
    Write !,"ROUTINEB - Y: ",Y
    Write !,"ROUTINEB - Z: ",Z
    Quit


    = = = = = = = = = = = = = = = = = = = = = = = = = = = = = = =


ROUTINEC
    Set Z="C"                      ;Z set to "C"
    Write !!,"ROUTINEC - X: ",X
    Write !,"ROUTINEC - Y: ",Y
    Write !,"ROUTINEC - Z: ",Z
    Quit
```

Example 2-17 shows three routines: ROUTINEA, ROUTINEB, and ROUTINEC. Each of the three routines modifies one or more of the variables X, Y, and Z.

**Example 2-18 Output from running the routines in Example 2-17**

```
 Do ^ROUTINEA

ROUTINEA - X: A
ROUTINEA - Y: A
ROUTINEA - Z: A

ROUTINEB - X: A
ROUTINEB - Y: B
ROUTINEB - Z: B

ROUTINEC - X: A
ROUTINEC - Y: B
ROUTINEC - Z: C

ROUTINEB - X: A
ROUTINEB - Y: B
ROUTINEB - Z: C

ROUTINEA - X: A
ROUTINEA - Y: B
ROUTINEA - Z: C
```

Example 2-18 demonstrates that no matter which of the three routines modifies the variables X, Y and Z, the modifications show up in all the routines in the *Call Stack*.

# Routines and Parameters

## Calling and Called Routines

In large computer systems, the execution path of code winds in and out of many routines. When the execution path progresses from one routine to another, the routine it passes from is the **Calling Routine**, and the routine it passes to is the **Called Routine.** In Example 2-17, ROUTINEA and ROUTINEB are both *Calling Routines*, and ROUTINEB and ROUTINEC are both *Called Routines*. Most routines become both *Called* and *Calling* routines as the code progresses.

## Parameter Passing

### Implicit Parameter Passing

*Variables* are **Parameters** when referred to as "being passed" from one routine to another. As previously stated, all variables or parameters may be modified by all routines in the *Call Stack*. This method of parameter passing is called **implicit parameter passing**. Implicit meaning: "implied, rather than expressly stated." In other words, the parameters are passed automatically without any special consideration.

## Explicit Parameter Passing

Parameters may also be passed **Explicitly** or passed with special consideration.

## Passed by Value and Passed by Reference

Two methods of *Explicit Parameter Passing*:

➤ **Passed by Value** - For parameters *Passed by Value,* the actual value of the parameter is passed from one routine to another.

➤ **Passed by Reference** - For parameters *Passed by Reference*, a pointer to the parameter is passed. Using this method, the called routine may modify and even delete the parameters passed to it.

## Parameters Passed by Value

For parameters *Passed by Value*, the actual value of the parameter is passed from one routine to another.

**Example 2-19 Parameter Passed by Value, ROUTINEA and ROUTINEB**

```
To run this code you must put the code in a routine, save the routine, and then
run the routine from the terminal. ROUTINEA and ROUTINEB need to be in separate
routines.

ROUTINEA
   Write !!,"ROUTINEA Starting"
   Set PARAM1="Value for Param1"
   Set PARAM2="Value for Param2"
   Write !,"ROUTINEA-PARAM1: ",PARAM1
   Write !,"ROUTINEA-PARAM2: ",PARAM2
   Do PROC^ROUTINEB(PARAM1,PARAM2) ;call passing PARAM1, PARAM2
   Write !!,"ROUTINEA-PARAM1: ",PARAM1
   Write !,"ROUTINEA-PARAM2: ",PARAM2
   Write !,"ROUTINEA Ending"
   Quit


   = = = = = = = = = = = = = = = = = = = = = = = = = = = = = = =


ROUTINEB
   ;
PROC(PAR1,PAR2)
   Write !!,"ROUTINEB Starting"
   Write !,"ROUTINEB-PAR1: ",PAR1
   Write !,"ROUTINEB-PAR2: ",PAR2
   Set PAR2="New value for PAR2"          ;ROUTINEB changes PAR2
   Write !!,"ROUTINEB-PAR1: ",PAR1
   Write !,"ROUTINEB-PAR2: ",PAR2
   Write !,"ROUTINEB Ending"
   Quit
```

Example 2-19 shows two routines, ROUTINEA and ROUTINEB. ROUTINEA calls the label PROC in ROUTINEB passing two parameters by value. Note that ROUTINEB is not required to name the parameters by the same name that ROUTINEA refers them. The values that PARAM1 and PARAM2 contained in ROUTINEA are the same values that PAR1 and PAR2 have in ROUTINEB. Now, if ROUTINEB modifies the values of PAR1 or PAR2, these modifications are not passed back to ROUTINEA.

**Example 2-20 Running ROUTINEA (parameters passed by value)**

```
 Do ^ROUTINEA
ROUTINEA Starting
ROUTINEA-PARAM1: Value for Param1
ROUTINEA-PARAM2: Value for Param2

ROUTINEB Starting
ROUTINEB-PAR1: Value for Param1
ROUTINEB-PAR2: Value for Param2

ROUTINEB-PAR1: Value for Param1
ROUTINEB-PAR2: New value for PAR2;ROUTINEB changes PAR2
ROUTINEB Ending

ROUTINEA-PARAM1: Value for Param1
ROUTINEA-PARAM2: Value for Param2
ROUTINEA Ending
```

Example 2-20 shows the output when ROUTINEA is run and calls ROUTINEB. Note that, even though ROUTINEB modifies the value of PAR2, this modification is not passed back to ROUTINEA.

## *Parameter Passed by Reference*

For parameters *Passed by Reference,* a pointer to the parameter is passed. Using this method, the called routine may modify and even delete the parameters passed to it.

**Example 2-21 Parameter Passed by Reference, ROUTINEA and ROUTINEB**

```
To run this code you must put the code in a routine, save the routine, and then
run the routine from the terminal. ROUTINEA and ROUTINEB need to be in separate
routines.
```

```
ROUTINEA
    Write !!,"ROUTINEA Starting"
    Set PARAM1="Value for Param1"
    Set PARAM2="Value for Param2"
    Write !,"ROUTINEA-PARAM1: ",PARAM1
    Write !,"ROUTINEA-PARAM2: ",PARAM2
    Do PROC^ROUTINEB(.PARAM1,.PARAM2)       ;Period or dot before PARAMS
    Write !!,"ROUTINEA-PARAM1: ",PARAM1
    Write !,"ROUTINEA-PARAM2: ",PARAM2
    Write !,"ROUTINEA Ending"
    Quit

    = = = = = = = = = = = = = = = = = = = = = = = = = = = = = =

ROUTINEB
    ;
PROC(PAR1,PAR2)
    Write !!,"ROUTINEB Starting"
    Write !,"ROUTINEB-PAR1: ",PAR1
    Write !,"ROUTINEB-PAR2: ",PAR2
    Set PAR2="New value for PAR2"
```

```
Write !!,"ROUTINEB-PAR1: ",PAR1
Write !,"ROUTINEB-PAR2: ",PAR2
Write !,"ROUTINEB Ending"
Quit
```

In Example 2-21, ROUTINEA calls the label PROC in ROUTINEB passing two parameters by reference. Notice the period or dot immediately preceding PARAM1 and PARAM2. This is the only indication that the parameter is passed by reference.

**Example 2-22 Running ROUTINEA (parameters passed by reference)**

```
 Do ^ROUTINEA
ROUTINEA Starting
ROUTINEA-PARAM1: Value for Param1
ROUTINEA-PARAM2: Value for Param2

ROUTINEB Starting
ROUTINEB-PAR1: Value for Param1
ROUTINEB-PAR2: Value for Param2

ROUTINEB-PAR1: Value for Param1
ROUTINEB-PAR2: New value for PAR2
ROUTINEB Ending

ROUTINEA-PARAM1: Value for Param1
ROUTINEA-PARAM2: New value for PAR2        ;new value passed back
ROUTINEA Ending
```

In Example 2-22, ROUTINEB has the label PROC that accepts two parameters passed by reference. Notice that the period immediately preceding PARAM1 and PARAM2 does not exist in the *Called Routine*. ROUTINEB modifies the value of the received parameters and passes the changes back.

## *Formats for Calling Routines*

**Table 2-1 Formats for Call Routines**

| Code to Call | Descriptions |
|---|---|
| Do ^Routine | Calling a routine |
| Do ^Routine(Param) | Calling a routine with a parameter |
| Write $$^Function | Calling a function |
| Set X=$$^Function(Param) | Calling a function with a parameter |
| Do Tag^Routine | Calling a routine at a tag |
| Do Tag^Routine(Param) | Calling a routine at a tag with a parameter |
| Write $$Tag^Function | Calling a function at a tag |
| Write $$Tag^Function(Param) | Calling a function at a tag with a parameter |

## Globals, Local Arrays and Variables

In COS, the term **Global** can be thought of as data stored on a computer disk. Global data is permanent or persistent, being stored on disk. A Global may be:

➤ **Scalar** (single value), as in a variable

➤ **Aggregate** (many elements), as in an array

An **Array** is a method of combining similar data together.

**Example 2-23 Array Example**

```
Set PEOPLE("DAVID")="DATA ABOUT DAVID"
Set PEOPLE("SUSAN")="DATA ABOUT SUSAN"
Set PEOPLE("MICHAEL")="DATA ABOUT MICHAEL"
Set PEOPLE("AMY")="DATA ABOUT AMY"
```

In Example 2-23, data is stored about four people. The person's name is the *Subscript* of the Array. The name of the Array is PEOPLE.

A *Global* refers to persistent or permanent (stored on disk) variables and arrays. *Variables* and *Arrays* typically are non-persistent, that is, not stored on disk. These *Variables* and *Arrays* cease to exist when the computer shuts down. We might use the term ***Local*** to refer to *Local Variables* and *Local Arrays*. When we refer to a *Local Variable*, we are simply referring to a *Variable*. When we refer to a *Local Array*, we refer to it simply as an *Array*. *Global Variables* and *Global Arrays* are handled just like *Local Variables* and *Local Arrays*. The only real difference is that *Local Variables* and *Local Arrays* exist only in memory. *Global Variables* and *Global Arrays* are persistent, and exist on disk. They are only removed when explicitly killed.

Refer to Table 2-2 for differences between *Global Arrays*, *Global Variables*, *Local Arrays* and *Local Variables* in a tabular display of this information.

**Table 2-2 Differences between Global Arrays, Global variable, Local Arrays and Local Variables**

| What | Description | |
|------|-------------|---|
| Global Arrays | Multi-dimensional using subscripts | Persistent, permanent, reside on disk |
| Global Variables | One-dimensional, Scalar, no subscripts | Persistent, permanent, reside on disk |
| Local Arrays | Multi-dimensional using subscripts | Temporary, reside only in memory |
| Local Variables | One-dimensional, Scalar, no subscripts | Temporary, reside only in memory |

## Example of setting Globals, Local Arrays and Variables

**Example 2-24 Setting Globals, Local Variables and Arrays**

```
Set ^X="ABC"           ;set a Global variable
Set ^X(1,2)="ABC"      ;set a Global array

Set X="ABC"            ;set a local variable
Set X(1,2)="ABC"       ;set a local array
```

Example 2-24 demonstrates how to set *Global Variable* and *Array*, and a *Local Variable* and *Array*.

Notice the Caret (^) immediately before the Global ^X.

Using the vernacular of other computer languages, *Globals* may be thought of as *files*. They reside on disk and are permanent, or persistent, until deleted. However, *Globals* are unique to COS. They are not read in a sequential manner like traditional files. See Chapters 6 and 7 on *Global Processing*. Be very careful when killing any *Global*. An entire database may be wiped out in an instant with one simple *Kill* command. Unfortunately, there is no warning that a Global is being deleted and no undelete capability. The *Kill Global* command may delete thousands or even millions of descendant nodes. The Kill is a powerful and dangerous command!

## Uniqueness of the Caché Global Structure or database

The Caché Database Structure is unique among databases; it was designed and created in the late 1960s to be used primarily with HealthCare applications. It has thrived in the Healthcare Industry as well as Financial Information systems. It was designed for use in multi-user database-driven applications. It predates "C" and most other current popular languages, and has a very different syntax and terminology.

The Caché Global Structure provides the programmer with a culture of unique freedom in accessing and modifying data without inefficient built-in safeguards. Rather, it relies on the programmer having a disciplined approach to data manipulation.

The Caché Global Structure is based on a **B-Tree** concept, which permits data to exist in a permanent sorted state, and allows for efficient searches, access, insertions, and deletions. In other words, the data is always sorted, (or indexed) which greatly improves the efficiency of data access.

The Caché Database Structure employees **Sparse Arrays**. A *Sparse Array* is an Array without data being populated to all entries. There is no wasted memory or hard disk space with Caché *Sparse Arrays*. Using *Sparse Arrays*, data can be inserted into the database quickly and efficiently.

Lastly, data stored in Globals is available to every Caché process running on the system. As soon as a Global or Global node is created, it is instantly available to all other processes on the system. This provides a freedom of data access without the excessive overhead of data and record locking seen in other databases. At first glance this may seem chaotic, but handled correctly by the programmer, it works and provides tremendous scalability of data, from a few bytes to terabytes with speeds that far exceed other technologies.

## Uniqueness of Caché Variables

Variables created by one routine are accessible by all routines in a session. This means that if RoutineA creates a variable, RoutineB can access, change or even delete that variable. This allows the programmer a certain freedom in his code. This strategy can be successful as long as the programmer is disciplined in his code writing and uses appropriate **Scoping** methods like the *New* command. See Chapter 9 on the *New* command. A **Scope** is the context within a computer program in which a variable name can be used. Outside of the scope of a variable, the variable's value is not accessible.

## Chapter 2 Summary

The first two chapters explained basic concepts of Caché ObjectScript (COS). This chapter covered: 1) Controlling Process Flow with the *Do, Goto* and *Quit* commands, *2)* Types of Routine lines: Label lines, Executable lines, Header lines and Comment lines, 3) *Inline Do, Nested Inline Do* commands and *Structured Code, 4) Calling* and *Called Routines, 5) Implicit* and *Explicit Parameter Passing, 6) Parameters Passed by Value* and *Reference, 7)* Formats for calling Routines, *8) Global Variables* and *Arrays,* 9) *Local Variables* and *Arrays* 10) Uniqueness of Caché Globals, and 11) Uniquness of Caché Variables.

*"Crashed and burning on the learning curve." – Dick Martel*

# Chapter 3 System-Supplied Functions I

Chapters 3 and 4 cover many **System-Supplied Functions** in Caché ObjectScript (COS). *System-Supplied Functions* are an extension of the base commands. They include string handling capabilities, numeric capabilities, as well as variable testing capabilities.

## System-Supplied Functions

**System-Supplied Functions** are "called routines" or subroutines that perform a specific task and return a value. They are an extension of the basic commands, a prefix of "**$**" identifies them.

## User-Defined Functions

**User-Defined Functions** are "called routines" or subroutines that perform a specific task and return a value. An application programmer creates them. A prefix of "**$$**" identifies them. By the use of *User-Defined Functions*, one can expand the capabilities of COS.

## System-Supplied Functions - Strings

COS has excellent string handling capabilities. *System-Supplied Functions* perform many of these string functions.

## $Length System-Supplied Function

### $Length (with one parameter) returns the length of a string

One of the simplest *System-Supplied Functions* is **$Length**, or **$L,** it returns the length of a string.

**Example 3-1 $Length Example**

```
 Write $L("Page Title")
10

 Set X="Page Title"
 Write $L(X)
10
```

Example 3-1 shows two ways of calculating the length of the string "Page Title".

## $Length to center text on a line

**Example 3-2 $Length to center text on a line**

```
Set X="Page Title"
Write ?(80-$L(X)/2),X
                              Page Title
```

Example 3-2 shows how to display the value of the string centered on an 80-character line. The tab character (?), (covered in Chapter 8) is set to 80 minus the length of X, divided by two. Since the length of X is 10, tab would be set to (80-10=70)/2=35. Therefore, the tab character is 35, which centers X on the line. This is a nice technique for centering page headings.

## $Length (with two parameters) returns the number of pieces in a string

*$Length* also accepts two parameters. Using this format, the first parameter is the string and the second parameter is a delimiter. *$Length* returns the number of pieces in the string separated by the delimiter.

## Delimiters and Delimited Strings

Typically, a **Delimiter** is a character not ordinarily used in text; it is used to separate text. A **Delimited String** is a string of text, which contains delimiters to separate the text into pieces. Here is an example of a string of text delimited by the Caret (^).

**Example 3-3 Delimited String of text**

```
Jack Sampson^123 Any Street^Any Town^USA^12045
```

Example 3-3 shows a delimited string of text. The delimiter is the Caret, (^). Piece one is "Jack Sampson", piece two is "123 Any Street" and so on.

## $Length to find the number of pieces in a string

**Example 3-4 $Length to find the number of pieces in a string**

```
Set X="This is a test"
Write $L(X," ")
4
```

In Example 3-4, *$Length* uses two parameters to display the number of pieces in the string: "This is a test", using the space character as a delimiter. There are four pieces (words) in this string.

### $Length to write each piece in a delimited string

This two parameter form of *$Length* may be combined with the *For Loop* command to elegantly write the pieces of a string.

**Example 3-5 $Length to write each piece in a delimited string**

```
Set String="Jack Sampson^123 Any Street^Any Town^USA^12045"
For I=1:1:$L(String,"^") Write !, $P(String,"^",I)

Jack Sampson
123 Any Street
Any Town
USA
12045
```

Example 3-5 shows a nice technique of writing the pieces of a delimited string of text. I know we have not covered **$Piece** yet, abbreviated *$P,* but the meaning of *$Piece* should be clear with this example and will be covered in Chapter 5.

---

### $Piece System-Supplied Function

The $Piece function selects text from a string based on a delimiter, for example:

```
Set X="Piece1^Piece2^Piece3"     ; Variable X is divided into 3 pieces
For I=1:1:3 Write !,$P(X,"^",I)
Piece1
Piece2
Piece3
```

---

## $Extract System-Supplied Function

The **$Extract** *System-Supplied Function* returns a substring from a string. *$Extract* may seem simple, but it has powerful capabilities, especially when combined with other *System-Supplied Functions*. *$Extract* accepts three parameters:

> ➤ The primary string, when only the first parameter is specified, the second and third parameters are assumed to be one

> ➤ The starting position of the substring being extracted, when only the first and second parameters are specified, the third parameter is assumed to be the same as the second

> ➤ The ending position of the substring to be extracted

## *$Extract selects a substring from a string*

**Example 3-6 $Extract selects a substring from a string**

```
 Set X="My dog Spot"
 Write !,$E(X,1,2)
My
```

In Example 3-6, a *Write* command uses *$Extract* to display the first two characters of the variable X. The first parameter in *$Extract* is the string X. The second parameter is the starting position, 1, and the third parameter is the ending position, 2. This command is saying to write the first two characters of the X variable.

**Example 3-7 $Extract selects a substring from a string**

```
 Set X="My dog Spot"
 Write !,$E(X,8,11)
Spot
```

In Example 3-7, a *Write* command invokes *$Extract* to display characters eight through eleven of variable X, "Spot".

## *$Extract with no second and third parameters, returns the first character*

When *$Extract* is not provided with the second and third parameters, they are assumed to be one.

**Example 3-8 $Extract with no second and third parameters**

```
 Set X="My dog Spot"
 Write !,$E(X)            ;with no second or third parameters
M                         ;the first character is returned

 Write !,$E(X,1,1)
M                         ;the first character is returned
```

In Example 3-8, a *Write* command invokes *$Extract* to display the first character of the string X. As you can see from this example, when the second and third parameters are missing, they are assumed to be one.

## *$Extract with no third parameter, becomes the same as the second parameter*

When *$Extract* is not provided with a third parameter, the third parameter becomes the same as the second parameter.

**Example 3-9 $Extract with no third parameter, becomes the same as the second parameter**

```
 Set X="My dog Spot"
 Write !,$E(X,4)          ;with no third parameter,
d                         ;the third becomes the same as the second

 Write !,$E(X,4,4)
d                         ;the fourth character is returned
```

In Example 3-9, a *Write* command invokes *$Extract* to display the fourth character of the string X. As you can see from this example, when the third parameter is missing, it becomes the same as the second.

## $Extract sets a variable

In addition to returning a substring from a string, *$Extract* also sets a variable to a substring.

**Example 3-10 $Extract sets a variable**

```
Set X="My dog Spot"
Set Y=$E(X,8,11)
Write !,Y
Spot
```

In Example 3-10, the variable Y is set to the eighth through the eleventh position of the string X, or "Spot".

## $Extract sets a substring in a string

**Example 3-11 $Extract sets a substring in a string**

```
Set X="My dog Spot"
Set $E(X,8,11)="Fred"
Write !,X
My dog Fred.
```

In Example 3-11, *$Extract* behaves a bit differently. Instead of extracting a string, *$Extract* sets a portion of the primary string X to "Fred".

## $Extract reformats a name

**Example 3-12 $Extract reformats a name**

```
Set NAME1="John Doe"
Set NAME2=$E(NAME1,6,8)_", "_$E(NAME1,1,4)
Write !,NAME2
Doe, John
```

In Example 3-12, *$Extract* swaps the first and last name to reformat the name.

## $Extract reformats a date

**Example 3-13 $Extract reformats a date**

```
Set DATE1="20092205"     ;A date string in the form "YYYYMMDD"
Set DATE2=$E(DATE1,7,8)_"/"_$E(DATE1,5,6)_"/"_$E(DATE1,3,4)
Write !,DATE2
05/22/09
```

In Example 3-13, *$Extracts* reformats a date from YYYYDDMM to MM/DD/YY.

## *$Extract deletes part of a variable string*

```
Set X="1111111111222222222223333333333"
Set $E(X,1,25)= ""
Write X
33333
```

In Example 3-14 *$Extract* deletes the first 25 characters of the X variable.

# *$Find System-Supplied Function*

*$Find* returns the location of a substring within a string. *$Find* requires two parameters but optionally may take a third.

- ➢ The string to be searched
- ➢ The substring to be searched for
- ➢ The optional third parameter is the starting position of the search. The default is to start at the beginning of the string (position one)

## *$Find to find the position of a substring in a string*

```
Set X="This is a test"
Write $F(X,"T")
2
```

In Example 3-15, *$Find* finds the position of "T". The position of "T" is 2 because *$Find* adds one to the ending position of the string found. This will be explained shortly.

```
Set X="This is a test"
Write $F(X,"is")
5
```

In Example 3-16 *$Find* locates the position of "is". The position of "is" is 5 because *$Find* adds one to the ending position of the string found. The "is" that is found is part of "This", not the whole word "is" which occurs later in the string.

```
Set X="This is a test"
Write $F(X,"ABC")
0
```

In Example 3-17, *$Find* finds the position of "ABC". Since "ABC" is not found *$Find* returns zero.

**Example 3-18 $Find locates "t" starting at the fifth position**

```
Set X="This is a test"
Write $F(X,"t",5)
12
```

In Example 3-18 *$Find* uses all three parameters. The third parameter is the starting position of the search. *$Find* locates the position of "t" starting from the fifth position; the answer is twelve. It locates the first "t" in the word "test".

## *$Find to find the second occurrence of a substring*

**Example 3-19 $Find finds the second occurrence of "is"**

```
Set X="This is a test"
Write $F(X,"is",$F(X,"is"))
8
```

In Example 3-19, *$Find* is compounded upon itself. *$Find* finds the second occurrence of "is". The inner *$Find* specifies the starting position of the search, which is the first occurrence of "is", or five. The answer is eight.

## *$Find to find the third occurrence of a substring*

**Example 3-20 $Find locates the third occurrence of "is"**

```
Set X="This is a test"
Write $F(X,"is",$F(X,"is",$F(X,"is")))
0
```

In Example 3-20, *$Find* is used three times. *$Find* attempts to locates the third occurrence of "is", which does not exist, so the answer is zero.

---

### *Why does $Find add one to its return value?*

Why does **$Find** add one to the ending position found?

Consider the following example:

```
Set STRING="My dog's name is Teddy."
Set X="Teddy"
Write $F(STRING,X)
23
```

The value 23 returned is actually the position following the string "Teddy". The reason for this, is that many times $Find is combined with $Length to find the starting position of a string.

```
Write $F(STRING,X)-$L(X)    ; 23 - 5 = 18
18
```

Eighteen is the starting position of "Teddy" in string.

---

## Exercises on $Length, $Extract and $Find

Here is your chance to try out what you have learned. The answers are shown after the questions. Assume the following:

Assume X="My dog's name is Teddy"

Write the code that:

> ➤ Displays the length of X

> ➤ Displays the number of pieces in X using space as the delimiter

> ➤ Displays the first two characters in X

> ➤ Displays characters four through eight in X

> ➤ Displays the starting position of "Teddy" in X

> ➤ Replace the name "Teddy" with the name "Trixie" in X

## Answers to Exercises on $Length, $Extract and $Find

**Example 3-21 Answers to Exercises on $Length, $Extract and $Find**

```
Displays the length of X
Write !,$L(X)
22

Displays the number of pieces in X using space as the delimiter
Write !,$L(X," ")
5

Displays the first two characters in X
Write !,$E(X,1,2)
My

Displays characters four through eight in X
Write !,$E(X,4,8)
dog's

Displays the starting position of "Teddy" in X
Write !,$F(X,"Teddy")-$L("Teddy")
18

Replace the name "Teddy" with "Trixie" in X
Set $E(X,18,22)="Trixie"
Write !,X
My dog's name is Trixie

The next line is a more advanced method of replacing "Teddy" with "Trixie"
when the position of "Teddy" is not known.

Set $E(X,$F(X,"Teddy")-$L("Teddy"),$F(X,"Teddy"))="Trixie"
Write !,X
My dog's name is Trixie

Or using the variable DOG for "Teddy":
Set DOG="Teddy"
```

```
Set $E(X,$F(X,DOG)-$L(DOG),$F(X,DOG))="Trixie"
Write !,X
My dog's name is Trixie
```

Example 3-21 demonstrates the answers to the exercises on *$Length*, *$Extract* and *$Find*. In the last two *$Extract* functions, the string "Teddy" is found. Then the length of "Teddy" is subtracted from the position returned by the *$Find*. This is done to find the starting position of the string "Teddy" in order to replace "Teddy" with "Trixie".

## Combining $Extract, $Find and $Length

The capabilities of *System-Supplied Functions* increase greatly when combined with each other. Here are some examples.

### Replace variable A with variable B

**Example 3-22 Replace variable A with variable B**

```
Set X="TEDDY IS A GREAT DOG"
Set A="GREAT"
Set B="BAD"
Set $E(X,$F(X,A)-$L(A),$F(X,A)-1)=B
Write X
TEDDY IS A BAD DOG
```

In Example 3-22, *$Extract, $Find* and *$Length* are combined to replace variable A with variable B when the position of A within variable X is not known. In addition, the length of variables A and B are unknown. There are three parameters to *$Extract*:

> ➤ X – the string we are dealing with

> ➤ $F(X,A)-$L(A) – the starting position of variable A

> ➤ $F(X,A)-1 – the ending position of variable A.

### Separating a name

**Example 3-23 Separating a name**

```
Set NAME1="John Q. Public"
Set FNAME=$E(NAME1,1,$F(NAME1," ")-2)
Set MI=$E(NAME1,$F(NAME1,".")-2,$F(NAME1,"."))
Set LNAME=$E(NAME1,$F(NAME1,".")+1,$L(NAME1))
Write !,FNAME
John
Write !,MI
Q.
Write !,LNAME
Public
```

In Example 3-23, *$Extract, $Find* and *$Length* are combined to take apart the various pieces of a name. First, FNAME is set by picking up all letters up to the first space. MI is obtained by searching for the period and backing up two characters. LNAME is set by searching for the period and extracting the remaining characters to the end of the line.

## $Replace System-Supplied Function

**$Replace** replaces one substring for another. It accepts up to six parameters:

➢ The source string

➢ The old substring

➢ The new substring

➢ The starting position (optional)

➢ The count or number of times to do the replacement (optional)

➢ Case sensitivity (optional)

### $Replace to replace a string

**Example 3-24 $Replace to replace a string**

```
Set TargetString="My dog is ugly"
Set OldString="ugly"
Set NewString="smart"
Set ChangedString=$Replace(TargetString,OldString,NewString)
Write !,ChangedString
My dog is smart
```

Example 3-24 demonstrates using *$Replace* with three parameters. The variable NewString "smart" replaces the variable OldString "ugly" in the variable TargetString.

### $Replace to replace a string starting at a specific location

**Example 3-25 $Replace to replace a string starting at a specific location**

```
Set TargetString="My dog is ugly and your dog is not"
Set OldString="dog"
Set NewString="cat"
Set ChangedString=$Replace(TargetString,OldString,NewString,16)
Write !,ChangedString
and your cat is not
```

Example 3-25 demonstrates using *$Replace* with four parameters. The fourth parameter, 16, tells *$Replace* to start replacing at the 16th character. As you can see, ChangedString displays only the 16th character to the end of the string. Therefore, in this example the starting position for replacement is also the starting position for any data in ChangedString.

## *$Replace to replace one occurrence of a string*

### Example 3-26 $Replace to replace one occurrence of a string

```
Set TargetString="My dog is ugly and your dog is not"
Set OldString="dog"
Set NewString="cat"
Set ChangedString=$Replace(TargetString,OldString,NewString,,1)
Write !,ChangedString
My cat is ugly and your dog is not
```

In Example 3-26 the string "cat" replaces the first occurrence of "dog" only.

## *$Replace with case sensitivity*

### Example 3-27 $Replace with case sensitivity

```
Set TargetString="My dog is ugly and your dog is not"
Set OldString="DOG"
Set NewString="cat"
Set ChangedString=$Replace(TargetString,OldString,NewString,,,0)
Write !,ChangedString
My dog is ugly and your dog is not
```

Example 3-27 demonstrates using *$Replace* with six parameters. The sixth parameter can be either -1 for case insensitivity or 0 for case sensitivity. The default is case sensitivity. As you can see from the example when sixth parameter is a 0 (case is sensitivity), "DOG" does not match "dog" and the replacement is not made.

## *$Replace with case insensitivity*

### Example 3-28 $Replace with case insensitivity

```
Set TargetString="My dog is ugly and your dog is not"
Set OldString="DOG"
Set NewString="cat"
Set ChangedString=$Replace(TargetString,OldString,NewString,,,1)
Write !,ChangedString
My cat is ugly and your cat is not
```

Example 3-28 demonstrates using *$Replace* with six parameters. The sixth parameter can be either 1 for case insensitivity or 0 for case sensitivity. The default is case sensitivity. As you can see from the example when the sixth parameter is a 1 for not case sensitive, "DOG" does match "dog" and the replacement is made even though the cases are different.

## $Translate System-Supplied Function

**$Translate** converts characters within a string. It changes characters in parameter two to characters in parameter three. *$Translate* is abbreviated to *$TR* because using just *$T* is not unique. There are also the *$TEST* and *$TEXT*.

*$Translate* accepts three parameters:

 ➢ The string to be converted

 ➢ The convert "from" characters

 ➢ The convert "to" characters, which is optional

### $Translate to remove a comma

**Example 3-29 $Translate to remove a comma**

```
Set X="123,456.00"
Set X=$TR(X,",")        ;remove comma
Write !,X
123456.00
```

Example 3-29 demonstrates *$Translate* with two parameters. The first parameter is the string to be converted. The second parameter contains the character(s) to be removed from the first parameter. The commas are removed from the variable X. If the third parameter is absent, it is assume to be null.

### $Translate to remove a comma and period

**Example 3-30 $Translate to remove a comma and period**

```
Set X="123,456.00"
Set X=$TR(X,",.")        ;remove commas and period
Write !,X
12345600
```

In Example 3-30, the comma and period characters are removed from the variable X. If the third parameter is absent, it is assume to be null.

### $Translate to reformat a date

**Example 3-31 $Translate with three parameters, reformates a date**

```
Set DATE="01/01/2003"
Set DATE=$TR(DATE,"/","-")        ;replaces "/" with "-"
Write !,DATE
01-01-2003
```

In Example 3-31 *$Translate* converts slashes (/) to dashes (-) to change the format of a date.

## $Zconvert System-Supplied Function

**$Zconvert** converts a data string. $Zconvert is abbreviated $ZCVT, it requires two parameters:

- ➢ The string to be converted
- ➢ "U" for uppercase and "L" for lowercase. There are other options for parameter two but they are beyond the scope of this book

## $Zconvert converts a string to Uppercase

**Example 3-32 Convert a string to Uppercase**

```
Set X="abc"
Set X=$ZCVT(X,"U")
Write !,X
ABC
```

In Example 3-32, $Zconvert converts the X string to uppercase. Notice the second parameters of "U" indicating the convert to uppercase.

## $Zconvert converts a string to Lowercase

**Example 3-33 Convert a string to Lowercase**

```
Set X="ABC"
Set X=$ZCVT(X,"L")
Write !,X
abc
```

In Example 3-33, $Zconvert converts the X string to lowercase. Notice the second parameter "L" for converting to lowercase.

## $Zstrip System-Supplied Function

$Zstrip strips characters from a data string, it requires two parameters:

- ➢ The target string
- ➢ What to strip

## *$Zstrip strips leading spaces*

**Example 3-34 Strip leading spaces**

```
Set X="    ABC    DEF    "
Set X=$ZSTRIP(X,"<W")
Write !,"-",X,"-"
-ABC    DEF    -
```

In Example 3-34, *$Zstrip* strips the leading spaces from a string. Notice the second parameter, "<W" or the "less than" character which means leading characters and the "W" to specify white spaces.

## *$Zstrip strips trailing spaces*

**Example 3-35 Strips trailing spaces**

```
Set X="    ABC    DEF    "
Set X=$ZSTRIP(X,">W")
Write !,"-",X,"-"
-    ABC    DEF-
```

In Example 3-35, *$Zstrip* strips the trailing spaces from a string. Notice the second parameter, ">W" or the "greater than" character which means trailing characters and the"W" to specify white spaces.

## *$Zstrip strips leading and trailing spaces*

**Example 3-36 Strip leading and trailing spaces**

```
Set X="    ABC    DEF    "
Set X=$ZSTRIP(X,"<>W")
Write !,"-",X,"-"
-ABC    DEF-
```

In Example 3-36, *$Zstrip* strips the leading and trailing spaces from a string. Notice the second parameter, "<>W", or the "less than" and "greater than" characters which means both leading and trailing characters and "W" for white spaces.

## *$Zstrip strips all spaces*

**Example 3-37 Strip all spaces**

```
Set X="    ABC    DEF    "
Set X=$ZSTRIP(X,"*W")
Write !,"-",X,"-"
-ABCDEF-
```

In Example 3-37, *$Zstrip* strips all spaces from a string. Notice the second parameter of *$Zstrip*, "*W", the asterisk character meaning all characters and "W" for white spaces. *$Zstrip* has other capabilities; refer to the Caché documentation from InterSystems, Inc., *www.intersystems.com*.

$Zstrip may also be used to strip characters.

### *$Zstrip Strips Characters*

**Example 3-38 $Zstrip Strip Characters**

```
Set X="ABC123DEF456"
Set X=$ZSTRIP(X,"*","123")
Write !,"-",X,"-"
-ABCDEF456-
```

In Example 3-36, *$Zstrip* strips the characters "123" from the variables X.


## *Chapter 3 Summary*

Chapters 3 and 4 cover many *System-Supplied Functions* in Caché ObjectScript (COS). This chapter covered: 1) *$Length* – returns the length of a string, or the number of pieces in a string, 2) *$Extract* – returns or sets a substring within a string, 3) *$Find* – finds the location of a substring within a string, 4) *$Replace* – replaces one substring for another, *5) $Translate* – converts characters in a string, 6) *$Zconvert* - converts string, 7) *$Zstrip* – strips characters from a string and 8) *Delimiters and Delimited strings*.

*"Few things are harder to put up with than the annoyance of a good example." – Mark Twain*

# Chapter 4 System-Supplied Functions II

Chapters 3 and 4 cover many **System-Supplied Functions** in Caché ObjectScript (COS). *System-Supplied Functions* are an extension of the base commands. They include string handling capabilities, numeric capabilities, as well as variable testing capabilities.

## System-Supplied Functions

**System-Supplied Functions** are "called routines" or subroutines that perform a specific task and return a value. They are an extension of the basic commands, a prefix of "**$**" identifies them.

## User-Defined Functions

**User-Defined Functions** are "called routines" or subroutines that perform a specific task and return a value. An application programmer creates them. A prefix of "**$$**" identifies them. By the use of *User-Defined Functions*, one can expand the capabilities of COS.

## System-Supplied Functions - Data

**Data System-Supplied Functions** provide information as to the existence and structure of data.

> - **$Data** – returns a numeric value describing the existence and structure of a Global or array node
> - **$Get** – determines the existence of a variable

## $Data System-Supplied Function

*$Data* returns a numeric value describing the existence and structure of a Global or array node.

**Table 4-1 $Data Table of Returned Values**

| What $Data Returns | Does the Array Node have Value? | Does the Array Node Have Descendants? |
|---|---|---|
| 0 | No | No |
| 1 | Yes | No |
| 10 | No | Yes |
| 11 | Yes | Yes |

Table 4-1 shows the four values returned by *$Data* as to the node's value and descendants.

Example 4-1 Local Array

```
Set A(1)="data"           ; this node has a value but no descendants

Set A(2)=""               ; this node has a null value but no descendants

Set A(3,1)="data"         ; this node has a value and by implication is a
                          ; descendant of the nonexistent node A(3)

Set A(4)="data"           ; this node has a value and descendants
Set A(4,1)="data"  ; this node is a descendant and has descendants
Set A(4,1,2)="data"       ; this node is a descendant
```

In

Example 4-1, we set up several different types of array nodes and descendants used in the following examples. Here we used a local array; we can get the same result from a Global array as well. Chapters 6 and 7 cover Globals.

## *Array node that has a value but no descendants*

Example 4-2 Array node that has a value but no descendants

```
Write !,$D(A(1))
1
```

In Example 4-2, one is returned because the array node A(1) has a value but no descendants.

## *Array node that has a null value and no descendants*

Example 4-3 Array node that has a null value and no descendants

```
Write !,$D(A(2))
1
```

In Example 4-3, the array node A(2) has a null value, this is valid as far as *$Data* is concerned. If A(2) did not exist, then *$Data* would return a zero.

## *Array node that has no value but has descendants*

Example 4-4 Array node that has no value but has descendants

```
Write !,$D(A(3))
10
```

In Example 4-4, the array node A(3) is nonexistent, but it does have a descendant of A(3,1), so a 10 is returned from *$Data*.

### Array node that has a value and descendants

**Example 4-5 Array node that has a value and descendants**

```
Write !,$D(A(4))
11
```

In Example 4-5, the array node of A(4) has both a value and descendants, hence *$Data* returns an 11.

### Array node that has a value but no descendants

**Example 4-6 Array node that has a value but no descendants**

```
Write !,$D(A(3,1))
1
```

In Example 4-6, array node A(3,1) has a value but no descendants.

### Array node that has a value and descendants

**Example 4-7 Array node that has a value and descendants**

```
Write !,$D(A(4,1))
11
```

In Example 4-7, array node A(4,1) has a value and descendants.

### Array node that does not exist and has no descendants

**Example 4-8 Array node does not exist and has no descendants.**

```
Write !,$D(A(5))
0
```

In Example 4-8, array node A(5) does not exist and has no descendants.

### *$Data with the If command*

Many times, the value that *$Data* returns is not specifically interrogated. In this situation, *$Data* returns true if its value is one, ten, or eleven and false if its value is zero.

**Example 4-9 $Data with the If command**

```
Set A(1)="data"
Set A(2)=""
Set A(3,1)="data"
Set A(4)="data"
Set A(4,1)="data"

If $D(A(1)) Write "True"  ;returns a 1, node has value but no descendants
True
If $D(A(2)) Write "True"  ;returns a 1, node has value but no descendants
```

```
True
If $D(A(3)) Write "True"  ;returns 10, node has no value but has descendants
True
If $D(A(3,1)) Write "True" ;returns 1, node has value but no descendants
True
If $D(A(4)) Write "True"  ;returns 11, node has value and descendants
True
If $D(A(5)) Write "True"  ;returns 0, node has no value nor descendants
<>
```

In Example 4-9, *$Data* is combined with the *If* command. If *$Data* returns a 1, 10, or 11, it is true. If *$Data* returns a 0, it is false.

## Exercises on $Data Exercises

Here is your chance to try out what you have learned. Try to guess what each of the *Write* commands will produce. The answers are shown after the questions.

  ➢ Kill A Write $D(A)

  ➢ If $D(A) Write "hit"

  ➢ Set A="" Write $D(A)

  ➢ Set A(1)="data" Write $D(A)

  ➢ Kill A Set A(1)="data" Write $D(A)

  ➢ If $D(A) Write "hit"

## Answer to Exercises on $Data

**Example 4-10 Answers**

```
Kill A
Write $D(A)              ;variable does not exist
0


If $D(A) Write "Hit"     ;variable does not exist
<>


Set A=""
Write $D(A)              ;variable exists but with a null value
1


Set A(1)="data"          ;both node and descendants exist
Write $D(A)
11

Kill A
Set A(1)="data"
Write $D(A)              ;node has no value but does have a descendant
10


If $D(A) Write "Hit"     ;node has no value but does have descendants
Hit
```

Example 4-10 gives the answers to the exercises.

## *$Get System-Supplied Function*

$Get determines the existence of a variable. $Get:

> ➤ returns the value if the variable has a value
>
> ➤ returns null if the variable has a null value
>
> ➤ returns null if the variable does not exist
>
> ➤ returns the default value if the variable's value does not exist

## *$Get returns the variable's value*

**Example 4-11 $Get returns the variables' value**

```
Set X="ABC"
Write !,$G(X)
ABC
```

In Example 4-11, *$Get* returns the value of variable X, "ABC"

## *$Get returns null*

**Example 4-12 $Get returns null**

```
Set Y=""
Write $G(Y)        ; Y has a value of null
<>

Kill Z
Write $G(Z)        ; Z does not exist
<>
```

In Example 4-12, null is returned because the variable does not exist nor has a null value.

## *$Get with a default parameter*

*$Get* may have an optional second parameter. The second parameter is the value to be returned if the variable does not exist.

**Example 4-13 $Get with a default parameter**

```
Set X=1
Write !, $G(X,"DEF")      ; If X has null as a value, the default is not used
1

Set X=""
Write !, $G(X,"DEF")      ; If X has null as a value, the default is not used
<>

Kill X
Write !, $G(X,"DEF")      ; If X does not exist, then the default is used
```

In Example 4-13, a second or default parameter is specified. When the variable X does not exist, the default parameter is used.  If the variable has a value or a null value, the default parameter is not used.

## System-Supplied Functions - Number formatting

COS has two *System-Supplied Functions* that format numbers.

➤ **$FNumber** – adds commas, decimal places, etc. to a number

➤ **$Justify** – right justifies a number and does some formatting

*$FNumber* and *$Justify* may be used separately or combined to format numbers.

## $FNumber System-Supplied Function

### $FNumber inserts commas in a number

**Example 4-14 $FNumber inserts commas in a number**

```
Write $FN(1234,",")
1,234

Set X=1234
Write $FN(X,",")
1,234
```

In Example 4-14, *$FNumber* inserts commas into a number.

### $FNumber inserts commas in a negative number

**Example 4-15 $FNumber inserts commas in a negative number**

```
Set X=-1234
Write $FN(X,",")
-1,234
```

In Example 4-15, *$FNumber* inserts commas into a negative number.

### $FNumber inserts a comma and a decimal point

**Example 4-16 $FNumber inserts a comma and a decimal point**

```
Set X=123456
Write $FN(X,",",2)          ; 2 - indicates 2 decimal places
123,456.00
```

In Example 4-16, *$FNumber* inserts commas and a decimal point into a number. The third parameter of "2" indicates 2 decimal places.

## $FNumber inserts commas and rounds a number

### Example 4-17 $FNumber inserts commas and rounds a number

```
Set X=123456.55
Write $FN(X,",",0).        ; 0 - indicates no decimal places
123,457
```

In Example 4-17, *$FNumber* inserts commas into the number and rounds to the nearest whole number. The third parameter of "0" indicates no decimal places and the 55 is rounded up.

# $Justify System-Supplied Function

## $Justify, Ten Character field, right justified

### Example 4-18 $Justify, Ten Character field, right justified

```
Set X=123657
Write $J(X,10)
    123657
```

In Example 4-18, *$Justify* returns a number in a ten character field, right justified.

## $Justify, Ten Character field, right justified with 2 decimal places

### Example 4-19 $Justify, Ten Character field, right justified with 2 decimal places

```
Set X=123657
Write $J(X,10,2)
 123657.00
```

In Example 4-19, *$Justify* returns a number in a ten character field, right justified with two decimal places. Note that the decimal point is included in the field size.

## $Justify, Ten Character field, alpha text, right justified

### Example 4-20 $Justify, Ten Character field, alpha text, right justified

```
Set X="ABCDEF"
Write $J(X,10)
    ABCDEF
```

In Example 4-20, *$Justify* returns an alpha text right justified in a ten character field.

## $Justify produces tabular output

### Example 4-21 $Justify produces tabular output

```
Set X1=123
Set X2=65432
Set X3=546.44
```

```
Set X4=0505.22
Write $J(X1,10,2)
Write $J(X2,10,2)
Write $J(X3,10,2)
Write $J(X4,10,2)
Write $J("----------",10)
Write $J((X1+X2+X3+X4),10,2)

    123.00
  65432.00
    546.44
    505.22
----------
  66606.66
```

In Example 4-21, *$Justify* produces a tabular output.

## $FNumber and $Justify Combined

### Format 12 digits, commas, right justified, 2 decimal

**Example 4-22 Format 12 digits, commas, right justified, 2 decimal**

```
Set X=12345
Write $J($FN(X,",",2),12)
   12,345.00
```

In Example 4-22, *$Justify* and *$FNumber* are combined to return a number in a twelve digit field, with commas, right justified and two decimal places.

### Format 12 digits, commas, right justified, 2 decimal, negative

**Example 4-23 Format 12 digits, commas, right justified, 2 decimal, negative**

```
Set X=-12345
Write $J($FN(X,"P,",2),12)
  (12,345.00)
```

In Example 4-23, *$Justify* and *$FNumber* are combined to return a number in a twelve digit field, with commas, right justified and two decimal places, using parentheses to signify negative. The middle parameter of "P," tells the function to use parentheses if negative and to insert commas.

### Format 12 digits, commas, right justified, 2 decimal, trailing minus sign

**Example 4-24 Format 12 digits, commas, right justified, 2 decimal, trailing minus sign**

```
Set X=-12345
Write $J($FN(X,"T,",2),12)
   12,345.00-
```

In Example 4-24, *$Justify* and *$FNumber* are combined to return a number in a twelve digit field, with commas, right justified and two decimal places using a trailing minus sign. The middle parameter of "T," tells the function to use a trailing minus sign if negative and to insert commas.

## Exercises on $FNumber and $Justify

Here is your chance to try out what you have learned. The answers are shown after the questions.

> Write this number with commas inserted
>
> Set X=1234

> Write this number with commas and two decimal places
>
> Set X=123456

> Write this number with no decimal places and round
>
> Set X=123456.55

> Write this number right justified in a 10 character field with 2 decimal places
>
> Set X=657

> Combine $Justify and $FNumber to give 12,345.00, right-justified, in a 12 character field
>
> Set X=12345

## Answer to Exercises on $FNumber and $Justify

**Example 4-25 $FNumber and $Justify Exercises answers**

```
Write this number with commas inserted
Set X=1234
Write $FN(X,",")
1,234

Write this number with commas and two decimal places
Set X=123456
Write $FN(X,",",2)
123,456.00

Write this number with no decimal places and round
Set X=123456.55
Write $FN(X,",",0)
123,457

Write this number right justified in a 10 character field with 2 decimal
places
Set X=657
Write $J(X,10,2)
    657.00

Combine $Justify and $FNumber to give 12,345.00, right-justified, in a
12 character field
Set X=12345
Write $J($FN(X,",",2),12)
   12,345.00
```

Example 4-25 contains the answers to the exercises.

# System-Supplied Functions - Character Representation

## $Ascii and $Char System-Supplied Functions

**$Ascii** converts a character to its ASCII equivalent numeric value. Every common character has an ASCII equivalent numeric value.

**$Char** converts an ASCII numeric value to its character equivalent.

**Example 4-26 $Ascii and $Char**

```
Write $Ascii("A")
65
Write $Char(66)
B
```

In Example 4-26 *$Ascii* displays the ASCII equivalent numeric value for uppercase "A", which is 65. The *$Char* converts the ASCII equivalent numeric value 66 to its respective character, which logically is uppercase "B".

A letter may be converted from uppercase to lowercase by adding 32 to its ASCII equivalent numeric value. In the same way, a lowercase letter may be changed to uppercase by subtracting 32 from its ASCII equivalent numeric value. Remembering that the uppercase letters come before the lowercase letters on the ASCII Table, makes it easier to remember when to add or subtract.

## Convert uppercase to lowercase

**Example 4-27 Convert uppercase to lowercase**

```
Set X=$ASCII("A")+32
Write $CHAR(X)
a
```

The code in Example 4-27 converts the uppercase "A" to lowercase "a" by adding 32 to its ASCII equivalent numeric value.

## Convert lowercase to uppercase

**Example 4-28 Convert lowercase to uppercase**

```
Set X=$ASCII("a")-32
Write $CHAR(X)
A
```

The code in Example 4-28, converts the lowercase "a" to an uppercase "A" by subtracting 32 from its ASCII equivalent numeric value.

# System-Supplied Functions - Decision Making

## $Case and $Select System-Supplied Functions

*$Case* and *$Select* do the same thing, but use different syntax. They provide a way of performing a series of decisions and selecting the first correct one. Multiple *If* commands can give the same result.

## $Select Example

**Example 4-29 $Select Example**

```
Write $S(X=1:"One",X=2:"Two",X=3:"Three",1:"None")

The above $Select command is equivalent to:
    If X=1 {Write "One"}
    ElseIf X=2 {Write "Two"}
    ElseIf X=3 {Write "Three"}
    Else {Write "None"}
```

In Example 4-29, the variable X is interrogated and depending upon its value, One, Two, Three, or None is displayed.

## $Case Example

**Example 4-30 $Case Example**

```
Write $CASE(X,1:"One",2:"Two",3:"Three",:"None")

The above $Case command is equivalent to:
For the variable X:
    If X=1 {Write "One"}
    ElseIf X=2 {Write "Two"}
    ElseIf X=3 {Write "Three"}
    Else {Write "None"}
```

The code in Example 4-30 interrogates the variable X, and depending upon its value, One, Two Three, or None is displayed.

## $Case Example for Days of Week

**Example 4-31 $Case Example for Day of Week**

```
To run this code you must put the code in a routine, save the routine, and then
run the routine from the terminal.

 Set DayOfWeek=2
 Set Day=$CASE(DayOfWeek,
              1:"Sunday",
              2:"Monday",
              3:"Tuesday",
              4:"Wednesday",
              5:"Thursday",
              6:"Friday",
```

```
                        7:"Saturday",
                          :"error")
Write !,Day
Monday
```

Example 4-31 demonstrates using *$Case* to display the day of the week.

## *$Test System-Supplied Function*

**$TEST** interprets the success or failure of the most recent command.

**Example 4-32 $Test with the Read command**

```
To run this code you must put the code in a routine, save the routine, and then
run the routine from the terminal.
```

```
 R "Prompt: ",X:3                  ;timed read command, 3 seconds
 If $Test {
    Write !,"The user answered the prompt"
 }
 Else {
    Write !,"The user did not answer the prompt"
 }
```

In Example 4-32, *$Test* is used with a *Timed-Read* command to see if the user answered the prompt rather than let the *Read* command time-out by itself. *$Test* may be combined with other commands, including the *Job, Lock, Open, Read and Close* commands.

# *System-Supplied Functions - Miscellaneous*

## *$Increment System-Supplied Function*

**$Increment** is a way to update a counter without employing the Lock command to obtain exclusive use of the Global variable or node. Since the *Lock* command is expensive, this function is desirable. The *Lock* command is covered in Chapter 7.

**Example 4-33 $Increment**

```
Set ^CNTR=""
Set X=$INCREMENT(^CNTR)
Write ^CNTR
1

Set X=$INCREMENT(^CNTR)
Write ^CNTR
2
```

In Example 4-33, *$Increment* updates the Global counter ^CNTR. The variable X is set to the return code. Another advantage of *$Increment* is that ^CNTR does not need to exist. If it does not exist, it is created.

## $Text System-Supplied Function

**$Text** is a way of referring to a line of code within a COS routine. One of its uses is when you want to include a short table in a routine.

**Example 4-34 $Text - Error code table**

```
To run this code you must put the code in a routine, save the routine, and then
run the routine from the terminal.

ROUTINEA
        For I=1:1:3 Write !,$T(TABLE+I)
        Q
TABLE
    ;;A01^Error code 1
    ;;A02^Error code 2
    ;;A03^Error code 3
```

In Example 4-34, a small error code table is included. When *$Text* refers to TABLE+I, it is referring to the Label TABLE and the +I is the number of lines from TABLE.

**Example 4-35 Error code table output**

```
    ;;A01^Error code 1
    ;;A02^Error code 2
    ;;A03^Error code 3
```

Example 4-35 shows the output of running the code in Example 4-34.

---

### Programmer's Tip: Display a Routine's Name

When a routine encounters an error, you should display where in the source code the error has occurred, such as the routine name. An excellent way to refer to a routine's name is to use *$Text*:

```
    Write !,$T(+0),"An error has occurred  . . ."
```

The advantage of this technique is that if a routine's name changes, the above code always displays the correct routine name. The routine's name is always on the first line.

---

## Chapter 4 Summary

Chapters 3 and 4 cover many *System-Supplied Functions* in Caché ObjectScript (COS). This chapter covered: 1) Functions relating to data: *$Data* and *$Get, 2)* Functions relating to numbers: *$FNumber* and *$Justify, 3)* Functions relating to Character Representation: *$Ascii and $Char* 4) Functions relating to Decision making: *$Case, $Select and $Test, and 4)* Miscellaneous functions:, *$Increment, and $Text.*

*"When the only tool you have is a hammer, everything looks like a nail." – Abraham H. Maslow*

# Chapter 5 List Processing

Chapter 5 covers the topic of **List Processing** in Caché ObjectScript (COS). Data elements grouped together are *Lists*. *List Processing* controls how data is stored, retrieved, compared, integrated and translated.

There are two primary ways to process lists in COS; with **$Piece**, or with the **ListBuild** set of *System-Supplied functions*. Since *ListBuild* has more capability, we shall consider them first. The *ListBuild* set of *System-Supplied Functions* include:

> $ListBuild       – ($LB) build a list
> $List             – ($LI) selects an element from the list, (similar to $Piece)

> $ListFind        – ($LF) finds an element in the list, (similar to $Find)
> $ListLength    – ($LL) returns the number of elements in a list, (similar to $Length with two
> parameters)

> $ListData       – ($LD) tests to see if an element exists in a list, (similar to $Data)
> $ListGet         – ($LG) returns a element in a list or null if the element does not exist, (similar
> to $Get)

> $ListNext       – ($LN) sequentially returns elements in a list
> $ListSame      – ($LS)  compares two lists

> $ListToString   – ($LTS) creates a string from a list
> $ListFromString – ($LFS) creates a list from a string

> $ListValid       – ($LV) is this a valid list?

Our first task is to define a list, **$ListBuild** will accomplish this task. There is more than one way to define a list.

# $ListBuild or $LB – build a list

## $ListBuild defines a list using literal parameters

### Example 5-1 $ListBuild defines a list of Pets using literal parameters

```
Set Pets=$LB("Dog","Cat","Fish")
Write !,Pets
DogCatFish
```

In Example 5-1, *$ListBuild* defines a list of Pets using literal parameters.

## $ListBuild defines a list using variable parameters

### Example 5-2 $ListBuild defines a list of Pets using variable parameters

```
Set Pet1="Dog"
Set Pet2="Cat"
Set Pet3="Fish"
Set Pets=$LB(Pet1,Pet2,Pet3)
Write !,Pets
DogCatFish
```

In Example 5-2, *$ListBuild* defines a list of Pets using variable parameters.

# $List or $LI - list

## $List displays elements from the list

### Example 5-3 $List displays elements from the list of Pets

```
Set Pets=$LB("Dog","Cat","Fish")
Write !,$LI(Pets,1)
Dog
Write !,$LI(Pets,2)
Cat
Write !,$LI(Pets,3)
Fish
```

In Example 5-3, *$List* displays the three elements from Pets.

## $List used to set variables

### Example 5-4 $List used to set variables

```
Set Pets=$LB("Dog","Cat","Fish")
Set Pet1=$LI(Pets,1)
Write !,Pet1
Dog
Set Pet2=$LI(Pets,2)
```

```
Write !,Pet2
Cat
Set Pet3=$LI(Pets,3)
Write !,Pet3
Fish
```

In Example 5-4, the three list elements from the list of Pets are set to variables named Pet1, Pet2 and Pet3 respectively.

## $List displays the list

**Example 5-5 $List displays the list of Pets**

```
Set Pets=$LB("Dog","Cat","Fish")
Write !,$LI(Pets,1,3)
DogCatFish
```

In Example 5-5, *$List* displays the list of Pets. Although it may seem like there is no separation between each of the elements, Caché uses unprintable characters to mark the separation between the elements.

## Display the entire list

**Example 5-6 Display the entire list of Pets**

```
Set Pets=$LB("Dog","Cat","Fish")
Write !,Pets
DogCatFish
```

In Example 5-6, the *Write* command displays the list of Pets.

## $List to add a fourth element to the list

**Example 5-7 $List to add a fourth element to the list of Pets**

```
Set Pets=$LB("Dog","Cat","Fish")
Set $LI(Pets,4)="Bird"
Write !,Pets
DogCatFishBird
```

In Example 5-7, a fourth element is added to the list of Pets using *$List*.

You will not always know if a list element exists. COS provides two *System-Supplied Functions* to deal with this situation:

# $ListData or $LD (similar to $Data)

## $ListData demonstration

**Example 5-8 $ListData demonstration**

```
Set Pets=$LB("Dog","Cat","Fish","")    ;4 elements are defined

If $LD(Pets,3) Write !,"Element 3 does exist"
Element 3 does exist

Write !,$LD(Pets,3)              ;$LD returns a 1 when the element exists
1

If $LD(Pets,4) Write !,"Element 4 is null but does exist"
Element 4 is null but does exist

Write !,$LD(Pets,4)             ;$LD returns a 1 when the element is null
1

If '$LD(Pets,5) Write !,"Element 5 does not exist" ;Single quote before the
Element 5 does not exist        ;$LD is a "not" and is interperted as
                                ;If $LD(Pets,5)=0. See Chapter 11 for
                                ;for more information on the "not"

Write !,$LD(Pets,5)             ;$LD returns a 0 when the element does
0                               ;not exist
```

In Example 5-8, *$LISTDATA* determines if elements 3, 4, and 5 exist. Element 3 does exist, so returns a one. Element 4 is null but still exists, so it returns a one. However, element five does not exist, so it returns a zero.

## $ListGet or $LG (similar to $Get)

### $ListGet demonstration

**Example 5-9 $ListGet demonstration**

```
Set Pets=$LB("Dog","Cat","Fish","")       ;4 elements are defined
Write !,$LG(Pets,3)
Fish

Write !,$LG(Pets,4)        ;$LG returns null because the element is null
<>

Write !,$LG(Pets,5)        ;$LG returns null because the element does not
exist
<>
```

In Example 5-9, *$ListGet* returns elements 3, 4 and 5. $LG returns "FISH" for element 3, null for elements 4 and 5. Element 4 is null and element 5 does not exist.

## $ListFind or $LF (similar to $Find)

### $ListFind returns the position of the element found

**Example 5-10 $ListFind returns the position of the element found**

```
Set Pets=$LB("Dog","Cat","Fish","")
Write !,$LF(Pets,"Cat")              ;"Cat" is the second element
2

Write !,$LF(Pets,"Snake")            ;"Snake" does not exist
0

Write !,$LF(Pets,"")                 ;null does exist
4
```

In Example 5-10, *$LISTFIND* finds the element "Cat" and returns a 2. In the second example, *$ListFind* tries to find the element "Snake" and returns a zero because "Snake" is not part of the list of Pets. For the third example, $LF finds a null in the fourth element.

### $ListFind returns the position of the element found after the third position

**Example 5-11 $ListFind returns the position of the element found after the third position**

```
Set Pets=$LB("Dog","Cat","Fish","Cat")
Write !,$LF(Pets,"Cat",3)        ;Find "Cat" after the third position
4
```

In Example 5-11, *$ListFind* finds the element "Cat" after the third position. There are two "Cats" in this list, one in the second position and one is in the fourth position.

## $ListFind in a compound find

```
Set Pets=$LB("Dog","Cat","Fish","Cat")
Write !,$LF(Pets,"Cat",$LF(Pets,"Cat"))
4
```

In Example 5-12, *$ListFind* is compounded upon itself and finds the second occurrence of the element "Cat". The first $LF finds the first occurrence of "Cat" at position 2. Using 2 as a starting point, $LF finds the second occurrence of "Cat" at position 4.

# $ListLength or $LL (similar to $Length with two parameters)

## $ListLength returns the number of elements

```
Set Pets=$LB("Dog","Cat","Fish")
Write !,$LL(Pets)
3
```

In Example 5-13, **$LISTLENGTH** returns the total number of elements in Pets.

## $ListLength and the For Loop command

```
Set Pets=$LB("Dog","Cat","Fish")
For I=1:1:$LL(Pets) Write !,$LI(Pets,I)
Dog
Cat
Fish
```

In Example 5-14, *$ListLength* is combined with the *$List* and the *For loop* command to list all elements in Pets.

# $ListNext or $LN - sequentially returns elements in a list.

## $ListNext displays all elements in a list

```
To run this code you must put the code in a routine, save the routine, and then
run the routine from the terminal.

Set Pets=$LB("Dog","Cat","","Fish")
Set Pointer=0                          ;Set pointer to 0 to start at top
While $ListNext(Pets,Pointer,Value) {
```

```
   Write !,Value
}

Dog
Cat
<>
Fish
```

In Example 5-15, *$ListNext* displays all elements in a list. Set the Pointer to zero to start at the top of the list.

## *$ListSame or $LS compares two lists*

### *$ListSame compares two lists*

**Example 5-16 $ListSame compares two lists**

```
Set Pets1=$LB("Dog","Cat","Fish")
Set Pets2=$LB("Dog","Cat","Fish")
If $LS(Pets1,Pets2) Write !,"The two lists are the same"
The two lists are the same

Write !,$LS(Pets1,Pets2)
1

Set Pets1=$LB("Dog","Cat")
Set Pets2=$LB("Dog","Cat","Fish")
If '$LS(Pets1,Pets2) Write !,"The two lists are not the same"
The two lists are not the same

Write !,$LS(Pets1,Pets2)
0
```

The code in Example 5-16 compares two lists. In the first example, the two lists are the same and in the second example, the two lists are different.

## *$ListToString or $LTS creates a string from a list*

### *$ListToString creates a string from a list*

**Example 5-17 $ListToString creates a string from a list**

```
Set Pets=$LB("Dog","Cat","Fish")
Set String=$LTS(Pets,"^")        ;delimiter ^
Write String
Dog^Cat^Fish


Set Pets=$LB("Dog","Cat","Fish")
Set String=$LTS(Pets,"~")        ;delimiter ~
Write String
Dog~Cat~Fish
```

In Example 5-17, **$ListToString** converts the Pets list to a delimited string. Note that the delimiter is specified by the second parameter to *$LTS*.

---

### *Delimiters*

Delimiters are special characters that separate pieces of data in a string. In the following string the delimiter is "^" and the pieces of data are Dog, Cat, Fish, and Turtle.

```
Dog^Cat^Fish^Turtle
```

---

## *$ListFromString or $LFS creates a list from a string*

### *$ListFromString creates a list from a string*

**Example 5-18 $ListFromString creates a list from a string**

```
Set String="Dog^Cat^Fish"        ;delimited string
Set Pets=$LFS(String,"^")         ;delimiter ^
Write Pets
DogCatFish                        ;list

Set String="Dog~Cat~Fish"         ;delimited string
Set Pets=$LFS(String,"~")         ;delimiter ~
Write Pets
DogCatFish                        ;list
```

In Example 5-18, **$LISTFROMSTRING** converts a delimited string to a list. Note that the delimiter is specified by the second parameter to *$LFS*.

## *$ListValid or $LV checks for a valid list*

### *$ListValid – checks for a valid list*

**Example 5-19 $ListValid – checks for a valid list**

```
Set String=$LB("Dog","Cat","Fish")
If $LV(String) Write !,"This is a valid list"
This is a valid list

Write !,$LV(String)               ;$LV returns a 1 if the list is valid
1

Set String=$LB("")                ;null list is still valid
If $LV(String) Write !,"This is a valid list"
This is a valid list
```

```
Write !,$LV(String)
1

Set String="ABC"
If '$LV(String) Write !,"This is NOT a valid list"
This is NOT a valid list

Write !,$LV(String)        ;$LV returns a 0 because the list is not valid
0
```

In Example 5-19, *$ListValid* determines if various lists are valid or not.

# Exercises on List Processing Exercises

## List Processing Exercise 1

Using anyone of the *ListBuild System-Supplied Functions*, write code that will create a list of Pets that includes "Dog"," "Cat", "Fish" and "" or null. Next, write the code to cycle through the Pets and display every element defined.

**Example 5-20 List Processing Exercise 1, First solution**

```
To run this code you must put the code in a routine, save the routine, and then
run the routine from the terminal.

Set Pets=$LB("Dog","Cat","Fish","")
For I=1:1:$LL(Pets) {
  If $LD(Pets,I)=1 Write !,$LI(Pets,I)
}
Dog
Cat
Fish
<>                    ;fourth element displayed, even though it is null
```

In Example 5-20, *$ListBuild* creates the list of Pets. Then a *For Loop* command traverses through all the elements of the Pets list. *The output from $ListData* decides if the specific element should be displayed or not. However, there is a problem here. If you remember *$Data,* a null value is still a valid value. The same is true of *$ListData*, null is a valid value. The fourth element is blank and returns a blank. For this type of test, *$ListGet* is a better choice.

**Example 5-21 List Processing Exercise 1, Second solution**

```
To run this code you must put the code in a routine, save the routine, and then
run the routine from the terminal.

Set Pets=$LB("Dog","Cat","Fish","")
For I=1:1:$LL(Pets) {
  If $LG(Pets,I)'="" Write !,$LI(Pets,I)
}
Dog
Cat
Fish
```

In Example 5-21, *$ListBuild* creates the list of Pets. Then a *For loop* command traverses through all the elements of the Pets list. The output from *$ListGet* decides if the specific element should be displayed or not.

**Example 5-22 List Processing Exercise 1, Third solution**

```
To run this code you must put the code in a routine, save 7the routine, and
then run the routine from the terminal.

Set Pets=$LB("Dog","Cat","Fish","")
For I=1:1:$LL(Pets) {
  If $LI(Pets,I)'="" Write !,$LI(Pets,I)
}
Dog
Cat
Fish
```

In Example 5-22, *$ListBuild* creates the list of Pets. Then a *For loop* command traverses through all the elements of the Pets list. *The output of $List decides* if the specific element should be displayed or not.

**Example 5-23 List Processing Exercise 1, Fourth solution**

```
To run this code you must put the code in a routine, save the routine, and then
run the routine from the terminal.

Set String="Dog^Cat^Fish"
Set Pets=$LFS(String,"^")
For I=1:1:$LL(Pets) {
  If $LI(Pets,I)'="" Write !,$LI(Pets,I)
}
Dog
Cat
Fish
```

In Example 5-23, *$ListFromString* creates the Pets list from a string. Then a *For loop* command traverses through all the elements of the Pets list. *The output of $List decides* if the specific element should be displayed or not.

**Example 5-24 List Processing Exercise 1, Fifth solution**

```
To run this code you must put the code in a routine, save the routine, and then
run the routine from the terminal.

Set String="Dog^Cat^Fish"
Set Pets=$LFS(String,"^")
Set Pointer=0
While $ListNext(Pets,Pointer,Value) {
  Write !,Value
}
Dog
Cat
Fish
```

In Example 5-24, *$ListFromString* creates the Pets list from a string. Then *$ListNext* traverses through all the elements of the Pets list.

## List Processing Exercise 2

Using any one of the *ListBuild System-Supplied Functions*, write code that will create a list of Pets that includes "Dog", "Cat" and "Fish". Next, search for the element "Dog" in Pets, and if that element exists, set that element to null.

**Example 5-25 List Processing Exercise 2, First solution**

```
To run this code you must put the code in a routine, save the routine, and then
run the routine from the terminal.

Set Pets=$LB("Dog","Cat","Fish")
For I=1:1:$LL(Pets) {
  If $LI(Pets,I)="Dog" Set $LI(Pets,I)=""
}

For I=1:1:$LL(Pets) Write !,$LI(Pets,I)

<>
Cat
Fish
```

In Example 5-25, *$ListBuild* creates the list of Pets. Then a *For Loop* command traverses through all the elements of the Pets list. *$List* interrogates each element, and when the one is found that contains "Dog", it is set to null. This example has the disadvantage of going through all the elements regardless of which element contains "Dog". If the list is particularly long, this will waste computer resources.

**Example 5-26 List Processing Exercise 2, Second solution**

```
To run this code you must put the code in a routine, save the routine, and then
run the routine from the terminal.

Set Pets=$LB("Dog","Cat","Fish")
Set Position=$LF(Pets,"Dog")                    ;List Find
If Position'=0 {
  Set $LI(Pets,Position)=""            ;Position of "Dog"
  Write !,"Position of ""Dog"" was: ",Position
}
Position of "Dog" was: 1

For I=1:1:$LL(Pets) Write !,$LI(Pets,I)

<>
Cat
Fish
```

In Example 5-26, *$ListBuild* creates the list of Pets. Then *$ListFind* finds the element that contains "Dog". If the element "Dog" is found, as signified by the variable Position not = zero, then replace the element with null using *$List*.

**Example 5-27 List Processing Exercise 2, Third solution**

```
To run this code you must put the code in a routine, save the routine, and then
run the routine from the terminal.

Set String="Dog^Cat^Fish"
Set Pets=$LFS(String,"^")
Set Position=$LF(Pets,"Dog")
If Position'=0 {
   Set $LI(Pets,Position)=""            ;Position of "Dog"
   Write !,"Position of ""Dog"" is: ",Position
}
Position of "Dog" is 1

For I=1:1:$LL(Pets) Write !,$LI(Pets,I)

<>
Cat
Fish
```

In Example 5-27, *$ListFromString* creates the Pets list from a string. Then *$ListFind* locates the element that contains "Dog". If the element "Dog" is found, as signified by the variable Position not = zero, then replace the element with null using *$List.*

## *List Processing Exercise 3*

Using any one of the *ListBuild System-Supplied Functions,* write code that will create a list of Pets that includes "Dog"," "Cat" and "Fish".  Next, write code that will find and switch the two elements "Dog" and "Fish" with each other. Assume that you do not already know the position of these elements. Note that the switch should be made only if both "Dog" and "Fish" are found in the list of Pets.

**Example 5-28 Switch Dog and Fish**

```
Set Pets=$LB("Dog","Cat","Fish")
Set Pos1=$LF(Pets,"Dog")               ;position of Dog
Set Pos2=$LF(Pets,"Fish")              ;position of Fish
If Pos1=0!(Pos2=0) Write "Not found"   ;if either Dog or Fish is not found
Quit
Set $LI(Pets,Pos1)="Fish"
Set $LI(Pets,Pos2)="Dog"
For I=1:1:$LL(Pets) Write !,$LI(Pets,I)
Fish
Cat
Dog
```

In Example 5-28, *$ListFind* finds the position of the elements "Dog" and "Fish". If either "Dog" or "Fish" is not found, then Quit; but if both "Dog" and "Fish" are found, then *$List* reverses these two elements.

## $Piece System-Supplied Function

The **$Piece** *System-Supplied Function* is an older method of processing lists. Much of the code in **Legacy** (older) systems uses *$Piece* extensively. I recommend using the *ListBuild* set of *System-Supplied Functions* for all new code since it does not have the restriction of having to define a delimiter.

Our first task is to define a delimited list, which can be done with or without *$Piece.*

## Define a delimited list

**Example 5-29 Defines delimited list of Pets**

```
Set Pets="Dog^Cat^Fish"
Write !,Pets
Dog^Cat^Fish
```

Example 5-29 defines a delimited list of Pets using a string, the delimiter caret (^) and the *Set* command.

## Delimited List

Note the difference between a *List* and a *Delimited List.* A *List* does not have a visible delimiter. The delimiter is an unprintable character controlled by the Caché system. In a *Delimited List*, the delimiter is defined by the programmer, which, in this case is a caret (^).

## Define a delimited list using variable parameters

**Example 5-30 Define a delimited list of Pets using variable parameters**

```
Set Pet1="Dog"
Set Pet2="Cat"
Set Pet3="Fish"
Set Pets=Pet1_"^"_ Pet2_"^"_ Pet3
Write !,Pets
Dog^Cat^Fish
```

Example 5-30 defines a delimited list of Pets using variables and the concatenation symbol (_).

## $Piece defines a delimited list

**Example 5-31 $Piece defines a delimited list**

```
Set Pets=""
Set $P(Pets,"^",1)="Dog"         ;define 1st piece
Set $P(Pets,"^",2)="Cat"         ;define 2nd piece
Set $P(Pets,"^",3)="Fish"        ;define 3rd piece
Write !,Pets
Dog^Cat^Fish
```

In Example 5-31, *$Piece* defines a delimited list of pets.

## $Piece displays elements in a delimited list

```
Set Pets="Dog^Cat^Fish"
Write !,$P(Pets,"^",1)          ;display the 1st piece
Dog
Write !,$P(Pets,"^",2)          ;display the 2nd piece
Cat
Write !,$P(Pets,"^",3)          ;display the 3rd piece
Fish
```

In Example 5-32, $Piece displays elements in the delimited list.

## $Piece breaks out elements from a delimited list

```
Set Pet1=$P(Pets,"^",1)         ;1st piece set to variable Pet1
Write !,Pet1
Dog
Set Pet2=$P(Pets,"^",2)         ;2nd piece set to variable Pet2
Write !,Pet2
Cat
Set Pet3=$P(Pets,"^",3)         ;3rd piece set to variable Pet3
Write !,Pet3
Fish
```

In Example 5-33, the three delimited list elements are set to their respective variables.

## $Piece displays all of the delimited list elements

```
Write !,$P(Pets,"^",1,3)
Dog^Cat^Fish
```

In Example 5-34, the entire delimited list is displayed using *$Piece* with four parameters. Note that the 1, 3 in *$Piece*, in this format it serves as a "From Piece" – "To Piece" and includes all pieces in between.

## Write command displays all the delimited list elements

```
Write !,Pets
Dog^Cat^Fish
```

In Example 5-35, the *Write* command displays all of the delimited list elements.

## *$Piece sets piece four*

**Example 5-36 $Piece sets piece four to "Bird"**

```
Set $P(Pets,"^",4)="Bird"
Write !,Pets
Dog^Cat^Fish^Bird
```

In Example 5-36, *$Piece* sets the fourth piece of the delimited list of pets to "Bird".

You will not always know if a delimited list element exists, so you must use two other *System-Supplied Functions* in combination with *$Piece*.

# *$Data – (similar to $ListData)*

With *$Data* and *$ListData*, a null ("") is considered to be a valid character.

## *$Data and $Piece*

**Example 5-37 $Data and $Piece**

```
Set Pets="Dog^Cat^Fish"
Set Pet3=$P(Pets,"^",3)
Write !,$D(Pet3)
1

Set Pet4=$P(Pets,"^",4)
Write !,$D(Pet4)
1
```

In Example 5-37, *$Data* is used to see if element three exists.  Element 3 exists so *$Data* returns a one. Next, piece four is set to the variable Pet4. You would expect that using *$Data* on Pet4 should return a zero, but since Pet4 is a valid variable with a value of null, *$Data* interprets this to be valid and a one is returned. If it is important that Pet4 be considered invalid if it contains a null, you must use *$Get*.

# *$Get – (similar to $ListGet)*

## *$Get and $Piece*

**Example 5-38 $Get and $Piece**

```
Set Pets="Dog^Cat^Fish"
Set Pet3=$P(Pets,"^",3)
Write !,$G(Pet3)
Fish

Set Pet4=$P(Pets,"^",4)
Write !,$G(Pet4)
<>
```

In Example 5-38, *$Get* obtains elements three and four. Element three from the delimited list exists so *$Get* returns "Fish", but element four does not exist so a null (""), is returned.

## Exercises on Delimited List Processing

Using *$Piece*, write code that will create a list of Pets that includes "Dog"," "Cat", "Fish" and null (""). Next, write the code to cycle through Pets and display every element defined.

**Example 5-39 Delimited List Processing Exercise**

```
To run this code you must put the code in a routine, save the routine, and then
run the routine from the terminal.

Set Pets=""
Set $P(Pets,"^",1)="Dog"
Set $P(Pets,"^",2)="Cat"
Set $P(Pets,"^",3)="Fish"
Set $P(Pets,"^",4)=""

For I=1:1:$L(Pets,"^") {
   If $P(Pets,"^",I)'="" Write !,$P(Pets,"^",I)
}
Dog
Cat
Fish
```

In Example 5-39, *$Piece* defines four elements in the Pets delimited list. Then a *For Loop* command traverses through all the elements of the Pets delimited list. The output of *$Piece* decides if the specific element should be displayed or not

## Delimiters

**DELIMITERS** are special characters that separate pieces of data in a string. With *$Piece*, you may specify your own delimiters. The problem with specifying your own delimiter is that the delimiter you specify may be in your raw data. If this happens, it will cause the count of pieces to be different from what one might expect.

### Delimited List problem demonstrated

**Example 5-40 Delimited problem demonstrated**

```
Set DOG="Rover"
Set CAT="Tiger"
Set FISH="Lamont"
Set PIG="Cud^dles"

Set $P(Pets,"^",1)=DOG
Set $P(Pets,"^",2)=CAT
Set $P(Pets,"^",3)=FISH
Set $P(Pets,"^",4)=PIG

For I=1:1:$L(Pets,"^") Write !,I," - ",$P(Pets,"^",I)
1 - Rover
```

```
2 - Tiger
3 - Lamount
4 - Cud
5 - dles
```

In Example 5-40, a list of Pets is set using four pet variables. However looking closely at the variable PIG, its name contains an embedded caret (^). The *For* command displays five elements instead of four. In addition, every element after the fourth will be off by one. This may become a serious error in any system that is dependent upon an expected piece count in a list.

The problem with an embedded delimiter is solved with list processing *($ListBuild, $List, $ListLength, $ListGet, $ListData)*. List processing uses it own unprintable delimiter.

## Delimited List Problem solved using $ListBuild

**Example 5-41 Delimited problem solved using the $ListBuild**

```
Set DOG="Rover"
Set CAT="Tiger"
Set FISH="Lamont"
Set PIG="Cud^dles"

Set Pets=$LB(DOG,CAT,FISH,PIG)

For I=1:1:$LL(Pets) Write !,I," - ",$LI(Pets,I)
1 - Rover
2 - Tiger
3 - Lamount
4 - Cud^dles
```

In Example 5-41, you can see that using list processing solves the problem of the unexpected delimiter.

Delimiters can be any character, ^ or * or & or |. Any delimiter chosen may show up in raw text and as such may introduce problems.

However, list processing has problems too. At times, a programmer sets a Global manually when fixing a problem. Take care when doing this in order that the special and unprintable delimiter is not overlaid. It is impossible to reproduce the *List's* delimiter on the keyboard.

## Correctly setting a Global array using $Piece or $ListBuild

**Example 5-42 Correctly setting a Global array using $Piece or $ListBuild**

```
Set ^Global1="Rover^Tiger^Lamount^Cuddles"
Set ^Global2=$LB("Rover","Tiger","Lamount","Cuddles")

Set $P(^Global1,"^",2)="Kitty"
Set $LI(^Global2,2)="Kitty"
```

Example 5-42 demonstrates the correct way to change elements in a Global created with *$Piece* and *$ListBuild*. Be careful to use the correct method when manually setting Global elements and do not mix the two.

## Compound $Piece and $ListBuild

A compound *$Piece* command is legal when retrieving data, but it is not legal when setting data.

## Retrieving an element using $Piece

**Example 5-43 Retrieving an element using $Piece**

```
Set ITEM="ABC^123*456^DEF"
Write $P($P(ITEM,"*",1),"^",2)
123
```

In Example 5-43, *$Piece* is compounded upon itself to retrieve an element defined within two delimiters.

## It is Illegal to set an element using $Piece in a compounded manner

**Example 5-44 It is Illegal to set an element using $Piece in a compounded manner.**

```
Set ITEM="ABC^123*456^DEF"

Set $P($P(ITEM,"*",1),"^",2)=789
^
<SYNTAX>
```

The code in Example 5-44 is attempting to set a variable using a compound *$Piece* and receives a <SYNTAX> error.

## Compound $ListBuild

## $ListBuild compounded upon itself

**Example 5-45 $ListBuild compounded upon itself**

```
Set Pets=$LB("Dogs",$LB("Rover","Teddy"),"Cats",$LB("Tiger","Kitty"))
```

The code in Example 5-45 uses *$ListBuild* compounded upon itself. The first element is "Dogs" with two sub-elements, "Rover" and "Teddy". The second element is "Cats" with two sub-elements, "Tiger" and "Kitty". This technique is not recommended unless it is known how the compound list was created. It may be difficult to determine how to break the list down. If you need to represent this kind of structure, use an array.

## Array to represent a compounded list

**Example 5-46 Array to represent a compounded list**

```
Set Pets("Dogs","Rover")=""
Set Pets("Dogs","Teddy")=""
Set Pets("Cats","Tiger")=""
```

```
Set Pets("Cats","Kitty")=""
```

In Example 5-46, we use an array to represent Pets instead of a compound list.

## Recommendations

I recommend that for all new development, you employ *the ListBuild* set of *System-Supplied Functions*. However, when working with legacy systems that use *$Piece* extensively, you should follow the standards already in place.

## List Processing versus Array Processing

When should you use *List Processing* as opposed to *Array Processing*? The determining factor should be readability and maintainability of the code. You should always ask the question "How easy will my code be for the next programmer to read and understand?" Code that is not easy to read and understand is a detriment to maintainability no matter how cleverly you use the various *List* functions. Moreover, a list does have a size limit. In the current version of Caché *Lists* are limited to 32k. If in your view the list is destined to expand beyond that, then arrays must be used.

## Chapter 5 Summary

In this chapter, we covered *List Processing*, more specifically 1) *ListBuild* functions, 2) *$List*, 3), *$ListFind*, 4) *$ListLength*, 5) *$ListData*, 6) *$ListGet*, 7) *$ListNext*, 8) *$ListSame*, 9) *$ListToString*, 10) *$ListFromString*, 11) *$ListValid* 12) *$Piece* and 13) *Delimited Strings*. This Chapter also addressed *List Processing* versus *Array Processing*.

*"Failure is not an option, it's included with the software."*

*– Murphy's Laws*

# Chapter 6 Global Processing I

Chapters 6 and 7 cover **Global Processing** in Caché ObjectScript (COS). Global Processing and storage is at the heart of what makes the Caché System unique in speed and massive scalability.

*Global Processing* and understanding how Globals are structured built and accessed is at the root of understanding the MUMPS "Global Structure" or in more modern terms the Caché "Multi-dimensional database." I encourage you to learn these two chapters well.

## Uniqueness of Caché Globals

As already stated in Chapter 2 and repeated here because of its importance; The Caché Database Structure is unique among databases; it was designed and created in the late 1960s to be used primarily with HealthCare applications. It has thrived in the Healthcare Industry as well as Financial Information systems. It was designed for use in multi-user database-driven applications. It predates "C" and most other current popular languages, and has a very different syntax and terminology.

The Caché Global Structure provides the programmer with a culture of unique freedom in accessing and modifying data without inefficient built-in safeguards. Rather, it relies on the programmer having a disciplined approach to data manipulation.

The Caché Global Structure is based on a **B-Tree** concept, which permits data to exist in a permanent sorted state, and allows for efficient searches, access, insertions, and deletions. In other words, the data is always sorted, (or indexed) which greatly improves the efficiency of data access.

The Caché Database Structure employees **Sparse Arrays**. A *Sparse Array* is an Array without data being populated to all entries. There is no wasted memory or hard disk space with Caché *Sparse Arrays*. Using *Sparse Arrays*, data can be inserted into the database quickly and efficiently.

Lastly, data stored in Globals is available to every Caché process running on the system. As soon as a Global or Global node is created, it is instantly available to all other processes on the system. This provides a freedom of data access without the excessive overhead of data and record locking seen in other databases. At first glance this may seem chaotic, but handled correctly by the programmer, it works and provides tremendous scalability of data, from a few bytes to terabytes with speeds that far exceed other technologies.

## Globals and Arrays

In Caché ObjectScript, the term **Global** is thought of as data stored on disk. Global data can be multi-dimensional (array) or scalar (single variable).

**Local Data** is non-persistent, only existing in memory. Local data can be multi-dimensional (array) or scalar (single variable).

Local Variables and Local Arrays are non-persistent, only existing in memory. When the computer is shutdown or when you exit from your current job or session, these Variables and Arrays cease to exist. Typically, any local variable is called a **Variable**. Moreover, any local array is called an **Array**.

Global Variables and Global Arrays are handled just like local variables and arrays. The only real difference is that Global variables and arrays are permanent; they are only deleted when explicitly killed. Both *Global Variables* and *Global Arrays* are called *Globals*.

**Table 6-1 Differences between Global Arrays, Global Variable, Local Arrays, and Local Variables**

| What | Description | |
|---|---|---|
| Global Arrays | Multi-dimensional using subscripts | Persistent, permanent, resides on disk |
| Global Variables | One-dimensional, Scalar, no subscripts | Persistent, permanent, resides on disk |
| Local Arrays | Multi-dimensional using subscripts | Temporary, resides only in memory |
| Local Variables | One-dimensional, Scalar, no subscripts | Temporary, resides only in memory |

Using the vernacular of other computer languages, *Globals* may be thought of as *Files*. They reside on disk and are permanent, or persistent, until deleted. However, *Globals* have a unique structure in Caché; they are not read in a sequential manner like traditional files. This unique structure is called the **Global Structure**.

## *Global Processing*

"Many people get turned off by Globals. They are a primitive structure. There are none of the controls, safety nets or value-added mechanisms that "proper" databases provide. As a result, MUMPS is often dismissed as irrelevant, insufficient or somehow, just plain wrong. To do so is to ignore a data storage mechanism that is lean, mean and totally malleable. In the right hands, that lack of baggage and overhead can be an incredibly liberating experience. In the wrong hands it can be a recipe for disaster."

M/Gateway Developments Ltd
Extreme Database Programming with MUMPS Globals
Version 1.1 : 15 May 2003
©2003, M/Gateway Developments Ltd.
Used with permission.

## *$Order and $Query System-Supplied Functions*

Perhaps, one of the most difficult concepts to comprehend in COS is the structure of the COS database, or *Global Structure*. By looking at the Global processing *System-Supplied Functions*, you can begin to understand the database structure. COS has two primary *System-Supplied Functions* that process Globals: **$Order** and **$Query**. We shall consider *$Order* first.

## $Order System-Supplied Function

The *Global Structure* is similar to a common Outline Structure. Consider the following outline of transportation machines in Table 6-2.

### Transportation Machines Outline Structure

**Table 6-2 Transportation Machines Outline Structure**

| Outline Structure Entries | Data or Information |
|---|---|
| I. Cars | Data about Cars |
| A. Domestic | |
| i. Dodge | |
| a. Caravan | |
| b. 150 Truck | |
| B. Foreign | |
| i. Toyota | Data about Toyota |
| a. Tercel | |
| ii. BMW | |
| II. Airplanes | |
| A. Military | |
| i. Jets | |
| a. F-14 | Data about F-14s |
| b. F-16 | |
| ii. Prop planes | |
| a. P-38 | |
| B. Commercial | Data about commercial planes |
| ii. Jets | |
| a. 707 | |
| b. 747 | Data about 747s |

Observations about the Outline Structure in Table 6-2:

➢ New entries may be added to any level at any time, and it would not affect the structure of the outline

➢ Data or information may be added to any level at any time, and it would not affect the structure of the outline. Data is added to the second column

➢ Each entry may or may not have associated data or information

Next, we will compare the Outline Structure from Table 6-2 with a similar Global Structure. In Table 6-3 the Outline Structure is on the left side and the Global Structure is and on the right side.

## *Outline Structure and Global Structure*

**Table 6-3 Outline Structure and Global Structure**

| Outline Structure Entries | Data | Global Structure |
|---|---|---|
| I. Cars | Data | ^TM("Cars")="Data" |
| A. Domestic | | ^TM("Cars","Domestic")="" |
| i. Dodge | | ^TM("Cars","Domestic","Dodge")="" |
| a. Caravan | | ^TM("Cars","Domestic","Dodge","Caravan")="" |
| b. 150 Truck | | ^TM("Cars","Domestic","Dodge","150 Truck")="" |
| B. Foreign | | ^TM("Cars","Foreign")="" |
| i. Toyota | Data | ^TM("Cars","Foreign","Toyota")="Data" |
| a. Tercel | | ^TM("Cars","Foreign","Toyota","Tercel")="" |
| ii. BMW | | ^TM("Cars","Foreign","BMW")="" |
| II. Airplanes | | ^TM("Airplanes")="" |
| A. Military | | ^TM("Airplanes","Military")="" |
| i. Jets | | ^TM("Airplanes","Military","Jets")="" |
| a. F-14 | Data | ^TM("Airplanes","Military","Jets","F-14")="Data" |
| b. F-16 | | ^TM("Airplanes","Military","Jets","F-16")="" |
| ii. Prop planes | | ^TM("Airplanes","Military","Prop planes")="" |
| a. P-38 | | ^TM("Airplanes","Military","Prop planes","P-38")="" |
| B. Commercial | Data | ^TM("Airplanes","Commercial")="Data" |
| ii. Jets | | ^TM("Airplanes","Commercial","Jets")="" |
| a. 707 | | ^TM("Airplanes","Commercial","Jets","707")="" |
| b. 747 | Data | ^TM("Airplanes","Commercial","Jets","747")="Data" |

## *Observations about the Outline Structure and Global Structure*

Observations about the Outline Structure and Global Structure in Table 6-3:

> ➢ "^TM" is the name of the Global array. "TM" is the actual name and, putting the caret (^) before the name, signifies that it is to be stored on disk, otherwise, it will be a local array stored only in memory. I use "TM" for brevity (Transportation Machines), actual Global names may be longer

- ➤ Each level of the Global structure is called a subscript; so "Cars", and "Airplanes" is the first subscript; "Domestic", "Foreign", "Military" and "Commercial" is the second subscript and so on
- ➤ The subscripts are separated from the Global name and surrounded by parentheses
- ➤ The equal sign (=) separates the Global and subscripts from the actual data or information
- ➤ As with the outline, new entries may be added to any level at any time and it would not affect the Global structure
- ➤ Data or information may be added to any level at any time and it would not affect the Global structure
- ➤ Each entry may or may not have associated data or information

## Traversing subscript one of a Global

We will now see how the *$Order System-Supplied Function* accesses the Global structure.

In Example 6-1, we traverse down subscript one.

**Example 6-1 Traversing subscript one of a Global**

```
Line 1: Set S1=""
Line 2: For  Do  Quit:S1=""              ;2 spaces after the For and Do
Line 3: . Set S1=$O(^TM(S1)) Quit:S1=""
Line 4: . Write !,"S1: ",S1
```

In Example 6-1, we start on line one by setting S1, or subscript one, to null. When a subscript is null it tells *$Order* to start at the top of that subscript. In line two a *Forever Do Loop* starts and will quit when S1 is null again. In other words, it will traverse through all the S1's. In line three, *$Order* obtains the next S1 entry. In line four, we display the value of S1.

**Example 6-2 Output from Example 6-1**

```
Airplanes
Cars
```

In Example 6-2, we show the output from the code in Example 6-1, the subscript-one entries.

## Structured Code – Traversing subscript one of a Global

**Example 6-3 Rewrite of Example 6-1 using Structured Code**

```
To run this code you must put the code in a routine, save the routine, and then
run the routine from the terminal.

Set S1="" Do {
  Set S1=$O(^TM(S1)) Quit:S1=""
  Write !,S1
} While S1'=""
```

Example 6-3 demonstrates how to write the same code as in Example 6-1 but using *Structured Code*, the *Do While* command. Notice the control parameter (S1'="") on the last line keeps the code processing while S1 is not null, so when S1 is null, the execution stops. Note that the *Do While* command will be covered in detail soon.

### Traversing subscripts one and two

So far, we have traversed the first subscript, next we will be going down subscript one, then jump over to subscript two and go down its level. When subscript two ends, we will jump back to get the next subscript one and then jump back and go down subscript two again, and so on.

**Example 6-4 Traversing subscripts one and two of a Global**

```
Line 1: Set S1=""
Line 2: For  Do  Quit:S1=""                ;2 spaces after the For and Do
Line 3: . Set S1=$O(^TM(S1)) Quit:S1=""
Line 4: . Write !,"S1: ",S1
Line 5: . Set S2=""
Line 6: . For  Do  Quit:S2=""              ;2 spaces after the For and Do
Line 7: . . Set S2=$O(^TM(S1,S2)) Quit:S2=""
Line 8: . . Write !,"  S2: ",S2
```

In Example 6-4, lines one through four are the same as in Example 6-1. Starting in line five, S2 (subscript two) is set to null. When a subscript is null, it tells *$Order* to start at the top of the subscript two (within subscript one). In line six, a *Forever Do Loop* starts and will quit when S2 is null again. In other words, it will traverse through all the S2s. In line seven, *$Order* obtains the next S2 entry. In line eight we display the value of S2 indented two spaces to help it stand out.

**Example 6-5, Output from Example 6-4**

```
S1: Airplanes
  S2: Commercial
  S2: Military
S1: Cars
  S2: Domestic
  S2: Foreign
```

In Example 6-5, the output from the code in Example 6-4 is displayed, for subscripts one and two entries.

### Do While and While commands

At this point we need to take a small detour and introduce two new commands.

➢ The **Do While** command

➢ The **While** command.

Both the *Do While* and *While* commands allows for a *Structured Code* multi-line looping mechanism in Caché ObjectScript. The only real difference is that the *Do While* command executes the code before checking the control expression while the *While* construct checks the control expression before the code is executed.

## Do While command

The *Do While* command executes the code, and then evaluates the control expression (after the "While"). If it is True (1), execution continues. If it is False (0), execution stops. The code that is executed is between the "Do" and the "While".

**Example 6-6 Do While command (Structured Code)**

```
To run this code you must put the code in a routine, save the routine, and then
run the routine from the terminal.

 Set Counter=0 Do {
    Set Counter=Counter+1
    Write !,Counter
 } While Counter'=5
```

In Example 6-6 we use the *Do While* command to count to 5. If the control expression says: "While Counter'=5", why is 5 printed? The answer goes back to how the *Do While* works, remember that it executes the code before checking the control expression, therefore 5 is printed

**Example 6-7 Output from code in Example 6-6**

```
To run this code you must put the code in a routine, save the routine, and then
run the routine from the terminal.

1
2
3
4
5
```

In Example 6-7 is the output from Example 6-6.

## Nested Do While command

**Example 6-8 Nested Do While command (Structured Code)**

```
To run this code you must put the code in a routine, save the routine, and then
run the routine from the terminal.

Set Counter=0 Do {
    Set Counter=Counter+1
    Set Counter2=0 Do {
          Set Counter2=Counter2+1
          Write !,"Counter: ",Counter
          Write !," Counter2: ",Counter2
    } While Counter2<3
} While Counter'=3
```

In Example 6-8 we use a Nested *Do While* command. The nesting can be several layers deep.

**Example 6-9 Output from code in Example 6-8**

```
To run this code you must put the code in a routine, save the routine, and then
run the routine from the terminal.

Counter: 1
  Counter2: 1
Counter: 1
  Counter2: 2
Counter: 1
  Counter2: 3
Counter: 2
  Counter2: 1
Counter: 2
  Counter2: 2
Counter: 2
  Counter2: 3
Counter: 3
  Counter2: 1
Counter: 3
  Counter2: 2
Counter: 3
  Counter2: 3
```

In Example 6-9 we see a nested *Do While* command. Note that the inner loop executes within the outer loop.

## While command

The *While* command evaluates the control expression *before* it executes the code, unlike the *Do While* command which evaluates the expression *after* it executes the code. If it is True (1), execution continues. If it is False (0), execution stops. The code that is executed is between the "While" and the curly bracket. The *While* command is not as intuitive as the *Do While* command.

**Example 6-10 While command (Structured Code)**

```
To run this code you must put the code in a routine, save the routine, and then
run the routine from the terminal.

Set Counter=0
While Counter'=5 {
    Set Counter=Counter+1
    Write !,Counter
  }
```

In Example 6-10 we use the *While* command to count to 5. If the control expression says: "While Counter'=5", why is 5 printed? The answer is that the Counter is incremented inside the loop and the control expression is not evaluated until it cycles back up again

**Example 6-11 Output from code in Example 6-10**

```
To run this code you must put the code in a routine, save the routine, and then
run the routine from the terminal.

1
2
3
4
5
```

In Example 6-11 is the output from Example 6-10.

**Example 6-12 Nested While command (Structured Code)**

```
To run this code you must put the code in a routine, save the routine, and then
run the routine from the terminal.

 Set Counter=0
 While Counter'=3 {
    Set Counter=Counter+1
    Set Counter2=0
    While Counter2<3 {
        Set Counter2=Counter2+1
        Write !,"Counter: ",Counter
        Write !," Counter2: ",Counter2
    }
 }
```

In Example 6-12 we use a Nested *While* command. The nesting can be several layers deep.

**Example 6-13 Output from code in Example 6-12**

```
To run this code you must put the code in a routine, save the routine, and then
run the routine from the terminal.

Counter: 1
   Counter2: 1
Counter: 1
   Counter2: 2
Counter: 1
   Counter2: 3
Counter: 2
   Counter2: 1
Counter: 2
   Counter2: 2
Counter: 2
   Counter2: 3
Counter: 3
   Counter2: 1
Counter: 3
   Counter2: 2
Counter: 3
   Counter2: 3
```

In Example 6-13 we see a nested *While* command. Note that the inner loop executes within the outer loop.

Now that our detour into *Do While* and *While* are complete, we will continue to traversing through the global.

## *Structured Code – Traversing subscripts one and two of a Global*

**Example 6-14 Rewrite of Example 6-4 using Structured Code**

```
To run this code you must put the code in a routine, save the routine, and then
run the routine from the terminal.
```

```
Set S1="" Do {
  Set S1=$O(^TM(S1)) Quit:S1=""
  Write !,"S1: ",S1
  Set S2="" Do {
    Set S2=$O(^TM(S1,S2)) Quit:S2=""
    Write !," S2: ",S2
  } While S2'=""
} While S1'=""
```

Example 6-14, we rewrite the same code as in Example 6-4 but using *Structured Code*, the *Do While* command. Notice the control parameters on the last two lines. Here for the first time we see nested *Do While* commands.

## *Traversing subscripts one, two and three*

Now we shall traverse the first, second and third subscripts. We will start with the first subscript, then within the first subscript we shall traverse down the second subscript, and then within the second subscript traverse down the third subscript. The method may continue for all the subscripts we have, but we will stop at this example with the third subscript.

**Example 6-15 Traversing subscripts one, two and three of a Global**

```
Line 1:   Set S1=""
Line 2:   For  Do  Quit:S1=""            ;2 spaces after the For and Do
Line 3:   . Set S1=$O(^TM(S1)) Quit:S1=""
Line 4:   . Write !,"S1: ",S1
Line 5:   . Set S2=""
Line 6:   . For  Do  Quit:S2=""          ;2 spaces after the For and Do
Line 7:   . . Set S2=$O(^TM(S1,S2)) Quit:S2=""
Line 8:   . . Write !," S2: ",S2
Line 9:   . . Set S3=""
Line 10:  . . For  Do  Quit:S3=""        ;2 spaces after the For and Do
Line 11:  . . . Set S3=$O(^TM(S1,S2,S3)) Quit:S3=""
Line 12:  . . . Write !,"    S3: ",S3
```

In Example 6-15 lines one through eight are the same as in Example 6-4. Starting in line nine, S3 is set to null. In line ten a *Forever Do Loop* starts and will quit when S3 is null again. In line eleven *$Order* obtains the next S3 entry. In line twelve we display the value of S3, indented four spaces to help it stand out.

**Example 6-16 Output from Example 6-15**

```
S1: Airplanes
   S2: Commercial
       S3: Jets
   S2: Military
       S3: Jets
       S3: Prop planes
S1: Cars
   S2: Domestic
       S3: Dodge
   S2: Foreign
       S3: BMW
       S3: Toyota
```

In Example 6-16, we display the output from the code in Example 6-15.

## Structured Code – Traversing subscripts one, two and three of a Global

**Example 6-17 Rewrite of Example 6-15 using Structured Code**

> To run this code you must put the code in a routine, save the routine, and then run the routine from the terminal.

```
Set S1="" Do {
  Set S1=$O(^TM(S1)) Quit:S1=""            ;get the next S1 subscript
  Write !,"S1: ",S1
  Set S2="" Do {
    Set S2=$O(^TM(S1,S2)) Quit:S2=""         ;get the next S2 subscript
    Write !,"  S2: ",S2
    Set S3="" Do {
      Set S3=$O(^TM(S1,S2,S3)) Quit:S3=""      ;get the next S3 subscript
      Write !,"      S3: ",S3
    } While S3'=""
  } While S2'=""
} While S1'=""
```

Example 6-17 demonstrates how to write the same code as in Example 6-15 but using *Structured Code*, the *Do While* command.

It may provide valuable experience for you to add the code that would traverse the fourth subscript as an exercise.

## GlobalSubscript Sort Order

> You may have noticed that Caché stores and prints your data in a different sort order than the order you entered the data. Data stored in Globals is sorted by the value of its subscripts with numeric items coming before strings. You can use the Binary Sorts After to compare two items as to their sort order. Binary Sorts After is covered in Chapter 11.

## *Five Command Structures to Traverse a Global*

Next, we will show five Command Structures to traverse a Global; there are more but these five will give you a good idea of what is available. Most programmers have their favorite. None of the Command Structures is better or more efficient than any other, and if you will be maintaining COS code you should be familiar with all five. We have covered two so far but to be complete we will list examples of all five.

### *Command Structure One for Traversing a Global*

**Example 6-18 Command Structure One for Traversing a Global**

```
To run this code you must put the code in a routine, save the routine, and then
run the routine from the terminal.

Set S1="" For  Do  Quit:S1=""              ;2 spaces after the For and Do
.Set S1=$O(^GLOBAL(S1)) Quit:S1=""
.Set S2="" For  Do  Quit:S2=""                ;2 spaces after the For and Do
..Set S2=$O(^GLOBAL(S1,S2)) Quit:S2=""
..Set S3="" For  Do  Quit:S3=""                  ;2 spaces after the For and Do
...Set S3=$O(^GLOBAL(S1,S2,S3)) Quit:S3=""
```

### *Command Structure Two for Traversing a Global*

**Example 6-19 Command Structure Two for Traversing a Global**

```
To run this code you must put the code in a routine, save the routine, and then
run the routine from the terminal.

Set S1="" For  Set S1=$O(^GLOBAL(S1)) Quit:S1=""  Do  ;2 sp after For and
before Do
.Set S2="" For  Set S2=$O(^GLOBAL(S1,S2)) Quit:S2=""  Do          ;ditto
..Set S3="" For  Set S3=$O(^GLOBAL(S1,S2,S3)) Quit:S3=""  Do      ;ditto
```

### *Command Structure Three for Traversing a Global*

**Example 6-20 Command Structure Three for Traversing a Global**

```
To run this code you must put the code in a routine, save the routine, and then
run the routine from the terminal.

Set (S1,S2,S3)=""
For  Set S1=$O(^GLOBAL(S1)) Quit:S1=""  Do       ;2 sp after For and before Do
.For  Set S2=$O(^GLOBAL(S1,S2)) Quit:S2=""  Do          ;ditto
..For  Set S3=$O(^GLOBAL(S1,S2,S3)) Quit:S3=""  Do       ;ditto
```

## Command Structure Four for Traversing a Global, the While command

**Example 6-21 Command Structure Four for Traversing a Global, the While command**

```
To run this code you must put the code in a routine, save the routine, and then
run the routine from the terminal.

Set S1=$O(^GLOBAL(""))                 ;initially set the S1 control param
While (S1'="") {                       ;S1'="" is the first control param
  Set S2=$O(^GLOBAL(S1,""))            ;initially set the S2 control param
  While (S2'="") {                     ;S2'="" is the second control param
    Set S3=$O(^GLOBAL(S1,S2,""))       ;initially set the S3 control param
    While (S3'="") {                   ;S3'="" is the third control param
      ; process data for S3
      Set S3=$O(^GLOBAL(S1,S2,S3))     ;get next S3
    }
    ; process data for S2
    Set S2=$O(^GLOBAL(S1,S2))          ;get next S2 entry
  }
  ; process data for S1
  Set S1=$O(^GLOBAL(S1))               ;get next S1 entry
}
```

Example 6-21 takes some explanation, and is difficult to understand. Since the *While* command checks the control parameter (S1) first, it needs to be set before the *While* command is started. That is why we had to issue a preliminary *$Order* before the *While* command. Then we do our processing for that specific subscript. Before we cycle back up to the *While* command we need to obtain the next subscript. This is done with the *$Order* at the end of the *While* command.

## Command Structure Five for Traversing a Global, the Do While command.

**Example 6-22 Command Structure Five for Traversing a Global, the Do While command**

```
To run this code you must put the code in a routine, save the routine, and then
run the routine from the terminal.

Set S1="" Do {
  Set S1=$O(^GLOBAL(S1)) Quit:S1=""
  Set S2="" Do {
    Set S2=$O(^GLOBAL(S1,S2)) Quit:S2=""
    Set S3="" Do {
      Set S3=$O(^GLOBAL(S1,S2,S3)) Quit:S3=""
    } While S3'=""
  } While S2'=""
} While S1'=""
```

## Accessing Global Data

So far, we have considered the Global Subscripts and how to traverse down the subscripts but we have only briefly mentioned how we might access the data. The next question is "how to access the data or information stored in a Global?" Example 6-15 is replicated in Example 6-23 and lines 4a, 8a, and 12a have been added to demonstrate how to access and display this data.

**Example 6-23 Accessing Global data**

```
To run this code you must put the code in a routine, save the routine, and then
run the routine from the terminal.

Line 1:    Set S1=""
Line 2:    For  Do  Quit:S1=""                    ;2 spaces after the For and
Do
Line 3:    . Set S1=$O(^TM(S1)) Quit:S1=""
Line 4:    . Write !,"S1: ",S1
Line 4a:   . Write " = ",^TM(S1)
Line 5:    . Set S2=""
Line 6:    . For  Do  Quit:S2=""                  ;2 spaces after the For and
Do
Line 7:    . . Set S2=$O(^TM(S1,S2)) Quit:S2=""
Line 8:    . . Write !," S2: ",S2
Line 8a:   . . Write " = ",^TM(S1,S2)
Line 9:    . . Set S3=""
Line 10:   . . For  Do  Quit:S3=""      ;2 spaces after the For and Do
Line 11:   . . . Set S3=$O(^TM(S1,S2,S3)) Quit:S3=""
Line 12:   . . . Write !,"  S3: ",S3
Line 12a:  . . . Write " = ",^TM(S1,S2,S3)
```

In Example 6-23, we've added lines 4a, 8a, and 12a, which will display the data or information associated with the Global subscripts.

**Example 6-24 Output from Example 6-23**

```
S1: Airplanes =
  S2: Commercial = Data
    S3: Jets =
  S2: Military =
    S3: Jets =
    S3: Prop planes =
S1: Cars = Data
  S2: Domestic =
    S3: Dodge =
  S2: Foreign =
    S3: BMW =
    S3: Toyota = Data
```

In Example 6-24, we display the output from Example 6-23. Certain lines may seem strange with the "=" and no data or information following the equal sign. If you look back at Table 6-2 you will notice that these Global references do not have data, it is not necessary for every Global subscript to have data.

## Structured Code, Do While command

```
To run this code you must put the code in a routine, save the routine, and then
run the routine from the terminal.

Set S1="" Do {
  Set S1=$O(^TM(S1)) Quit:S1=""
  Write !,"S1: ",S1
  Write " = ",^TM(S1)
  Set S2="" Do {
    Set S2=$O(^TM(S1,S2)) Quit:S2=""
    Write !,"  S2: ",S2
    Write " = ",^TM(S1,S2)
    Set S3="" Do {
      Set S3=$O(^TM(S1,S2,S3)) Quit:S3=""
      Write !,"    S3: ",S3
      Write " = ",^TM(S1,S2,S3)
    } While S3'=""
  } While S2'=""
} While S1'=""
```

Example 6-25 demonstrates how to write the same code as in Example 6-23 but using *Structured Code*, the *Do While* command

## Modifying Global Data

One of the more powerful features in the Caché Global Structure is how its Global subscripts and data can be modified, added to, and deleted without having to reformat the Global Structure. Consider the following examples:

**Example 6-26 Setting up a simple Global Array of Pets**

```
Set ^Pets("Dog","Boxer","Male","Buddy")="9^0"
Set ^Pets("Dog","Lab","Female","Loverly")="6^0"
Set ^Pets("Dog","Lab","Male","Tiny")="5^1"
Set ^Pets("Cat","Burmese","Male","BoyCat")="3^0"
Set ^Pets("Cat","Burmese","Female","TomBoy")="3^0"
Set ^Pets("Cat","Korat","Female","Fancy")="5^1"
```

Example 6-26 defines a Global array of dogs and cats. Subscript one is either "Dog" or "Cat", subscript two is the breed, subscript three is the sex and subscript four is the name. Piece one of the data is the animal's age and piece two is either a one or a zero. A one if the animal is available for adoption and zero if the animal is not available for adoption.

**Example 6-27 Code to traverse and display the Global created in Example 6-26**

> To run this code you must put the code in a routine, save the routine, and then run the routine from the terminal.

```
Set Animal="" Do {
  Set Animal=$O(^Pets(Animal)) Quit:Animal=""
  Set Breed="" Do {
    Set Breed=$O(^Pets(Animal,Breed)) Quit:Breed=""
    Set Sex="" Do {
      Set Sex=$O(^Pets(Animal,Breed,Sex)) Quit:Sex=""
      Set Name="" Do {
        Set Name=$O(^Pets(Animal,Breed,Sex,Name)) Quit:Name=""
        Set Data=^Pets(Animal,Breed,Sex,Name)
        Set Age=$P(Data,"^",1)
        Set Adoption=$P(Data,"^",2)
        If Adoption=1 Set Available="is"
        If Adoption=0 Set Available="is not"
        Write !,Animal," named ",Name,", Breed ",Breed,", Sex ",Sex
        Write ", ",Age," years old, ",Available," available for adoption"
      } While Name'=""
    } While Sex'=""
  } While Breed'=""
} While Animal'=""
```

**Example 6-28 Output from the routine in Example 6-27 based on the Global created in Example 6-26**

```
Cat named TomBoy, Breed Burmese, Sex Female, 3 years old, is not available
for adoption
Cat named BoyCat, Breed Burmese, Sex Male, 3 years old, is not available for
adoption
Cat named Fancy, Breed Korat, Sex Female, 5 years old, is available for
adoption
Dog named Buddy, Breed Boxer, Sex Male, 9 years old, is not available for
adoption
Dog named Loverly, Breed Lab, Sex Female, 6 years old, is not available for
adoption
Dog named Tiny, Breed Lab, Sex Male, 5 years old, is available for adoption
```

Example 6-28 shows the output from the routine in Example 6-27.

Now lets' make some modifications to the Global.

**Example 6-29 Modification to the ^Pets Global created in Example 6-26**

```
Kill ^Pets("Dog","Lab","Female","Loverly")

Set $P(^Pets("Cat","Korat","Female","Fancy"),"^",2)=0

Set ^Pets("Rat","Rodent","Male","Ben")="2^1"
```

In Example 6-29, first we kill the Global subscript for Loverly, the Female Dog. Next, we make the Cat named Fancy not available for adoption and lastly add a new Pet, Ben the Rat.

```
Cat named TomBoy, Breed Burmese, Sex Female, 3 years old, is not available
for adoption
Cat named BoyCat, Breed Burmese, Sex Male, 3 years old, is not available for
adoption
Cat named Fancy, Breed Korat, Sex Female, 5 years old, is not available for
adoption
Dog named Buddy, Breed Boxer, Sex Male, 9 years old, is not available for
adoption
Dog named Tiny, Breed Lab, Sex Male, 5 years old, is available for adoption
Rat named Ben, Breed Rodent, Sex Male, 2 years old, is available for adoption
```

In Example 6-30 first notice that the Dog Loverly no longer displays because it is no longer in the Global. Next, the Cat named Fancy is no longer available for adoption. Finally, we have a new addition, Ben the rat.

The above changes were made to the ^Pets Global. The Caché system automatically reformats and resorts the Global Structure. It actually does not resort nor reformat, but just adds, changes, and deletes, database pointers. As mentioned before this is one of the more powerful features in the Caché Global Structure.

## *$Query System-Supplied Function*

So far, we have seen how to traverse down three levels of subscripts in a Global array, using the *$Order System-Supplied Function*. Another way to traverse a Global is by using the *$Query System-Supplied Function*. *$Query* traverses a Global a bit differently. Unlike *$Order*, with *$Query* you do not need to specify the subscripts. *$Query* makes extensive use of *Indirection* (see Chapter 18, under Dynamic Code).

### *$Query to traverse a Global array*

**Example 6-31 Using $Query to traverse a Global array**

```
To run this code you must put the code in a routine, save the routine, and then
run the routine from the terminal.

Set TM="^TM"
For  Do  Quit:TM=""              ;2 spaces after the For and Do
. Set X=$Q(@TM) Quit:TM=""
. Write !,TM," = ",@TM
```

In Example 6-31, *$Query* traverses all subscripts of the TM Global in one *Forever Do* command. Notice the interesting use of *Indirection* (@). *Indirection* is a difficult concept and you may not fully understand it at this point.

**Example 6-32 Output from Example 6-31**

```
^TM("Airplanes") =
^TM("Airplanes","Commercial") = Data
^TM("Airplanes","Commercial","Jets") =
^TM("Airplanes","Commercial","Jets",707) =
^TM("Airplanes","Commercial","Jets",747) = Data
```

```
^TM("Airplanes","Military") =
^TM("Airplanes","Military","Jets") =
^TM("Airplanes","Military","Jets","F-14") = Data
^TM("Airplanes","Military","Jets","F-16") =
^TM("Airplanes","Military","Prop planes") =
^TM("Airplanes","Military","Prop planes","P-38") =
^TM("Cars") = Data
^TM("Cars","Domestic") =
^TM("Cars","Domestic","Dodge") =
^TM("Cars","Domestic","Dodge","150 Truck") =
^TM("Cars","Domestic","Dodge","Caravan") =
^TM("Cars","Foreign") =
^TM("Cars","Foreign","BMW") =
^TM("Cars","Foreign","Toyota") = Data
^TM("Cars","Foreign","Toyota","Tercel") =
```

Example 6-32 shows the output of *$Query* used in Example 6-31. *$Query* returns all parts of a Global node, including the Global name, subscripts, and data. Although it requires fewer commands to access the Global, using *$Query* it is more difficult to segregate, or break out the subscripts and data. Actual use of *$Query* is somewhat rare, whereas *$Order* is used extensively in traditional applications. *$Query* should not be confused with *$Quit*.

In older or *Legacy* systems, you may see a Global array accessed with the *$N ($Next) System-Supplied Function*. Do not use *$Next*. *$Order* is the current *System-Supplied Function* for traversing a Global array.

So far, all subscripts in the Globals we have considered have been variables. At times, you may encounter subscripts that are constants and not variables.

## Constant Subscripts

A *Constant* is a data item that does not change its value, whereas a *Variable*, as the name implies, varies its value. A data item in quotes is considered to be a *Constant,* because its value does not vary.

**Example 6-33 Using Constant Subscripts**

```
Kill ^Pets2

Set SUB1="First Subscript"
Set SUB3="Third Subscript"

Set ^Pets2(SUB1,"Dog",SUB3)=""
Set ^Pets2(SUB1,"Cat",SUB3)=""
Set ^Pets2(SUB1,"Fish",SUB3)=""
Set ^Pets2(SUB1,"Turtle",SUB3)=""
```

In Example 6-33, we set up variable subscripts SUB1 and SUB3. The second subscript, "Dog", "Cat", "Fish", and "Turtle" are constant subscripts and do not vary..

## Traverse a Global with Constant Subscripts

**Example 6-34 Traverse a Global with Constant Subscripts**

```
To run this code you must put the code in a routine, save the routine, and then
run the routine from the terminal.

Set (SUB1,SUB2,SUB3)=""
For  Set SUB1=$O(^Pets2(SUB1)) Quit:SUB1=""  Do          ;2 spaces after the
. For  Set SUB2=$O(^Pets2(SUB1,SUB2)) Quit:SUB2=""  Do         ;For and
before
. . For  Set SUB3=$O(^Pets2(SUB1,SUB2,SUB3)) Quit:SUB3=""  Do ;the Do
. . . Write !,SUB1," - ",SUB2," - ",SUB3
Quit

First Subscript - Cat - Third Subscript
First Subscript - Dog - Third Subscript
First Subscript - Fish - Third Subscript
First Subscript - Turtle - Third Subscript
```

Example 6-34 demonstrates how to traverse a Global that contains constant subscripts. It is no different than traversing a Global with variable subscripts.

At times you may know in advance the constant subscripts of a Global and need to traverse them. For example, our Global ^Pets2 has constant subscripts of "Dog", "Cat", "Fish" and "Turtle". You can use the following *For Loop* command (for SUB2) to traverse this Global.

**Example 6-35 Traversing a Global specifying with Constant Subscripts**

```
To run this code you must put the code in a routine, save the routine, and then
run the routine from the terminal.

Set (SUB1,SUB3)=""
For  Set SUB1=$O(^Pets2(SUB1)) Quit:SUB1=""  Do
. For  SUB2="Dog","Cat","Turtle" Do     ;specify what values to look up
. . For  Set SUB3=$O(^Pets2(SUB1,SUB2,SUB3)) Quit:SUB3=""  Do
. . . Write !,SUB1," - ",SUB2," - ",SUB3
Quit

First Subscript - Dog - Third Subscript
First Subscript - Cat - Third Subscript
First Subscript - Turtle - Third Subscript
```

In Example 6-35, we see how the *For Loop* command (for SUB2) specifies subscript constants. Please notice two things about this example as compared to Example 6-34: 1) the sort order is according to how we specify SUB2, and 2) we did not specify "Fish" so "Fish" does not come out in the display.

## *Building a Database*

Now that we have a rudimentary knowledge of the Caché Global Structure, how should we apply it in a real world situation?

Suppose we have a database of people and we want to store information about these people and access them by Name, Social Security Number, Medical Record Number, City, State and Zip code. Note that the Social Security Number and Medical Record Number are unique; there is only one per person. Whereas, the other data items are not unique, multiple people can have the same data items. Here is one possible way to organize our database.

Theoretically, Globals fall into two types; *Data Globals* and *Index Globals*. In reality, most Globals are a combination of both.

## *Building a Data Global*

The first step is to build a data Global containing the information about people.

**Example 6-36 Building a Data Global**

```
Set ^People(1)=$LB("Doe","John","5545-56-2322","1234","Los
Angeles","CA","95111")
Set ^People(2)=$LB("Doe","Jane","5544-20-2232","2345","Los
Angeles","CA","95111")
Set ^People(3)=$LB("Jacobs","Dawn","7894-11-
4545","3456","Harvard","MA","01666")
Set ^People(4)=$LB("Dover","Ilene","1190-56-
0933","4567","Dallas","TX","75211")
Set ^People(5)=$LB("Johnson","Mike","3406-44-3344","5678","Ink","AR","71933")
Set ^People(6)=$LB("Dover","Ben","3434-24-
3344","6789","Inkwell","AR","71955")
```

Example 6-36 shows the basics of a Data Global. First, the subscript is a sequential number, 1,2,3,4.....n. The numeric subscript allows for as many additional entries as needed. Second, all data is to the right of the equal sign, in this way, adding additional data to the end of the *$LB ($ListBuild)* is no problem. A Global like this can grows in number and in size.

Now, how do we access this Global in an efficient manner, especially if there are millions of subscripts? Obviously, it would not be efficient to traverse the Global from top to bottom sequentially looking for the data we want. We need fast, efficient access. The answer is an *Index Global*.

# *Building an Index Global*

Example 6-37 Building an Index Global

> To run this code you must put the code in a routine, save the routine, and then run the routine from the terminal.

```
Set Num="" Do {
  Set Num=$O(^People(Num)) Quit:Num=""
  Set Data=^People(Num)
  Set Ln=$Li(Data,1)                    ;last name
  Set Fn=$Li(Data,2)                    ;first name
  Set SSN=$Li(Data,3)                   ;social security number
  Set MRN=$Li(Data,4)                   ;medical record number
  Set City=$Li(Data,5)                  ;City
  Set State=$Li(Data,6)                 ;State
  Set Zip=$Li(Data,7)                   ;Zip
  Set ^PeopleIndex("Name",Ln_","_Fn,Num)=""
  Set ^PeopleIndex("Ln",Ln,Num)=""
  Set ^PeopleIndex("SSN",SSN)=Num
  Set ^PeopleIndex("MRN",MRN)=Num
  Set ^PeopleIndex("City",City,Num)=""
  Set ^PeopleIndex("State",State,Num)=""
  Set ^PeopleIndex("Zip",Zip,Num)=""
} While Num'=""
```

We see in Example 6-37 the code to build an Index Global, called ^PeopleIndex. First we go through the ^People Global sequentially extracting the data elements we want to index. Second, we set ^PeopleIndex using these data elements.

Example 6-38 Resulting Global from executing the routine in Example 6-37

```
ZW ^PeopleIndex
^PeopleIndex("City","Dallas",4)=""
^PeopleIndex("City","Harvard",3)=""
^PeopleIndex("City","Ink",5)=""
^PeopleIndex("City","Inkwell",6)=""
^PeopleIndex("City","Los Angeles",1)=""
^PeopleIndex("City","Los Angeles",2)=""
^PeopleIndex("Ln","Doe",1)=""
^PeopleIndex("Ln","Doe",2)=""
^PeopleIndex("Ln","Dover",4)=""
^PeopleIndex("Ln","Dover",6)=""
^PeopleIndex("Ln","Jacobs",3)=""
^PeopleIndex("Ln","Johnson",5)=""
^PeopleIndex("MRN",1234)=1
^PeopleIndex("MRN",2345)=2
^PeopleIndex("MRN",3456)=3
^PeopleIndex("MRN",4567)=4
^PeopleIndex("MRN",5678)=5
^PeopleIndex("MRN",6789)=6
^PeopleIndex("Name","Doe,Jane",2)=""
^PeopleIndex("Name","Doe,John",1)=""
^PeopleIndex("Name","Dover,Ben",6)=""
^PeopleIndex("Name","Dover,Ilene",4)=""
^PeopleIndex("Name","Jacobs,Dawn",3)=""
^PeopleIndex("Name","Johnson,Mike",5)=""
^PeopleIndex("SSN","1190-56-0933")=4
```

```
^PeopleIndex("SSN","3406-44-3344")=5
^PeopleIndex("SSN","3434-24-3344")=6
^PeopleIndex("SSN","5544-20-2232")=2
^PeopleIndex("SSN","5545-56-2322")=1

^PeopleIndex("SSN","7894-11-4545")=3
^PeopleIndex("State","AR",5)=""
^PeopleIndex("State","AR",6)=""
^PeopleIndex("State","CA",1)=""
^PeopleIndex("State","CA",2)=""
^PeopleIndex("State","MA",3)=""
^PeopleIndex("State","TX",4)=""
^PeopleIndex("Zip",71933,5)=""
^PeopleIndex("Zip",71955,6)=""
^PeopleIndex("Zip",75211,4)=""
^PeopleIndex("Zip",95111,1)=""
^PeopleIndex("Zip",95111,2)=""
^PeopleIndex("Zip","01666",3)=""
```

In Example 6-38 we see the resulting ^PeopleIndex Global. How do we use this Index Global to access the data in the ^People Global?

## Accessing data through an Index Global

### List People sorted by State

**Example 6-39 List People sorted by State**

```
To run this code you must put the code in a routine, save the routine, and then
run the routine from the terminal.

Set State="" Do {
  Set State=$O(^PeopleIndex("State",State)) Quit:State=""
  Set Num="" Do {
    Set Num=$O(^PeopleIndex("State",State,Num)) Quit:Num=""
    Set Data=^People(Num)
    Set Ln=$Li(Data,1)
    Set Fn=$Li(Data,2)
    Write !,Fn," ",Ln," lives in: ",State
  } While Num'=""
} While State'=""

Mike Johnson lives in: AR
Ben Dover lives in: AR
John Doe lives in: CA
Jane Doe lives in: CA
Dawn Jacobs lives in: MA
Ilene Dover lives in: TX
```

Example 6-39 demonstrates the code to traverse through the ^PeopleIndex("State") Global and show all the people who live in the various states. By using the State index, only 6 subscripts need to be read. This process is more efficient than going though the entire ^People Global.

## List Zip Codes

**Example 6-40 List all the Zip Code for all people whose last name begins with a "D"**

```
To run this code you must put the code in a routine, save the routine, and then
run the routine from the terminal.

Set Ln="D" Do {
  Set Ln=$O(^PeopleIndex("Ln",Ln)) Quit:$E(Ln,1,1)'="D"
  Set Num="" Do {
    Set Num=$O(^PeopleIndex("Ln",Ln,Num)) Quit:Num=""
    Set Data=^People(Num)
    Set Fn=$Li(Data,2)
    Set Zip=$Li(Data,6)
    Write !,Fn," ",Ln," has a Zip Code: ",Zip
  } While Num'=""
} While $E(Ln,1,1)="D"

John Doe has a Zip Code: 95111
Jane Doe has a Zip Code: 95111
Ilene Dover has a Zip Code: 75211
Ben Dover has a Zip Code: 71955
```

The code in Example 6-40 demonstrates how to select from the ^PeopleIndex Global, all people whose last names begin with a "D". Note that I don't need to know the exact Last Name to position the first read at the "D"s. I need only initially set the Ln to "D" and the first $Order will go to the correct subscript.

### $Order

Setting the Last Name to "D" may possibly could problems. Since $Order returns the next node in a Global, setting the Last Name to "D" may bypass a node if the first Last Name is just "D". For this reason, it may be better to set the last name to something like "Cz", so the next $Order will pick up the very first name starting with "D".

However, another possible solution is to set the LastName to "D" and do a reverse $Order, which would go backwards one node. The code to do a reverse $Order is:

```
Set Ln="D"
Set Ln=$O(^PeopleIndex("Ln",Ln),-1)
```

Now, can you tell me the difference between the SSN and MRN indexes and the other indexes?

## Two types of Global Indexes

**Example 6-41 Subscripts in the ^PeopleIndex Global**

```
; These indices have 3 subscripts and have no data to the right
; of the equal sign

^PeopleIndex("City","Los Angeles",2)=""
78^PeopleIndex("Name","Dover,Ben",6)=""
^PeopleIndex("State","TX",4)=""
^PeopleIndex("Zip","01666",3)=""


; These indices have 2 subscripts and have data to the right
; of the equal sign

^PeopleIndex("SSN","7894-11-4545")=3
^PeopleIndex("MRN",4567)=4
```

In Example 6-41, we see that the SSN and MRN indexes have 2 subscripts, whereas the other indexes have 3 subscripts. We may ask why this is. In the other subscripts we will have multiple numbers or pointers to the ^People Global because there are duplicate values, but the Name and SSN are unique to the Person, and we do not need multiple numbers.

Hence we have two types of Global Indexes:

> ➤ Those that have duplicates, like State and Zip

> ➤ Those that do not have duplicates, like SSN and Name

---

### Data Global and Indexed Global

The concept of having a Data Global indexed by a single numeric subscript and one or more Index Globals pointing into the Data Global is sound. The Index Global can always be rebuilt to reflect the current business model without ever having to change the Data Global. Having all the data indexed by a single numeric subscript means that the Data Global will never have to be reformatted and will always be stable.

---

## Chapter 6 Summary

Chapters 6 and 7 cover *Global Processing* in Caché ObjectScript (COS). In this chapter, we covered the *MUMPS Global*, or *Global Structure*, or its newer name *Caché Multi-dimensional Database*. We demonstrated how to define, traverse, access and modify a Global. First, we compared the *Global Structure* with an Outline Structure. Then we learned how to Traverse a Global down through its various subscripts with *$Order*. Two new *Structured Code* commands were demonstrated, *the Do While* and *While* command. We saw five ways or command structures that may be used to traverse a Global. We considered a second way of traversing a Global, using the *$Query*. Lastly, we saw how to build a Global database, using *Data Globals* and *Index Globals*.

# Chapter 7 Global Processing II

Chapters 6 and 7 cover **Global Processing** in Caché ObjectScript (COS). Global Processing and storage is at the heart of what makes the Caché System unique in speed and massive scalability.

*Global Processing* and understanding how Globals are structured, built and accessed is at the root of understanding the MUMPS "Global Structure" or in more modern terms the Caché "Multi-dimensional database." I encourage you to learn these two chapters well.

## Namespaces

Caché systems are divided into **Namespaces**. Think of Namespaces as separate folders on a Windows computer. If you are on a Caché system you will have a default Namespace. Many times when the system prompts you for a command it will display the *Namespace* as the prompt.

## Default Namespaces

**Example 7-1 Default Namespaces**

```
USER>                        ;namespace USER

SAMPLES>                     ;namespace SAMPLES

%SYS>                        ;namespace %SYS
```

In Example 7-1, three typical *Namespaces* are shown as prompts.

If you do not know your default *Namespace* you can issue the **$ZU(5)** *System-Supplied Function* to display the default *Namespace*. In newer versions of Caché, *$ZU(5)* is obsolete, the new command is Write $SYSTEM.SYS.NameSpace()

## Display the default Namespace

**Example 7-2 Display the default namespace**

```
Write $ZU(5)                    ;older way to display the default namespace
USER

Write $SYSTEM.SYS.NameSpace()   ;newer way to display the default namespace
USER
```

Example 7-2 demonstrates *$ZU(5)* and $SYSTEM.SYS.NameSpace() to display the default *Namespace*.

## Changing Namespaces

**Example 7-3 Changing Namespaces**

```
ZN "SAMPLES"                    ;change your Namespace to SAMPLES

ZNSpace "SAMPLES"               ;change your Namespace to SAMPLES

Set  X=$ZU(5,"SAMPLES")         ;change your Namespace to SAMPLES
                                ;Note; the $ZU command is obsolete in
                                ;newer versions of Caché

Do ^%CD                         ;%CD, utility to change Namespaces
Namespace: SAMPLES              ;%CD will ask for a Namespace
```

Example 7-3 demonstrates several ways of changing your *Namespace*.

## Show all Namespaces

**Example 7-4 Show all Namespaces**

```
Do ^%CD             ;%CD, utility to change namespaces
Namespace: ?        ;enter a question mark here

    '?' for help.
    '@' (at-sign) to edit the default, the last namespace
        name attempted.  Edit the line just as if it were
        a line of code.
    <RETURN> will leave you in the current namespace.
Here are the defined namespaces:
    %SYS
    DOCBOOK
    SAMPLES
    USER
```

In Example 7-4 **^%CD** shows all *Namespaces* available on a system.

## Extended Syntax

**Extended Syntax** is a variable or constant surrounded by square brackets [] that proceed a Global name to specify a Global in another *Namespace*.

**Example 7-5 Extended Syntax**

```
Write ^["USER"]GLOBAL           ;constant used as Extended Syntax, this
Global
                                ;is in the Namespace USER


Set  EXTSYN="USER"
Write ^[EXTSYN]GLOBAL           ;variable used as Extended Syntax, this
Global
                                ;is in the Namespace USER
```

In Example 7-5, demonstrates *Extended Syntax*. By using *Extended Syntax*, you are telling the system that this Global exists in another *Namespace* other than the one you currently reside in. If there is no

*Extended Syntax* prefix to a Global, then the Global is assumed to be in the current *Namespace*, unless the Caché System Manager has that Global mapped to another *Database*.

## Temporary Globals

There are times when you need to process large amounts of temporary data, much more than can be held in memory with a variable array. In situations like these, you have several options:

- ➢ ^CacheTempUser – a special Global created by InterSystems that has the speed of memory access but without the limitation of exceeding your memory allotment
- ➢ Process Private Globals – Globals that may only be accessed by the current process
- ➢ Use a regular Global such as ^TMP or ^TEMP with $J as the first subscript. $J is unique to your process and by its use you will avoid trampling on other processes' data.

## CacheTempUser

**CacheTempUser** is a Global name created by InterSystems that makes use of the in-memory buffer pool. The real name is *CacheTemp*, but since Caché uses that name for its own purposes, InterSystems recommends using CacheTempUser. When you use CacheTempUser you must use $J as the first subscript. $J is unique to your process and by its use you will avoid trampling on other processes' data.

**Example 7-6 ^CacheTempUser($J)**

```
Kill ^CacheTempUser($J)              ;clean your own allotment of CacheTempUser
Set ^CacheTempUser($J)="Abc"
Set ^CacheTempUser($J,"Sub1")="Def"

Write ^CacheTempUser($J)
Abc
Write ^CacheTempUser($J,"Sub1")
Def

Kill ^CacheTempUser($J)              ;clean up before you exit
Quit
```

In Example 7-6, ^CacheTempUser($J) is first killed, then you do your processing and at the end kill it once again to clean up the space you used.

While using ^CacheTempUser, you should keep the following points in mind:

- ➢ It is a temporary Global and may not exist after your process exits
- ➢ CacheTempUser is not written to disk, however, if large amounts of data are written to it, it may be automatically flushed to disk and later be reinstated when needed
- ➢ CacheTempUser is not logged to a journal
- ➢ It cannot be depended upon in a restartable situation
- ➢ When Caché is restarted, ^CacheTemp is wiped out

> Any Global name starting with "^CacheTemp" will automatically go to this special global. So you could have ^CacheTempUserAPI, or ^CacheTempUserSORT, etc.

## Process-Private Globals

**Process-Private Globals**, as the name implies can only be accessed by the process that creates them. These Globals are deleted when the process that created them ceases to exist.

They are specified by their unique syntax:

> ^||Global

**Example 7-7 Process-Private Globals**

```
                            ;initially no need to kill the Global
Set ^||Global="Abc"
Set ^||Global("SUB1")="Def"

Write ^||Global
Abc
Write ^||Global("SUB1")
Def
                            ;no need to kill the Global at the end of
processing
Q
```

In Example 7-7, *Process-Private Globals* are used in the same way as CacheTempUser, with the exception that $J does not need to be the first subscript because only your process may access them. Also *Process-Private Globals* do not need to be killed before and after they are used.

## *^TMP or ^TEMP as a temporary Global*

**Example 7-8 ^TMP($J) or ^TEMP($J)**

```
Kill ^TMP($J)                ;clean your own allotment of ^TMP
Set ^TMP($J)="Abc"
Set ^TMP($J,"Sub1")="Def"

Write ^TMP($J)
Abc
Write ^TMP($J,"Sub1")
Def

Kill ^TMP($J)                ;clean up before you exit
Quit
```

In Example 7-8, ^TMP is first killed, then you do your processing and at the end kill it once again to clean up the space you used.

## *Naked Indicators or Naked References*

A **Naked Indicator** is a way to refer to a Global node in a short-hand fashion.

**Example 7-9 Naked Indicators or Naked References**

```
Kill
Set ^X("SUB1","SUB2","SUB3")="X-Data"
Write ^("SUB3")                    ;Naked Indicator reference
X-Data
```

Example 7-9 demonstrates the use of *Naked Indicators*. At first, a *Naked Indicator* may seem beneficial, but there are problems. They always refer to the very last Global referenced. If another Global is inserted between the full Global reference and the *Naked Indicator*, the *Naked Indicator* would refer to the new Global reference.

**Example 7-10 Naked Indicators, new full reference inserted**

```
Kill
Set ^X("SUB1","SUB2","SUB3")="X-Data"
Set ^Y("SUB3")="Y-Data"
Write ^("SUB3")                    ;Naked Indicator reference
Y-Data
```

In Example 7-10, another Global reference is inserted between the full reference and the Naked Indicator. The *Naked Indicator* will automatically attempt to reference the new Global; unless a programmer is paying very close attention this will cause problems. I have seen systems where *Naked Indicators* are used extensively with little or no problems, but for the novice programmer it is not recommended.

---

### *Use Naked Indicator /Naked References with caution*

Naked Indicators may be useful, but use with caution. Naked Indicators refer to the immediately preceding full Global reference. This can be trouble when, unknowingly, another Global reference is inserted before the naked indicator, use carefully.

---

## The Merge command

The **Merge** command will copy an array, either local or Global, and all descendant subscripts to another array. Since the *Merge* command executes synchronously (it executes real time, as you wait), depending upon the size of the array, this command may take some time.

**Example 7-11 Merge command**

```
Kill

Set X(1,2)=12
Set X(1,3)=13

Set Y(2,1)=21
Set Y(2,2)=22
Merge Y=X
          ;After the Merge above, the Y array is as follows:
```

```
Write
X(1,2)=12
X(1,3)=13
Y(1,2)=12
Y(1,3)=13
Y(2,1)=21
Y(2,2)=22
```

In Example 7-11, the X array is merged with the Y array. The Y array stays intact unless individual subscripts are overridden by the X array. The *Merge* command always copies from the operand on the right of the equal sign to the operand on the left.

The *Merge* command is not as straightforward as it seems at first glance. It uses the subscripts specified in the *Merge* command to decide where to actually do the merge. Consider the next few examples.

**Example 7-12 Merge command**

```
Kill
Set X("A","B1")="AB1"
Set X("A","B2")="AB2"

Set Y("C")="C"

Merge Y=X
            ;After the Merge above, the Y array is as follows:
Write
X("A","B1")="AB1"
X("A","B2")="AB2"
Y("A","B1")="AB1"
Y("A","B2")="AB2"
Y("C")="C"
```

In Example 7-12, we see two arrays, X and Y, and in the *Merge* command, the X array is copied over the Y array and you can see the results.

**Example 7-13 Merge command**

```
Kill
Set X("A","B1")="AB1"
Set X("A","B2")="AB2"

Set Y("C")="C"

Merge Y("C")=X

            ;After the Merge above, the Y array is as follows:

Write
X("A","B1")="AB1"
X("A","B2")="AB2"
Y("C")="C"
Y("C","A","B1")="AB1"
Y("C","A","B2")="AB2"
```

In Example 7-13, the X array is copied over the Y("C") array, so all additions to the Y array are added after the "C" subscript.

**Example 7-14 Merge command**

```
Kill
Set X("A","B1")="AB1"
Set X("A","B2")="AB2"

Set Y("C","D")="C"

Merge Y("C")=X
            ;After the Merge above, the Y array is as follows:
Write
X("A","B1")="AB1"
X("A","B2")="AB2"
Y("C","A","B1")="AB1"
Y("C","A","B2")="AB2"
Y("C","D")="C"
```

In Example 7-14, we see a combination of *Merge* commands. The *Merge* command can be tricky and you should experiment with it until you get a good understanding of what it does. In the last few examples, we have used the *Merge* command on local arrays, but they work the same on Global arrays.

## *Problems with the Merge command*

The *Merge* command has one difficulty.

**Example 7-15 Merge command difficulty**

```
Kill ARRAY1
Merge ARRAY2=ARRAY1
Write $D(ARRAY2)
0
```

In Example 7-15, we kill ARRAY1 and you would expect an <UNDEFINED> error message from the *Merge* command, but there will be no error message. Therefore, if ARRAY1 is undefined, ARRAY2 will be undefined as well, as $Data shows. You cannot assume that ARRAY2 is defined just because the *Merge* command does not error.

## *The Lock command*

The **Lock** command is a way to reserve a Global variable or array for exclusive modification or update.

**Example 7-16 Lock command**

```
Lock ^X
```

In Example 7-16, the *Lock* command reserves the Global "X" for exclusive modification. Any other process that attempts to lock this Global will hang or wait until this process releases the Global.

## Multiple Lock commands

Example 7-17 Multiple Lock commands

```
Lock ^X,^Y,^Z
```

In Example 7-17, we lock several Global variables at one time.

When a new lock is executed, all previous locks are released. You may keep previous locks in place by use of an **Incremental Lock**.

## Incremental Lock command

Example 7-18 Incremental Lock command

```
Lock +^Y
```

In Example 7-18, the Global variable "Y" is locked without releasing any prior locks.

## Incremental Unlock command

Example 7-19 Incremental Unlock command

```
Lock -^Y
```

In Example 7-19, the Global variable "Y" is released without affecting any prior locks.

## Unlock All command

Example 7-20 Unlock All command

```
Lock
```

In Example 7-20, the *Lock* command with no parameters releases all previous locks.

When a Global array is locked, the entire array is locked.

## Lock a Global Array

Example 7-21 Lock a Global Array

```
Set ^A(SUB1)=1
Set ^A(SUB1,SUB2)=2
Set ^A(SUB1,SUB2,SUB3)=3
Lock ^A
```

In Example 7-21, locking of the ^A array locks the entire Global array. This is true even if the ^A Global array has millions of descendants.

## Lock part of a Global Array

```
Set ^A(SUB1)=1
Set ^A(SUB1,SUB2)=2
Set ^A(SUB1,SUB2,SUB3)=3
Lock ^A(SUB1,SUB2,SUB3)
```

In Example 7-22, only the specific Global node is locked, the rest of the Global is not affected.

---

### Possible Problems with the Lock command

Note that when a Global is "Locked", only those processes that also use the Lock command are prevented from accessing it. Another process, not using the Lock command, may sneak in, access and modify this Global. I see this as a weakness in COS and hope that it is addressed. You should also review the System-Supplied Function $Increment which has the capability of updating a Global counter without using the Lock command. $Increment and the Lock command are incompatible, either use $Increment or the Lock command, do not mix the two. It is recommended to use $Increment where it applies.

ZAllocate is another name for Lock.

---

## The Kill command

The **Kill** command deletes a variable or array, either local or Global, and all its descendants.

Example 7-23 Kill command

```
Set ^X=1
Set ^X("A")=2
Set ^X("B","C")=3
Kill ^X
ZW ^X
<>
```

Example 7-23 demonstrates killing the X Global and all its descendants.

## Kill a Global Array

Example 7-24 Kill a Global Array

```
Set ^A(SUB1)=1
Set ^A(SUB1,SUB2)=2
Set ^A(SUB1,SUB2,SUB3)=3
. . . many sets representing many descendants
Kill ^A
ZW ^A
<>
```

In Example 7-24, killing of the ^A Global array kills the entire Global array. This is true even if the ^A Global array has millions of descendants.

When you kill a Global array, execution control returns immediately. It may seem that the *Kill* command executes very fast, but that is not the case. When you kill a large Global array, the kill execution is handed off to a system process that goes through, deletes the entire array, and ensures the database integrity remains intact.

One tip on the efficiency of killing large Globals: it is normally better to do one kill near the top of the array rather than many kills further down the array. When a large kill is performed in addition to removing the data blocks, the remaining blocks need to be stitched back together, and it is more efficient to do this once rather than many times.

---

## Kill command Warning

You must be exceedingly careful with killing any Global array. An entire database may be wiped out in an instant with one Kill command. There is no warning nor undelete. The command:

```
Kill ^GLOBAL
```

May delete thousands or even millions of descendants and span many disk packs. This is a dangerous command indeed!

---

"This permanently and immediately deletes the specified global record from disc. Be very careful with the **KILL COMMAND** – it's both extremely simple to use and incredibly dangerous. If you specify fewer subscripts, all lower-level subscripts will be deleted. If you specify no subscripts at all, the entire global will be deleted."

Rob Tweed
M/Gateway Developments Ltd
Extreme Database Programming with MUMPS Globals
Version 1.1 : 15 May 2003
©2003, M/Gateway Developments Ltd.
Used with permission.

## Exercises on Globals

**Example 7-25 Global of Pets**

```
Set ^Pets("Dog","Boxer","Male","Buddy")="9^0"
Set ^Pets("Dog","Lab","Female","Loverly")="6^0"
Set ^Pets("Dog","Lab","Male","Tiny")="5^1"
Set ^Pets("Cat","Burmese","Male","BoyCat")="3^0"
Set ^Pets("Cat","Burmese","Female","TomBoy")="3^0"
Set ^Pets("Cat","Korat","Female","Fancy")="5^1"
```

Example 7-25 defines a Global array of dogs and cats. Subscript one is either "Dog" or "Cat", subscript two is the breed, subscript three is the sex and subscript four is the name. Piece one of the data is the animal's age and piece two is either a one or a zero. A one if the animal is available for adoption and zero if the animal is not available for adoption.

Write the code that will:

- Traverse down all four subscripts of the Pets Global using *$Order* and display each subscript and both pieces of data

- Traverse down the Global using *$Query* and display the subscripts on the left side of the equal sign and the data on the right side

- Lock and unlock the Pets Global at the top level

- Merge the Pets Global into a Pets2 Global

The next 5 examples demonstrate the answers to the above questions in each of the Command Structures for Traversing the ^Pets Global defined in Example 7-25. The File Command Structures were covered in Chapter 6.

## *Answers to Exercises on Globals – Command Structure One for Traversing a Global*

**Example 7-26 Answers to the Exercises using Command Structure One for Traversing a Global**

```
To run this code you must put the code in a routine, save the routine, and then
run the routine from the terminal.

;1. Traverse down all four subscripts of the Pets Global using
;$Order and display each subscript and both pieces of data.

Set S1="" For  Do  Quit:S1=""                    ;two spaces after the For and
Do
. Set S1=$O(^Pets(S1)) Quit:S1=""
. Set S2="" For  Do  Quit:S2=""
. . Set S2=$O(^Pets(S1,S2)) Quit:S2=""
. . Set S3="" For  Do  Quit:S3=""
. . . Set S3=$O(^Pets(S1,S2,S3)) Quit:S3=""
. . . Set S4="" For  Do  Quit:S4=""
. . . . Set S4=$O(^Pets(S1,S2,S3,S4)) Quit:S4=""
. . . . Set Data=^Pets(S1,S2,S3,S4)
. . . . Set Age=$P(Data,"^",1)
. . . . Set Adoption=$P(Data,"^",2)
. . . . If Adoption=1 Set Available="is"
. . . . If Adoption=0 Set Available="is not"
. . . . Write !,S1," named ",S4,", Breed ",S2,", Sex ",S3
. . . . Write ", ",Age," years old, ",Available," available for adoption"

;2. Traverse down the Global using $Query and display the
;subscripts on the left side of the equals sign and the data
```

```
;on the right side of the equals sign

Set Pets="^Pets"
For  Do  Quit:Pets=""              ;2 spaces after the For and Do
. Set Pets=$Q(@Pets) Quit:Pets=""
. Write !,Pets," = ",@Pets

;3. Lock and unlock the Pets Global at the top level
Lock ^Pets             ; lock
Lock                   ; unlock
                                ; OR
Lock +^Pets            ; lock
Lock -^Pets            ; unlock

;4. Merge the Pets Global into a Pets2 Global
Merge ^Pets2=^Pets
```

Example 7-26 demonstrates the answers to the exercises using Command Structure One for traversing a Global.

## *Answers to Exercises on Globals – Command Structure Two for Traversing a Global*

**Example 7-27 Answers to the Exercises using Command Structure Two for Traversing a Global**

```
To run this code you must put the code in a routine, save the routine, and then
run the routine from the terminal.
```

```
;1. Traverse down all four subscripts of the Pets Global using
;$Order and display each subscript and both pieces of data.

Set S1="" For  Set S1=$O(^Pets(S1)) Quit:S1="" Do          ;two spaces after
the For and before the Do
. Set S2="" For  Set S2=$O(^Pets(S1,S2)) Quit:S2="" Do
. . Set S3="" For  Set S3=$O(^Pets(S1,S2,S3)) Quit:S3="" Do
. . . Set S4="" For  Set S4=$O(^Pets(S1,S2,S3,S4)) Quit:S4="" Do
. . . . Set Data=^Pets(S1,S2,S3,S4)
. . . . Set Age=$P(Data,"^",1)
. . . . Set Adoption=$P(Data,"^",2)
. . . . If Adoption=1 Set Available="is"
. . . . If Adoption=0 Set Available="is not"
. . . . Write !,S1," named ",S4,", Breed ",S2,", Sex ",S3
. . . . Write ", ",Age," years old, ",Available," available for adoption"

;2. Traverse down the Global using $Query and display the
;subscripts on the left side of the equals sign and the data
;on the right side of the equals sign

Set Pets="^Pets"
For  Set Pets=$Q(@Pets) Quit:Pets="" Do
. Write !,Pets," = ",@Pets

;3. Lock and unlock the Pets Global at the top level
;Same as prior example

;4. Merge the Pets Global into a Pets2 Global
;Same as prior example
```

Example 7-27 demonstrates the answer to the exercises using Command Structure Two for traversing a Global.

## Answers to Exercises on Globals – Command Structure Three for Traversing a Global

**Example 7-28 Answers to the Exercises using Command Structure Three for Traversing a Global**

```
To run this code you must put the code in a routine, save the routine, and then
run the routine from the terminal.

;1. Traverse down all four subscripts of the Pets Global using
;$Order and display each subscript and both pieces of data.

Set (S1,S2,S3,S4)=""
For  Set S1=$O(^Pets(S1)) Quit:S1=""  Do ;two spaces after the For and before
the Do
. For  Set S2=$O(^Pets(S1,S2)) Quit:S2=""  Do
. . For  Set S3=$O(^Pets(S1,S2,S3)) Quit:S3=""  Do
. . . For  Set S4=$O(^Pets(S1,S2,S3,S4)) Quit:S4=""  Do
. . . . Set Data=^Pets(S1,S2,S3,S4)
. . . . Set Age=$P(Data,"^",1)
. . . . Set Adoption=$P(Data,"^",2)
. . . . If Adoption=1 Set Available="is"
. . . . If Adoption=0 Set Available="is not"
. . . . Write !,S1," named ",S4,", Breed ",S2,", Sex ",S3
. . . . Write ", ",Age," years old, ",Available," available for adoption"

2. Traverse down the Global using $Query and display the
;subscripts on the left side of the equals sign and the data
;on the right side of the equals sign
;Same as prior example

;3. Lock and unlock the Pets Global at the top level
;Same as prior example

;4. Merge the Pets Global into a Pets2 Global
;Same as prior example
```

Example 7-28 demonstrates the answer to the exercises using Command Structure Three for traversing a Global.

## Answers to Exercises on Globals – Command Structure Four for Traversing a Global

**Example 7-29 Answers to the Exercises using Command Structure Four for Traversing a Global, the While command**

```
To run this code you must put the code in a routine, save the routine, and then
run the routine from the terminal.

;1. Traverse down all four subscripts of the Pets Global using
;$Order and display each subscript and both pieces of data.
Set S1=$O(^Pets(""))
While (S1'="") {
```

```
    Set S2=$O(^Pets(S1,""))
  While (S2'="") {
    Set S3=$O(^Pets(S1,S2,""))
    While (S3'="") {
      Set S4=$O(^Pets(S1,S2,S3,""))
      While (S4'="") {
        Set Data=^Pets(S1,S2,S3,S4)
        Set Age=$P(Data,"^",1)
        Set Adoption=$P(Data,"^",2)
        If Adoption=1 Set Available="is"
        If Adoption=0 Set Available="is not"
        Write !,S1," named ",S4,", Breed ",S2,", Sex ",S3
        Write ", ",Age," years old, ",Available," available for adoption"
        Set S4=$O(^Pets(S1,S2,S3,S4))
      }
      Set S3=$O(^Pets(S1,S2,S3))
    }
    Set S2=$O(^Pets(S1,S2))
  }
  Set S1=$O(^Pets(S1))
}

;2. Traverse down the Global using $Query and display the
;subscripts on the left side of the equals sign and the data
;on the right side of the equals sign
Set Pets="^Pets"

Set Pets=$Q(@Pets)
While (Pets'="") {
  Write !,Pets," = ",@Pets
  Set Pets=$Q(@Pets)
}

;3. Lock and unlock the Pets Global at the top level
;Same as prior example

;4. Merge the Pets Global into a Pets2 Global
;Same as prior example
```

Example 7-29 demonstrates the answer to the exercises using Command Structure Four for traversing a Global, the *While* command.

## Answers to Exercises on Globals – Command Structure Five for Traversing a Global

**Example 7-30 Answers to the Exercises using Command Structure Five for Traversing a Global, the Do While command**

```
To run this code you must put the code in a routine, save the routine, and then
run the routine from the terminal.

;1. Traverse down all four subscripts of the Pets Global using
;$Order and display each subscript and both pieces of data.

Set S1="" Do {
  Set S1=$O(^Pets(S1)) Quit:S1=""
  Set S2="" Do {
    Set S2=$O(^Pets(S1,S2)) Quit:S2=""
    Set S3="" Do {
```

```
        Set S3=$O(^Pets(S1,S2,S3)) Quit:S3=""
        Set S4="" Do {
          Set S4=$O(^Pets(S1,S2,S3,S4)) Quit:S4=""
          Set Data=^Pets(S1,S2,S3,S4)
          Set Age=$P(Data,"^",1)
          Set Adoption=$P(Data,"^",2)
          If Adoption=1 Set Available="is"
          If Adoption=0 Set Available="is not"
          Write !,S1," named ",S4,", Breed ",S2,", Sex ",S3
          Write ", ",Age," years old, ",Available," available for adoption"
        } While S4'=""
      } While S3'=""
    } While S2'=""
} While S1'=""

;2. Traverse down the Global using $Query and display the
;subscripts on the left side of the equals sign and the data
;on the right side of the equals sign

Set Pets="^Pets"
Do {
  Set Pets=$Q(@Pets) Quit:Pets=""
  Write !,Pets," = ",@Pets
} While Pets'=""

;3. Lock and unlock the Pets Global at the top level
;Same as prior example

;4. Merge the Pets Global into a Pets2 Global
;Same as prior example
```

Example 7-30 demonstrates the answer to the exercises using Command Structure Five for traversing a Global, the *Do While* command.

## *A note on using Globals*

> "Globals are faster than local storage for large arrays for several reasons. Addressing of variables in local storage is optimized for a large number of relatively small unrelated data points. Addressing of globals is optimized for a small number of related, large data structures. . . . unless your buffer pool is extremely small, you are never working directly with, nor waiting for, the storage medium anyway. The global pages being referenced are loaded into the buffer memory, and all your activity will happen in memory anyway. Journaling might affect performance with globals, but process private globals are not journalled, so that is not an issue. "

Mark Sires . . . used with permission.

## *Chapter 7 Summary*

Chapters 6 and 7 cover **Global Processing** in Caché ObjectScript (COS). In this chapter, we covered the *MUMPS Global*, or *Global Structure*, or its newer term *Caché Multi-dimensional Database*. We also covered: 1) *Namespaces, 2) Extended Syntax, 3) Temporary Globals (CacheTempUser and Process Private Globals), 4) Naked References, 5) Merge command, 6) Lock command, 7) Kill command and 8) Five Command Structures for Traversing a Global.*

*"We are not satisfied, until you are not satisfied."*
*– www.despair.com*

# Chapter 8 Commands Revisited

This chapter expands upon some of the commands covered in previous chapters. Discussed are additional capabilities to the *Read* and *Write* commands, *If/Else*, *ElseIf* and *Endif* commands. Two *Structured Code* commands are reviewed, the *Do While* and *While* command

## Read and Write commands

The *Read* command sets a variable to a value, (similar to the *Set* command.) The *Write* command displays the value of a variable.

## Basic Read command

Typically, the *Read* command accepts input from the screen or terminal. It also has the capability to display a prompt before accepting the input.

**Example 8-1 The Basic Read command**

```
Read X
My dog has fleas
Write X
My dog has fleas

Read "Prompt: ",X                    ;display "Prompt: "
Prompt: My dog has fleas
Write X
My dog has fleas
```

Example 8-1 shows the two formats of the basic *Read* command. The first format accepts input from the screen or terminal without a prompt, the second format displays a prompt before accepting input.

At times, you need to convert the user's input to uppercase, regardless of the case the user is currently using. There are various ways of converting text to uppercase. The **$ZCVT** *System-Supplied Function* accomplishes this. Chapters 3 and 4 cover *System-Supplied Function*s.

## Read and convert to uppercase

**Example 8-2 Read and convert to uppercase**

```
Read X
My dog has fleas
Set X=$ZCVT(X,"U")           ;convert to uppercase
Write X
MY DOG HAS FLEAS
```

In Example 8-2, *$ZCVT* is used to convert the user input to uppercase.

## Basic Write command

The *Write* command displays the value of a variable.

**Example 8-3 The Basic Write command**

```
Set X="ABC"
Write X
ABC
```

Example 8-3 demonstrates the basic *Write* command.

---

## Read and Write commands used with external files

The Read and Write commands may be used with external files, which are covered in Chapter 12 on File Processing.

---

## Advanced Read and Write commands

### Exclamation point (!), Read or Write with carriage return, line feed

The The Exclamation point character may be combined with the *Read* and *Write* commands to issue a *Carriage Return*, and *Line Feed*.

**Example 8-4 Read or Write with carriage return, line feed**

```
Read !!,"Prompt: ",X
<carriage return, line feed>
<carriage return, line feed>
Prompt: My dog has fleas

Write !,X,!
<carriage return, line feed>
My dog has fleas
<carriage return, line feed>
```

Example 8-4 shows the Exclamation point (!), or carriage return, line feed. The Exclamation point may be repeated as many times as needed in the *Read* or *Write* commands.

### Hash symbol (#), Read or Write with form feed

The Hash symbol may be combined with the *Read* and *Write* commands to issue a *Form Feed*. A *Form Feed* will advance to the top of the next page.

**Example 8-5 Read or Write with form feed**

```
Read #,"Prompt: ",X
<Form Feed inserted here>
Prompt: My dog has fleas
```

```
Write #,X,!
<Form Feed inserted here>
My dog has fleas
```

Example 8-5 shows the Hash symbol (#) character to issue a *Form Feed*.

### *Question mark (?), or Tab, Read or Write advancing a number of spaces/*

The Question mark character, also called Tab, may be combined with the *Read* or *Write* commands to advance a number of horizontal spaces. The Tab character requires an associated integer. The integer is the number of spaces to advance from the start of the line.

**Example 8-6 Read or Write advancing a number of spaces**

```
Read ?10,"Prompt: ",X
        Prompt:

Write ?10,"New",?20,"Title"
        New       Title
```

In Example 8-6, the question mark character, also call Tab is used to advance across the page 10 spaces for the *Read* command, and then both 10 and 20 horizontal spaces for the *Write* command."

The integer used after the question mark is always the number of spaces from the beginning of the line, not from the last position written on the line.

**Example 8-7 Improper use of the Tab in the Write command**

```
Write ?10,"New",?10,"Title"
        NewTitle
```

In Example 8-7, why is "New" and "Title" next to each other?

Answer; both "New" and "Title" are written after advancing 10 spaces from the beginning of the line. Or, more properly stated, 10 spaces from the beginning of the line, or the nearest blank position available after 10 spaces.

### *Colon (:), Read command timer*

The Colon character combined with the *Read* command functions as a timer. The colon character requires an associated integer. This integer is the number of seconds to wait before the *Read* terminates, unless a <Return> or <Enter> key is hit first.

**Example 8-8 Read command Timer**

```
Read X:5
```

In Example 8-8, the *Read* command will terminate after waiting five seconds unless a <Return> or <Enter> key is hit.

### *Hash symbol (#), Read a specified number of characters*

The Hash symbol combined with the *Read* command limits the number of characters read from the screen or terminal. The hash symbol requires an associated integer. This integer is the number of characters to accept before the *Read* terminates, unless a <Return> or <Enter> key is hit.

**Example 8-9 Read a specified number of characters**

```
Read X#6
My dog<character acceptance is stopped here>

Write !,X
My dog
```

In Example 8-9, when the X variable is followed by "#6", the *Read* command will terminate after the first six characters are accepted, unless a <Return> or <Enter> key is hit.

## *Advanced Read and Write command Exercises*

Write the code that will:

> ➢ Read a value into the variable X, with the prompt "Please enter value:"
>
> ➢ Read a value into X after advancing to the next page
>
> ➢ Read a value into X after advancing 5 lines
>
> ➢ Read a value into X from column 20
>
> ➢ Read a value into X, if after 5 seconds no value is entered, continue
>
> ➢ Read a value into X, but only accept 5 characters
>
> ➢ Write "My dog's name is Teddy" after advancing to the next page
>
> ➢ Write "My cat's name is fluffy" after advancing 5 lines
>
> ➢ Write "I have too many pets" after moving across the page 10 spaces

## *Advanced Read and Write command Exercise Answers*

**Example 8-10 Advanced Read and Write command Exercise Answers**

```
Read a value into the variable X, with the prompt "Please enter value:"
Read "Please enter value:",X

Read a value into X after advancing to the next page.
Read #,X

Read a value into X after advancing 5 lines.
Read !!!!!,X

Read a value into X from column 20.
Read ?20,X
```

```
Read a value into X, if after 5 seconds no value is entered, continue.
Read X:5

Read a value into X, but only accept 5 characters.
Read X#5

Write "My dog's name is Teddy" after advancing to the next page.
Write #,"My dog's name is Teddy"

Write "My cat's name is fluffy" after advancing 5 lines.
Write !!!!!,"My cat's name is fluffy"

Write "I have too many pets" after moving across the page 10 spaces.
Write ?10,"I have too many pets"
```

# If, ElseIf and Else commands

As we have seen before, the *If* command is the primary decision maker in COS.

## If and Else commands in the older style of MUMPS

This first example will show the *If* and *Else* commands as used in the older style of MUMPS.

Note; starting with this example and in all examples using the *If, ElseIf* and *Else* commands, that the code is indented. These examples are meant to be used in routines and cannot just be typed interactively. Remember the first space of any COS routine line is reserved for the Label.

**Example 8-11 If and Else commands in the older style of MUMPS**

```
To run this code you must put the code in a routine, save the routine, and then
run the routine from the terminal.

Set X=1
If X=1 Write !,"X=1"
Else  Write !,"X is not = 1"        ;Else must be followed by two spaces
```

In Example 8-11, the *If* and its associated *Else* command are on two adjacent lines. The important thing to remember is that two spaces must follow the "E" (*Else* command).

## If and Else commands in Structured Code

The next example shows the same *If* and *Else* commands in *Structured Code*.

**Example 8-12 If and Else commands in Structured Code.**

```
To run this code you must put the code in a routine, save the routine, and then
run the routine from the terminal.

; First Method
Set X=1
If X=1 {
  Write !,"X=1"
}
Else {
```

```
   Write !,"X is not = 1"
}

; Second Method
Set X=1
If X=1 {Write !,"X=1"}
Else {Write !,"X is not = 1"}

; Third Method
Set X=1
If X=1 {Write !,"X=1"} Else {Write !,"X is not = 1"}
```

In Example 8-12, notice the three methods of the *If* and *Else* commands; all three methods are identical in execution. It depends upon your preference and readability as to which of the three you use. However, for all three methods; there must be a pair of curly brackets {} after the *If* command and after the *Else* command. Spacing and multiple lines do not matter.

## Nested If and Else commands with Structured Code

The next example will demonstrate *Nested If* and *Else* commands in *Structured Code*.

**Example 8-13 Nested If and Else commands in Structured Code**

To run this code you must put the code in a routine, save the routine, and then run the routine from the terminal.

```
; First Method
Set X=1,Y=2
If X=1 {
  Write !,"X=1"
  If Y=2 {
    Write !,"Y=2"
  }
  Else {
    Write !,"Y is not = 2"
  }
}
Else {
  Write !,"X is not = 1"
  If Y=2 {
    Write !,"Y=2"
  }
  Else {
    Write !,"Y is not = 2"
  }
}

; Second Method
Set X=1,Y=2
If X=1 {Write !,"X=1"
  If Y=2 {Write !,"Y=2"}
  Else {Write !,"Y is not = 2"}
}
Else {Write !,"X is not = 1"
  If Y=2 {Write !,"Y=2"}
  Else {Write !,"Y is not = 2"}
}
```

```
; Third Method
Set X=1,Y=2
If X=1 {Write !,"X=1" If Y=2 {Write !,"Y=2"} Else {Write !,"Y is not = 2"}}
Else {Write !,"X is not = 1" If Y=2 {Write !,"Y=2"} Else {Write !,"Y is not =
2"}}
```

In Example 8-13 notice, again, the three methods of the *Nested If* and *Else* commands; all three methods are identical in execution. It depends upon your preference and readability as to which of the three you use.

These methods demonstrate that using nested *If* and *Else* commands can become unruly quickly; use with care to ensure easy readability of the code. Also play close attention to the indentation of commands, which helps with readability.

## *If, ElseIf and Else commands in Structured Code*

The next example will demonstrate *If, ElseIf* and *Else* commands in *Structured Code*.

**Example 8-14 If, ElseIf and Else commands in Structured Code**

```
To run this code you must put the code in a routine, save the routine, and then
run the routine from the terminal.

; First Method
Set X=1
If X=1 {
   Write !,"X=1"
}
ElseIf X=2 {
   Write !,"X=2"
}
Else {
   Write !,"X not = 1 or 2"
}

; Second Method
Set X=1
If X=1 {Write !,"X=1"}
ElseIf X=2 {Write !,"X=2"}
Else {Write !,"X not = 1 or 2"}
```

Example 8-14 demonstrates two methods of using the use of the *If, ElseIf* and *Else* commands.

The *ElseIf* command can be repeated many times to cover the appropriate situations, but if you find yourself using too many *ElseIf* commands, perhaps you would be better off using the *$Case* or *$Select System-Supplied Functions*, see Chapter 4.

## *If, (multiple) ElseIf and Else commands in Structured Code*

Example 8-15 If, (multiple) ElseIf and Else command in Structured Code.

```
To run this code you must put the code in a routine, save the routine, and then
run the routine from the terminal.

Set Day=1
If Day=1 {Write !,"Today is Sunday"}
ElseIf Day=2 {Write !,"Today is Monday"}
ElseIf Day=3 {Write !,"Today is Tuesday"}
ElseIf Day=4 {Write !,"Today is Wednesday"}
ElseIf Day=5 {Write !,"Today is Tursday"}
ElseIf Day=6 {Write !,"Today is Friday"}
ElseIf Day=7 {Write !,"Today is Saturday"}
Else {Write !,"If don't know what day it is!"}
```

Example 8-15 shows how to use the *If, ElseIf* and *Else* commands to display the day of the week in *Structured Code*.

*Structured Code* does take some getting used to and experimentation until you know exactly what it is doing. There have been times I have assumed it is doing what it was not. Using a good debugger or adding lots of write statements to your code is a good idea until you are thoroughly comfortable with it.

## *While and Do While command*

**The While** and the **Do While** commands are one of COS contributions to the MUMPS programming language. Used properly and with understanding they are nice additions. They are by their very nature *Structured Code*.

For example, suppose you want to ask the user for input and only accept Yes or No (Y or N) as valid answers. Using the *If* command you might write something like this:

Example 8-16 Using the If command to verify user input

```
AskUser    ;
  Read !,"Please enter 'Y'es or 'N' ",Answer      ;ask user for answer
  Set Answer=$ZCVT(Answer,"U")                     ;convert to upper case
  If $E(Answer)'="Y",($E(Answer)'="N") Goto AskUser  ;$E looks at the
                                                    ;first char
```

In Example 8-16, the *If* command verifies the users input. It is straightforward coding. However, it does require a Label (AskUser) and it does require a *Goto* command that we try to avoid if possible.

If we wish to rewrite this code using the *While* command, it would look something like:

**Example 8-17 Using the While command to verify user input**

```
To run this code you must put the code in a routine, save the routine, and then
run the routine from the terminal.

Set Answer=""
While $E(Answer)'="Y",($E(Answer)'="N")   {
  Read !,"Please enter 'Y'es or 'N' ",Answer        ;ask user for answer
  Set Answer=$ZCVT(Answer,"U")                       ;convert to upper case
}
```

In Example 8-17, the *While* command verifies the users input. Note that the Label and *Goto* command is missing. Some programmers prefer this type of structure because the *While* command control parameters ($E(Answer)'="Y",($E(Answer)'="N") ) are at the top and not buried in the procedure.

If we wish to rewrite this code using the *Do While* command, it would look something like:

**Example 8-18 Using the Do While command to verify user input**

```
To run this code you must put the code in a routine, save the routine, and then
run the routine from the terminal.

Set Answer=""
Do {
  Read !,"Please enter 'Y'es or 'N' ",Answer        ;ask user for answer
  Set Answer=$ZCVT(Answer,"U")                       ;convert to upper case
} While $E(Answer)'="Y",($E(Answer)'="N")
```

In Example 8-18, the *Do While* command verifies users input. Note that the *Do While* command control parameters ($E(Answer)'="Y",($E(Answer)'="N") are after the last curly bracket } and after the key word "While".

## Difference between the While and Do While commands

The question that may be in your mind, what is the difference between the *While* command and *Do While* command? In the *While* command the control parameters are checked before the procedure is run, whereas, in the *Do While* command, the control parameters are check after the procedure is run.

## Secret Escape Hatch in Structured Code

*Structured Code* has a secret escape hatch, so to speak, embedding a *Quit* command in the middle of this *Structured Code*, the control parameters are ignored and the *While* command or *Do While* command exits.

**Example 8-19 Do While command with embedded Quit command**

```
To run this code you must put the code in a routine, save the routine, and then
run the routine from the terminal.

Set Answer=""
Do {
  Read !,"Please enter 'Y'es or 'N' ",Answer        ;ask user for answer
  If Answer="" Q
  Set Answer=$ZCVT(Answer,"U")                       ;convert to upper case
} While $E(Answer)'="Y", ($E(Answer)'="N")
```

In Example 8-19, the *Quit* command on the fourth line will cause the *Do While* command to exit regardless of the control parameters. Be very careful when using a *Quit* command inside *Structured Code*. See Chapter 16 for a more complete explanation of *Structured Code*.

## Chapter 8 Summary

In this chapter, we covered some of the more advanced features of various commands; specifically we expanded upon the *Read* and *Write* commands with convert to uppercase, line and page feed, tabs and a timer. We saw how to read a specific number of characters. In addition we looked at the *If/ElseIf/Else* commands *and nested If/ElseIf/Else* commands *in older style (legacy) MUMPS as well as in the new Structured Code. We covered two new* commands *only available in Caché ObjectScript, the While*, and the *Do While* commands and talk about their differences and problems.

# Chapter 9 New Command

This chapter covers the New command. The *New* command limits a variable's scope or range of use. In theory the *New* command in simple, in reality the *New* command is powerful and needs to be respected and understood.

The intention of the *New* command is to not inadvertently over-write variables already defined. The effect of the *New* command ceases once a *Quit* command is encountered. In essence, the *New* command provides a new version of a variable.

The *New* command cannot be used in *Procedures* (Chapter 15) and *Methods* (Chapter 32) where *Private Variables* eliminate the need for the *New* command.

There are three variations of the *New* command:

➢ When used without variables

➢ When used with variable(s)

➢ When used with variables in parenthesis

## New command used without variables

**Example 9-1 New command used without variables**

```
New              ; all variables created will be new
Set X=1
Quit             ; New command cancelled
```

Example 9-1 demonstrates the *New* command without variables. The result of this command is that from this point until the *Quit* command, all variables created will be new. Old variables and their values are gone but will be restored when the *Quit* command is encountered. Note that the extensive use of this form of the *New* command may be costly to computer resources, especially if there are many variables.

## Newcommand Routine (New command without variables)

**Example 9-2 Newcommand Routine**

```
To run this code you must put the code in a routine, save the routine, and then
run the routine from the terminal.

Newcommand          ; New command Routine
Start
    Set X=1,Y=2,Z=3
    Write !!,"X: ",X
    Write !,"Y: ",Y
    Write !,"Z: ",Z
    Do SubRoutine
```

```
    Write !!,"X: ",X
    Write !,"Y: ",Y
    Write !,"Z: ",Z
    Quit

SubRoutine          ; SubRoutine
    New                       ; "New" all variables
    Set X=100,Y=200,Z=300
    Write !!,"X: ",X
    Write !,"Y: ",Y
    Write !,"Z: ",Z
    Quit                      ; All variables revert back to their original value
```

In Example 9-2, variables X, Y and Z are set to 1, 2 and 3 respectively. Upon calling the SubRoutine, all variables are "Newed", and then variables X, Y and Z are changed. When the *Quit* command executes, all variables revert to their original value.

## Running the Newcommand Routine (New command without variables)

**Example 9-3 Running the Newcommand Routine**

```
Do ^Newcommand

X: 1                ;first X,Y,Z are set to 1,2,3 respectively
Y: 2
Z: 3

X: 100      ;within SubRoutine, X,Y,Z are reset to 100,200,300 respectively
Y: 200
Z: 300

X: 1                ;after the quit command in the Subroutine, X,Y,X revert
Y: 2
Z: 3
```

In Example 9-3, you can see the results of running the Newcommand routine. Although the SubRoutine changes the value of the variables, when the SubRoutine exits, the variables revert back to their previous value.

## New command used with Arrays

**Example 9-4 New command used with Arrays**

```
To run this code you must put the code in a routine, save the routine, and then
run the routine from the terminal.

Newcommand          ; New command Routine
Start                     ;
    Set Array(1)=1
    Set Array(2)=2
    Set Array(3)=3
    Write !!,"Array(1): ",Array(1)
    Write !,"Array(2): ",Array(2)
    Write !,"Array(3): ",Array(3)
```

```
    Do SubRoutine
    Write !!,"Array(1): ",Array(1)
    Write !,"Array(2): ",Array(2)
    Write !,"Array(3): ",Array(3)
    Quit

SubRoutine
    New                    ;"New" all variables and arays
    Set Array(1)=100
    Set Array(2)=200
    Set Array(3)=300
    Write !!,"Array(1): ",Array(1)
    Write !,"Array(2): ",Array(2)
    Write !,"Array(3): ",Array(3)
    Quit               ;All variables and arrays revert back to their original
value
```

In Example 9-4, Array nodes (1), (2), and (3) are set to 1, 2 and 3 respectively. Upon calling the SubRoutine, all variables and arrays are "Newed", and then Array nodes (1), (2), and (3) are changed. When the *Quit* command executes, all variables and arrays revert to their original value.

**Example 9-5 Running the Newcommand Routine**

```
Do ^Newcommand

Array(1): 1        ;first Array(1),(2),(3) are set to 1,2,3 respectively
Array(2): 2
Array(3): 3

Array(1): 100  ;within SubRoutine, Array(1),(2),(3) are reset to 100,200,300
Array(2): 200
Array(3): 300

Array(1): 1     ;after the quit command in Subroutine, Array(1),(2),(3) revert
Array(2): 2
Array(3): 3
```

In Example 9-5, you can see the results of running the Newcommand routine. Although the SubRoutine changes the value of the Array nodes, when the SubRoutine exits, the Array nodes revert back to their previous value.

---

### *New command has no effect on Globals*

Note that the New command has no effect on Global Variables or Global Arrays.

---

It is interesting to note, that when you call a routine or subroutine with parameters (*Passed by value*), the specified parameters implicitly are *Newed*.

## New command and parameter passing (Passed by value)

**Example 9-6 Calling with parameters (passed by value) creates an implicit New**

```
To run this code you must put the code in a routine, save the routine, and then
run the routine from the terminal.
```

```
Newcommand              ; New command Routine
 Start     ;
    Set X=1,Y=2,Z=3
    Write !!,"X: ",X
    Write !,"Y: ",Y
    Write !,"Z: ",Z
    Do SubRoutine(X,Y,Z)   ;X,Y,Z Parameter Passing
    Write !!,"X: ",X
    Write !,"Y: ",Y
    Write !,"Z: ",Z
    Quit
    ;

SubRoutine(X,Y,Z)  ;Subroutine with Parameter Passing
    Set X=100,Y=200,Z=300
    Write !!,"X: ",X
    Write !,"Y: ",Y
    Write !,"Z: ",Z
    Quit                    ;All variables revert back to their original value
```

In Example 9-6, variables X, Y and Z are set to 1, 2 and 3 respectively. Then the SubRoutine is called with parameters X, Y and Z (note the variables are not explicitly *Newed*). Then variables X, Y and Z are changed. When the *Quit command* executes, all variables revert back to their original value.

**Example 9-7 Running the Newcommand Routine with Parameter Passing**

```
Do ^Newcommand

X: 1          ;first X,Y,Z are set to 1,2,3 respectively
Y: 2
Z: 3

X: 100        ;within SubRoutine, X,Y,Z are reset to 100,200,300 respectively
Y: 200
Z: 300

X: 1          ;after the quit command in the Subroutine, X,Z,X revert
Y: 2
Z: 3
```

In Example 9-7, you can see the result of running the Newcommand routine using Parameter Passing. Although the SubRoutine changes the value of the variables, when the SubRoutine exits, the variables revert back to their previous value.

However, when you call a routine or subroutine with parameters - *Passed by reference*, the Subroutine changes the values and these changes are passed back to the calling routine.

# New command and parameter passing – (Passed by reference)

**Example 9-8 Calling with parameters - passed by reference**

```
To run this code you must put the code in a routine, save the routine, and then
run the routine from the terminal.

Newcommand                  ; New command Routine
 Start       ;
    Set X=1,Y=2,Z=3
    Write !!,"X: ",X
    Write !,"Y: ",Y
    Write !,"Z: ",Z
    Do SubRoutine(.X,.Y,.Z)          ;X,Y,Z Parameter Passing (by reference)
    Write !!,"X: ",X
    Write !,"Y: ",Y
    Write !,"Z: ",Z
    Quit
    ;
 SubRoutine(X,Y,Z)             ;Subroutine with Parameter Passing (by reference)
    Set X=100,Y=200,Z=300
    Write !!,"X: ",X
    Write !,"Y: ",Y
    Write !,"Z: ",Z
    Quit                       ;All variables do not revert back
```

In Example 9-8, variables X, Y and Z are set to 1, 2 and 3 respectively. Then the SubRoutine is called with parameters X, Y and Z *Passed by reference*. The variables X, Y and Z are changed. When the *Quit* command is executed, the variables <u>do not revert back</u> to their original value but maintain the new values.

**Example 9-9 Running Newcommand Routine**

```
Do ^Newcommand

X: 1        ;first X,Y,Z are set to 1,2,3 respectively
Y: 2
Z: 3

X: 100      ;within SubRoutine, X,Y,Z are reset to 100,200,300 respectively
Y: 200
Z: 300

X: 100      ;after the quit command in Subroutine, X,Y,Z do not revert
Y: 200
Z: 300
```

In Example 9-9, you can see the result of running the Newcommand routine. When the SubRoutine changes the value of the variables, this new value is maintained in the calling code.

So far, we have seen that *a New* command is only effective until the next *Quit* command. Nevertheless, what about an implicit *Quit* as used in an *Inline Do* command?

## New command used with Inline Do command or Implicit Quit

**Example 9-10 New command used with Inline Do command or Implicit Quit**

```
To run this code you must put the code in a routine, save the routine, and then
run the routine from the terminal.

Newcommand                          ;New command Routine
Start    ;
   Set X=1,Y=2,Z=3
   Write !!,"X: ",X
   Write !,"Y: ",Y
   Write !,"Z: ",Z
   ;
   Do                               ;inline Do
   . New
   . Set X=100,Y=200,Z=300
   . Write !!,"X: ",X
   . Write !,"Y: ",Y
   . Write !,"Z: ",Z
   ;                                ;implicit quit
   Write !!,"X: ",X
   Write !,"Y: ",Y
   Write !,"Z: ",Z
   Quit
```

In Example 9-10, variables X, Y and Z are set to 1, 2 and 3 respectively. Then an *Inline Do* command executes and variables X, Y and Z are changed. When the *Implicit Quit* command is executed, the variables revert back to their original value. Therefore, the effect of the *Implicit Quit* is the same as the *Explicit Quit*.

**Example 9-11 Running Newcommand Routine**

```
Do ^Newcommand

X: 1        ;first X,Y,Z are set to 1,2,3 respectively
Y: 2
Z: 3

X: 100      ;within SubRoutine, X,Y,Z are reset to 100,200,300 respectively
Y: 200
Z: 300

X: 1        ;after the Implicit quit in Subroutine, X,Y,Z do revert
Y: 2
Z: 3
```

In Example 9-11, you can see the result of running the Newcommand routine. The effect of the *Implicit Quit* is the same as the *Explicit Quit*.

# New command used with variables

**Example 9-12 New command used with variables**

```
New X,Y
```

In Example 9-12, the *New* command is used with variables. The result of this command is that, from this point until a *Quit* command executes, the variables specified at the command line will be new. The old values of these variables are gone and restored when a *Quit* command executes. All other variables are unaffected.

# Newcommand Routine (New command with variables)

**Example 9-13 Newcommand Routine**

```
To run this code you must put the code in a routine, save the routine, and then
run the routine from the terminal.

Newcommand          ; New command Routine
Start
    Set X=1,Y=2,Z=3
    Write !!,"X: ",X
    Write !,"Y: ",Y
    Write !,"Z: ",Z
    Do SubRoutine
    Write !!,"X: ",X
    Write !,"Y: ",Y
    Write !,"Z: ",Z
    Quit

SubRoutine         ;
    New X,Y                 ; "New" X and Y variables only
    Set X=100,Y=200,Z=300
    Write !!,"X: ",X
    Write !,"Y: ",Y
    Write !,"Z: ",Z
    Quit                    ; Only X and Y variables revert back to their
                            ; original value
```

In Example 9-13, variables X, Y and Z are set to 1, 2 and 3 respectively. Upon calling the SubRoutine, variables X and Y are "Newed", and then variables X, Y and Z are changed. When the *Quit* command executes, variables X and Y revert to their original value, variable Z is unaffected

# Running the Newcommand Routine (New command:With variables)

**Example 9-14 Running the Newcommand Routine**

```
Do ^Newcommand
```

```
X: 1              ;first X,Y,Z are set to 1,2,3 respectively
Y: 2
Z: 3

X: 100            ;within SubRoutine, X,Y,Z are reset to 100,200,300 respectively
Y: 200
Z: 300

X: 1              ;after the quit command in the Subroutine, only X and Y revert
Y: 2
Z: 300
```

In Example 9-14, you can see the results of running the Newcommand routine. Although the SubRoutine changes the value of the variables, when the SubRoutine exits, only X and Y revert back to their previous value but Z maintains its changed value.

## *This form of the New command is hard to maintain*

This form of the *New* command can be hard to maintain. The programmer must identify all variables to be *Newed* in the affected code. Then later on, if changes are made to the code, the programmer must make an extra effort to identify any new variables used and be sure to include them in the *New* command. New variables are easily missed.

**Example 9-15 New command used with variables**

```
To run this code you must put the code in a routine, save the routine, and then
run the routine from the terminal.

SubroutineA;
  New X,Y,Z,A,B,D
  Set X=1
  Set Y=2
  Set Z=3
  Set A=4
  Set B=5
  Set D=6
  Quit
```

Example 9-15 shows SubroutineA with several variables, the programmer must ensure all appropriate variables are in the New command.

**Example 9-16 New command used with variables**

```
SubroutineA;
  New X,Y,Z,A,B,D
  Set W=0
  Set X=1
  Set Y=2
  Set Z=3
  Set A=4
  Set B=5
  Set C=4
  Set D=6
  Quit
```

Example 9-16 is the same as Example 9-15 except for a few new variables. Can you spot the new variables? When adding new variables to a subroutine, the programmer has to be diligent to include the new variables in the *New* command.

## New command used with Variables and Arrays

Although you can specify an Array using this form of the *New* command, you cannot specify an Array Node.

**Example 9-17 New command used with Variables and Arrays**

```
New X              ;if X is an array this command is legal

New X(1)           ;this command is illegal
```

Example 9-17 demonstrates using the *New* command with an Array, however using the *New* command with an Array Node is illegal.

## New command may exhaust Memory

Used improperly the *New* command can easily exhaust available memory.

**Example 9-18 New command exhausts Memory**

```
To run this code you must put the code in a routine, save the routine, and then
run the routine from the terminal.

For I=1:1:10000 New X Do
. Set X=I
. Write !,X
<FRAMESTACK>
```

Example 9-18 demonstrates improper use of the *New* command. The variable X is continually "Newed" until memory is exhausted.

**Example 9-19 New command exhausts Memory - Corrected**

```
To run this code you must put the code in a routine, save the routine, and then
run the routine from the terminal.

For I=1:1:10000 Do
. New X
. Set X=I
. Write !,X
```

Example 9-19 moves the *New* command down into the body of the *Do*, this way, when the *Do* ends each iteration with an implied *Quit*, the *New* command is cancelled.

# New command used with variables in parentheses

```
New (X,Y)
```

Example 9-20 shows the *New* command with variables in parenthesis. The result of this command is that until the *Quit* command, all variables except those in the parenthesis will be new. The old values of these variables are gone and will be restored when a *Quit* command is encountered. The variables inside the parenthesis are not affected.

This form of the *New* command has the advantage over the previous one in that if new variables are added later they will automatically be *Newed* unless explicitly included within the parenthesis.

Again, note that the extensive use of this form of the *New* command may be expensive with regard to computer resources, especially if there are a large number of variables.

# Newcommand Routine (New command with variables in parenthesis)

```
To run this code you must put the code in a routine, save the routine, and then
run the routine from the terminal.

Newcommand                    ; New command Routine
Start
    Set X=1,Y=2,Z=3
    Write !!,"X: ",X
    Write !,"Y: ",Y
    Write !,"Z: ",Z
    Do SubRoutine
    Write !!,"X: ",X
    Write !,"Y: ",Y
    Write !,"Z: ",Z
    Quit

SubRoutine                    ;
    New (X,Y)                       ; "New" all variables except X and Y
    Set X=100,Y=200,Z=300
    Write !!,"X: ",X
    Write !,"Y: ",Y
    Write !,"Z: ",Z
    Quit                      ; All variables except X and Y variables revert
                              ; back to their original value
```

In Example 9-21, variables X, Y and Z are set to 1, 2 and 3 respectively. Upon calling the SubRoutine, all variables except X and Y are "Newed", and then variables X, Y and Z are changed. When the *Quit* command executes, all variables except X and Y revert to their original value.

## Running the Newcommand Routine (New command:With variables in parenthesis)

**Example 9-22 Running the Newcommand Routine**

```
Do ^Newcommand

X: 1          ;first X,Y,Z are set to 1,2,3 respectively
Y: 2
Z: 3

X: 100        ;within SubRoutine, X,Y,Z are reset to 100,200,300 respectively
Y: 200
Z: 300

X: 100        ;after the quit command in the Subroutine, X and Y do not revert
Y: 200
Z: 3
```

In Example 9-22 you can see the results of running the Newcommand routine. Although the SubRoutine changes the value of the variables, when the SubRoutine exits, X and Y do not revert back to their previous value, however the variable Z does revert.

## New command used improperly

**Example 9-23 New command used improperly**

```
To run this code you must put the code in a routine, save the routine, and then
run the routine from the terminal.

Newcommand ;
 Loop           ;
    N X,Y
    Set X=$G(X)+1
    Set Y=$G(Y)+1
    Set Z=$G(Z)+1
    G Loop
```

In Example 9-23, can you spot the problem? If you would run this routine what sort of error would you get? If you say the problem is that the *New* command is not paired with a *Quit* command you are correct and the error would be a <FRAMESTACK> error, or more basically this routine will exhaust the computer memory.

## *Examples of the New command*

"Throw away variables" like I or X should always be Newed before use.

**Example 9-24 Examples of not using a New command**

```
To run this code you must put the code in a routine, save the routine, and
then run the routine from the terminal.

For I=1:1:10 D Proc1
Quit

Proc1      ;
  Write !,"Processing I of: ",I
  Do Proc2
  Quit

Proc2      ;
  For I=1:1:5 {
    Write !,"I number: ",I
  }
  Quit
```

Can you spot the problem in Example 9-24? This code will go into an infinite look, it will never stop running. The problem of course is the top level control uses the variable "I" as its control variable. The Label Proc2 also uses "I" as a control variable. Therefore, whoever wrote their code first, *Assumed* that the variable "I" was not in use. What is the solution? Whenever you use a throw away variables like "I" as a control variable always *New* the variable.

This error was easy to spot, but very often the two pieces of code are separated by hundreds and may be thousands of lines of code and many routines.

**Example 9-25 Solution to assuming a variable is not in use Variable**

```
To run this code you must put the code in a routine, save the routine, and
then run the routine from the terminal.

New I                       ;New I
For I=1:1:10 Do Proc1
Quit

Proc1      ;
  Write !,"Processing I of: ",I
  Do Proc2
  Quit

Proc2      ;
  New I
  For I=1:1:5 {
    Write !,"I number: ",I   ;New I
  }
  Quit
```

Example 9-25 demonstrates the solution. Although the *Newing* of "I" at the top is not necessary, it is good programming practice.

## New command warnings

The ramification of the *New* command is far reaching and needs to be used wisely. Without the *New* command, all variables are accessible to all routines that run in the same process. The *New* command is an attempt to limit this scope. It may be of good use in utility routines and functions that should not change the value of any previously defined variables. You need to experiment and run tests with this command to understand it.

## Chapter 9 Summary

In this chapter, we covered the *New* command and it's pairing with the *Quit* command and their affect on scoping variables. Specifically, we looked at the *New* command/*Quit* command pair when used: 1) without variables, 2) when used with variables and 3) when used with variables in parenthesis. We explored the *New* commands affect on arrays, and variables passed by value and by reference. In addition we covered the subject of the *New* command and maintenance. Lastly we demonstrated how the *New* command could exhaust memory.

The *New* command cannot be used in *Procedures* (Chapter 15) and *Methods* (Chapter 32) where *Private Variables* eliminate the need for the *New* command.

*"The human brain starts working the moment you are born and never stops until you stand up to speak in public."*

*- Sir George Jessel*

# *Chapter 10 Pattern Matching*

This chapter covers the topic of **Pattern Matching** in Caché ObjectScript (COS). *Pattern Matching* is a powerful subset of COS capabilities. It is a bit cryptic but once understood provides the programmer with capabilities difficult to perform otherwise.

In COS, *Pattern Matching* is a way of validating data, it looks for a match on a pattern of characters. For example; suppose you wanted to verify an American Social Security Number? The Social Security Number is in nnn-nn-nnnn format.

## *Validate an American Social Security Number with Pattern Matching*

**Example 10-1 Validate an American Social Security Number with Pattern Matching**

```
If SSN?3N1"-"2N1"-"4N Write !,"Valid Social Security Number"
```

Example 10-1 compares a Social Security Number to a pattern.

The pattern ?3N1"-"2N1"-"4N means:

> ➢ ? – the question mark signifies the start of a pattern, do not confuse this with the *Tab* character which also uses the question mark

> ➢ 3N – three numeric digits, the first three characters of the ssn

> ➢ 1"-" – one dash, the dash coming after the first three characters of the ssn

> ➢ 2N – two numeric digits coming after the first dash in the ssn

> ➢ 1"-" – one dash, the dash coming after the two numeric's in the middle of the ssn

> ➢ 4N – four numeric digits coming at the end of the ssn

Example 10-1 uses "N" for a numeric code, there are other codes, as seen in Table 10-1.

## Pattern Matching Codes

*Pattern Matching* uses several codes to represents the type of characters to be matched.

**Table 10-1 *Pattern Matching* Codes**

| Code | Meaning |
|------|---------|
| A | Alphabetic characters, A thru Z, uppercase and lowercase |
| U | Uppercase characters |
| L | Lowercase characters |
| N | Numeric digits |
| P | Punctuation characters |
| C | Control Character |
| E | Any Character |

In addition to *Pattern Matching* Codes to represent characters, the length of a pattern may also be specified.

## Pattern Length

**Table 10-2 Pattern Length**

| Length | Meaning |
|--------|---------|
| 4 | exactly four |
| 1.4 | from one to four |
| .4 | up to four |
| 4. | at least 4 |
| . | any number including zero |

In this next example, we will look at using *Pattern Matching* to validate a Alpha Characters.

## *Validating Alpha Characters*

**Example 10-2 Validating Alpha Characters**

```
; Pattern Matching "A" - alpha characters, uppercase and lowercase

Set Data="ABCDEabcde"          ;Data contains all alpha characters
Set Pattern=".A"               ;Pattern of any number of alpha characters
Write Data?@Pattern            ;checks for all alpha characters
1                              ;if the data conforms to the pattern
                               ; - a 1 (true) is returned

Set Data="ABCDEabcde"          ;Data contains all alpha characters
If Data?.A Write !,"The data conforms to the pattern"
The data conforms to the pattern
```

Example 10-2 demonstrates two methods of validating Alpha Characters according to a pattern. The pattern construct, ".A" indicates all alpha characters, both uppercase and lowercase.

The pattern construct for uppercase ".U" and lowercase ".L" work the same way as the pattern construct for Alpha, ".A".

## *Validating Uppercase Characters*

**Example 10-3 Validating Uppercase Characters**

```
; Pattern Matching "U" - uppercase characters

Set Data="ABCDE"          ;Data contains all uppercase characters
Set Pattern=".U"          ;Pattern of any number of uppercase characters
Write Data?@Pattern       ;checks for all uppercase characters
1                         ;if the data conforms to the pattern
                          ; - a 1 (true) is returned

Set Data="ABCDE"          ;Data contains uppercase characters
If Data?.U Write !,"The data conforms to the pattern"
The data conforms to the pattern
```

Example 10-3 demonstrates two methods of validating data according to a pattern. The pattern construct, ".U" indicates all uppercase characters.

The pattern construct for uppercase ".U" and lowercase ".L" work the same way as the pattern construct for alpha, ".A". The pattern construct for lowercase, ".L" is not demonstrated; use the uppercase examples and change the pattern construct from ".U" to ".L" if you wish to check for lowercase characters.

Now, what if you want to validate a capitalized word?

## Validating a Capitalized Word

**Example 10-4 Validating a Capitalized Word**

```
Set Data="California"          ;Data contains a capitalized word
Set Pattern="1U.L"             ;Pattern for capitalized word
Write Data?@Pattern
1                              ;if the data conforms to the pattern
                              ; - a 1 (true) is returned
```

Example 10-4 demonstrates validating a capitalized word. The pattern of "1U.L" indicates 1 uppercase and any number of lowercase characters.

## Validating Numeric Digits

**Example 10-5 Validating Numeric Digits**

```
; Pattern Matching "N" - Numeric Digits

Set Data="1234"           ;Data contains all Numeric Digits
Set Pattern=".N"          ;Pattern for any number of Numeric Digits
Write Data?@Pattern       ;checks for all Numeric Digits
1                         ;if the data conforms to the pattern
                         ; - a 1 (true) is returned

Set Data="1234"           ;Data contains all Numeric Digits
If Data?.N Write !,"The data conforms to the pattern"
The data conforms to the pattern
```

Example 10-5 demonstrates two methods of validating data according to a pattern. The pattern construct, ".N" indicates all Numeric Digits.

---

### Use "N" for Integers in Patterns

You will notice that Pattern Matching uses "N" for numeric digits. However, "N" is really restricted to Integers. If you try to use Pattern Matching with a numeric digit and a decimal point, the decimal point will be seen as a length operand. Therefore don't think of the "N" for numeric digits, but for Integers only.

---

Now, what if you want to validate a number with two decimal positions?

## Validating a Numeric with Two Decimal Positions

**Example 10-6 Validating a Numeric with Two Decimal Positions**

```
Set Data="12.34"                ;Data contains Numerics, decimal and 2
numerics
Set Pattern=".N1""."2N"  ;Pattern for Numerics, decimal and 2 numerics
Write Data?@Pattern
1                                ;if the data conforms to the pattern
                                 ;a 1 (true) is returned

Set Data="12.34"                ;Data contains Numerics, decimal and 2
numerics
If Data?.N1"."2N Write !,"The data conforms to the pattern"
The data conforms to the pattern
```

Example 10-6 demonstrates two methods of validating a numeric, decimal point and two numeric digits.

## Validating Punctuation Characters

**Example 10-7 Validating Punctuation Characters**

```
; Pattern Matching "P" - Punctuation characters

Set Data="., ;"           ;Data contains all Punctuation characters
Set Pattern=".P"          ;Pattern for any number of Punctuation characters
Write Data?@Pattern       ;checks for all Punctuation characters
1                         ;if the data conforms to the pattern
                          ; - a 1 (true) is returned

Set Data="., ;"           ;Data contains all Punctuation characters
If Data?.P Write !,"The data conforms to the pattern"
The data conforms to the pattern
```

Example 10-7 demonstrates two methods of validating punctuation characters according to a pattern. The pattern construct, ".P" indicates all punctuation characters.

At this point we will search a string for a substring with *Pattern Matching*.

## Search a string for a substring

**Example 10-8 Search a string for a substring**

```
Set String="Jack and Jill went down the hill."
Set Pattern=".E1.P1""Jill""1P.E"            ;search for "Jill"
Write String?@Pattern
1

Set String="Jack and Jill went down the hill."
If String?.E1P1"Jill"1P.E Write !,"The string is found"
The string is found
```

Example 10-8 demonstrates how to search for a substring using *Pattern Matching*. The other way of searching for a substring within a string is with the *$Find System-Supplied Function*. The pattern reads: any number of any characters, followed by 1 punctuation, followed by "Jill", followed by 1 punctuation and ending with any number of any characters. This code searches the *String* for the word "Jill".

I included the following examples on *Control Characters* just to be consistent with the previous examples. Typically, you would only scan a string for control characters if you have reason to believe the control characters will impact further processing.

## Validating Control Characters

**Example 10-9 Validating Control Characters**

```
; Pattern Matching "C" - Control Characters

; The $Char System Supplied Function below produces the Bell (7),
; Backspace (8), Linefeed (10), Formfeed (12) and Carriage Return (13)
; Control Characters

Set Data=$C(7)_$C(8)_$C(10)_$C(12)_$C(13) ;Data contains Control Characters
Set Pattern=".C"          ;Pattern for any number of Control Characters
Write Data?@Pattern       ;checks for all Control Characters
1                         ;if the data conforms to the pattern
                          ; - a 1 (true) is returned

Set Data=$C(7)_$C(8)_$C(10)_$C(12)_$C(13) ;Data contains Control Characters
If Data?.C Write !,"The data conforms to the pattern"
The data conforms to the pattern
```

Example 10-9 demonstrates two methods of validating data according to a pattern. The pattern construct, ".C" indicates all control characters.

So far in our examples we have looked to see if the data contained or did not contain Alpha, Uppercase, Lowercase, Numeric, Punctuation and Control Characters regardless of the length. In the following examples, we will specify the length.

Before we do, I need to mention one more *Pattern Matching* type, that of any character, or every character, or "E".

## Pattern Matching to Validate Data of Specific Lengths

In *Pattern Matching* the way you specify the length is with the period, ".". The number before the period is the "From" number and the number after the period is the "To" number.

> ➤ "2.4" means a length of from 2 to 4 characters

> ➤ ".5" means a length from 0 to 5 characters

> ➤ "5." means a length from 5 to any number of characters

> ➤ "." means any length

> ➤ "3" means a length of 3 characters

## Pattern Matching Numeric Digits using Specific Lengths

Example 10-10 *Pattern Matching* Numeric Digits using Specific Lengths

```
Set Data="12"
If Data?1.5N Write !,"Data has numeric digits from 1 to 5 in length"
Data has numeric digits from 1 to 5 in length6

Set Data="54321"
If Data?.10N Write !,"Data has numeric digits from 0 to 10 in length"
Data has numeric digits from 0 to 10 in length

Set Data="123454321"
If Data'?1.5N Write !,"Data does not have numeric digits from 1 to 5 in
length"
Data does not have numeric digits from 1 to 5 in length
```

Example 10-10 demonstrates matching Numeric Digits of varying lengths.

## Pattern Matching Alpha Characters using Specific Lengths

Example 10-11 *Pattern Matching* Alpha Characters using Specific Lengths

```
Set Data="ABC"
If Data?1.3A Write !,"Data has Alpha characters from 1 to 3 in length"
Data has Alpha characters from 1 to 3 in length

Set Data="ABCDE"
If Data'?1.3A Write !,"Data does not have Alpha characters from 1 to 3 in
length"
Data does not have Alpha characters from 1 to 3 in length
```

Example 10-11 demonstrates Alpha Characters of varying lengths.

# More complex Pattern Matching

## Pattern Matching using Parenthesis, or Logical "OR"

Using Parenthesis inside a pattern introduces a logical "OR" into the pattern.

Example 10-12 *Pattern Matching* using Parenthesis or Logical "OR"

```
Set Name="Jack"
If Name?1(1"Jack",1"Jill",1"Fred") Write 1 ;Name must be Jack or Jill or Fred
1

Set Name="Jill"
If Name?1(1"Jack",1"Jill",1"Fred") Write 1 ;Name must be Jack or Jill or Fred
1

Set Name="Fred"
If Name?1(1"Jack",1"Jill",1"Fred") Write 1 ;Name must be Jack or Jill or Fred
1
```

Example 10-12 demonstrates using parenthesis inside a pattern to represent a Logical "OR". The pattern matches if the name is "Jack", "Jill" or "Fred."

---

### Pattern Matching parenthesis

Inside Pattern Matching parenthesis, a comma represents a Logical OR, meaning if any comma delimited string (inside the parenthesis) is true, the whole expression is true. However, in regular MUMPS and COS code, a comma normally is interpreted as a Logical AND, where all comma delimited strings (inside the parenthesis) must be true for the whole expression to be true. More on Logical ORs and ANDs in Chapter 11.

---

## Pattern Matching using Parenthesis, or Logical "OR" for Zip Code (Postal Code)

**Example 10-13** *Pattern Matching* using Parenthesis or Logical "OR" for Zip Code (Postal Code)

```
Set Zip="16063"
If Zip?1(5N,5N1"-"4N) Write 1
1

Set Zip="16063-3015"
If Zip?1(5N,5N1"-"4N) Write 1
1
```

Example 10-13 demonstrates using parenthesis inside a pattern to represent a Logical "OR". The pattern matches a Zip Code regardless if the Zip Code is 5 characters or 10 characters long.

## Numeric Pattern Matching

**Example 10-14 Numeric** *Pattern Matching*

```
Set value=1234
If value?1N.N Write !,"Valid numeric"    ;length from 1 numeric to any
Valid numeric                            ;length of numerics

   = = = = = = = = = = = = = = = = = = = = = = = = = = = = = = =

Set value="abc"
If value'?1N.N Write !,"Not numeric"         ;"Not" numeric of any length
Not numeric

   = = = = = = = = = = = = = = = = = = = = = = = = = = = = = = =

Set value=1234
If value?2N.4N Write !,"Valid numeric"   ;numeric of length 2 to 4
Valid numeric
```

Example 10-14 shows several example of *Pattern Matching* for numeric digits of differing lengths.

## Zip Code (Postal Code) Pattern Matching

**Example 10-15 Zip Code (Postal Code) *Pattern Matching***

```
; zip code in nnnnn or nnnnn-nnnn format
set pattern="5N"
If $l(zip)=10 set pattern="5N1""-""4N"
If zip?@pattern Write !,"Valid zip code"         ;valid zip code
If zip'?@pattern Write !,"Invalid zip code"      ;invalid zip code
```

Example 10-15 shows *Pattern Matching* for a 5 or 9 digit Zip Code.

## Date Pattern Matching

**Example 10-16 Date *Pattern Matching***

```
; date format in mm/dd/yy or mm/dd/yyyy format
If date?1.2N1"/"1.2N1"/"2.4N Write !,"Valid date format"    ;valid format
If date'?1.2N1"/"1.2N1"/"2.4N Write !,"Invalid date format" ;invalid format
```

Example 10-16 shows *Pattern Matching* for date verification. The date can be either in MM/DD/YY or MM/DD/YYYY format

**Example 10-17 Complex Date *Pattern Matching***

```
;date format in mm/dd/yy or mm-dd-yy or mm.dd.yy
If date?1.2N1(1"."1.2N1".",1"/"1.2N1"/",1"-"1.2N1"-")2.4N W !,"valid format"
If date'?1.2N1(1"."1.2N1".",1"/"1.2N1"/",1"-"1.2N1"-")2.4N Write !,"invalid
format"
```

Example 10-17 shows a *Pattern Matching* for date verification. The date can have several different formats as shown in the example

## Phone Number Pattern Matching

**Example 10-18 Phone Number *Pattern Matching***

```
Set pattern="3N1""-""4N"
Set phone=$TR(phone," ")                              ;remove spaces
If $l(phone)=14 Set pattern="1N1""(""3N1"")""3N1""-""4N"
If phone?@pattern Write !,"Valid phone format"        ;valid phone
If phone'?@pattern Write !,"Invalid phone format"     ;invalid phone number

;phone format nnn-nnnn or nnn.nnn.nnnn or (nnn)nnn-nnnn
If (PH?3N1"-"4N)!(PH?3N1"."3N1"."4N)!(PH?1"("3N1")"3N1"-"4N) Write !,"valid
phone"
```

Example 10-18 shows a pattern matching for a phone number verification. The phone number can have several different formats as shown in the example.

## Dollar Number Pattern Matching

**Example 10-19 Dollar Number *Pattern Matching* Examples**

```
Set dol="100,000,000.00"

If (dol?.3N1"."2N)!(dol?.3N1","3N1"."2N)!(dol?.3N1","3N1","3N1"."2N) Write
"Valid"
```

Example 10-19 shows pattern matching for a dollar amount up to 999 million. This examples uses Parenthesis and the Logical "OR".

# Exercises on Pattern Matching

1. Write a pattern that could be used to verify a name in the format: LAST, FIRST MI. All letters need to be uppercase.

2. Modify the previous pattern to ensure that each of words is capitalized: Last, First Mi. Allow for the Middle initial to be either a 1 character initial or an entire name.

3. Write a pattern that could be used to verify an insurance number of the format: 1 uppercase alpha, 6 numbers, 1 dash followed by 3 to 7 numbers, i.e. U657823-123.

4. Write a pattern that could be used to verify a dollar amount include a dollar sign, dollars, cents, decimal point and commas.

# Answers to Exercises on Pattern Matching

**Example 10-20 Answers to Exercises on *Pattern Matching***

```
; Write a pattern that could be used to verify a name in the format:
; LAST, FIRST MI. All letters need to be uppercase.
Set Name="DOE, JOHN M."
If Name?.U1", ".U1" "1U1"." W "Format Valid"
Format Valid

; Modify the previous pattern to ensure that each of words is capitalized:
; Last, First Mi. Allow for the Middle initial to be either a 1 character
; initial or an entire name.
Set Name="Doe, John Michael"
If Name?1U.L1", "1U.L1" "1U.L Write "Format Valid"
Format Valid

; Write a pattern that could be used to verify an insurance number of the
; format: 1 uppercase alpha, 6 numbers, 1 dash followed by 3 to 7 numbers,
; U657823-123.
Set Number="U657823-123"
If Number?1U6N1"-"3.7N Write "Format Valid"
Format Valid

; Write a pattern that could be used to verify a dollar amount include
; a dollar sign, dollars, cents, decimal point and commas.
```

```
Set AMT1="$25.50"
Set AMT2="$23,125.50"
Set AMT3="$6,789,325.50"
If $L(AMT1)<8,AMT1?1"$"1.3N1"."2N Write "Format Valid"
Format Valid
If $L(AMT2)<12,AMT2?1"$"1.3N1","3N1"."2N Write "Format Valid"
Format Valid
If $L(AMT3)<16,AMT3?1"$"1.3N1","3N1","3N1"."2N Write "Format Valid"
Format Valid
```

## *Chapter 10 Summary*

In this chapter, we covered various ways to use *Pattern Matching*. Specifically; we looked at patterns for *Alpha* characters, *Uppercase*, *Lowercase*, *Numeric digits*, *Punctuation*, and *Control* characters. We also looked at specific examples of how to validate an American Social Security Number, Zip Codes, Capitalized Words, Dollar amounts, Dates and Phone numbers. In addition we demonstrated how to use *Pattern Matching* to search for a string and validate data of specific lengths.

*Customer: "My mouse is at the edge of my desk, what should I do?"*

*Tech Support: "Get a bigger desk!"*

*-Scott Adams*

# *Chapter 11 Comparison Operators*

This chapter covers the topic of **Comparison Operators** in Caché ObjectScript (COS). Using the correct *Comparison Operator* is important to achieve accurate outcomes when comparing two data items.

*Comparison Operators* are characters that act on associated **Operands**. The *operands* may be either numeric digits or alphanumeric text, or a variable that represents numeric digits or alphanumeric text. For correct results in your code using the right *Comparison Operator* is essential.  Examples of comparison operators are *equal to* (=), *greater than* (>) and *contains* "[".

## *Table of Comparison Operators*

**Table 11-1 Table of Comparison Operators**

| Operator | Character | Type of Operands | Description |
|---|---|---|---|
| Unary NOT | ' | Numeric digits | Reverses the value of the operand |
| Binary Greater Than | > | Numeric digits | Tests whether the left operand is numerically greater than the right operand |
| Binary Less Than | < | Numeric digits | Test whether the right operand is numerically greater than the left operand |
| Binary And | & and && | Numeric digits and Alphanumeric Text | Test whether both operands are true |
| Binary Or | ! and \|\| | Numeric digits and Alphanumeric Text | Test whether either operand is true |
| Binary Equal To | = | Numeric digits and Alphanumeric Text | Tests two operands for equality* |
| Binary Contains | [ | Alphanumeric Text | Test whether the characters in the right operand is a substring of the left operand |
| Binary Follows | ] | Alphanumeric Text | Tests whether the characters in the left operand comes after the characters in the right operand according to the ASCII collating sequence. |
| Binary Sorts After | ]] | Numeric digits and Alphanumeric Text | Tests whether the left operand sorts after the right operand in subscript collating sequence. |

***Equal Sign***

*The Equal Sign may be used as a comparison operator or an assignment operator.

An example of a comparison operator is:  If A=B then . . .

An example of an assignment is:  Set A=B

---

Before we start looking at *Comparison Operators* we need to cover some basic principles of how COS interprets True and False.

## How COS Interprets True and False

In COS, a 0 is always false and any other number is always true.

**Example 11-1 True and False respectively**

```
Set X=1
If X Write "True"        ;1 is always true and 0 is always false
True

Set X=0
If X Write "True"        ;1 is always true
<>

If 'X Write "False"      ;0 is always false
False

Set X=10
If X Write "True"        ;Any number other than 0 is always true
True

Set X=-10
If X Write "True"        ;Any number other than 0 is always true
True
```

Example 11-1 demonstrates that in COS any number other than 0 is always true and 0 is always false.

Does this same rule apply to alphanumeric text data?

**Example 11-2 Alphanumeric text True and False**

```
Set X="1"
If X Write "True"        ;1 is always true even in Alphanumeric text
True

Set X="0"
If X Write "True"        ;1 is always true even in Alphanumeric text
<>

If 'X Write "False       ;0 is always false even in Alphanumeric text
False
```

```
Set X="1ABC"
If X Write "True"          ;The 1 is used and the rest of the text is ignored
True

Set X="0ABC"
If X Write "True"          ;The first numeric is used and the
<>
                           ;rest of the text is ignored

If 'X Write "False
False

Set X="ABC1"               ;If the numeric is not first in the text it is
If X Write "True"          ;ignored and any text comes back as 0 or false
<>

Set X="ABC0"
If X Write "True"          ;If the numeric is not first in the text it is
<>                         ;ignored and any text comes back as 0 or false

If 'X Write "False
False
```

From Example 11-2, what can we learn about how COS interprets True and False with alphanumeric text?

> When alphanumeric text (quoted string) contains only a numeric it is evaluated as pure numeric

> When alphanumeric text (quoted string) has as it first characters a numeric, the numeric is used as a pure numeric, and the rest of the alphanumeric text is ignored

> When alphanumeric text (quoted string) has as it first characters an alphanumeric text character, the whole string is evaluated as 0 or false

# Unary NOT Operator (')

The **Unary NOT Operator** reverses the truth-value and is intended for Numeric Operands.

## Unary NOT Operator (') used on numeric digits

**Example 11-3 Unary NOT Operator used on numeric digits**

```
Set X=1
If X Write "True"          ;1 is always true and 0 is always false
True

Set X=0
Write 'X                   ;X is 0, so "Not X" is 1 or true
1

Set X=1
Write 'X                   ;X is 1, so "Not X" is 0 or false
0
```

```
Set X=0
If 'X Write "True"           ;X is 0 so "Not X" is 1 and 1 is true
True

Set X=5                      ;Any "Non Zero" value is true
If X Write "True"
True

Set X=5
Write 'X                     ;"Not X", or "Not 5", is 0 or false
0
```

Example 11-3 demonstrates some uses of the *Unary NOT Operator*. Note that 1 is always true and 0 is always false. If the variable X is 0, when we write "Not X", we write 1. In the same manner if the variable X is 1 and we write "Not X", we write 0. Not only is 1 true, but any "Non Zero" number is true. So when we "Not" any non-zero value, zero is always produced.

The *Unary NOT Operator* is used on numeric digits, but what happens when we attempt to use it on alphanumeric text?

## Unary NOT Operator (') used on Alphanumeric text

**Example 11-4 Unary NOT Operator used on Alphanumeric text**

```
Set X="1"
If X Write "True"            ;1 is always true even with Alphanumeric text
True

Set X="0"
Write 'X                     ;X is 0, so "Not X" is 1 even with Alphanumeric
1                            ;test

Set X="1"
Write 'X                     ;X is 1, so "Not X" is 0 even with Alphanumeric
0

Set X="0ABC"                 ;The first numeric is used and the
If 'X Write "True"           ;rest of the text is ignored
True

Set X="5ABC"                 ;"Not X", or "Not 5", is 0 or false
Write 'X                     ;The first numeric is used and the rest is ignored
0

Set X="ABC0"                 ;If the numeric is not the first character in
If 'X Write "True"           ;the text it is ignored and any text comes back
True                         ;as 0 or false. Since the If command uses a "Not"
                             ;it comes back as true.
```

Example 11-4 demonstrates some uses of the *Unary NOT Operator* on Alphanumeric text.

## Unary NOT Operator (') and $Data

One area you are likely to see True and False *If* commands is with the *$Data System-Supplied Function*. By way of review here is the *$Data* table from Chapter 4.

**Table 11-2 $Data table of returned values**

| What $Data Returns | Array Item has Value | Array Item has Descendants |
|:---:|:---:|:---:|
| 0 | No | No |
| 1 | Yes | No |
| 10 | No | Yes |
| 11 | Yes | Yes |

**Example 11-5 True and False with $Data**

```
Set A(1)="data"
Set A(2)=""
Set A(3,1)="data"
Set A(4)="data"
Set A(4,1)="data"

If $D(A(1)) Write "True"          ;this will return a 1 or true
True

If '$D(A(1)) Write "True"         ;this is not true
<>

If $D(A(3)) Write "True"          ;this will return a 10 or true
True

If '$D(A(3)) Write "True"         ;this is not true
<>

If $D(A(4)) Write "True"          ;this will return a 11 or true
True

If '$D(A(4)) Write "True"         ;this is not true
<>

If $D(A(5)) Write "True"          ;this will return a 0 or false
<>

If '$D(A(5)) Write "True"         ;this is true
True

If $D(A(2)) Write "True"          ;this will return a 1 or true, even though
True                              ;the data is blank or null
```

Example 11-5 shows the *Unary NOT Operator, $Data* with various array values.

## Exercises on True, False, Not and $Data

For each of the expressions below, determine whether the variable X is true or false.

- ➢ Set X=1
- ➢ Set X=0
- ➢ Set X=10
- ➢ Set X=-10
- ➢ Set X="1"
- ➢ Set X="0"
- ➢ Set X="1ABC"
- ➢ Set X="0ABC"
- ➢ Set X="ABC1"
- ➢ Set X='1
- ➢ Set X='0
- ➢ Set X=5
- ➢ Set X='5

    For the following assume:

      Set A(1)="data"

      Set A(2)=""

      Set A(3,1)="data"

      Set A(4)="data"

      Set A(4,1)="data"

- ➢ Set X=$D(A(1))
- ➢ Set X='$D(A(1))
- ➢ Set X=$D(A(3))
- ➢ Set X=$D(A(5))
- ➢ Set X=$D(A(2))

# Answers to Exercises on True, False, Not and $Data

```
Set X=1                                True

Set X=0                                False

Set X=10                               True

Set X=-10                              True

Set X="1"                              True

Set X="0"                              False

Set X="1ABC"                           True

Set X="0ABC"                           False

Set X="ABC1"                           False

Set X='1                               False

Set X='0                               True

Set X=5                                True

Set X='5                               False

For the following assume:
    Set A(1)="data"
    Set A(2)=""
    Set A(3,1)="data"
    Set A(4)="data"
    Set A(4,1)="data"

Set X=$D(A(1))                         True

Set X='$D(A(1))                        False

Set X=$D(A(3))                         True

Set X=$D(A(5))                         False

Set X=$D(A(2))                         True
```

## Binary Greater Than and Binary Less Than

**Binary Greater Than** and **Binary Less Than** are used on numeric operands, but they can be used on alpha operands as well, but the results are less than satisfying.

## Simple Numeric Comparisons

**Example 11-7 Simple Numeric Comparisons**

```
If 2>1 Write "True"      ;2 is greater than 1
True

If 1<2 Write "True"      ;1 is less than 2
True

If 1'>2 Write "True"     ;1 is not greater than 2
True

If 2'<1 Write "True"     ;2 is not less than 1
True
```

Example 11-7 demonstrates simple numeric comparisons using *Binary Less Than* and *Binary Greater Than*.

## Binary Less Than and Binary Greater Than used on quoted numeric text

**Example 11-8 Binary Less Than and Binary Greater Than used on quoted numeric text**

```
If "2">"1" Write "True"    ;2 is greater than 1
True

If "1"<"2" Write "True"    ;1 is less than 2
True

If "1"'>"2" Write "True"   ;1 is not greater than 2
True

If "2"'<"1" Write "True"   ;2 is not less than 1
True
```

Example 11-8 demonstrates quoted numeric comparisons. The *Binary Greater Than* and *Binary Less Than Operators* also work on variables that contain quoted numbers.

### Binary Less Than and Greater Than with variables that contain quoted numbers

**Example 11-9 Binary Less Than and Greater Than with variables that contain quoted numbers.**

```
Set A="1"
Set B="2"
If B>A Write "True"        ;B or 2 is greater than A or 1
True

If A<B Write "True"        ;A or 1 is less than B or 2
True

If A'>B Write "True"       ;A or 1 is not greater than B or 2
True

If B'<A Write "True"       ;B or 2 is not less than A or 1
True
```

Example 11-9 demonstrates using variables that contain numeric values. So far so good with no surprises. Nevertheless, what if the variables hold non-numeric values?

### Binary Less Than and Greater Than used on quoted alphanumeric text

**Example 11-10 Binary Less Than and Greater Than used on alphanumeric text**

```
Set A="A"
Set B="B"
If B>A Write "True"        ;Any alphanumeric text is assumed to be 0
<>

If A<B Write "True"        ;Any alphanumeric text is assumed to be 0
<>

If A'>B Write "True" ;"Not Greater Than" is the same as equal to or less than
True                 ;and 0 is equal to 0

If B'<A Write "True" ;"Not Less Than" is the same as equal to or greater than
True                 ;and 0 is equal to 0
```

Example 11-10 demonstrates the problems with using Numeric Operators to compare alphanumeric variables. Variable A, with the value of "A" is converted to its equivalent number, which is zero. Variable B, with the value of "B" is also converted to zero. So with A and B being zeros, the comparisons do work, sort of.

**Example 11-11 Binary Less Than and Greater Than used on alphanumeric text**

```
Set A="1A"
Set B="2B"
If B>A Write "True"        ;As we saw before, the leading number is used and
True                       ;the rest is ignored

If A<B Write "True"        ;Ditto
True

If A'>B Write "True"       ;Is 1 not greater than 2, yes it is
True
```

```
If B'<A Write "True"      ;Is 2 not less than 1, yes it is
True

If B'>A Write "True"      ;Is 2 not greater than 1, no
<>

If A'<B Write "True"      ;Is 1 not less than 2, no
<>
```

Example 11-11 demonstrates using variables that start with numbers but have alphanumeric characters following. In this situation, the leading numbers are used in the comparisons and the trailing text is ignored.

Comparing alphanumeric text is better suited for the **Binary Follows** and **Binary Sorts After** OPERATORS.

## *Exercises on Binary Less Than and Greater Than*

For each of the expressions below, determine whether the expression true or false.

> ➤ 2>1

> ➤ 1<2

> ➤ If 1'>2

> ➤ 2'<1

> ➤ If "2">"1"

> ➤ If "1"<"2"

For the following assume:
    Set A="1"
    Set B="2"

> ➤ B>A

> ➤ A'>B

For the following assume:
    Set A="A"
    Set B="B"

> ➤ B>A

> ➤ A<B

> ➤ A'>B

> ➤ B'<A

# Answers to Exercises on Binary Less Than and Greater Than

**Example 11-12 Answers to Exercises on Binary Less Than and Greater Than**

```
2>1                                  True

1<2                                  True

If 1'>2                              True

2'<1                                 True

If "2">"1"                           True

If "1"<"2"                           True

For the following assume:
    Set A="1"
    Set B="2"

B>A                                  True

A'>B                                 True

For the following assume:
    Set A="A"
    Set B="B"

B>A                                  False

A<B                                  False

A'>B                                 True

B'<A                                 True
```

# Binary And and Binary Or

**Binary And** and **Binary Or** are for use on numeric and alphanumeric operands. They are both straightforward but a few points need to be mentioned.

# Binary And

*Binary And* must have both its operands to be true for it to return a true value

*Binary And* is represented by three characters, &, && and "," (comma)

## Binary And using numbers

Example 11-13 Binary And using numbers

```
If 1&1 Write "True"        ;Both 1 and 1 are true so the result is true
True

If 5&5 Write "True"        ;Any non 0 value is considered true
True

If 1&0 Write "True"        ;Both have to be true and 0 is not true
<>

If 1&'0 Write "True"       ;Both have to be true and "Not 0" is true
True

If '1&'1 Write "True"      ;Not 1 is 0, and "0 AND 0" is not true
<>

If 1,1 Write "True"        ;Both 1 and 1 are true so the result is true
True

If 5,5 Write "True"        ;Any non 0 value is considered true
True

If 1,0 Write "True"        ;Both have to be true and 0 is not true
<>

If 1,'0 Write "True"       ;Both have to be true and "Not 0" is true
True

If 1,0 Write "True"        ;Both have to be true and 0 is not true
<>

If '1,'1 Write "True"      ;Not 1 is 0, and "0 AND 0" is not true
<>
```

Example 11-13 demonstrates the *Binary And Operator* using the & character and the "," (comma) character on numbers.

## Binary And using variables

Example 11-14 Binary And using variables

```
Set A=1
Set B=1
If A&A Write "True"        ;Both A and B are true so the result is true
True

Set A=5
Set B=5
If A&B Write "True"        ;Any non 0 value is considered true
True

Set A=1
Set B=0
If A&B Write "True"        ;Both have to be true and B is not true
<>
```

```
Set A=1
Set B=0
If A&'B Write "True"      ;Both have to be true and "Not B" is true
True

Set A=1
Set B=1
If A,B Write "True"       ;Both A and B are true so the result is true
True

Set A=5
Set B=5
If A,B Write "True"       ;Any non 0 value is considered true
True

Set A=1
Set B=0
If A,B Write "True"       ;Both have to be true and B is not true
<>

Set A=1
Set B=0
If A,'B Write "True"      ;Both have to be true and "Not B" is true
True
```

Example 11-14 demonstrates the *Binary And Operator* using the & character and the "," (comma) character on variables.

We have looked at the *Binary And Operator* with literals and variables using characters & and "," (comma). We have another character used in the *Binary And*, the "&&" characters, how does this differ from the other two?

> The & and "," (comma) characters looks at both operands and returns False if either operand is 0. Otherwise, it returns true

> The && character looks at the left operand and returns false if it is 0. Only if the left operand is non-zero will it look at the right operand

I will not demonstrate using the *Binary And Operator* on Alphanumeric texts; I have shown the results of such operations using the *Unary NOT Operator*, the *Binary Greater Than* and *Less Than Operators* and it all work the same.

Keep in mind what operators are meant for Numeric's and what operators are meant for alphanumeric text and you will not have a problem. Refer to Table 11-1 for a review.

## Binary Or

**Binary Or** must have one of its operands to be true for it to return a true value

**Binary Or** is represented by two characters, ! (exclamation point), and || (two vertical bars)

## Binary Or using numbers

**Example 11-15 Binary Or using numbers**

```
If 1!1 Write "True"      ;If either literal is true the result is true
True

If 1!0 Write "True"      ;If either literal is true the result is true
True

If 5!0 Write "True"      ;Any non 0 value is considered true
True

If 0!0 Write "True"      ;At least one operand needs to be true
<>

If 0!'0 Write "True"     ;"Not 0" is considered true
True

If '1!'1 Write "True"    ;Not 1 is 0, and "0 or 0" is not true
<>
```

Example 11-15 demonstrates the *Binary Or Operator* using the ! (exclamation point) character on numbers.

## Binary Or using variables

**Example 11-16 Binary Or using variables**

```
Set A=1
Set B=1
If A!B Write "True"      ;If either variable is true the result is true
True

Set A=1
Set B=0
If 1!0 Write "True"      ;If either variable is true the result is true
True

Set A=5
Set B=0
If A!B Write "True"      ;Any non 0 variable is considered true
True

Set A=0
Set B=0
If A!B Write "True"      ;At least one operand needs to be true
<>

Set A=0
Set B=0
If A!'B Write "True"     ;"Not 0" is considered true
```

```
True

Set A=1
Set B=1
If 'A!'B Write "True"     ;Not 1 is 0, and "0 or 0" is zero and not true
<>
```

Example 11-16 demonstrates the *Binary Or Operator* using the ! (exclamation point) character on variables.

We have looked at the *Binary Or Operators* with literals and variables using character ! (exclamation point). We have another character used in the *Binary Or*, the "||" (two vertical bars), how does this differ from the other two?

> ➤ The ! (explanation point) character looks at both operands and returns True if either operand is 1. Otherwise it returns false

> ➤ The || (two vertical bars) characters looks at the left operand and returns true if it is 1. Only if the left operand is zero will it look at the right operand.

## Multiple Binary ORs and Binary ANDs

**Example 11-17 Multiple Binary ORs and Binary ANDs**

```
Set A=1
Set B=2
Set C=3

If A=1!B=2!C=3 Write "True"
<>

If A=1&B=2&C=3 Write "True"
<>
```

Example 11-17 shows two *If* commands using multiple *Binary ORs* and multiple *Binary ANDs* that should work, but do not. Why? It has to do with how COS strictly interprets a command from left to right. This demonstrates the importance of using parentheses.

**Example 11-18 Multiple Binary ORs and Binary ANDs**

```
Set A=1
Set B=2
Set C=3

If (A=1)!(B=2)!(C=3) Write "True"
True

If (A=1)&(B=2)&(C=3) Write "True"
True
```

Example 11-18 is the same as Example 11-17 except parentheses are used to segregate each operand, as you can see this now works correctly. Parentheses are not always necessary but a good programmer should be in the habit of using them. This is especially true when using the *Binary Or*.

## Exercises on Binary And and Binary Or

For each of the expressions, below and determine whether it is true or false.

- 1&1
- 5&5
- 1&0
- 1&'0
- '1&'1
- 1,1
- 1,0

For the following assume:
    Set A=1
    Set B=1

- A&B

For the following assume:
    Set A=1
    Set B=0

- A&B
- A&'B
- A,B
- A,'B
- 1!1
- 1!0
- 0!0
- 0!'0
- '1&'1

For the following assume:
    Set A=0
    Set B=0

- If A!'B

For the following assume:
    Set A=1
    Set B=1

➤ 'A&'B

For the following assume:
    Set A=1
    Set B=2
    Set C=3

➤ A=1!B=2!C=3

➤ A=1&B=2&C=3

➤ (A=1)!(B=2)!(C=3)

➤ (A=1)&(B=2)&(C=3)


# Answers to Exercises on Binary And and Binary Or

**Example 11-19 Answers to Exercises on Binary And and Binary Or**

```
1&1                       True

5&5                       True

1&0                       False

1&'0                      True

'1&'1                     False

1,1                       True

1,0                       False

For the following assume:
    Set A=1
    Set B=1

A&B                       True

For the following assume:
    Set A=1
    Set B=0

A&B                       False

A&'B                      True

A,B                       False

A,'B                      True

For the following assume:
    Set A=1
    Set B=1

1!1                       True
1!0                       True
```

```
0!0                   False
0!'0                  True
'1&'1                 False

For the following assume:
    Set A=0
    Set B=0

If A!'B               True

For the following assume:
    Set A=1
    Set B=1

'A&'B                 False

For the following assume:
    Set A=1
    Set B=1
    Set C=1

A=1!B=2!C=3           False
A=1&B=2&C=3           False
(A=1)!(B=2)!(C=3)     True
(A=1)&(B=2)&(C=3)     True
```

## Binary Equals

The **Equal Sign** (=) is used in two ways:

> ➢ As an assignment operator

> ➢ As a comparison operator between two operands

## Equal sign as an assignment operator

When used as an assignment operator the equal sign "sets" the variable or Global on the left side of the equal sign to the expression on the right side of the equal sign.

**Example 11-20 Equal sign as an assignment operator**

```
Set A=1              ;set variable A to 1
Write !,A
1

Set B="Text"         ;set variable B to Text
Write !,B
Text

Set C=1+2+3          ;set variable C to 6
Write !,C
6

Set ^Global(0)=6/3;set ^Global(0) to 2
Write ^Global(0)
2
```

```
Set D=^Global(0)        ;set variable D to the data contained in ^Global(0)
or 2
Write !,D
2

Set $E(E,3,4)=55        ;set the 3rd and 4th character E to 5
Write !,E
  55

Set $P(F,"^",2)=10;set the second piece of variable F to 10
Write !,F
^10
```

Example 11-20 demonstrates a number of ways that the *Equal Sign* operator is used as an assignment operator.

## Equal sign as a comparison operator between two operands

When used as a comparison operator the *Equal Sign* compares two operands for equality, the operands can be numeric or alphanumeric text.

**Example 11-21 Equal sign as a comparison operator between two operands**

```
If 1=1 Write !,"Equal"
Equal

If 1'=1 Write !,"Equal"
<>

If "Text"="Text" Write !,"Equal"
Equal

If 1+2+3=1+2+3 Write !,"Equal"
Equal

If 1="1" Write "Equal"
Equal

If 1+1="2" Write "Equal"
Equal

If 1+1="1+1" Write "Equal"       ;Quoting numbers does make a difference
<>

If "003"="3" Write !,"Equal"
<>

If 003=3 Write !,"Equal"
Equal

Set $E(E,3,4)=55
If E=E Write !,"Equal"
Equal

Set $P(F,"^",2)=10
If $P(F,"^",2)=$P(F,"^",2) Write !,"Equal"
Equal
```

Example 11-21 demonstrates a number of ways that the *Equal Sign* operator may be used. Be careful using quotes around numeric digits as shown in this example.

## *Binary Contains*

**Binary Contains** tests whether the second operand is contained in the first operand.

**Example 11-22 Binary Contains**

```
If "This is our Country"["Country" Write !,"Contains"
Contains

If "This is our Country"["is our" Write !,"Contains"
Contains

If "This is our Country"["this is" Write !,"Contains"    ;cases must match
<>

If "This is our Country"'["ABC123" Write !,"Not Contains"    ;not contains
Not Contains

If 002[2 Write !,"Contains"
Contains

If 2[002 Write !,"Contains"        ;the 002 is reduced to 2
Contains
```

Example 11-22 shows several examples of how the *Binary Contains* works. Pay special attention to the numeric contains

# *The Binary Follows Operator and Binary Sort After Operator*

The **Binary Follows Operator** and the **Binary Sort After Operator** are similar but contain some important differences.

## *Binary Follows*

The *Binary Follows Operator* tests whether left operand comes after the right operand in ASCII collating sequence.

### *Binary Follows with alpha data*

**Example 11-23 Binary Follows with alpha data**

```
Write $Ascii("A")        ;ASCII value of "A"
65

Write $Ascii("B")        ;ASCII value of "B"
66

If "B"]"A" Write "True"   ;ASCII value of "B" follows the ASCII value of "A"
True
```

In Example 11-23 , the ASCII value of "B" follows the ASCII Value of "A".

## Binary Follows with numeric data

**Example 11-24 Binary Follows Operator with numeric data**

```
Write $Ascii(2)
50

Write $Ascii(1)
49

If 2]19 Write "True"
True
```

In Example 11-24, does 2 come after 19 in ASCII collating sequence? Bear in mind that the 2 is compared to the 1 in 19 and the test stops there. So, 2 comes after 1 in ASCII collating sequence. Since the 2 is only one character long the test will only be one character long, the 9 in 19 is ignored. Thus, 2 does come after 19.

## Binary Sort After Operator

The **Binary Sorts After Operator** tests whether the left operand sorts after the right operand in numeric subscript collation sequence.

### Numeric subscript collation sequence

What is "numeric subscript collation sequence"? It is a collation sequence whereas the null string comes first, followed by canonic numbers in numeric order with negative numbers first, zero next and positive numbers, followed lastly by non-numeric values.

Let us look at it another way, consider this example:

**Example 11-25 Setting the ^TMP Global**

```
Set ^TMP("ABC")=""
Set ^TMP(1)=""
Set ^TMP(0)=""
Set ^TMP(-1)=""
```

Example 11-25 uses four different subscripts in setting the ^TMP Global, when we display the Global, what do we see?

**Example 11-26 How a Global is sorted**

```
D ^%G
Global ^TMP
    ^TMP(-1)=""
    ^TMP(0)=""
    ^TMP(1)=""
    ^TMP("ABC")=""
```

Example 11-26 shows how the Global is sorted, in other words, the subscripts of Globals are sorted in "numeric subscript collation sequence". The *Binary Sort After Operator* just mimics how Globals are sorted.

**Example 11-27 Binary Sort After Operator**

```
I "-1"]]"" Write "True"    ;"-1" Sorts After ""
True

I "0"]]"-1" Write "True" ;"0" Sorts After "-1"
True

I "1"]]"0" Write "True"    ;"1" Sorts After "0"
True

I "ABC"]]"1" Write "True" ;"ABC" Sorts After "1"
True
```

Example 11-27 shows several *Binary Sort After Operators*. Remember, it is the first operand that Sorts After the second operand.

## *Chapter 11 Summary*

In this chapter, we considered all the various comparison operators available in Caché. Specifically; 1) How COS Interprets True and False, 2) *Unary NOT Operator* reverses the truth value, 3) *Binary Greater Than* and *Binary Less Than* are used for simple numeric comparisons, 4) *Binary And* & *Binary Or* are used on both numeric and alpha numeric operands, 5) Multiple *Binary Ands* and *Binary Ors*, 6) Uses for the *Binary Equal*, 7) *Binary Contains* and 8) Differences between the *Binary Follows* and *Binary Sorts After*.

# *Chapter 12 File Processing*

This chapter covers the topic of **File Processing** in Caché ObjectScript (COS). *File Processing* allows the programmer to access external files. See Chapter 34 for how to do *File Processing* using Caché Objects.

Normally Caché ObjectScript (COS) saves and retrieves data from Globals, but there are times when it is necessary to access external files. External files are typically those used by the associated Operating System. External files can be any file type on any computer, but for the sake of simplicity, we will deal with "Text" files with a file extension of "TXT".

The first part of the chapter will deal with accessing external files. The second part will demonstrate miscellaneous file functions.

## *Read and writ an external file*

COS uses the following commands to process external files.

  - ➤ *Open* – open an external file
  - ➤ *Close* – close an external file
  - ➤ *Read* – read a record from an external file
  - ➤ *Write* – write a record to an external file
  - ➤ *Use* – sets the specified device as the current device

## *Write an External file*

**Example 12-1 Write to an External File**

```
Line1:
    WriteFile     ;
Line2:
        Set OutFile="FILE.TXT"        ;name of out file - FILE.TXT
Line3:
        Close OutFile                 ;close a file before you open it
Line4:
        Open OutFile:"WNS":10         ;open the file for writing,
                                      ;WNS - write, new, stream
                                      ;timeout of 10 seconds
Line5:
        If '$Test Write !,OutFile," cannot be opened." Quit ;cannot open
Line6:
        Use OutFile                   ;Sets OutFile as the current device
Line7:
        Write "First Record"
Line8:
        Write !,"Second Record"
Line9:
```

```
                Write !,"Third Record"
Line10:
                Use 0 Write !,"End of Program reached"
Line11:
                Quit
```

Example 12-1 demonstrates writing an external file. Consider the following observations:

- ➢ Line1: – Program Name
- ➢ Line2: – Set variable OutFile to the actual file name
- ➢ Line3: – Close the file first, always a good idea just in case it is open
- ➢ Line4: – Open the file for writing using attributes of WNS; Write, New, Stream. Also I have included a timeout of 10 seconds
- ➢ Line5: – Test with the *$Test* special variable, if the file is open, *$Test* will be 1, otherwise it would be 0
- ➢ Line6: – Use command, sets OutFile as the current device
- ➢ Line7: –No carriage return/line feed on the first record, but on subsequent records
- ➢ Line10: – Use command sets Zero or the terminal as the current device

---

### Closing a File before Opening it

It is always a good idea to close a file before opening it. This is more for debugging than production. More than once I have interrupted a process to debug it, and have forgotten that the file was still open. Having an open file created further confusion in debugging. So I made it a habit to always close a file before opening it, it makes debugging easier and less confusing.

---

### Time Out

When opening a file for reading or writing it is important to include a time out. Although you may expect the file to be there, or expect to be able to write to it, there are many circumstances when you cannot. The disk may be full or someone may have changed the device's protection so you no longer have access. In Chapter 14 on Testing and  Debugging and Chapter 17 on Writing Robust Code I talk about assumptions. To assume you will always be able to access or write to a file is poor programming. When a whole production run suddenly freezes and you are called in, in the middle of the night to find out why, and your process is waiting on a file is a painful lesson on using a Time Out.

---

Now we will read the file we just created.

## Read a file and display its records

**Example 12-2 Read a file and display its records**

```
Line1:
    ReadFile        ;
Line2:
            Set InFile="FILE.TXT"           ;name of infile - FILE.TXT
Line3:
            Close InFile                    ;close a file before you open it
Line4:
            Open InFile:"R":10              ;open file for read, timeout 10 sec
Line5:
            If '$Test Write !,InFile," cannot be opened." Quit
Line6:
            Set InCount=0                   ;init counter of records read
Line7:
            Set X=$ZU(68,40,1)              ;enable the $ZEOF special variable
Line7a:
            Set system.Process.SetZEOF(1)   ;enable the $ZEOF special variable
Line8:
            Set EOF=0 Do {                  ;EOF is end of file switch
Line9:
              Use InFile                    ;sets InFile as the Current Device
Line10:
              Read InRecord                 ;read record from file
Line11:
              If $ZEOF=-1 Set EOF=1 Quit    ;$ZEOF=-1 when end of file reached
Line12:
              Set X=$Increment(InCount)     ;increment counter
Line13:
              Use 0 Write !,InRecord        ;display record
Line14:
            } While EOF=0                   ;read until end of file
Line15:
            Use 0 Write !,InCount," Records read"
Line16:
            Use 0 Write !,"End of File reached"
Line17:
            Quit
```

Example 12-2 demonstrates reading an external file and displaying each record read. Consider the following observations:

> ➤ Line1 – Program Name

> ➤ Line2 – Set variable InFile to the actual file name

> ➤ Line3 – Close the file first, always a good idea just in case it is open

> ➤ Line4: – Open the file for Reading, with a timeout of 10 seconds

- ➢ Line5: – Test with the *$Test* special variable, if the file is open, *$Test* will be 1, otherwise it would be 0
- ➢ Line6: – Set the input record counter to zero
- ➢ Line7: – Enable the *$ZEOF* special variable
- ➢ Line7a: - Enable the $ZEOF special variable

    Line 7 and 7a accomplish the same thing. The code for line 7a is more advanced and may not work on earlier Caché instances.

- ➢ Line8: – Set the EOF variable to 0, this is the control variable
- ➢ Line9: – *Use* command sets InFile as the current device
- ➢ Line10: - Read the next record
- ➢ Line11: – Test the *$ZEOF* special variable, if it is -1, then we have reached end of file and set the EOF variable to 1 to exit the loop
- ➢ Line12: – Increment the input record counter
- ➢ Line13: – Use command sets Zero or the terminal as the current device, and displays the record just read
- ➢ Line14: – End of loop, check to see if End of File has been reached
- ➢ Line15: – The *Use* command sets the current device to the terminal, and displays the input record count
- ➢ Line16: – Display end of file reached

## Running Routine ^ReadFile

**Example 12-3 Running Routine ^ReadFile**

```
Do ^ReadFile
First Record
Second Record
Third Record
3 Records read
End of File reached
```

In Example 12-3 we run the Routine ^ReadFile created in Example 12-2.

## Read and Write a file

Now instead of just displaying each record read, we will read an input file and then write an output file.

**Example 12-4 Read and Write a file**

```
ReadAndWrite        ;
    Set InFile="FILE.TXT"        ;name of infile - FILE.TXT
    Set OutFile="FILE2.TXT"      ;name of outfile - FILE2.TXT
    Close InFile,OutFile         ;close a file before you open it

    Open InFile:"R":10           ;open the file for reading, timeout 10 sec
    If '$Test Write !,InFile," cannot be opened." Quit    ;cannot open file
    Open OutFile:"WNS":10        ;open file for write, new, timeout of 10 sec
    If '$Test Write !,OutFile," cannot be opened." Quit    ;cannot open file

    Set (InCount,OutCount)=0     ;init counter of records read and write
    Set X=$ZU(68,40,1)           ;enables the $ZEOF special variable
    ;Set system.Process.SetZEOF(1) ;enable the $ZEOF special variable


    Set EOF=0 Do {               ;EOF is the end of file switch
        Use InFile               ;sets InFile as the current device
        Read InRecord            ;read record from file
        If $ZEOF=-1 Set EOF=1 Quit    ;$ZEOF=-1 when end of file reached
        Set X=$Increment(InCount)     ;increment counter
        Use 0 Write !,InRecord         ;display record
        Set X=$Increment(OutCount)     ;increment counter
        Use OutFile              ;sets OutFile as the current device
        Write InRecord,!
    } While EOF=0                ;read until end of file
    Use 0 Write !,InCount," Records read"
    Use 0 Write !,OutCount," Records written"
    Use 0 Write !,"End of File reached"
    Quit
```

Example 12-4 demonstrates reading and writing a file.

### $ZEOF Special Variable

The $ZEOF Special Variable identifies an End of File situation when used with sequential read. The variable will be zero during normal reads and -1 when End of File has been reached. To use this variable you must disable the <ENDOFFILE> error for sequential files.
To do this: Set X=$ZU(68,40,1)

## *Running Routine ^ReadAndWrite*

**Example 12-5 Running Routine ^ReadAndWrite**

```
Do ^ReadAndWrite
First Record
Second Record
Third Record
```

```
3 Records read
3 Records written
End of File reached
```

In Example 12-5 we run the Routine ^ReadAndWrite created in Example 12-4.

## Use command

The **Use** command sets the specified device as the current device.  There can only be one current device at a time.

➢ Use 0 – sets the specified device, or Zero as the current device, Zero normally being the terminal or default output device

➢ Use File – sets the specified device, the variable File as the current device

## Cycle through several Files

**Example 12-6 Cycle through several files**

```
To run this code you must put the code in a routine, save the routine, and then
run the routine from the terminal.

CycleThruFiles    ;
    For File="FILE1.TXT","FILE2.TXT","FILE3.TXT" {
    Open File:"WNS"
    Close File
    }

    Set File=("FILE*.TXT");use * as a wildcard
    Set File=$ZSearch(File)
    Write !,File
    Do {
        Set File=$ZSearch("")  ;use a blank parameter to get next file
        If File="" Q
        Write !,File
    } While File'=""
```

Example 12-6 first creates three files, FILE1.TXT, FILE2.TXT, and FILE3.TXT. Then it uses *$ZSearch* to cycle through each of the three files using an asterisk as a wildcard after the file name. Note we call *$ZSearch* with a blank parameter in the loop, this is the way of telling *$ZSearch* to get the next file in the list. You should always cycle completely through the list to avoid locking up the list of files.

## Running Routine ^CycleThruFiles

**Example 12-7 Running Routine ^CycleThruFiles**

```
Do ^CycleThruFiles

C:\Cache2010\mgr\user\FILE.TXT
C:\Cache2010\mgr\user\FILE1.TXT
C:\Cache2010\mgr\user\FILE2.TXT
C:\Cache2010\mgr\user\FILE3.TXT
```

In Example 12-7 we run the Routine ^CycleThruFiles created in Example 12-6. Note that we picked up an unexpected file (FILE.TXT) that was created earlier.

## Search multiple files for a specific string

Now let us search through several files for a specific string.

**Example 12-8 Search multiple files for a specific string**

To run this code you must put the code in a routine, save the routine, and then run the routine from the terminal.

```
SearchForString
    For File="FILE1.TXT","FILE3.TXT","FILE5.TXT" {  ;three empty files
            Open File:"WNS"
            Close File
    }
    For File="FILE2.TXT","FILE4.TXT","FILE6.TXT" {  ;three files with "fleas"
            Open File:"WNS"
            Use File Write !,"My dog has fleas"
            Close File
    }

    Set File=("FILE*.TXT") ;set initial files to search
    Set File=$ZSearch(File) ;set initial search
    Do {
            Set File=$ZSearch("")                    ;get next file
            If File="" Quit                          ;end of file list
            Open File:"R":10 ;open files
            If '$Test Write !,File," cannot be opened." Quit
            Set X=$ZU(68,40,1)                       ;set up $ZEOF
            Set EOF=0 Do {
                    Use File                 ;set File as current device
                    Read Inrec               ;read record
                    If $ZEOF=-1 Set EOF=1 Quit
                    If Inrec["fleas" {
                            Use 0 Write !,"File: "
                            Write File," contains string 'fleas'."
                    }
            } While EOF=0
            Close File
    } While File'=""
```

Example 12-8 first creates six files with three of them containing the string "fleas." Then it searches all files: "FILE*.TXT" and reads through all records looking for the string "fleas."

## Running Routine ^SearchForString

**Example 12-9 Running Routine ^SearchForString**

```
Do ^SearchForString

File: C:\Cache2010\mgr\user\FILE2.TXT contains string 'fleas'.
File: C:\Cache2010\mgr\user\FILE4.TXT contains string 'fleas'.
```

```
File: C:\Cache2010\mgr\user\FILE6.TXT contains string 'fleas'.
```

In Example 12-9 we run the Routine ^SearchForString created in Example 12-8.

## Miscellaneous File Functions

Following are a number of miscellaneous and useful related file functions.

### Finding a File

**Example 12-10 Finding a File**

```
Set File=$ZSearch("FILE.TXT")                ;Find a File that exists
Write !,File
C:\Cache2010\mgr\user\FILE.TXT

Set File=$ZSearch("FILEXXX.TXT")             ;Find a file that does not
exist
Write !,File
<>
```

Example 12-10 uses **$ZSearch** to find the file we created earlier.

### Retrieve Date information about a file

**Example 12-11 Retrieve date information about a File**

```
Set File="FILE.TXT"
Write $ZU(140,3,File)                        ; Create Date/Time
61371,68318

Write $ZDatetime($ZU(140,3,File))
01/10/2009 18:58:38

Write $ZU(140,2,File)                        ; Modified Date/Time
61371,68318

Write $ZDateTime($ZU(140,2,File))
01/10/2009 18:58:38
```

Example 12-11 uses **$ZU(140)** to retrieve the created and modified date and time of a file.

### Check on the existence of a file

**Example 12-12 Check on the existence of a File**

```
Set File="FILE.TXT"
Write $ZU(140,4,File)              ; Existence of File
0                                  ; 0  - file exists

Set File="FILEXXX.TXT"
Write $ZU(140,4,File)              ; Existence of File
-2                                 ; -2 - file does not exist
```

Example 12-12 uses *$ZU(140)* to verify the existence of a file.

## Copying a file

**Example 12-13 Copying a file**

```
Set File="FILE.TXT"
Set NewFile="NEWFILE.TXT"

Write $ZU(140,11,File,NewFile)     ; Copy FILE.TXT to NEWFILE.TXT
0                                  ; copy successfull

Set File="NEWFILE.TXT"
Write $ZU(140,3,File)              ; Create Date/Time of the new file
61372,35519
```

Example 12-13 shows how to copy one filename to another.

## Renaming a file

**Example 12-14 Renaming a file**

```
Set File="FILE.TXT"
Set NewFile="NEWFILE.TXT"

Write $ZU(140,6,File,NewFile)     ; Rename FILE.TXT to NEWFILE.TXT

Set File="FILE.TXT"
Write $ZU(140,4,File)             ; Check the existence of File
-2                                ; Old file does not exist,
                                  ; it has been renamed

Set File="NEWFILE.TXT"
Write $ZU(140,4,File)             ; Check the existence of File
0                                 ; New file does exist
```

Example 12-14 uses **$ZU(140)** to rename the file FILE.TXT to NEWFILE.TXT.

## Delete a File

**Example 12-15 Delete a File**

```
Set File="NEWFILE.TXT"
Write $ZU(140,5,File)             ; Delete a file
0                                 ; 0  - delete successful

Set File="NEWFILE.TXT"
Write $ZU(140,5,File)             ; Delete a file
-2                                ; -2  - delete unsuccessful
                                  ; already deleted the file
```

Example 12-15 deletes NEWFILE.TXT. It attempts to delete it again but since the file is already deleted, it receives a -2 return code specifying that the second delete failed.

## *Chapter 12 Summary*

In this chapter, we considered *File Processing*. We saw how to:

 ➢  Write to an External file ,

 ➢  Read a file and display its records,

 ➢  Read from one file and write to another,

 ➢  Employ the *Use* command,

 ➢  Cycle through several Files,

 ➢  Search multiple files for a string,

 ➢  Find a file,

 ➢  Retrieve Date information about a file,

 ➢  Check on the existence of a file,

 ➢  Copying a file,

 ➢  Renaming a file, and

 ➢  Delete a file.

We also covered why it is a good idea to Close a file before Opening it and the reason for the $ZEOF Special Variable. As I stated at the beginning of this chapter the $ZU commands were depreciated in Caché version 2010. Appendix A demonstrates *File Processing* using Object Calls instead of $ZU.

# *Chapter 13 Error Processing*

An indispensable and crucial part of software development is to capture and report upon all foreseen and unforeseen errors. However, all too often, like documentation, it is deferred until later and often forgotten.

## *Introduction*

*Error Processing* in Caché ObjectScript (COS) can be complex and a thorough treatment of it is well beyond the scope of this book. However, the programmer needs a working knowledge of *Error Processing*, which I will try to provide.

## *Why take all this trouble with Errors?*

A Computer System is always more expensive to maintain than develop. Therefore, the more quickly errors can be discovered and resolved the less maintenance it will require. This reason alone should justify developing good comprehensive Error Processing.

## *Error Processing*

*Error Processing* should consist of at least four elements:

- Identify the Error
- Capture or Trap the Error
- Report upon the Error
- Handle the Error

## *Identify the Error*

Predictable Errors are *Foreseen Errors* and relatively easy to handle. These would include a Device that refuses to open and a bad return value from a called procedure. Unpredictable Errors are *Unforeseen Errors* and are more difficult to identify and handle.

## *Foreseen Errors*

The programmer can test for *Foreseen Errors;* these include checking return codes from calls, verifying input parameters, checking timeouts on opens and the like. Application errors also come under *Foreseen Errors.*

## Testing for File Open

**Example 13-1 Testing for File Open**

```
To run this code you must put the code in a routine, save the routine, and then
run the routine from the terminal.

Set File="File.txt"
Close File                ;good practice to close a file before opening it
Open File:"RS":5
If '$Test {               ;test to see if the file is open
   Write "File "_File_" not open"
   ;do some sort of error handling
}
Quit
```

In Example 13-1 after the command to open an external file we test to ensure it is open. We cannot just "assume" that the file will be open.

## Testing for the existence of Parameters

**Example 13-2 Testing for the existence of Parameters**

```
To run this code you must put the code in a routine, save the routine, and then
run the routine from the terminal.

Do Procedure1("Par1","")
Quit

Procedure1(Param1,Param2)

  If $G(Param1)="" {
        Write "Parameter 1 is null."
        ;do some sort of error handling

  }

  If $G(Param2)="" {
        Write "Parameter 2 is null."
        ;do some sort of error handling

  }
  Quit
```

In Example 13-2 we test to ensure that both Param1 and Param2 exist. Again, we cannot "assume" that the parameters will exist.

## Testing the Status returned from a Call

**Example 13-3 Testing the Status Code that is returned from calling another routine**

```
To run this code you must put the code in a routine, save the routine, and then
run the routine from the terminal.

Set Statuscode=^SomeRoutine
If $G(Statuscode)'=1 {
    Write "Bad Statuscode returned from call to ^SomeRoutine"
    ;do some sort of error handling
}
```

```
Quit
```

Example 13-3 tests the status code that is returned from call another routine. We cannot just "assume" the returned status code will be good.

The last few examples demonstrate testing for common *Foreseen Errors*. It is extremely important to test for these errors as close to where they originate as possible and not just assume the obvious; that the file is open, or the parameter is valid, or that the call is successful. Errors are like a pinball in a pinball machine, they move about the system and show up far from where they originate. Errors are more difficult to identify and resolve when they show up far from their source.

## Unforeseen Errors

*Unforeseen Errors*, by their very definition are difficult to handle. Typically these are handled with an *Error Trap*. An *Error Trap*, as the name implies is like a Mouse Trap. A trap is set, and when an error occurs, the trap is snapped and the error is caught. It needs to be reset to be used again.

## Error Trapping

InterSystems provides a utility for trapping errors:

> ➤ **^%ETN** – Application Error Trap

### Setting the Error Trap

**Example 13-4 Setting the Error Trap**

```
Set $ZT="^%ETN"    ; $ZT is the error trap special variable, it says when an
                   ; error occurs, go to this routine, ^%ETN
```

Example 13-4 demonstrates setting the Error Trap. The default InterSystems Application Error Trap utility is *^%ETN*. Once the *$ZT* (Z Trap) special variable is set to *^%ETN,* the trap is set. Then when an error occurs, the routine *^%ETN* takes control and saves the relevant data for later analysis. Once the error trap is sprung, it needs to be reset again.

### Springing the Error Trap

**Example 13-5 Springing the Error Trap**

```
To run this code you must put the code in a routine, save the routine, and then
run the routine from the terminal.

RoutineA
  ;
  Set $ZT="^%ETN" ; $ZT is the error trap special variable, it says when
                  ; an error occurs, go to this routine, ^%ETN

  Kill X
  Write X         ; variable X does not exist so trying to write variable X
                  ; springs the error trap
```

Example 13-5 shows how to deliberately spring the error trap. Here we set $ZT (the error trap special variable) to ^%ETN (the default InterSystems Application Error Trap utility). Next we Kill the variable X, and then attempt to write X. Since X does not exist, attempting to write X produces an error condition.

**Example 13-6 Running RoutineA to Spring the Error Trap**

```
Run ^RoutineA

Error has occurred: <UNDEFINED> at 10:30 AM
```

In Example 13-6 we run RoutineA and the result is as expected, and Undefined error.

---

### ^%ETN

Be aware that when ^%ETN is invoked, that after it has recorded the error it will log the process out of Caché.

---

## *Report upon the Error*

> ➤ **^%ERN** – Application Error Trap Report

**Example 13-7 Report upon the Error**

```
Do ^%ERN

For Date: T  26 Oct 2008   3 Errors

Error: ?

    Select one of the errors for this date.  Enter ?L to list
    all the errors which are defined for 26 Oct 2008.
    Enter * to enter a comment relating to all the errors
         which exist for this date (e.g. 'all fixed')
    Enter tag^routine to list this date's errors which
         occurred in a specific routine.
    Enter [text to list this date's errors which had 'text'
         in either the error, line of code or comment.
    Enter <error to list the errors with the specified error.

Error: ?L

 1. <UNDEFINED>RoutineA+5^RoutineA *X  at  9:55 am.    $I=|TRM|:|2524($X=0
$Y=136)
      $J=2524   $ZA=0   $ZB=$c(13)    $ZS=47630 ($S=48618256)
              Write X                   ;variable X does not exist

Error: 1

 1. <UNDEFINED>RoutineA+5^RoutineA *X  at  9:55 am.    $I=|TRM|:|2524($X=0
$Y=136)
```

```
    $J=2524   $ZA=0    $ZB=$c(13)    $ZS=47630 ($S=48618256)
            Write X                        ;variable X does not exist

Variable: ?

    Enter the name of the variable you wish to view.
    Enter the stack level you wish to view.
    Enter ?# to view the variables defined for stack level #
    Enter ?var to list levels  where variable 'var' is defined
    Enter *S to view all the Process State Variables ($S,etc)
    Enter *F to view the execution Frame Stack
    Enter *C to enter a Comment for this error
    Enter *L to Load the variables into the current partition
    Enter *P to Print the Stack & Symbol information to a device
    Enter *A to to print ALL information, state variables, Stack
            Frames, and Local Variables to a device.
    Enter *V to trace selected variables through the frame stack
    Enter *? to redisplay the error information


Variable:
```

Example 13-7 demonstrates how to look up a specific error and begin to investigate. At this point I leave further investigating up to the reader. Refer to InterSystems' documentation at *www.intersystems.com* for more information on error reporting.

## Handling the Error

Typically when a system encounters an error, the normal response is to quit or halt. By setting *$ZT="^%ETN"* the error will be recorded and the processing will stop and the session is halted. But what about less serious errors, errors that you want to record, but then continue processing? You could call an error processing routine of your own.

### Error Processing Routine for Other (less serious) Errors

**Example 13-8 Error Processing Routine for Other (less serious) Errors**

```
To run this code you must put the code in a routine, save the routine, and then
run the routine from the terminal.

RoutineA
   ;
   Write !,"RoutineA starting"
   ;
Label1
   Write !,"RoutineA at Label1"
   Set $ZT="ErrorProcessing"    ; $ZT is the error trap special
                                ; variable, it says when an error
                                ; occurs, go to this label

   Set ReturnLabel="RestartPoint1"    ; This is the restart label
                                      ; label after an error occurs
   Kill X
   Write X             ; variable X does not exist so trying to write
                       ; variable X springs the error trap

RestartPoint1
```

```
        Write !,"RoutineA at RestartPoint1"
        Set $ZT="ErrorProcessing"     ; $ZT is the error trap special
                                      ; variable, it says when an error
                                      ; occurs, go to this label

        Set ReturnLabel="RestartPoint2"    ; This is the restart label
                                           ; label after an error occurs
        Kill X
        Write X                 ; variable X does not exist so trying to write
                                ; variable X springs the error trap

RestartPoint2
        Write !,"RoutineA at RestartPoint2"

        Write !,"RoutineA exiting"
        Quit

ErrorProcessing(Location,Message)
        Write !,"RoutineA at ErrorProcessing"
        Write !,$ZE
        Set DateTime=$ZDATETIME($H)
        Set ^ApplError(DateTime)=$ZE
        Write !,DateTime," ",$ZE
        Goto @ReturnLabel               ; branch back to the restart point.
```

Example 13-8 demonstrates one method of having your own Error Processing code that records the error and then passes control back to a restart point. Note the restart point is changed as the routine progresses. The Error Processing routine uses *Indirection* (see Chapter 18, under Dynamic Code) to branch back to the restart point.

**Example 13-9 Output from Example 13-8**

```
To run this code you must put the code in a routine, save the routine, and then
run the routine from the terminal.

RoutineA starting
RoutineA at Label1
RoutineA at ErrorProcessing
<UNDEFINED>Label1+8^ROUTINEA *X
06/09/2011 21:15:37 <UNDEFINED>Label1+8^ROUTINEA *X
RoutineA at RestartPoint1
RoutineA at ErrorProcessing
<UNDEFINED>RestartPoint1+8^ROUTINEA *X
06/09/2011 21:15:37 <UNDEFINED>RestartPoint1+8^ROUTINEA *X
RoutineA at RestartPoint2
RoutineA exiting
```

## Terms regarding Errors

- **Errors** – whenever the Caché system encounters a situation that it cannot handle it will produce an "Error" and stop processing, unless that Error is trapped (see *Error Trap* below) and handled. There are literally hundreds of possible errors, but we shall consider only the most frequent

- **Error Trap** – most complex Caché systems have *Error Traps*. The *Error Trap* attempts to trap the error, store all relevant data and make it available for later analysis. It also may attempt to handle the error and continue processing

- **Call Stack** or **Frame Stack** – as computer routines run they call other routines, and these routines call still more routines, these *Calling Chains* may become quite long. Information about the current state of these "calling" and "called" routines are stored in the *Call Stack*

## Errors

Some of the more common errors you may encounter are:

- **Syntax Error** – this error indicates there is something wrong with the syntax or structure of the code

- **Undefined Error** – a local or Global variable or array node is not defined

- **Subscript Error** – a variable that is being used as a subscript in a local or Global array is blank

- **EndOfFile Error** – there has been an attempt to read past the end-of-file marker in a file

- **Divide Error** – divide by zero is attempted, which is illegal

- **Parameter Error** - the number of parameters passed from a calling routine is not the same as the number of parameters expected by the called routine

- **NoLine Error** – a line or label in a routine being called does not exist, or perhaps the routine is "private" and the tag is hidden

- **NoRoutine Error** – a routine being called does not exist

- **Edited Error** – while a routine was running, it was edited or modified. In more recent versions of Caché this is handled by the Caché Operating System

## Syntax Error

A **Syntax Error** indicates there is something wrong with the syntax or structure of the code.

## Examples of Syntax Errors

**Example 13-10 Example of Syntax Errors**

```
Set Set X=1               ;Two "Set" commands
<SYNTAX>

Set X=$O(^GLOBAL(X)       ;Missing a second right parentheses
<SYNTAX>

Write $F(X)               ;$Find needs more parameters
<SYNTAX>

Write $E(X,1,1,2)         ;$Extract has too many parameters
<SYNTAX>

Write $P(X,,1)            ;$Piece is missing the middle parameter
<SYNTAX>

QUIT:                     ;Quit is missing a post-conditional
<SYNTAX>
```

Example 13-10 shows several syntax errors, these errors are normally easier to find and fix than other type of errors, but not always. It is helpful to have an editor, like InterSystems Studio (http://www.intersystems.com) or GeorgeJames' Serenji (http://www.georgejames.com) that highlights syntax errors in your code.

Typically it is not wise to write a whole routine before checking for syntax errors. It is much better to write a few lines of code and then check to ensure they are free of syntax errors.

## Undefined Error

An **Undefined Error** occurs when a local or Global variable or array node is not defined.

## Examples of Undefined Errors

**Example 13-11 Examples of Undefined Errors**

```
Kill X
Write X                   ;variable X is not defined
<UNDEFINED>

Kill Y
Write X=Y                 ;variable Y is not defined
<UNDEFINED>

Kill ^Global(Sub1)
Write ^Global(Sub1)       ;Global node does not exist
<UNDEFINED>

Kill Sub1
```

```
    Write ^Global(Sub1)          ;it may be difficult to tell which is undefined,
                                  ;the variable used as a subscript, or the Global
node
<UNDEFINED>
```

Example 13-11 shows several undefined errors. From looking at this example it would seem that *Undefined Errors* are straightforward, but variables or Globals may be defined in a different routine. Hunting down where a variable or Global should be defined may be an exhaustive experience. One way to avoid these errors is to use the *$Get* or *$Data* System-Supplied function with variables and Globals respectively. However, some consider this "sloppy" code.

## Undefined Errors and the New command

**Example 13-12 Undefined Errors and the New command**

```
    Set X=123                   ;variable X is just defined

    New X                       ;New command

    Write X          ;variable X is not defined because it was just Newed
<UNDEFINED>
```

Example 13-12 shows how the *New* command can precipitate an *Undefined Error*.

## Subscript Error

A **Subscript Error** occurs when a variable used as a subscript in a local or Global array is blank.

## Examples of Subscript Errors

**Example 13-13 Examples of a Subscript Error**

```
    Set Sub1=""
    Set ^Global(Sub1)=""   ;Sub1 is blank
<SUBSCRIPT>

    Kill Sub1
    Set ^Global(Sub1)="" ;If Sub1 did not exist,an <UNDEFINED> error is produced
<UNDEFINED>
```

Example 13-13 demonstrates a subscript error. A *Subscript Error* is when an array subscript is blank or null. If the subscript did not exist, an *Undefined Error* would be produced, understanding this distinction will aid in debugging routines.

## EndOfFile Error

An **EndOfFile** error occurs when there is an attempt to read past the end-of-file marker of an external file. File processing is covered in Chapter 12 but enough is repeated here for this example.

Suppose we had an external file with 5 records in it, when we attempt to read the 6$^{th}$ record we will get an *EndOfFile* error. The file contains the following records:

> First record in the file
> Second record in the file
> Third record in the file
> Fourth record in the file
> Fifth record in the file

### Example of an EndOfFile Error

Example 13-14 Example of an EndOfFile Error

```
To run this code you must put the code in a routine, save the routine, and then
run the routine from the terminal.

ReadFile   ;
  Set File="C:\FILE.DAT"
  Open File:"R":10                    ;open the file with a timeout of 10 sec
  If '$T Write !,"Cannot open file" Q   ;quit if the file cannot be open
  Set RecordCount=0
Loop
  Set RecordCount=RecordCount+1
  Use File R Rec
  Use 0 Write !,Rec,"   Record count: ",RecordCount
  Go Loop
```

Example 13-14 shows a routine set up to read a file and receives an *EndOfFile* Error when it reads past the fifth record.

Example 13-15 Example of running the routine ^ReadFile

```
Do ^ReadFile

First record in the file   Record count: 1
Second record in the file   Record count: 2
Third record in the file   Record count: 3
Fourth record in the file   Record count: 4
Fifth record in the file   Record count: 5
  Use File R Rec
                 ^
<ENDOFFILE>Loop+2^ReadFile
```

Example 13-15 runs the ^ReadFile routine and receives an *EndOfFile Error* when attempting to read the 6$^{th}$ record.

## Divide Error

A **Divide Error** is when division by zero is attempted.

### Example of Divide Error

**Example 13-16 Example of a Divide Error**

```
 Write 1/0
<DIVIDE>
```

Example 13-16 demonstrates a *Divide Error*. It occurs when division by zero is attempted. Mathematically it is illegal to divide by zero.

## NoLine Error

This **NoLine Error** occurs when a routine attempts to reference a Tag or Label that does not exist.

### Example of a NoLine Error

**Example 13-17 Example of a NoLine Error**

```
RoutineA    ;
    ;
Start       ;
    Do Process^RoutineB          ;The Label Process does not exist in
RoutineB
<NOLINE>
```

In Example 13-17 RoutineA does a call to the label *Process* in RoutineB. However, if label *Process* in RoutineB does not exist we receive a *NoLine Error*.

## NoRoutine Error

This error occurs when a routine attempts to call another Routine that does not exist.

### Example of a NoRoutine Error

**Example 13-18 Example of a NoRoutine Error**

```
RoutineA    ;
    ;
Start       ;
    Do ^RoutineD              ;RoutineD does not exist
<NOROUTINE>
```

In Example 13-18 RoutineA does a call to RoutineD, but if RoutineD does not exist we receive a *NoRoutine Error*.

### Edited Error

This error occurs when a routine that is currently being run (or the routine is in a stack of routines being run) is edited or changed by another process.

I know we have not talked about a **Call Stack** yet, but it does apply here, consider the next example.

### Example of a Call Stack

**Example 13-19 Example of a Call Stack**

```
To run this code you must put the code in a routine, save the routine, and then
run the routine from the terminal.

RoutineA   ;
    Do ^RoutineB
    Quit


    = = = = = = = = = = = = = = = = = = = = = = = = = = = = = =


RoutineB
    Do ^RoutineC
    Quit
    ;


    = = = = = = = = = = = = = = = = = = = = = = = = = = = = = =


RoutineC
    ;                   ;we shall consider the call stack at this point
    Quit
```

In Example 13-19 we have three routines:

> ➢ RoutineA calls RoutineB

> ➢ RoutineB calls RoutineC

In Routine C we have a *Call Stack* of 3 routines, or think of it as a ladder, RoutineA is the top rung, RoutineB is the second rung and RoutineC is the bottom rung of the ladder. For most ladders we start at the bottom then go up and back down. In this ladder we start at the top, then go down and back up. Suppose while RoutineC is processing someone changes RoutineA. Even though RoutineA still exists, or more properly a new copy of RoutineA exists, it is no longer where we left it, so, the top rung of the ladder is now missing. As we attempt to go back up the ladder, climb the *Call Stack*, when we get to RoutineA we will receive an *Edited Error*.

In more recent versions of Caché this is handled by the Caché Operating System.

## Call Stack or Frame Stack

As a computer processes a routine, the routine will call another routine, which in turn calls another routine, and that routine calls another routine, and so on. These **Calling Chains** may become quite long and the system needs to keep track of this information because what goes down a chain must climb back up. Information about the current state of these calling chains is stored in the **Call Stack**.

**Example 13-20  Four Routine Call Stack**

| |
|---|
| RoutineW |
| RoutineZ |
| RoutineY |
| RoutineZ |
| ^%STACK |

## Call Stack Demonstration

**Example 13-21 Call Stack Demonstration**

```
To run this code you must put the code in a routine, save the routine, and then
run the routine from the terminal.

RoutineW
    ;
    Write !,$T(+0)," Start"
    Do ^RoutineX
    Write !,$T(+0)," Finish"
    Quit


    = = = = = = = = = = = = = = = = = = = = = = = = = = = = = = = =

RoutineX
    ;
    Write !,$T(+0)," Start"
    Do ^RoutineY
    Write !,$T(+0)," Finish"
    Quit


    = = = = = = = = = = = = = = = = = = = = = = = = = = = = = = = =

RoutineY
    ;
    Write !,$T(+0)," Start"
    Do ^RoutineZ
    Write !,$T(+0)," Finish"
    Quit


    = = = = = = = = = = = = = = = = = = = = = = = = = = = = = = = =

RoutineZ
    ;
```

```
Write !,$T(+0)," Start"
Do ^%STACK
Write !,$T(+0)," Finish"
Quit
```

In Example 13-21 RoutineW calls RoutineX, and RoutineX calls RoutineY, and RoutineY calls RoutineZ, and finally RoutineZ calls **^%STACK**. The routine *^%STACK* is an InterSystems utility to display and integrate the call stack. You can learn more about the *%STACK* utility from www.intersystems.com

### Call Stack Demonstration – running RoutineW

**Example 13-22 Call Stack Demonstration – running RoutineW**

```
Do ^RoutineW

RoutineW Start
RoutineX Start
RoutineY Start
RoutineZ Start  6
Process Stack:

Level  Type     Line                      Source
   1   SIGN ON
   2   DO                                       ~D ^RoutineW
   3   DO        RoutineW+3^RoutineW        ~D ^RoutineX
   4   DO        RoutineX+3^RoutineX        ~D ^RoutineY
   5   DO        RoutineY+3^RoutineY        ~D ^RoutineZ
   6   DO        RoutineZ+3^RoutineZ        ~D ^%STACK
```

In Example 13-22 we see what *^%STACK* displays. A thorough explanation of this output is beyond the scope of this book, refer to the InterSystems documentation for more information, www.intersystems.com.

## Chapter 13 Summary

In Chapter 13 we covered *Error Processing.* We talked about why we should bother with *Error Processing*, how to Identify an error, whether Foreseen or Unforeseen. Next we looked at the InterSystems error trap and error reporting utility and how to handle an error. Finally we defined some Error Terms and covered some of the more common errors as well as the *Call Stack.*

# Chapter 14 Testing and Debugging

*Testing* and *Debugging* is a methodical process of executing code to find and reduce the number of bugs or defects and ensure the code executes as intended.

## Objective of Testing - Quality

Testing measures the Quality of the software, is the software:

- Correct or accurate
- Complete - nothing missing
- Reliable and dependable
- Efficient without wasting resources
- Written within established standards
- Portable - movable to other systems
- Maintainable – easily modified

## Scope of Testing

Reams of books have been written on software testing, but where does the individual programmer start? The programmer should start with *Unit Testing*. *Unit Testing* is testing the smallest segment or piece of code, just one line, or a piece of a line. Here are various types of testing each with a different scope:

- Unit Testing – testing the smallest piece of code
- Code Block Testing – testing a block of code
- Module or Subroutine Testing – testing a module or subroutine
- Routine Testing – testing at a routine level
- Sub-System Testing – testing at a sub-systems level, or a group of logically connected routines
- System Testing – testing the system as a whole
- Interface Testing - testing the systems where inputs and outputs are involved
- Regression Testing – does the new code work with already established code
- User Testing – having the end user test the system
- Integration Testing – does the new code work with its environment

*A Unit Test is the basis for all these,* if the individual Unit is not correct; the other testing is suspect.

The great ocean liner Titanic failed in large part because of sub-standard rivets. *The quality of the code at the Unit level* is comparable to the quality of the rivets on the Titanic.

## Types of Testing: Static and Dynamic

➢ *Static Testing* - code walkthroughs or peer reviews where others inspecting the code for weaknesses

➢ *Dynamic Testing* - actually running the program

In the next section, we are going to look at dynamic testing.

## Debugging (Dynamic Testing)

How is *Unit Testing* done? Using some of the debugging tools that follow, test every assumption, command, function of every line of code so that you are 100% sure it does what you expect it to do. Is this a lot of work? Yes, but it is necessary to have bug free code. However, even when you do all this work, you may still have bugs in your code.

---

**There is always one more bug – one of Murphy's Laws**

---

Debugging involves stopping executing code at a particular point and examining every assumption, command, function, and logic to ensure it is correct. It also involves examining Globals, variables, and arrays to ensure they contain the values you expect them to contain.

If you have access to the Caché Studio from InterSystems (*www.intersystems.com*) or Serenji from GeorgeJames (*www.georgejames.com)*, these two products have Graphic User Interfaces that help greatly in debugging. Otherwise, you will need to use the old tried-and-true methods, which we will cover next.

## Debugging commands

➢ Break command

➢ Break command based on the DEBUG variable

➢ Break command with Line Stepping

➢ Disable the Break command

➢ ZBreak command

➢ ZBreak command with Line Stepping

➢ Setting Watchpoints with the ZBreak command

➢ On-line Help with the ZBreak command

## Break command

When the *Break* command is inserted into a routine, it will suspend processing and allow the programmer to examine or modify variables and arrays.

**Example 14-1 Break command**

```
To run this code you must put the code in a routine, save the routine, and then
run the routine from the terminal.

RoutineDebug        ;
    Set X=1
    Set Y=2
    Set Z=3
    Set A=Y*Z
    Break                       ;Break command
    Write !,X
    Write !,Y
    Write !,Z
    Write !,A
```

In Example 14-1, we have a routine called RoutineDebug. After several lines of code, we see the *Break* command. The *Break* command will suspend processing at this point.

**Example 14-2 Executing the Break command**

```
D ^RoutineDebug

 Break                          ;Break command
 ^
<BREAK>RoutineDebug+5^RoutineDebug
USER 2d0>Write X                ;at this point the programmer has control
1
USER 2d0>Write Y
2
USER 2d0>Write Z
3
USER 2d0>Write A
6
USER 2d0>G                      ;Go command given, the routine takes
                                ;back control
1
2
5
6
```

In Example 14-2, the user runs the routine *RoutineDebug* with the *Break* command. After variables X, Y, Z and A are set we arrive at the *Break* command and the programmer received control. The programmer writes out several variables and changes the Z variable. Then he issues the *Go* command to continue processing. Processing will continue to the end of the routine or to the next *Break* command.

The *Break* command may be based on a variable. Some programmers establish a *DEBUG* variable. If *DEBUG* equals 1 (Set DEBUG=1) each *Break* command is executed, if the *DEBUG* variable does not exist or equals 0 (Set DEBUG=0), the *Break* command is not executed.

## Break command based on the DEBUG variable

**Example 14-3 Break command based on the DEBUG variable**

```
To run this code you must put the code in a routine, save the routine, and then
run the routine from the terminal.

RoutineDebug        ;
    Set X=1
    Set Y=2
    Set Z=3
    Set A=Y*Z
    If $G(DEBUG)=1 Break            ;Break command and DEBUG variable
    Write !,X
    Write !,Y
    Write !,Z
    Write !,A
```

Example 14-3 is an example of a *Break* command with the *DEBUG* variable. If the *DEBUG* variable equals 1 each *Break* command is executed, if the *DEBUG* variable does not exist or equals 0, the *Break* command is not executed. This is a nice way to leave *Break* commands in your code and turn them off and on as needed.

## Break command with Line Stepping

**Example 14-4 Break command with Line Stepping**

```
To run this code you must put the code in a routine, save the routine, and then
run the routine from the terminal.

RoutineDebug        ;
    Set X=1
    Set Y=2
    Set Z=3
    Set A=Y*Z
    Break "L"                       ;Break command with Line Stepping
    Write !,X
    Write !,Y
    Write !,Z
    Write !,A
```

In Example 14-4, we use the *Break* command with the *Line Stepping* option. For each *Go* command it will only step to the next line, this way you can step through your code one line at a time.

**Example 14-5 Break command with Line Stepping Demonstrated**

```
Do ^RoutineDebug

Write !,X
^
<BREAK>RoutineDebug+6^RoutineDebug
USER 2d0>G                                ;Go command

1
Write !,Y
```

```
^
<BREAK>RoutineDebug+7^RoutineDebug
USER 2d0>G                              ;Go command

2
Write !,Z
^
<BREAK>RoutineDebug+8^RoutineDebug
USER 2d0>G                              ;Go command

3
Write !,A
^
<BREAK>RoutineDebug+9^RoutineDebug
USER 2d0>G                              ;Go command

6
USER>
```

In Example 14-5, we use the *Break* command with the *Line Stepping* option. Notice that for each *Go* command it will only continue to the next line, this way you can step through your code one line at a time.

If you need to disable all breaks, just issue the *Break Off* command and then issue the *Go* command.

## Disable the Break command

**Example 14-6 Disable the Break command**

```
Do ^RoutineDebug

Write !,X
^
<BREAK>RoutineDebug+6^RoutineDebug
USER 2d0>G                              ;Go command

1
Write !,Y
^
<BREAK>RoutineDebug+7^RoutineDebug
USER 2d0>Break "OFF"                    ;break off command

USER 2d0>G                              ;Go command

2
3
6
```

Example 14-6 demonstrates disabling the *Break* command.

We have covered the basics of the *Break* command, for more options see the InterSystems documentation, www.intersystems.com.

## ZBreak command

A serious drawback with the *Break* command is that the routine must be edited to insert the *Break* command. You will not always have access to edit the routine, especially those routines running in a production system. In addition, it is far too easy to forget to remove the *Break* command.

As an alternative we have the *ZBreak* command, with the *ZBreak* command modifying the routine to insert a break is not necessary.

**Example 14-7 ZBreak command**

```
To run this code you must put the code in a routine, save the routine, and then
run the routine from the terminal.

RoutineDebug        ;
Start       ;
    Set X=1
    Set Y=2
    Set Z=3
    Set A=Y*Z
    Write !,X
    Write !,Y
    Write !,Z
    Write !,A
    Quit
```

In Example 14-7, we have the original routine but without the *Break* command.

The *ZBreak* command is not inserted into the routine, but is given before we execute the routine.

**Example 14-8 Invoking the ZBreak command**

```
ZBreak Start+1^RoutineDebug        ;break at Start+1
Do ^RoutineDebug
Set X=1
^
<BREAK>Start+1^RoutineDebug
USER 2d0>G                                ;Go command

1
2
3
6
```

In Example 14-8, *ZBreak* is set before the routine is run, then when the routine is run; it breaks at the Start label+1. *ZBreak* is known as a *Soft Break* because it does not require editing of the routine and will not exist after you HALT from the system with the *Halt* command.

## ZBreak command with Line Stepping

**Example 14-9 ZBreak command with Line Stepping**

```
ZBreak Start+1^RoutineDebug:"L"

Do ^RoutineDebug
Set X=1
```

```
^
<BREAK>Start+1^RoutineDebug
USER 2d0>G
Set Y=2
^
<BREAK>Start+2^RoutineDebug
USER 2d0>G
Set Z=3
^
<BREAK>Start+3^RoutineDebug
USER 2d0>G
Set A=Y*Z
^
<BREAK>Start+4^RoutineDebug
USER 2d0>G
Write !,X
^
<BREAK>Start+5^RoutineDebug
USER 2d0>G
1
Write !,Y
^
<BREAK>Start+6^RoutineDebug
USER 2d0>G
2
Write !,Z
^
<BREAK>Start+7^RoutineDebug
USER 2d0>G
3
Write !,A
^
<BREAK>Start+8^RoutineDebug
USER 2d0>G
6

USER>
```

In Example 14-9, *ZBreak* is set using the *Line Stepping Option*, similar to the *Line Stepping Option* used in the *Break* command.

## Setting Watchpoints with the ZBreak command

Breakpoints stop routine execution whenever a specific location is reached. *Watchpoints* however, stop routine execution whenever the value of a specified variable changes.

Using the same routine used in Example 14-7 we shall see how *Watchpoints* work:

**Example 14-10 Setting Watchpoints**

```
USER>ZBreak *Y     ;set a watchpoint whenever the Y variable is modified

USER>Do ^RoutineDebug

Set Y=2
^
<BREAK>Start+2^RoutineDebug
USER 2d0>G
```

```
1
2
3
6
USER>
```

In Example 14-10, a *Watchpoint* is set to stop routine execution when the Y variable is changed.

## On-line Help with the ZBreak command

**Example 14-11 ZBreak On-line help**

```
ZBreak ?

ZB location{:parms}    Set breakpoint
ZB -location{#delay}   Disable breakpoint
ZB +location           Enable breakpoint
ZB --location          Remove breakpoint


location is a line reference, or *variable, or $

parms is action:{condition}:{execute}

action is B, L, L+, S, S+, T, or N  which mean
 BREAK, Line step, Single step, Trace, or No action
condition is a truth-valued expression
execute is code to be executed

/CLEAR                       Remove all breakpoints
/DEBUG{:device}              Clear or set debug device
/TRACE:{ON,OFF,ALL}{:device} Enable or disable trace, or trace all lines
/ERRORTRAP:{ON,OFF}          Enable or disable $ZTRAP and $ETRAP
/INTERRUPT:{NORMAL,BREAK}    Specify Control-C action
```

Example 14-11 demonstrates on-line help with the *ZBreak* command.

I have covered just the basics of *Testing* and *Debugging*. For more information, see the on-line documentation for InterSystems Inc., *www.intersystems.com*.

# *Chapter 14 Summary*

This chapter covers *Testing* and *Debugging*. The Objective of Testing is Quality, testing has a different Scope depending upon the objective of each test. Dynamic Debugging is the process of walking down through code using the various commands available to ensure the code is doing what is intended. Specifically the commands are: 1) *Break*, 2) *ZBreak*, and 3) *Watchpoints*.

# *Chapter 15 Procedures*

This chapter covers the topic of **Procedures** in Caché ObjectScript (COS). *Procedures* enforce structure and variable scoping missing in Legacy MUMPS code. *Procedure* protocol is also used in Caché Object Methods.

## *Procedures*

InterSystem's suggests using Caché ObjectScript *Procedures* as a replacement for user written legacy subroutines and functions. *Procedures* offer significant improvements over older legacy code structures. *Procedures* enforce needed structure, control, and scope that legacy subroutines and functions lack. Specifically:

➢ By default all variables used in Procedures are private, this eliminates Newing variables, or in many cases forgetting to New variables

➢ Procedures identifies all Public Variables, either through Parameters or the Public Variable List

➢ Within Procedures no two Tags or Labels can be the same, thus eliminating potential bugs

➢ A Procedure may act as a Subroutine (does not return a value) or a Function (returns a value)

➢ A Procedure cannot be called using the Tag+offset format, eliminating a buggy option

➢ The code of a Procedure is contained within curly brackets, { }

➢ A Procedure may be Public or Private, by default they are Private

Caché ObjectScript *Procedures* represents a major step in making Caché ObjectScript code more robust. Many of the same features *Procedures* offer are used in Caché Methods. I suggest that all new developments use them.

However, using *Procedures* correctly takes time and practice, and may be frustrating at first.

## Definitions

- ➤ A Routine is a computer program, a separate entity that may contain *Procedures*, Subroutines, and Functions

- ➤ A Subroutine is a block of code called at a Tag or Label and ends with a *Quit* command. It does not pass back a value. A Subroutine exists inside a Routine

- ➤ A Function is the same as a Subroutine but does pass back a value. A Function exists inside a Routine

- ➤ A *Procedure* may mimic both a Subroutine and a Function but has more stringent and enforced structure. A *Procedure* exists inside a Routine

## Elements of a COS Procedure

A COS *Procedure* is a block of Caché ObjectScript code, written by application programmers, having a specific structure, control, scope, and syntax to accomplish an objective. It can be public or private and may or may not return a value.

The elements of a COS *Procedure* are:

- ➤ Procedure Name
- ➤ Parameters
- ➤ List of Public Variables
- ➤ *Procedure* access declaration (public or private)
- ➤ Code
- ➤ Return Value

## Template of a COS Procedure

**Example 15-1 Template of a COS Procedure**

```
To run this code you must put the code in a routine, save the routine, and then
run the routine from the terminal.

RoutineA
;
ProcedureABC(Param1,Param2) [PubVar1,PubVar2]  Public  {
  Write !,"Param1: ",Param1
  Write !,"Param2: ",Param2
  Write !,"PubVar1: ",PubVar1
  Write !,"PubVar2: ",PubVar2
}
```

Observations regarding the template of a COS *Procedure* in Example 15-1:

➤ The name of the routine containing the *Procedure* is RoutineA

➤ The name of this *Procedure* is ProcedureABC

➤ This *Procedure* accepts two parameters, Param1 and Param2

➤ This *Procedure* defines two variables as public, PubVar1 and PubVar2

➤ The word "Public" just before the "{" can be either "Public" or "Private" and refers to the *Procedure* itself

➤ This *Procedure* may exit either with a *Quit* command, or the "}" but must end with the "}"

Now lets' explore and experiment with this *Procedure*. We will start with the code that would call the *Procedure*

## Calling a COS Procedure

**Example 15-2 Calling a COS Procedure**

```
Set Param1=2
Set Param2=3
Set PubVar1=5                                ;public variable
Set PubVar2=5                                ;public variable
Do ProcedureABC^RoutineA(Param1,Param2)     ;calling a Procedure
Param1: 2
Param2: 3
PubVar1: 5
PubVar2: 5
```

Example 15-2 demonstrates calling a public *Procedure* (as shown in Example 15-1) with parameters and two public variables. The public *Procedure* ProcedureABC, contained within RoutineA displays parameters and public variables.

## Public and Private Procedures

*Procedures* may be *Public* or *Private*. A *Private Procedure* can only be called from within the Routine in which it lives; *Public Procedure* can be called from any routine. The first line of the *Procedure* defines whether it is public or private. Just before the beginning curly bracket it may say "Public" or "Private". The default is private if not specified.

## Template of a Public Procedure

**Example 15-3 Template of a Public Procedure**

```
RoutineA
;
ProcedureABC(Param1,Param2) [PubVar1,PubVar2]   Public   {
```

Example 15-3 demonstrates the first line of a *Public Procedure*. Note the word "Public" just before the "{".

## Template of a Private Procedure

**Example 15-4 Template of a Private Procedure**

```
RoutineA
;
ProcedureABC(Param1,Param2) [PubVar1,PubVar2]   Private   {
```

Example 15-4 demonstrates the first line of a *Private Procedure*. Note the word "Private" just before the "{".

Most of the following examples use *Public Procedures; Private Procedures* are demonstrated later in this chapter.

# Parameters

Parameters passed by a calling process are always within parentheses.

## Parameters passed by a calling process

**Example 15-5 Parameters passed by a calling process**

```
Do ProcedureABC^RoutineA(Param1,Param2)  ;calling a Procedure
```

The process in Example 15-5 is calling ProcedureABC (contained within routine RoutineA) passing two parameters, Param1 and Param2. This parameter list on the *Procedure* call is known as the *Actual Parameter List.*

Parameters received by a called *Procedure* are always within parentheses.

## Parameters received by a called Procedure

```
RoutineA
    ;
ProcedureABC(Param1,Param2) [PubVar1,PubVar2]  Public  {
```

RoutineA in Example 15-6 contains ProcedureABC, which accepts two Parameters, Param1, and Param2. The names of the parameters in the called *Procedure* and the names in the calling process are not required to be the same. This parameter list on the *Procedure* definition line is known as the *Formal Parameter List.*

---

### "New" command Unnecessary in Procedures

When a Procedure is called with parameters, these parameters are automatically Newed, issuing a New command on the parameters is unnecessary.

Variables created within a Procedure are by default Private, eliminating the need for a New command on new variables.

---

The parameters passed to a *Procedure* are by default *Passed by Value*. This means that whatever changes the *Procedure* makes to the parameters will be lost when the *Procedure* exits.

## Calling a Procedure with Parameters Passed by Value

```
Set Param1=2
Set Param2=3
Set PubVar1=5
Set PubVar2=5
Do ProcedureABC^RoutineA(Param1,Param2)
;
Write !,"Param1: ",Param1
Write !,"Param2: ",Param2

(RoutineA) Param1: NewValue1
(RoutineA) Param2: NewValue2

Param1: 2          ;original value displayed
Param2: 3          ;original value displayed

   = = = = = = = = = = = = = = = = = = = = = = = = = = = = = =

To run this code you must put the code in a routine, save the routine, and then
run the routine from the terminal.

RoutineA
    ;
```

```
ProcedureABC(Param1,Param2) [PubVar1,PubVar2]  Public  {
  ;
  Set Param1="NewValue1"  ;set Param1 to a new value
  Set Param2="NewValue2"  ;set Param2 to a new value
  Write !,"(RoutineA) Param1: ",Param1
  Write !,"(RoutineA) Param2: ",Param2
}
```

Example 15-7 demonstrates calling a *Procedure* with two parameters passed by value. Even though the *Procedure* changes the values of Param1 and Param2, when the *Procedure* exits, those parameters revert to their original value.

## Calling a Procedure with Parameters Passed by Reference

When a *Procedure* modifies parameters passed by reference, these modifications are passed back to the calling process.

**Example 15-8 Calling a Procedure with Parameters Passed by Reference**

```
Set Param1=2
Set Param2=3
Set PubVar1=5
Set PubVar2=5
Do ProcedureABC^RoutineA(.Param1,.Param2)       ;Period before Params, which
;                                               ;indicates passed by
reference
Write !,"Param1: ",Param1
Write !,"Param2: ",Param2

(RoutineA) Param1: NewValue1
(RoutineA) Param2: NewValue2

Param1: NewValue1           ;modified value displayed
Param2: NewValue2           ;modified value displayed

   = = = = = = = = = = = = = = = = = = = = = = = = = = = = = =
```

To run this code you must put the code in a routine, save the routine, and then run the routine from the terminal.

```
RoutineA
   ;
ProcedureABC(Param1,Param2) [PubVar1,PubVar2]  Public  {
  ;
  Set Param1="NewValue1"  ;set Param1 to a new value
  Set Param2="NewValue2"  ;set Param2 to a new value
  Write !,"(RoutineA) Param1: ",Param1
  Write !,"(RoutineA) Param2: ",Param2
}
```

Example 15-8 demonstrates calling a *Procedure* with two parameters passed by reference. Note the "Period" before Param1 and Param2 when calling the *Procedure*. This "Period" is what signifies that a Parameter is passed by reference, there is no other indication. The *Procedure* changes the values of Param1 and Param2, when the *Procedure* exits those parameters do not revert back to their original values, but maintains their new values.

## Calling a Procedure using Default Parameters

In some cases, the calling process may not define all the necessary parameters. When this happens, the called *Procedure* can set a default value for the Parameters.

**Example 15-9 Calling a Procedure using Default Parameters**

```
Set Param2=3
Set PubVar1=5
Set PubVar2=5
Do ProcedureABC^RoutineA(,Param2);Comma indicates no first parameter

(RoutineA) Param1: Default1
(RoutineA) Param2: 3

    = = = = = = = = = = = = = = = = = = = = = = = = = = = = = = = = = = =

To run this code you must put the code in a routine, save the routine, and then
run the routine from the terminal.

RoutineA
    ;
ProcedureABC(Param1="Default1",Param2="Default2") [PubVar1,PubVar2]   Public
{
    ;
  Write !,"(RoutineA) Param1: ",Param1
  Write !,"(RoutineA) Param2: ",Param2
}
```

Example 15-9 demonstrates calling a *Procedure* using Parameter defaults. Notice that the calling process does not define Param1. When ProcedureABC is called, Param1 uses the default value, (Default1) and Param2 uses the value passed to it.

## Calling a Procedure with the wrong number of Parameters

The number of parameters in the *Formal Parameter List* and the *Actual Parameter List* do not necessarily have to match. However, it is good programming discipline to always ensure they match.

## Calling a Procedure with the Actual Parameter List less than the Formal Parameter List

Example 15-10 Calling a Procedure with the Actual Parameter List less than the Formal Parameter List

```
Set Param1=2
Set Param2=3
Set PubVar1=5
Set PubVar2=5
Do ProcedureABC^RoutineA(Param1) ;Actual Parameter List

(RoutineA) Param1: 2
(RoutineA) Param2:
Write !,"(RoutineA) Param2: ",Param2
                         ^
<UNDEFINED>ProcedureABC+3^RoutineA *Param2


   = = = = = = = = = = = = = = = = = = = = = = = = = = = = = =

To run this code you must put the code in a routine, save the routine, and then
run the routine from the terminal.

RoutineA
    ;
    ; (formal parameter list)
ProcedureABC(Param1,Param2) [PubVar1,PubVar2]  Public  {
    ;
  Write !,"(RoutineA) Param1: ",Param1
  Write !,"(RoutineA) Param2: ",Param2
}
```

Example 15-10 demonstrates calling a *Procedure* with a *Formal Parameter List* less than the *Actual Parameter List*. This is a real concern because the called *Procedure* expects that Param2 is defined, and when it attempts to write Param2 the result is an **Undefined Error**.

This would be a good example of using **Default** values for Parameters as demonstrated earlier in this chapter. If *Default Parameters* values are not used, It is good technique to check all expected parameters with *a $Get or $Data* system-supplied function.

## Calling a Procedure with the Actual Parameter List less than the Formal Parameter List

**Example 15-11 Calling a Procedure with the Actual Parameter List less than the Formal Parameter List**

```
Set Param1=2
Set Param2=3
Set PubVar1=5
Set PubVar2=5
Do ProcedureABC^RoutineA(Param1)

(RoutineA) Param1: 2
(RoutineA) Param2:


     = = = = = = = = = = = = = = = = = = = = = = = = = = = = = = = = = =

To run this code you must put the code in a routine, save the routine, and then
run the routine from the terminal.

RoutineA
    ;
ProcedureABC(Param1,Param2) [PubVar1,PubVar2]  Public  {
  Set Param1=$G(Param1)
  Set Param2=$G(Param2)
    ;
  Write !,"(RoutineA) Param1: ",Param1
  Write !,"(RoutineA) Param2: ",Param2
}
```

Example 15-11 demonstrates calling a *Procedure* with a *Formal Parameter List* less than the *Actual Parameter List*. The called *Procedure* does not fail because a *$Get* is issued against the Parameters.

# Public Variables

Now let us consider the *Public Variables* specified in the header line of the *Procedure*. Note the two public variables [PubVar1, PubVar2] in the example below.

## Template of a COS Procedure with Public Variables

**Example 15-12 Template of a COS Procedure with Public Variables**

```
To run this code you must put the code in a routine, save the routine, and then
run the routine from the terminal.

RoutineA
;
ProcedureABC(Param1,Param2) [PubVar1,PubVar2]  Public  {
  Write !,"Param1: ",Param1
  Write !,"Param2: ",Param2
  Write !,"PubVar1: ",PubVar1
  Write !,"PubVar2: ",PubVar2
}
```

In Example 15-12 the variables between the square brackets are public and the *Procedure* has full access to these variables. If the *Procedure* modifies these variables, the modifications are passed back to the calling process.

All other variables not listed within the square brackets are *Private Variables* and the called *Procedure* has no access to them.

## *Calling a Procedure with Public Variables*

**Example 15-13 Calling a Procedure with Public Variables**

```
Set PubVar1=2
Set PubVar2=3
Do ProcedureABC^RoutineA()
(RoutineA) PubVar1: NewValue1
(RoutineA) PubVar2: NewValue2

Write !,"PubVar1: ",PubVar1
Write !,"PubVar2: ",PubVar2
PubVar1: NewValue1        ;new value displayed
PubVar2: NewValue2        ;new value displayed


   = = = = = = = = = = = = = = = = = = = = = = = = = = = = = = =

To run this code you must put the code in a routine, save the routine, and
then run the routine from the terminal.

RoutineA
   ;
ProcedureABC() [PubVar1,PubVar2]  Public  {
   ;
  Set PubVar1="NewValue1"                    ;set PubVar1 to a new value
  Set PubVar2="NewValue2"                    ;set PubVar2 to a new value
  Write !,"(RoutineA) PubVar1: ",PubVar1
  Write !,"(RoutineA) PubVar2: ",PubVar2
}
```

Example 15-13 demonstrates calling a *Procedure* with two Public Variables, PubVar1, and PubVar2. ProcedureABC modifies these variables and the modifications are passed back to the calling process.

---

## *% Variables*

Variables that begin with % are always considered Public.

---

## Private Variables

You may think of *Private Variables* in one of two ways:

➢ Variables created and used outside of the called *Procedure*

➢ Variables created and used inside the called *Procedure*

## Variables created and used outside the called Procedure

Variables created and used outside of the called *Procedure* are not accessible to the called *Procedure* and if the called *Procedure* attempts to access these variables, it will receive an undefined error message.

For variables created and used outside the called *Procedure* that are not included in the *Public Variable List,* the called *Procedure* has no access to them.

**Example 15-14 Variables created and used outside the called Procedure**

```
Set Param1=1
Set Param2=2
Set PubVar1=1
Set PubVar2=2
Set OutVar1=2
Set OutVar2=3
Do ProcedureABC^RoutineA(Param1,Param2)
<UNDEFINED>ProcedureABC+2^RoutineA *OutVar1


    = = = = = = = = = = = = = = = = = = = = = = = = = = = = = = =

To run this code you must put the code in a routine, save the routine, and then
run the routine from the terminal.

RoutineA
    ;
ProcedureABC(Param1,Param2) [PubVar1,PubVar2]  Public  {
  ;
  Write OutVar1
  Write OutVar2
}
```

Example 15-14 demonstrates variables created and used outside the *Procedure*. As soon as ProcedureABC attempts to access a variable created outside the called *Procedure*, it receives an error.

## Variables created inside the called Procedure

For variables created inside the called *Procedure* that are not included in the Public Variable List, it is similar (but not the same) as *Newing* the variables. The variables are destroyed as soon as the called *Procedure* exits.

**Example 15-15 Variables created inside the called Procedure**

```
Set Param1=1
Set Param2=2
Set PubVar1=1
Set PubVar2=2

Do ProcedureABC^RoutineA(Param1,Param2)
Write !,"PrivateVar1: ",PrivateVar1
PrivateVar1:
Write !,"PrivateVar1: ",PrivateVar1
                     ^
<UNDEFINED> *PrivateVar1

Write !,"PrivateVar2: ",PrivateVar2
Quit


    = = = = = = = = = = = = = = = = = = = = = = = = = = = = = = = = = =
```

To run this code you must put the code in a routine, save the routine, and then run the routine from the terminal.

```
RoutineA
  ;
ProcedureABC(Param1,Param2) [PubVar1,PubVar2]  Public  {
  ;
  Set PrivateVar1=1
  Set PrivateVar2=2
  Write !,"PrivateVar1: ",PrivateVar1
  Write !,"PrivateVar2: ",PrivateVar2
}
```

Example 15-15 demonstrates attempting to access variables created inside the called *Procedure*.

## Variables created inside a called Procedure are not passed to other Modules

One of the differences between Subroutines, Functions, etc. and *Procedures*, is that variables created inside the *Procedure* **are not passed to other Modules (Subroutines, Functions or Procedures).**

**Example 15-16 Variables created inside the called Procedure are not passed to other Modules**

```
Set Param1=1
Set Param2=2
Set PubVar1=1
Set PubVar2=2
Do ProcedureABC^RoutineA(Param1,Param2)

(RoutineA) PrivateVar1: 1
(RoutineA) PrivateVar2: 2
```

```
(RoutineB) PrivateVar1:
<UNDEFINED>ProcedureDEF+2^RoutineB *PrivateVar1                    ^


   = = = = = = = = = = = = = = = = = = = = = = = = = = = = = = = = =
```

To run this code you must put the code in a routine, save the routine, and then
run the routine from the terminal.

```
RoutineA
   ;
ProcedureABC(Param1,Param2) [PubVar1,PubVar2]  Public  {
   ;
   Set PrivateVar1=1
   Set PrivateVar2=2
   Write !,"(RoutineA) PrivateVar1: ",PrivateVar1
   Write !,"(RoutineA) PrivateVar2: ",PrivateVar2
   ;
   Do ProcedureDEF^RoutineB()
}


   = = = = = = = = = = = = = = = = = = = = = = = = = = = = = = = = =


RoutineB
   ;
ProcedureDEF() Public  {
   ;
   Write !,"(RoutineB) PrivateVar1: ",PrivateVar1
   Write !,"(RoutineB) PrivateVar2: ",PrivateVar2
   ;
}
```

Example 15-16 shows RoutineA, RoutineB, and the process that calls RoutineA. ProcedureABC
(inside RoutineA) defines two *Private Variables*, PrivateVar1, and PrivateVar2. ProcedureABC then calls
ProcedureDEF (inside RoutineB). When ProcedureDEF attempts to access the *Private Variables*, it
received an error.

The only way for a *Procedure* to pass *Private Variables* is through *Parameter Passing* or including the
variables in the *Public Variable List*.

## Variables created inside the called Procedure passed to other Procedures through Parameters

**Example 15-17 Variables created inside the called Procedure passed to other Procedures through Parameters.**

```
Set Param1=1
Set Param2=2
Set PubVar1=1
Set PubVar2=2
Do ProcedureABC^RoutineA(Param1,Param2)

(RoutineA) PrivateVar1: 1
(RoutineA) PrivateVar2: 2
(RoutineB) PriVar1: 1
(RoutineB) PriVar2: 2


   = = = = = = = = = = = = = = = = = = = = = = = = = = = = = = = = =
```

```
RoutineA
    ;
ProcedureABC(Param1,Param2) [PubVar1,PubVar2]  Public  {
  ;
  Set PrivateVar1=1
  Set PrivateVar2=2
  Write !,"(RoutineA) PrivateVar1: ",PrivateVar1
  Write !,"(RoutineA) PrivateVar2: ",PrivateVar2
  ;
  Do ProcedureDEF^RoutineB(PrivateVar1,PrivateVar2)
}

    = = = = = = = = = = = = = = = = = = = = = = = = = = = = =

RoutineB
    ;
ProcedureDEF(PriVar1,PriVar2) Public  {
  ;
  Write !,"(RoutineB) PriVar1: ",PriVar1
  Write !,"(RoutineB) PriVar2: ",PriVar2
  ;
}
```

Example 15-17 shows RoutineA, RoutineB, and the process that calls RoutineA. ProcedureABC (inside RoutineA) defines two *Private Variables*, PrivateVar1, and PrivateVar2. ProcedureABC then calls ProcedureDEF (inside RoutineB) passing the two Private Variables through the Parameters. When ProcedureDEF attempts to access the *Private Variables*, it is allowed.

## *Variables created inside the called Procedure passed to other Procedures through the Public List*

Example 15-18 Variables created inside the called Procedure passed to other Procedures through the Public List.

```
Set Param1=1
Set Param2=2
Set PubVar1=1
Set PubVar2=2
Do ProcedureABC^RoutineA(Param1,Param2)

  (RoutineA) PrivateVar1: 1
   (RoutineA) PrivateVar2: 2
   (RoutineB) PrivateVar1: 1
   (RoutineB) PrivateVar2: 2
    = = = = = = = = = = = = = = = = = = = = = = = = = = = = = = = = =
```

```
RoutineA
    ;
ProcedureABC(Param1,Param2) [PubVar1,PubVar2, PrivateVar1,PrivateVar2]
Public  {
  ;
  Set PrivateVar1=1
```

```
  Set PrivateVar2=2
  Write !,"(RoutineA) PrivateVar1: ",PrivateVar1
  Write !,"(RoutineA) PrivateVar2: ",PrivateVar2
  ;
  Do ProcedureDEF^RoutineB(Param1,Param2)
}


  = = = = = = = = = = = = = = = = = = = = = = = = = = = = = =

RoutineB
    ;
ProcedureDEF(Param1,Param2) [PrivateVar1,PrivateVar2]  Public  {
  ;
  Write !,"(RoutineB) PrivateVar1: ",PrivateVar1
  Write !,"(RoutineB) PrivateVar2: ",PrivateVar2
  ;
}
```

Example 15-18 shows RoutineA, RoutineB, and the process that calls RoutineA. ProcedureABC (inside RoutineA) defines two *Private Variables*, PrivateVar1, and PrivateVar2. ProcedureABC then calls ProcedureDEF (inside RoutineB) passing the two *Private Variables* through the *Public Variable List*. When ProcedureDEF attempts to access the *Private Variables,* it is allowed. Note that the two *Private Variables* must be in ProcedureABC and ProcedureDEF *Public Variable List*.

In addition, if the original calling process wants to receive back these two variable, it must include them in its *Public List*. In other words, to have access to variables in the *Public List*, the calling and all called Procedures must have the same *Public List*.

## Private Procedures

*Procedures* may be **Public** or **Private**. A *Private Procedure* can only be called from within the Routine in which it lives; a *Public Procedure* can be called from any routine. The first line of the *Procedure* defines whether it is *public* or *private*. Just before the beginning curly bracket it may say "Public" or "Private". The default is private if not specified.

## Calling a Private Procedure

**Example 15-19 Calling a Private Procedure**

```
Set Param1=1
Set Param2=2
Set PubVar1="1"
Set PubVar2="2"
Do ProcedureABC^RoutineA(Param1,Param2)

Set Param2=2
Set PubVar1="1"
Set PubVar2="2"
Do ProcedureABC^RoutineA(Param1,Param2)  ;Calling a Private Procedure
Do ProcedureABC^RoutineA(Param1,Param2)
^
<NOLINE>

  = = = = = = = = = = = = = = = = = = = = = = = = = = = = = =
```

```
RoutineA
    ;
ProcedureABC(Param1,Param2) [PubVar1,PubVar2]  Private  {
  ;
  Set PrivateVar1=1
  Set PrivateVar2=2
  Write !,"(RoutineA) PrivateVar1: ",PrivateVar1
  Write !,"(RoutineA) PrivateVar2: ",PrivateVar2
  ;
}
```

In Example 15-19 the process calls ProcedureABC and receives a <NOLINE> error because ProcedureABC is a *Private Procedure*.

## Return Value

A COS *Procedure* may return a value like a *Function* or not return a value like a *Subroutine*.

### Calling a Procedure like a Function

**Example 15-20 Calling a Procedure like a Function**

```
Set PubVar1=3
Set PubVar2=4
Write $$ProcedureABC^RoutineA(1,2)        ;Called as a Function
(RoutineA) Param1: 1
(RoutineA) Param2: 2
(RoutineA) PubVar1: 3
(RoutineA) PubVar2: 4
1

Do ProcedureABC^RoutineA(1,2)     Called as a Subroutine
(RoutineA) Param1: 1
(RoutineA) Param2: 2
(RoutineA) PubVar1: 3
(RoutineA) PubVar2: 4


    = = = = = = = = = = = = = = = = = = = = = = = = = = = = = = = =
```

```
RoutineA
    ;
ProcedureABC(Param1,Param2) [PubVar1,PubVar2]  Public  {
  ;
  Write !,"(RoutineA) Param1: ",Param1
  Write !,"(RoutineA) Param2: ",Param2
  Write !,"(RoutineA) PubVar1: ",PubVar1
  Write !,"(RoutineA) PubVar2: ",PubVar2,!
  Quit 1
}
```

Example 15-20 calls the same *Procedure* (ProcedureABC) both as a *Subroutine* and as a *Function*. As a reminder, a *Subroutine* does not return a value whereas a *Function* does return a value.

## Miscellaneous Notes on the COS Procedures

➤ Passing by reference is the only way an array can be passed

➤ One may only call a *Procedure* from the top. Access to the *Procedure* through "tag+offset" syntax is not allowed

➤ Duplicate Tags or Labels are not permitted within a *Procedure*

➤ *Indirection* and the *Xecute* command are not directly supported by *Procedures*. They are not executed within the scope of the *Procedure* because by default all variables are *Private*. If you invoke variable X with *Indirection* inside a *Procedure*, it will attempt to invoke a *Public* Variable X instead of your *Private* Variable X. The discussion of *Indirection* and *Xecute* used within a *Procedure* is outside the scope of this book and I refer you to the InterSystems documentation at www.intersystems.com.

## Exercise on a COS Procedure

Write a new COS *Procedure* from scratch. First create a new routine called MyRoutine. Inside MyRoutine include the code to call the *Procedure*. Name your COS *Procedure* "MyProcedure". Pass MyProcedure four parameters of your own naming. Two of the Parameters should be *Called by Value* and two *Called by Reference*. Change the value for all four parameters inside your procedure. Include two variables in the *Public Variable List*. Display the value of the Parameters as well as the variables in the *Public Variable List* before calling MyProcedure, inside MyProcedure and after calling MyProcedure. Compile and run MyRoutine and ensure you get correct output.

Your assignment should look something like the following:

**Example 15-21 Exercise on COS Procedure**

```
MyRoutine  ;
;
Set PubVar1="PubVar1"
Set PubVar2="PubVar2"
Set Param1="Param1"
Set Param2="Param2"
Set Param3="Param3"
Set Param4="Param4"
Write !,"Before calling MyProcedure - Param1: ",Param1
Write !,"Before calling MyProcedure - Param2: ",Param2
Write !,"Before calling MyProcedure - Param3: ",Param3
Write !,"Before calling MyProcedure - Param4: ",Param4
Write !,"Before calling MyProcedure - PubVar1: ",PubVar1
Write !,"Before calling MyProcedure - PubVar2: ",PubVar2

Do MyProcedure(Param1,Param2,.Param3,.Param4)
```

```
Write !,"After calling MyProcedure - Param1: ",Param1
Write !,"After calling MyProcedure - Param2: ",Param2
Write !,"After calling MyProcedure - Param3: ",Param3
Write !,"After calling MyProcedure - Param4: ",Param4
Write !,"After calling MyProcedure - PubVar1: ",PubVar1
Write !,"After calling MyProcedure - PubVar2: ",PubVar2
Quit
```

To run this code you must put the code in a routine, save the routine, and then run the routine from the terminal.

```
MyProcedure(Param1,Param2,Param3,Param4) [PubVar1,PubVar2]  Public  {
  Set PubVar1="PubVar100"
  Set PubVar2="PubVar200"
  Set Param1="Param100"
  Set Param2="Param200"
  Set Param3="Param300"
  Set Param4="Param400"

  Write !,"Inside MyProcedure - Param1: ",Param1
  Write !,"Inside MyProcedure - Param2: ",Param2
  Write !,"Inside MyProcedure - Param3: ",Param3
  Write !,"Inside MyProcedure - Param4: ",Param4
  Write !,"Inside MyProcedure - PubVar1: ",PubVar1
  Write !,"Inside MyProcedure - PubVar2: ",PubVar2
}


Do ^MyRoutine

Before calling MyProcedure - Param1: Param1
Before calling MyProcedure - Param2: Param2
Before calling MyProcedure - Param3: Param3
Before calling MyProcedure - Param4: Param4
Before calling MyProcedure - PubVar1: PubVar1
Before calling MyProcedure - PubVar2: PubVar2
Inside MyProcedure - Param1: Param100
Inside MyProcedure - Param2: Param200
Inside MyProcedure - Param3: Param300
Inside MyProcedure - Param4: Param400
Inside MyProcedure - PubVar1: PubVar100
Inside MyProcedure - PubVar2: PubVar200
After calling MyProcedure - Param1: Param1
After calling MyProcedure - Param2: Param2
After calling MyProcedure - Param3: Param300
After calling MyProcedure - Param4: Param400
After calling MyProcedure - PubVar1: PubVar100
After calling MyProcedure - PubVar2: PubVar200
```

## *Chapter 15 Summary*

In this chapter, we covered Caché ObjectScript *Procedures* as a replacement for user written legacy subroutines and functions. *Procedures* offer significant improvements over older legacy code structures. *Procedures* enforce needed structure, control, and scope that legacy subroutines and functions lack. *Procedures* are closely related to *Object Methods* covered later in this book.

# Chapter 16 Structured Code

This chapter covers the topic of Caché ObjectScript (COS) **Structured Code**. *Structured Code* is a more contemporary way of coding and matches up nicely with other computer programming languages. It provides better readability than the old legacy style of MUMPS programming.

The first chapter introduced *Structured Code* and examples appear throughout this book. This chapter will review *Structured Code* and introduce some new concepts.

## If command with Structured Code

**Example 16-1 If command with Structured Code**

```
Set X=12
If (X=12) {Set X=13}
Write X
13
```

In Example 16-1, notice the placement of the parentheses () and curly brackets {}. The format of this new *Structured Code* using the *If* command is:

> If (decision code) {action code}

The decision code is inside the parentheses, and the action code is inside the curly brackets. If the *decision code* is true, the *action code* executes. Using *Structured Code*, the curly brackets can occur on any line and include multiple lines of code. Also the parentheses are optional. The key to this new structure is readability.

## For Loop commands with Structured Code

**Example 16-2 Loop commands with Structured Code**

```
To run this code you must put the code in a routine, save the routine, and then
run the routine from the terminal.

For I=1:1:3 {
  Write !,"First Level: ",I
  For II=1:1:3 {
    Write !,"  Second Level: ",I+II
  }
}
Write !,"End of For Loop"
```

Example 16-2 demonstrates nested *For Loop* commands with *Structured Code*. Note the placement of the curly brackets, {}. They define the start and end of each section of repeating code.

Example 16-3 Output from Example 16-2

```
First Level: 1
  Second Level: 2
  Second Level: 3
  Second Level: 4
First Level: 2
  Second Level: 3
  Second Level: 4
  Second Level: 5
First Level: 3
  Second Level: 4
  Second Level: 5
  Second Level: 6
End of For Loop
```

Example 16-3 shows the output from Example 16-2.

The next two examples come from Chapter 6 on Global Processing.

## Setting up the TM (Transportation Machines) Global

Example 16-4 Setting up the (Transportation Machines) Global

```
Set ^TM("Cars")="Data"
Set ^TM("Cars","Domestic")=""
Set ^TM("Cars","Domestic","Dodge")=""
Set ^TM("Cars","Domestic","Dodge","Caravan")=""
Set ^TM("Cars","Domestic","Dodge","150 Truck")=""
Set ^TM("Cars","Foreign")=""
Set ^TM("Cars","Foreign","Toyota")="Data"
Set ^TM("Cars","Foreign","Toyota","Tercel")=""
Set ^TM("Cars","Foreign","BMW")=""
Set ^TM("Airplanes")=""
Set ^TM("Airplanes","Military")=""
Set ^TM("Airplanes","Military","Jets")=""
Set ^TM("Airplanes","Military","Jets","F-14")="Data"
Set ^TM("Airplanes","Military","Jets","F-16")=""
Set ^TM("Airplanes","Military","Prop planes")=""
Set ^TM("Airplanes","Military","Prop planes","P-38")=""
Set ^TM("Airplanes","Commercial")="Data"
Set ^TM("Airplanes","Commercial","Jets")=""
Set ^TM("Airplanes","Commercial","Jets","707")=""
Set ^TM("Airplanes","Commercial","Jets","747")="Data"
```

In Example 16-4, we setup the TM Global. The next few examples use this Global.

## Traversing a Global Array with the Do While command and Structured Code

Example 16-5 Traversing a Global Array with the Do While command and Structured Code

```
To run this code you must put the code in a routine, save the routine, and then
run the routine from the terminal.

Set S1="" Do {
   Set S1=$O(^TM(S1)) Q:S1=""          ;get the next S1 subscript
   Write !,"S1: ",S1
   Set S2="" Do {
      Set S2=$O(^TM(S1,S2)) Q:S2=""       ;get the next S2 subscript
      Write !,"  S2: ",S2
      Set S3="" Do {
         Set S3=$O(^TM(S1,S2,S3)) Q:S3=""        ;get the next S3 subscript
         Write !,"    S3: ",S3
      } While S3'=""
   } While S2'=""
} While S1'=""
```

Example 16-5 demonstrates how to access a Global Array with three levels of subscripts with the *Do While* command and *Structured Code*.

Example 16-6 Output from Example 16-5

```
S1: Airplanes
   S2: Commercial
      S3: Jets
   S2: Military
      S3: Jets
      S3: Prop planes
S1: Cars
   S2: Domestic
      S3: Dodge
   S2: Foreign
      S3: BMW
      S3: Toyota
```

Example 16-6 shows the output from Example 16-5.

## Traversing a Global Array with the While command and Structured Code

Example 16-7 Traversing a Global Array with the While command and Structured Code

```
To run this code you must put the code in a routine, save the routine, and then
run the routine from the terminal.

Set S1=$O(^TM(""))        ; set S1 control parameter
While (S1'="") {          ; S1'="" is the first control parameter
   Write !,"S1: ",S1
   Set S2=$O(^TM(S1,"")) ; set S2 control parameter
   While (S2'="") {              ; S2'="" is the second control parameter
         Write !,"  S2: ",S2
```

```
            Set S3=$O(^TM(S1,S2,""))        ; set S3 control parameter
            While (S3'="") {                ; S3'="" - third control parameter
                    Write !,"    S3: ",S3
                    Set S3=$O(^TM(S1,S2,S3))        ;get next S3 entry
            }
            Set S2=$O(^TM(S1,S2))                   ;get next S2 entry
            }
    Set S1=$O(^TM(S1))                              ;get next S1 entry
}
```

The *While* command in Example 16-7 needs some explanation. Since the *While* command checks the control parameter (S1) first, it needs to be set before the *While* command is started. That is why we had to issue a preliminary *$Order* before the *While* command. Then we do our processing for that specific subscript. Before we cycle back up to the *While* command we need to obtain the next subscript and this is done with the *$Order* at the end of the *While* command. Like I said back in Chapter 6, the *Do While* command is more intuitive than the *While* command.

**Example 16-8 Output from Example 16-7**

```
S1: Airplanes
  S2: Commercial
    S3: Jets
  S2: Military
    S3: Jets
    S3: Prop planes
S1: Cars
  S2: Domestic
    S3: Dodge
  S2: Foreign
    S3: BMW
    S3: Toyota
```

Example 16-8 shows the output from Example 16-7.

## *If and Else commands with Structured Code*

**Example 16-9 If and Else commands with Structured Code**

```
To run this code you must put the code in a routine, save the routine, and then
run the routine from the terminal.

; First Method
Set X=1
If X=1 {
  Write !,"X=1"
}
Else {
  Write !,"X is not = 1"
}

; Second Method
Set X=1
If X=1 {Write !,"X=1"}
Else {Write !,"X is not = 1"}

; Third Method
```

```
Set X=1
If X=1 {Write !,"X=1"} Else {Write !,"X is not = 1"}
```

In Example 16-9, note there are three methods of the *If* and *Else* commands, all three methods are identical in execution. It depends upon your preference and readability as to which of the three you use. However, for all three methods; there must be a pair of curly brackets {} after the *If* command and after the *Else* command. Spacing and multiple lines do not matter.  Please note that the only difference between the three methods is spacing and line feeds.

## Nested If and Else commands with Structured Code

**Example 16-10 Nested If and Else commands with Structured Code**

```
To run this code you must put the code in a routine, save the routine, and then
run the routine from the terminal.
```

```
; First Method
 Set X=1,Y=2
 If X=1 {
   Write !,"X=1"
   If Y=2 {
        Write !,"Y=2"
   }
   Else {                          ;this Else matches If Y=2
        Write !,"Y is not = 2"
   }
}
Else {                            ;this Else matches If X=1
   Write !,"X is not = 1"
        If Y=3 {
             Write !,"Y=3"
        }
        Else {                    ;this Else matches If Y=3
           Write !,"Y is not = 3"
        }
}

; Second Method
Set X=1,Y=2
If X=1 {Write !,"X=1"
   If Y=2 {Write !,"Y=2"}
   Else {Write !,"Y is not = 2"}
}
Else {Write !,"X is not = 1"
   If Y=3 {Write !,"Y=3"}
   Else {Write !,"Y is not = 3"}
}

; Third Method
Set X=1,Y=2
If X=1 {Write !,"X=1" If Y=2 {Write !,"Y=2"} Else {Write !,"Y is not = 2"}}
Else {Write !,"X is not = 1" If Y=3 {Write !,"Y=3"} Else {Write !,"Y is not
= 3"}}
```

In Example 16-10 note the three methods of the *Nested If* and *Else* commands; all three methods are identical in execution. It depends upon your preference and readability as to which of the three you use. However, multiple *If, Else's* can be difficult to read regardless of the method you choose and their use restrictive. Please note that the only difference between the three methods is spacing and line feeds.

## *If, ElseIf and Else commands with Structured Code*

Example 16-11 If, ElseIf and Else commands with Structured Code

```
To run this code you must put the code in a routine, save the routine, and then
run the routine from the terminal.

; First Method
Set X=1
If X=1 {
    Write !,"X=1"
}
ElseIf X=2 {
    Write !,"X=2"
}
Else {
    Write !,"X not = 1 or 2"
}

; Second Method
Set X=1
If X=1 {Write !,"X=1"}
ElseIf X=2 {Write !,"X=2"}
Else {Write !,"X not = 1 or 2"}
```

Example 16-11 demonstrates two methods of using the *If, ElseIf* and *Else* commands.

The *ElseIf* command can be repeated many times to cover the appropriate situations, but if you find yourself using too many *ElseIf* commands, perhaps you would be better off using the *$Case* or *$Select* System-Supplied Function. Please note that the only difference between the two methods is spacing and line feeds.

## *If, (multiple) ElseIf and Else commands with Structured Code*

Example 16-12 If, (multiple) ElseIf and Else command with Structured Code

```
To run this code you must put the code in a routine, save the routine, and then
run the routine from the terminal.

Set Day=1
If Day=1 {Write !,"Today is Sunday"}
ElseIf Day=2 {Write !,"Today is Monday"}
ElseIf Day=3 {Write !,"Today is Tuesday"}
ElseIf Day=4 {Write !,"Today is Wednesday"}
ElseIf Day=5 {Write !,"Today is Tursday"}
ElseIf Day=6 {Write !,"Today is Friday"}
ElseIf Day=7 {Write !,"Today is Saturday"}
Else {Write !,"I don't know what day it is!"}
```

Example 16-12 shows the use of *If, ElseIf* and *Else* commands to display the day of the week in *Structured Code*.

*Structured Code* does take some getting used to and experimentation until you know exactly what it is doing. There have been times I have assumed it is doing what it was not. Using a good debugger or adding many write statements to your code is a good idea until you are thoroughly comfortable with it.

## Comparison between Inline Do command and Structured Code

There is one fundamental behavior of the Inline *Do* command that is not the same in *Structured Code*.

**Example 16-13 Simple Inline Do command with For Loop commands**

To run this code you must put the code in a routine, save the routine, and then run the routine from the terminal.

```
For Num=1:1:3 Do
. If Num=2 Quit
. Write !,Num
```

If you save the above code in a routine and then run the it from the Terminal, you should get the following output.

```
1                       ;first 1 is written
3                       ;then 3 is written, 2 is skipped
```

When Example 16-13 is run, two numbers will be written, 1 and 3. The *If* command on line 2 will prevent further execution of the code for Num=2 ONLY. The code will continue for the third iteration and write 3.

What will happen when we rewrite this example using *Structured Code*?

**Example 16-14 For Loop command in Structured Code**

To run this code you must put the code in a routine, save the routine, and then run the routine from the terminal.

```
For Num=1:1:3 {
   If Num=2 Quit
   Write !,Num
}
```

If you save the above code in a routine and then run the it from the Terminal, you should get the following output.

```
1                       ;first 1 is written
                        ;2 and 3 are not written
```

Example 16-14 shows the same *For Loop* command, but this time in *Structured Code*. Note carefully that only 1 is written, 2 and 3 are not. *The Quit* command in line 2 effectively stops the execution of the rest of the loop.

How would this code be rewritten to accomplish the same effect as Example 16-13?

**Example 16-15 Structure Code rewritten**

```
To run this code you must put the code in a routine, save the routine, and then
run the routine from the terminal.

 For Num=1:1:3 {
   If Num'=2 {
      Write !,Num
   }
 }

If you save the above code in a routine and then run the it from the Terminal,
you should get the following output.

1                    ;first 1 is written
3                    ;3 is written but 2 is not
```

In Example 16-15, the *Structured Code* is rewritten to accomplish the same effect as Example 16-13

There is another technique to solve this problem with *Structured Code*, the **Continue** command.

## *Continue command*

**Example 16-16 Structured Code using the Continue command**

```
To run this code you must put the code in a routine, save the routine, and then
run the routine from the terminal.

 For Num=1:1:3 {
   If Num=2 Continue
   Write !,Num
 }
```

Example 16-16 demonstrates the *Continue* command, which in certain cases can replace the *Quit* command used in older code.

The technique of quitting in the middle of an Inline *Do* command is widespread in COS programming. If you decide to rewrite this code into *Structured Code*, bear this important difference in mind.

**Example 16-17 Simple Inline Do command with For Loop command**

```
To run this code you must put the code in a routine, save the routine, and then
run the routine from the terminal.

 Set X=1
 If X=1 Do
 . Write !,1
 . Write !,2
 . Quit
 Write !,3
 Write !,4
 Quit
```

In Example 16-17 the *Quit* command on line 5 only quits from the Inline *Do* command, the code continues to the write 3 and 4.

The next example will show the same code from Example 16-17 but using *Structured Code*.

**Example 16-18 Code from Example 16-17 using Structured Code**

```
To run this code you must put the code in a routine, save the routine, and then
run the routine from the terminal.

Set X=1
If X=1 {
  Write !,1
  Write !,2
  Quit
}
Write !,3
Write !,4
Quit
```

In Example 16-18 the *Quit* command on line 5 stops the entire subroutine. The 3 and 4 after the right curly bracket "}" never gets written.

The rule of thumb: While in *Structured Code*, be very careful how you use the *Quit* command, and test your assumptions.

## *Chapter 16 Summary*

In this chapter, we explored *Structured Code, a more contemporary way of coding. Structured Code* is more readable than older style Legacy code. This chapter gives many examples of *Structured Code*, in traversing down a multi-dimensional Global with the *For Loop, While* and *Do While* as well as nested *If/ ElseIf and Else* structures. *Structured Code* has one significant difference from Legacy code in the way *Quits* are handled in a loop the programmer needs to be aware of. Lastly the *Continue* command is introduced.

*"No one has a finer command of language than the person who keeps his mouth shut." —Sam Rayburn*

# Chapter 17 Writing Robust Code

Chapter 17 covers the topic of **Writing Robust Code** in Caché ObjectScript (COS). *Robust Code* responds well to unexpected events and seldom will break. *Writing Robust* Code takes a special attentive mindset.

---

### Definition of Robust

strong,

hardy in constitution,

constructed or designed to be sturdy,

durable, and able to recover from unexpected conditions

---

This chapter explains how to write Robust Caché code. By applying robust techniques, your code can be more bug free and reliable.

## Programming Goals

A programmers' goal should be to write code that is:

> ➤ Carefully designed
>
> ➤ Logical and methodical
>
> ➤ Thoroughly tested
>
> ➤ Well Documented
>
> ➤ Maintainable
>
> ➤ Readable
>
> ➤ **ROBUST**

## What is Robust Code?

**Robust Code** is able to handle unexpected situations and respond appropriately. Any programmer can write code for anticipated situations. Writing *Robust Code* requires more deliberation, time, and effort.

Much has been written on *Robust Code*. In this chapter the main points are summarized and examples given.

## Overview of Robust Code

One way of writing *Robust Code* is to consider all **Assumptions** and test all **Logic Paths.**

- ➤ To *Assume* is to believe that a thing is true before there is proof
- ➤ *Logic Paths* are paths that code could travel down including all branches of *If* commands, *Case or Select* commands, *Do* commands, etc.

A bug-ridden system continually breaks, produces wrong data, and is generally unreliable. A system written with robust concepts can handle almost any contingency. However, there is a cost to *Robust Code*. When a programmer sets out to consider all logic paths and carefully examines all assumptions, coding and testing time doubles.

Writing *Robust Code* is not easy. Programmers are optimists and assume their code will work correctly. Sadly, this is rarely the case. Not anticipating the unexpected causes grief and embarrassment.

## Mr. Murphy

Let me introduce you to an acquaintance of mine: Mr. Murphy of Murphy's Law fame. Learn to listen to him, and he will save you much trouble. He will be your constant companion in coding. If you pay close attention to him, he will give you clues. Here are some sayings attributed to him:

- ➤ Anything that can go wrong, will go wrong
- ➤ Never assume
- ➤ The subtlest bugs cause the greatest damage
- ➤ A working program is one that has only unobserved bugs
- ➤ Debugging is at least twice as hard as writing the program in the first place

Here are are some sayings of my own:

- ➤ Test every line of code. You may not find anything wrong with it, but the process of testing may reveal other problems.
- ➤ When editing a routine, save it often. There is nothing worse than to agonize over getting the code just right, only to have a brief power hit destroy all your hard work.
- ➤ Document your code as you write it. When you are interrupted, unless you have it documented, you will lose your train of thought. Another advantage of documenting your code as you write it, your documentation will most likely be correct. If your code is not correct, comparing it with your methodical documentation will reveal inconsistencies.
- ➤ When you are having trouble seeing or coding a concept, bring in a second pair of eyes. It is uncanny how easily someone else can spot your trouble.

> After writing a section of code, review it several times. You will find simpler ways of writing it.

> The mark of a well-written system is how easily another programmer can assume maintenance of it.

## Plan of Action

A necessary first step in writing *Robust Code* is having a **Plan of Action.**

Elements of a *Plan of Action* should include:

> Well-defined specifications

> An agreement on **Specification Creep**

> Walkthroughs or peer reviews

> Testing, testing, testing

## Specifications

**Specifications** explain what is to be created or changed. Normally, specifications come from the users of the software and are reviewed by the technical staff. At times, users need help knowing what a system can do. It is imperative that the users and technical staff agree on detailed *Specifications* and not just a "high level agreement."

## Specification Creep

**Specification Creep** is what happens when either the users or technical staff wants to change the specifications. Prior agreement on how to handle these changes is necessary. There also needs to be an agreement as to whether the milestone dates should be adjusted.

## Walkthroughs

**Walkthroughs** should be done at every level of system development. These are peer reviews. They involve the planner showing his plan, logic, module, or code to his peers. His peers then should offer gentle constructive criticism.

## Testing

**Testing** should be done at all levels starting with the smallest logical unit, and progressing upwards. The users also need to devote significant time testing the system. There is nothing worse than to hear, several months after a system has been implemented, that "this system is not what we had in mind."

## Debugging Examples

Here we will go over some sample code. This first example involves accepting input from the user.

### Accepting User Input

**Example 17-1 Customer Procedure version 1**

```
This code cannot be run from the Terminal, it needs to be put in a Routine and
then run the Routine.

Customer  ;
  Write !!,"1 - Customer Registration"
  Write !,"2 - Customer Name Change"
  Write !,"3 - Customer Complaints"
  Read !,"Enter 1,2 or 3 : ",Option

  If Option=1 {Do CustReg}
  Elseif Option=2 {Do CustName}
  Elseif Option=3 {Do CustComplaint}
  Quit
```

How many problems can you spot in Example 17-1? There is the obvious one; no provision is made if the user enters something other than 1, 2, or 3. There is a second problem. What if the user never enters anything? The *Read* command will just sit there forever. Lastly, the modules CustReg, CustName, and CustComplaint are not defined, but we are going to ignore those.

**Example 17-2 Customer Procedure version 2**

```
This code cannot be run from the Terminal, it needs to be put in a Routine and
then run the Routine.

Customer  ;
  Write !!,"1 - Customer Registration"
  Write !,"2 - Customer Name Change"
  Write !,"3 - Customer Complaints"
  Read !,"Enter 1,2 or 3 : ",Option:60          ;give user 60 second time out

  If Option=1 {Do CustReg}
  Elseif Option=2 {Do CustName}
  Elseif Option=3 {Do CustComplaint}
  Else {Write !,"Invalid input" Goto Customer}  ;check for invalid input
  Quit
```

Does Example 17-2 look better? We have taken care of any invalid input with the last *Else* command and have put a time-out on the *Read* command. Are we all set? Well, not really. In online systems, we need to give the user a way out or *exit point*. We could just assume that if the user hits <Enter> they will exit, but we need to be more explicit. Also, if the user never enters an option, this code will go into a infinite loop.

**Example 17-3 Customer Procedure version 3**

```
This code cannot be run from the Terminal, it needs to be put in a Routine and
then run the Routine.

Customer   ;
  Write !!,"1 - Customer Registration"
  Write !,"2 - Customer Name Change"
  Write !,"3 - Customer Complaints"
  Write !,"""Exit"" to quit"
  Read !,"Enter 1,2 or 3 : ",Option:60          ;give user 60 second time out

  If Option=1 {Do CustReg}
  Elseif Option=2 {Do CustName}
  Elseif Option=3 {Do CustComplaint}
  Elseif Option="Exit" {Quit}
  Else {Write !,"Invalid input" Goto Customer}
  Quit
```

In Example 17-3, we have added code to exit the process. Is this a complete bug-free routine? This is a good example of fixing one bug and causing another. Now that the user can enter text as well as numbers, what Case will the user use? It is safest to convert the user input into uppercase.

The situation of causing more bugs when you are fixing one is something all programmers must constantly watch for. This is very problematic! It happens to the best of us quite often.

---

## One of Murphy's Law's

If a computer program has five bugs, and they are all fixed, a sixth bug will promptly appear

---

**Example 17-4 Customer Procedure version 4**

```
This code cannot be run from the Terminal, it needs to be put in a Routine and
then run the Routine.

Customer   ;
  Write !!,"1 - Customer Registration"
  Write !,"2 - Customer Name Change"
  Write !,"3 - Customer Complaints"
  Write !,"""Exit"" to quit"
  Read !,"Enter 1,2 or 3 : ",Option:60   ;give user 60 second time out

  Set Option=$ZCVT(Option,"U")                  ;convert to uppercase
  If Option=1 {Do CustReg}
  Elseif Option=2 {Do CustName}
  Elseif Option=3 {Do CustComplaint}
  Elseif Option="EXIT" {Quit}                   ;check against uppercase Exit
  Else {Write !,"Invalid input" Goto Customer}
  Quit
```

Is Example 17-4 a complete bug-free routine? What if the user leaves for the night, does not log out and this code is running, what will happen? I leave this problem for you to figure out. And, by the way, we still have the infinite loop problem, how would you solve it.

## *Wrong Assumptions*

To *Assume* is to believe that a thing is true before there is any proof.

Here are some common assumptions.

### *Assuming a Variable is not in use*

**Example 17-5 Assuming a Variable is not in use**

```
This code cannot be run from the Terminal, it needs to be put in a Routine and
then run the Routine.

  For I=1:1:10 Do Proc1
  Quit

Proc1     ;
  Write !,"Processing I of: ",I
  Do Proc2
  Quit

Proc2     ;
  For I=1:1:5 {
    Write !,"I number: ",I
  }
  Quit
```

Can you spot the problem in Example 17-5? This code will go into an infinite loop; it will never stop running. The problem, of course, is that the top level uses the variable "I" as its control variable. The *label Proc2* also uses "I" as a control variable. Therefore, whoever wrote this code, *assumed* that the variable "I" was not in use. What is the solution? Whenever you use a common variable like "I", as a control variable; always *New* the variable.

This error was easy to spot, but very often, the two pieces of code are separated by hundreds and may be thousands of lines of code and many routines.

**Example 17-6 Solution to assuming a variable is not in use**

```
This code cannot be run from the Terminal, it needs to be put in a Routine and
then run the Routine.

  New I                          ;New I
  For I=1:1:10 Do Proc1
  Quit

Proc1     ;
  Write !,"Processing I of: ",I
  Do Proc2
  Quit

Proc2     ;
```

```
New I                                    ;New I
For I=1:1:5 {
  Write !,"I number: ",I
}
Quit
```

Example 17-6 demonstrates the solution. Although the *Newing* of "I" at the top is not necessary, it is good programming practice.

## Assumptions concerning the Tab Character

The question mark, also called Tab, is used in the *Write* command to advance a number of horizontal spaces. The Tab character requires an associated integer. The integer is the number of spaces to advance from the start of the line.

**Example 17-7 Wrong Assumption concerning the Tab Character**

```
Write ?10,"TAB",?10,"Character",?10,"Example"
```

What is wrong with Example 17-7? Let us run it and see the results.

**Example 17-8 Wrong Assumption concerning the Tab Character**

```
Write ?10,"TAB",?10,"Character",?10,"Example"
          TABCharacterExample
```

The text in Example 17-8 is pushed together, why? The answer lies in a wrong assumption concerning the Tab Character. The Tab Character advances a number of horizontal spaces from the beginning of the line, not from where the last text stopped.

**Example 17-9 Wrong Assumption concerning the Tab Character, Solution**

```
Write ?10,"TAB",?20,"Character",?40,"Example"
          TAB       Character         Example
```

Example 17-9 demonstrates the correct use of the Tab Character.

## Assumption concerning the User's Response

**Example 17-10 Assumption concerning the User's Response Version I**

```
Write !,"This is an important message to the user!"
Hang 10
```

What is wrong with Example 17-10? Nothing is wrong with the code, but there is a problem in the assumption concerning the user. The programmer is assuming that in the 10 seconds the code is hanging, or waiting, the user will be paying attention to the screen and not doing something else.

**Example 17-11 Assumption concerning the User's Response Version II**

```
Write !,"This is an important message to the user!"
Read !,"Hit <Enter> to to acknowledge this message",X
```

Example 17-11 demonstrates a better way. Using the *Read* command, the code waits until the user acknowledges the message before it continues. However, adding the *Read* command creates another problem. There should be a time out on every read.

**Example 17-12 Assumption concerning the User's Response Version III**

```
Write !,"This is an important message to the user!"
Read !,"Hit <Enter> to to acknowledge this message",X:120
```

Example 17-12 includes a time out of 120 seconds. However, you say, is this not the same as Example 17-10? Yes, something more needs to be done.

If it is imperative that the user see the message you can use *$Test*.

**Example 17-13 Assumption concerning the User's Response Version IV**

```
This code cannot be run from the Terminal, it needs to be put in a Routine and
then run the Routine.

    Set Tries=0
Tryagain
    Set Tries=Tries+1
    Write !,"This is an important message to the user!"
    Read !,"Hit <Enter> to to acknowledge this message",X:120
    If '$Test {
            If Tries>3 Write "at this point do some sort of error processing"
            If Tries'>3 Goto Tryagain
    }
```

Example 17-13 uses a loop and *$Test* to try to ensure the user responds to the message. If the user does not respond to the message then some error processing needs to be done. See Chapter 13 on Error Processing.

## Assumption concerning the Open command

If an *Open* command does not have a time out qualifier and there is a problem the open will just hang.

**Example 17-14 Assumption concerning the Open Command, Solution**

```
Set INFILE="INFILE.TXT"
Open INFILE:"R":10
If '$Test Write !,"Cannot open file: ",INFILE Quit
```

Example 17-14 shows an *Open* command with a time out. If the file does not exist or is protected, it cannot be opened and the *$Test* will be triggered. It is not pleasant to be called into work in the middle of the night for a frozen production system, only to find out someone has failed to put a *$Test* on an *Open* command.

## Assumptions concerning Parameter passing

In other computer programming languages, the calling routine and the called routine both must agree on the number of parameters to be passed. If the correct number of parameters is not passed and received, there is an error. In COS, the calling routine may call the called routine with either more or less than the expected number of parameters within limitations. The real problem here is that the called routine cannot depend upon all parameters being defined.

**Example 17-15 Assumptions concerning Parameter Passing**

```
To run this code you must put the code in a routine, save the routine, and then
run the routine from the terminal. RoutineA and RoutineB need to be in separate
routines.

RoutineA    ;
   Set PARM1=1
   Set PARM2=2
   Do PROC^RoutineB(PARM1,PARM2)
   Quit


   = = = = = = = = = = = = = = = = = = = = = = = = = = = = = = = = = =

RoutineB    ;
PROC(PARM1,PARM2,PARM3)
   Write !,PARM1
   Write !,PARM2
   Write !,PARM3
   Quit
```

Example 17-15 demonstrates incorrect assumptions concerning parameter passing. In this example, RoutineA calls the Label "PROC" in RoutineB passing two parameters. However, the Label "PROC" in RoutineB is expecting three parameters, and when it goes to write the third parameter it will get an <UNDEFINED> *error.*

**Example 17-16 Undefined error from wrong number of Parameters**

```
Do ^RoutineA

1
2

Write !,PARM3
         ^
<UNDEFINED>PROC+3^RoutineB *PARM3
USER 3d1>
```

Example 17-16 demonstrates the <UNDEFINED> *error* from Example 17-15.

## Data Validation

**Data Validation** ensures that a routine operates on accurate and acceptable data. Erroneous, incomplete, or non-existent data will cause frequent problems in a system. Data validation verifies that the data is valid, appropriate, and correct for the application before proceeding.

### When should Data Validation be done?

Data Validation should be done when data enters the system, either through user input, electronic feeds or other methods. If Data Validation is done when data enters the system, processes that follow can assume the data is correct and processing will continue without incident. However, if Data Validation is not complete and comprehensive at the front end, processes that follow will be plagued with data problems.

## Types of Data Items

All permanent data item in a system should be assigned a type:

> Numeric – every data item classified as numeric must be numeric. If an alpha character were to slip into a numeric data type, it would cause havoc

> Integer – integers need to be integers, not a numeric (numbers with decimal places), not alpha characters and not blank

> Alpha characters – these, should be alpha, not numeric, not blank, not unprintable characters or control characters

> Alpha-Numeric – need I say more?

If a data item was classified as Alpha and used as a subscript to a Global, and that data item was blank, the routine would receive a <SUBSCRIPT> *error*. If there was an assumption that a data item was defined and it was not defined, the routine would produce an <UNDEFINED> *error*. If a numeric item had alpha characters in it and arithmetic were performed on it, the item would become zero and the arithmetic results would be suspect.

One of the best weapons in data validation is *Pattern Matching*; it is covered in Chapter 10.

## Chapter 17 Summary

In this chapter, we covered the importance of writing *Robust Code*. First, we defined what is meant as *Robust Code:* 1) Consider all assumptions and 2) Test all logic paths. *Robust Code* also includes elements of a) Careful design, b) Being logical and methodical, c) Thoroughly tested, d) Well documented, e) Maintainable, and f) Readable. Next, we introduced Mr. Murphy and enlisted his help in writing *Robust Code*. A plan of action should include 1) Well-defined specification, 2) An agreement on specification creep, 3) Walkthroughs, and 4) Testing. Finally, we considered an example of accepting user input and demonstrated a series of wrong assumptions.

# *Chapter 18 Miscellaneous Topics*

Chapter 18 contains **Miscellaneous** Topics found in Caché ObjectScript (COS).

## *How can I learn to read Caché ObjectScript code?*

Reading and understanding Caché ObjectScript code (COS) or older MUMPS legacy code is challenging for most programmers. This is especially true when the code uses excessively long lines or is unusually cryptic and contains few comments, but there are a few "tricks of the trade", so to speak.

## *Use a Graphical User Interface (GUI) Editor/Debugger*

One technique in reading Caché ObjectScript code is to use Caché Studio or an online editor/debugger like Serenji (available from GeorgeJames.com). Both of these products color-code different parts of the code for easy identification. Also with Studio or Serenji in debugger mode, you can walk through the code systematically examining variables and observing exactly what various commands do.

When running Caché Studio or Serenji is not an option, another technique is to use *Break* or *ZBreak* commands (see Testing and Debugging, Chapter 14) and walk through the code, however it is more cumbersome than using Caché Studio or Serenji.

## *Set Temporary Globals*

If you have write access to the code you can set temporary Global nodes at various points and see the path the code takes.

**Example 18-1 Setting Temporary Globals**

```
This code cannot be run from the Terminal, it needs to be put in a Routine and
then run the Routine.

START ;
    Set VARA=1,VARB=2,VARC=3
    Do STEP1
    Do STEP2
    Do STEP3
    Quit
STEP1 ;
    Set ^TMP($J,$H,"STEP1")="" ;global to mark this step
    ; . . . normal processing code . . .
    ; . . . normal processing code . . .
    ; . . . normal processing code . . .
    Set ^TMP($J,$H,"STEP1","VARA")=VARA ;global to reveal the value of VARA
    Set ^TMP($J,$H,"STEP1","VARB")=VARB ;global to reveal the value of VARB
    Set ^TMP($J,$H,"STEP1","VARC")=VARC ;global to reveal the value of VARC
    Quit
```

```
STEP2 ;
    Set ^TMP($J,$H,"STEP2")="" ;global to mark this step
    ; . . . normal processing code . . .
    ; . . . normal processing code . . .
    ; . . . normal processing code . . .
    Set ^TMP($J,$H,"STEP2","VARA")=VARA ;global to reveal the value of VARA
    Set ^TMP($J,$H,"STEP2","VARB")=VARB ;global to reveal the value of VARB
    Set ^TMP($J,$H,"STEP2","VARC")=VARC ;global to reveal the value of VARC
    Quit
STEP3 ;
    Set ^TMP($J,$H,"STEP3")="" ;global to mark this step
    ; . . . normal processing code . . .
    ; . . . normal processing code . . .
    ; . . . normal processing code . . .
    Set ^TMP($J,$H,"STEP3","VARA")=VARA ;global to reveal the value of VARA
    Set ^TMP($J,$H,"STEP3","VARB")=VARB ;global to reveal the value of VARB
    Set ^TMP($J,$H,"STEP3","VARC")=VARC ;global to reveal the value of VARC
    Quit
```

In Example 18-1, we set a temporary Global to mark the time we hit each Step and also display the value of various variables to ensure they are what were expected.

The novice COS programmer must realize that reading code is an art that requires practice, as frustrating as that may seem at times. The temptation is always there to rewrite the code in your own style, and although this has been done many times, it is dangerous. First, if you don't understand the code as written, how can you re-write it in your own style? Second, the very process of rewriting the code introduces more errors. When errors do occur, you have no idea if they are part of the original code or part of your rewriting process. Thus, it does nothing to advance your skill in reading and understanding code.

## Function, SubRoutine and $Quit

A *Function* always returns a value and a *SubRoutine* does not.

One of Caché ObjectScripts newer structures, a *Procedure* (covered in Chapter 15) imitates a *Function* and a *SubRoutine*.

However, a technique may be employed whereby a *Function* and *SubRoutine* may imitate each other. It all has to do with a little known special variable, *$Quit*.

## $Quit

**Example 18-2 $Quit**

```
If $Q=1 Quit 1      ;If $Q is 1, then we are inside a function and must
                    ;return a value

If $Q=0 Quit        ;If $Q is 0, then we are inside a subroutine and
                    ;nothing is returned
```

In Example 18-2, the *$Quit* special variable is tested. If we are inside a function, *$Quit* will return a one, and if we are inside a subroutine, *$Quit* will return zero.

If *$Quit* returns a one, we are inside a function and must quit passing back a value. In addition, if *$Quit* returns a zero we are inside a subroutine and quit without passing back a value.

**Example 18-3 $Quit Demonstrated**

```
This code cannot be run from the Terminal, it needs to be put in a Routine and
then run the Routine.

     Do Module()          ;called as a SubRoutine, nothing is passed back

     Write $$Module()     ;called as a Function, 1 is passed back
     1
     Quit

Module()
     ;
     ; do processing
     ;
     If $Q=1 Quit 1       ;If $Q is 1, then we are inside a function and must
                          ;return a value

     If $Q=0 Quit         ;If $Q is 0, then we are inside a Subroutine and
                          ;nothing is returned
```

In Example 18-3, *Module* is called twice, once as a *SubRoutine* and once as a *Function.*

## When should I use Post-Conditionals?

**Post-Conditionals** are appropriate at the beginning of a line when you do not want the *If* command affecting the rest of the line. They are mainly used in older legacy code with longer lines.

**Example 18-4 Post-Conditional If Command**

```
This code cannot be run from the Terminal, it needs to be put in a Routine and
then run the Routine.

Start    ;
    Set X=2
    If X=1 Set Y="ABC" Do NextProc1    ;NextProc1 will not be executed
                                       ;if X is not 1
    Set X=2
    Set:X=1 Y="ABC"  Do NextProc2      ;NextProc2 will always be executed
                                       ;regardless of the value of X

    Quit

NextProc1  ;
    Write !,"NextProc1"
    Quit

NextProc2  ;
    Write !,"NextProc2"
    Quit
```

In Example 18-4, the variable X is set to 2. The first *If* command is dependent up X being 1 and therefore will not be executed. However, the second *If* command, using the *Post-Conditional* method, NextProc2 will always be executed. Whenever a *Post-Conditional* is used, it only applies to the immediate command and does not apply to commands later on the same line. The *Post-Conditional* was used in older code when very long lines were the norm.

**Example 18-5 Other examples of Post Conditional commands**

```
Write:X=1 "ABC"          ;Write "ABC" if X=1

Do:X=1 Proc              ;Do Proc if X=1

Read:X=1 Var             ;Read Variable if X=1

Kill:X=1 Var             ;Kill Variable if X=1

Quit:X=1                 ;Quit if X=1
```

Example 18-5 shows some of the other ways *Post-Conditional* commands may be used.

# When should I use dynamic code?

We write computer routines in English-like text, then the computer converts this text into computer readable instructions. The English-like text is known as **Source Code**. The computer readable instructions are known as **Object Code**. Compilation of *source code* into *object code* is normally done immediately after you save the source code. When you use **Dynamic Code**, compilation of the code is not done until the routine actually runs, which is known as **Run Time**.

*Dynamic code* generation is a way of creating and executing code at run time. This is done in two ways:

> ➤ **Indirection** the at sign, (@)
>
> ➤ The **Xecute** command or just X

*Dynamic code* provides interesting ways of writing routines, but care should be taken; *Dynamic Code* comes at a price. Each time dynamic code is encountered the computer must re-compile this dynamic code, this uses additional computer resources. There are proper uses of dynamic code, but excessive use should be avoided.  With time and experience the COS programmer learns what is and is not a proper use of dynamic code.

## Indirection, the at sign, (@)

*Indirection* is a method of depositing code in a variable and then executing that variable.

**Example 18-6 Indirection**

```
Set TITLE="COS"
Set X="TITLE"

Write @X                 ;Write the variable that X contains, which is TITLE
COS

Write X
TITLE
```

Example 18-6 shows one way of using *Indirection*. What *Indirection* actually does is execute the contents of a variable. The variable X contains another variable, TITLE, and *indirection* says to write the variable that X contains. TITLE contains the string "COS" and this is written. The second *Write* command shows that X still contains the value "TITLE".

**Example 18-7 Indirection Part 2**

```
For X="CNT1","CNT2","CNT3" Set @X=0
Write
```

If you run the above from the Terminal, you should get the following output.

```
CNT1=0
CNT2=0
CNT3=0
X="CNT3"
```

Example 18-7 uses *Indirection* in a slightly different way. The command Set @X=0 sets the variable that X contains to zero. Using the *For Loop* command, the command Set @X=0 is executed once for each unique value of X. Therefore, CNT1, CNT2 and CNT3 all get set to zero, one at a time.

## Xecute Command

The *Xecute* command is similar to *Indirection* but the syntax is a bit different. The abbreviation for the *Xecute* command is just "X".

**Example 18-8 Xecute command**

```
Set TITLE="COS"
Set X="Write TITLE"
Xecute X
COS
```

Example 18-8 shows one way of using the *Xecute* command. The " *Xecute* X" in line three is read: "Execute the code contained in variable X." The code in variable X is "Write TITLE", therefore the variable TITLE is written.

Liberal use of *Dynamic Code* often makes routines more difficult to understand and maintain. Just because you know how to use *Dynamic Code* does not mean you use it at every opportunity.

## Percent sign (%)

In COS systems, you will notice variables, routines and Globals preceded by a percent sign (%). When you see these it means they are used for a special purpose. Normally the system sets up and uses variables, routines and Globals proceeded by a percent sign (%). However, the application programmer is not prevented from setting and using them, but, it is not normally a good idea.

## $Data Revisited

The way the **$Data** works is different depending upon what parameter is passed to it:

**Example 18-9 $Data**

```
Set X="" Write $D(X)
1

Write $D(^A(X))
<SUBSCRIPT>
```

In Example 18-9, when a variable is null, and *$Data* is used on that variable, a one is returned because null is considered a value. However, when the same variable is used as a subscript in an array, the same *$Data* will produce a programming error.

**Example 18-10 $Data**

```
Set ITEM="ABC"
Write $D(ITEM)
1
```

In Example 18-10, the plain vanilla version of *$Data* is demonstrated.

Following is a slightly different use of *$Data* that some programmers seem to be unaware of.

**Example 18-11 $Data revisited**

```
Kill X
Set ITEM="ABC"
Write $D(ITEM,X)          ;value of ITEM put into X
1
Write !,X
ABC
```

In Example 18-11, *$Data* performs two functions, 1) specifying that state of the ITEM variable, and 2) inserting the contents of the ITEM variable (if it has contents) into the variable X. If the ITEM variable does not exist, neither will the X variable.

**Example 18-12 $Data revisited2**

```
Kill ITEM
Write $D(ITEM,X)
0
Write !,X
<UNDEFINED>
```

In Example 18-12, *$Data* interrogates the ITEM variable, which does not exist, and the X variable does not exist as one would expect.

## Job Command – start another process

The **Job** command starts another process that will run in parallel to the one that started it.

**Example 18-13 Job Command to run a Routine: ^RTN**

```
Job ^RTN
```

In Example 18-13, the *Job* command is used to start the ^RTN routine. ^RTN will run in parallel with the current job.

**Example 18-14 Job Command to run a Label: PROC^RTN**

```
Job PROC^RTN
```

In Example 18-14, the *Job* command is use to start the ^RTN routine at the PROC label.

**Example 18-15 Job PROC^RTN(PARAM1,PARAM2)**

```
Job PROC^RTN(PARAM1,PARAM2)
```

In Example 18-15, the *Job* command is used to start the ^RTN routine at the label PROC passing it parameters PARAM1 and PARAM2.

It is difficult to monitor a job that is created by the *Job* command. One way around this is for the jobbed process to periodically write some sort of status message to a Global, then by looking at the Global you can determine the progress.

Long running processes can be divided into specific parts if they are not sequentially dependent upon each other. The *Job* command can be used to speed it up by running the specific parts in parallel. This is known as **Parallel Processing.**

## Chapter 18 Summary

In this chapter, we discussed a number of miscellaneous topics that did not fit into other chapters. In particular:  1) Reading Caché ObjectScript code, 2) Functions, Subroutines and $Quit, 3) Post-Conditionals, 4) Dynamic Code, 5) Percent sign, 6) $Data Revisited, 7) Job command.

"There is no reason anyone would want a computer in their home."

-Ken Olson, president, chairman and founder of Digital Equipment Corporation, in 1977

# Chapter 19 Miscellaneous Examples

Chapter 19 contains **Miscellaneous Examples** of Caché ObjectScript (COS).

## Examples using Strings

### Replace multiple spaces with a single space

**Example 19-1 Replace multiple spaces with a single space**

```
Set X="ABC     DEF"
For  Quit:X'["  "  Set X=$E(X,1,$F(X,"  ")-2)_$E(X,$F(X,"  "),$L(X))
Write !,X
```

If you run the above code from the Terminal, you should get the following output.

```
ABC DEF
```

= = = = = = = = = = = = = = = = = = = = = = = = = = = = = = =

```
Set X="ABC     DEF     XYZ"
 For  Quit:X'["  "   Set X=$E(X,1,$F(X,"  ")-2)_$E(X,$F(X,"  "),$L(X))
 Write !,X
```

If you run the above code from the Terminal, you should get the following output.

```
ABC DEF XYZ
```

In Example 19-1, all the multiple spaces in variable X are replaced with a single space. With the above code, any number of multiple spaces will be replaced with a single space. Note the two spaces after the "For" and after the "Quit".

## Fill a line with words

Sometimes a programmer may be required to write a routine that will fill a line with words without going beyond the right margin. Assume variable A is a list of words separated by spaces and variable X is the line you wish to fill, up to 80 characters.

**Example 19-2 Fill a line with words**

This code cannot be run from the Terminal, it needs to be put in a Routine and then run the Routine.

```
Set A="When in the Course of human events, it becomes necessary for one "
Set A=A_"people to dissolve the political bands which have connected them "
Set A=A_"with another, and to assume among the powers of the earth, the "
Set A=A_"separate and equal station to which the Laws of Nature and of "
Set A=A_"Nature's God entitle them, a decent respect to the opinions of "
Set A=A_"mankind requires that they should declare the causes which impel "
Set A=A_"them to the separation."
Set X=""

For I=1:1:$L(A," ") {
    If $L(X)+$L($P(A," ",I))+1<81 {
    If X="" {
        Set X=X_$P(A," ",I)
    }
    Else {
        Set X=X_" "_$P(A," ",I)
    }
    }
    Else {
        Write !,X
        Set X=$P(A," ",I)
    }
}
If X'="" Write !,X
```

If you save the above code in a routine and then run the it from the Terminal, you should get the following output.

```
When in the Course of human events, it becomes necessary for one people to
dissolve the political bands which have connected them with another, and to
assume among the powers of the earth, the separate and equal station to which
the Laws of Nature and of Nature's God entitle them, a decent respect to the
opinions of mankind requires that they should declare the causes which impel
them to the separation.
```

In Example 19-2, a *For Loop* is used to bounce through the words in variable A. The next word in variable A is concatenated with variable X to determine if the total length is less than 81. If the total length is less than 81 the next word from variable A is concatenated to variable X. Otherwise variable X is written and set to the outstanding piece of variable A. At the end, whatever is left over in variable X is written.

## Count the number of words or characters on a line

It is a simple task to count the number of words or characters on a line or in a string variable.

**Example 19-3 Count Words or characters on a line or in a string variable**

```
Set A="The slow lazy dog could not jump over his bed."
Write $L(A)                 ; number of characters in variable A
54

Write $L(A," ")            ; number of words in variable A
11
```

Example 19-3 demonstrates how to count the number of characters and words in a string variable.

## Scan and replace text in a string variable

**Example 19-4 Scan and replace text in a string variable**

```
Set A="The slow lazy dog could not jump over his bed."
Set FROM="slow lazy"
Set TO="very fast"
Set $E(A,$F(A,FROM)-$L(FROM),$F(A,FROM))=TO_" "
Write A
```

If you run the above code from the Terminal, you should get the following output.

```
The very fast dog could not jump over his bed.
```

In Example 19-4, *$Extract, $Find*, and *$Length* are all used in combination to replace the FROM variable with the TO variable in the string A. The same function can be performed with *$Replace* which is covered in Chapter 3.

## Scan and replace text in a string variable using $Replace

**Example 19-5 Scan and replace text in a string variable using $Replace**

```
Set A="The slow lazy dog could not jump over his bed."
Set FROM="slow lazy"
Set TO="very fast"
Set A=$Replace(A,FROM,TO)
Write A
```

If you run the above code from the Terminal, you should get the following output.

```
The very fast dog could not jump over his bed.
```

In Example 19-5 uses *$Replace* to achieve the same result as Example 19-4.

## Find a value in a List multiple times

**Example 19-6 Find a value in a List multiple times.**

```
Set NUM=$LB("ONE","TWO","ONE","TWO","ONE")
Set X=0 Do {
  Set X=$LF(NUM,"ONE",X) Q:X=0
  Write !,X," ",$LI(NUM,X)
} While X'=""
```

If you run the above code from the Terminal, you should get the following output.

```
1 ONE
3 ONE
5 ONE
```

In Example 19-6, a list named "NUM" is created by using *$ListBuild*. Next, we use *$ListFind* and go through the list and find the three positions for the string "ONE". The variable X is initially set to zero and then set each time the string "ONE" is found so that we don't count the same item twice. As used in the *$ListFind*, the X variable is the starting position of each search.

## Create a line of characters

**Example 19-7 Create a line of characters**

```
Write ! For I=1:1:30 Write "="          ;method one
==============================

Set $P(LINE,"=",31)=""                   ;method two
Write !,LINE
==============================
```

Example 19-7 demonstrates two methods of creating a line of characters.

## Find a variable string with spaces

Here are several methods of discovering if a variable string contains spaces.

**Example 19-8 Find a variable string with spaces**

```
Set X=" "
If X?1" " Write "Hit"        ;pattern matching for one space
Hit

Set X="     "
If X?1.5" " Write "Hit"       ;pattern matching for one to five space
Hit

Set X="          "
If X?." " Write "Hit"         ;pattern matching for any number of spaces
```

```
Hit
```

In Example 19-8, pattern matching is used to see if the variable string contains various number of spaces. Remember that the period (.) in pattern matching represents a range. In the last example, when the period (.) is used alone, as in this case, the range is infinite.

## Find the last piece in a string of pieces

Here is one method of finding the last piece in a string.

**Example 19-9 Find the last piece in a string of pieces**

```
Set X="FIRST^SECOND^THIRD^FOURTH"
Set LastPiece=$P(X,"^",$L(X,"^"))
Write !,LastPiece
FOURTH
```

In Example 19-9, the *$Piece* and *$Length* functions are used to find the last piece in a list of pieces. Here the two parameter format of *$Length* is used to point to the last piece number.

## Find the last piece in a list (created by $ListBuild)

If a list was built by *$ListBuild*, you may use this method to find the last piece.

**Example 19-10 Find the last piece in a list (created by $ListBuild**

```
Set X=$LB("FIRST","SECOND","THIRD","FOURTH")
Set LastPiece=$LI(X,$LL(X))
Write !,LastPiece
FOURTH
```

In Example 19-10, *$List* and *$ListLength* are used to find the last piece in a list built by *$ListBuild*. *$ListLength* replaces the two parameter format of the *$Length* function in Example 19-9.

# Examples using Globals

## Search a Global

**Example 19-11 Traversing a Global using Indirection and $Query**

```
This code cannot be run from the Terminal, it needs to be put in a Routine and
then run the Routine.

Set ^Global="start"
Set ^Global(1)="Sub1=1"
Set ^Global(1,2)="Sub1=1,Sub2=2"
Set ^Global(2)="Sub1=2"
Set ^Global(2,3,4)="Sub1=2,Sub2=3,Sub3=4"
Set ^Global(3)="Sub1=3"
Set ^Global(4)="Sub1=4"

Set X="^Global"
```

```
Do {
  Set X=$Q(@X) Q:X=""
    Write X," = ",@X,!
} While X'=""
```

```
^Global(1) = Sub1=1
^Global(1,2) = Sub1=1,Sub2=2
^Global(2) = Sub1=2
^Global(2,3,4) = Sub1=2,Sub2=3,Sub3=4
^Global(3) = Sub1=3
^Global(4) = Sub1=4
```

In Example 19-11, we use *Indirection* and *$Query* to traverse through an entire Global regardless of the nodes or their levels.

**Example 19-12 Searching a Global for a string**

```
Set ^Global="start"
Set ^Global(1)="Sub1=1"
Set ^Global(1,2)="Sub1=1,Sub2=2"
Set ^Global(2)="Sub1=2"
Set ^Global(2,3,4)="Sub1=2,Sub2=3,Sub3=4"
Set ^Global(3)="Sub1=3"
Set ^Global(4)="Sub1=4"

Set X="^Global"
Set String="Sub2"               ;set String to "Sub2"
Do {
  Set X=$Q(@X) Q:X=""
  If X[String!(@X[String) {      ;does X contain "Sub2" or the contents of X
    Write X," = ",@X,!           ;contain "Sub2"
  }
} While X'=""
```

```
^Global(1,2) = Sub1=1,Sub2=2
^Global(2,3,4) = Sub1=2,Sub2=3,Sub3=4
```

Example 19-12 is the same as Example 19-11 except we are searching the Global for the contents of the variable "string" which is "Sub2."

## Examples using Variables

### Set a List of variables to null

**Example 19-13 Set a list of variables to null**

```
For X="VAR1","VAR2","VAR3" Set @X=""
Write                              ;Write the variable just created
```

If you run the above code from the Terminal, you should get the following output.

```
VAR1=""
VAR2=""
VAR3=""
X="VAR3"
```

In Example 19-13, a *For Loop* command and *Indirection* are used to set a list of variable names to null (""). The variable names are VAR1, VAR2, and VAR3. More variables may be added to the list.

### Set a number of variables or counters to zero

**Example 19-14 Set a number of variables to zero**

```
For X="VAR1","VAR2","VAR3" Set @X=0
Write                              ;Write the variable just created
```

If you run the above code from the Terminal, you should get the following output.

```
VAR1=0
VAR2=0
VAR3=0
X="VAR3"
```

In Example 19-14, a *For Loop* command and *Indirection* are used to set a list of variables or counters to zero. The variable, or counter names, are VAR1, VAR2 and VAR3.

**Example 19-15 Set a number of variables to zero**

```
Set COUNTERS="CNT1,CNT2,CNT3"
For I=1:1:$L(COUNTERS,",") Set @($P(COUNTERS,",",I))=0
Write                              ;Write the counters just created
```

If you run the above code from the Terminal, you should get the following output.

```
CNT1=0
CNT2=0
CNT3=0
COUNTERS="CNT1,CNT2,CNT3"
I=3
```

In Example 19-15, a *For Loop* command, *Indirection*, *$Length* and *$Piece* are used to set a list of counters to zero. Notice how the indirection is used. Also notice the two parameter format of *$Length* which returns the number of pieces in the string. One advantage of this approach is that more counters may be added to the COUNTERS variable name and the *For Loop* command is able to handle it without modification.

**Example 19-16 Set a number of variables to zero, the easy way**

```
Set (CNT1,CNT2,CNT3)=0
Write
```

If you run the above code from the Terminal, you should get the following output.

```
CNT1=0
CNT2=0
CNT3=0
```

It is nice to experiment with *Indirection* to set counters, but perhaps the simplest way is to use the code in in Example 19-16.

## Set a List of variables to zero

**Example 19-17 Set a List of variables to zero**

```
Set COUNTERS=$LB("CNT1","CNT2","CNT3")
For I=1:1:$LL(COUNTERS) Set @$LI(COUNTERS,I)=0
For I=1:1:3 Write !,@$LI(COUNTERS,I)
```

If you run the above code from the Terminal, you should get the following output.

```
0
0
0
```

In Example 19-17, a *For Loop* command and the *List* System-Supplied functions are used to set a list of counters to zero. The *$ListBuild* is used here to build a list. Then *$ListLength* is used with *$List* to set the counters. Notice how *$ListLength* is used as the list limit, similar to *$Length* with two parameters.

## Display a number of variables

**Example 19-18 Display a number of Pets**

```
Set DOG="Rover"
Set CAT="Tiger"
Set FISH="Lamont"
For X="DOG","CAT","FISH" Write !,X,": ",@X
```

If you run the above code from the Terminal, you should get the following output.

```
DOG: Rover
CAT: Tiger
FISH: Lamont
```

In Example 19-18, a *For Loop* command and *Indirection* are used to display a list of Pets. Notice that writing the X variable gives DOG, CAT, and FISH, whereas writing the @X variable gives Rover, Tiger and Lamont, this is a good demonstration of how indirection works.

## Display a number of counters

**Example 19-19 Display a number of counters**

```
Set CNT1=54
Set CNT2=65
Set CNT3=71
Set CNTRS="CNT1,CNT2,CNT3"
For I=1:1:$L(CNTRS,",") Write !,$P(CNTRS,",",I),": ",@($P(CNTRS,",",I))
```

If you run the above code from the Terminal, you should get the following output.

```
CNT1: 54
CNT2: 65
CNT3: 71
```

In Example 19-19, a *For Loop* command, *Indirection*, *$Length* and *$Piece* are used to display a list of counters. Notice how the indirection is used. Also notice the two parameter format for *$Length* which gives the number of pieces in a string. One advantage of this approach is that more variables may be added to the CNTRS variable and the *For Loop* command is able to handle it without modifications.

## Display a List of counters

**Example 19-20 Display a list of counters**

```
Set CNT1=54
Set CNT2=65
Set CNT3=71
Set COUNTERS=$LB("CNT1","CNT2","CNT3")
For I=1:1:$LL(COUNTERS) Write !,$LI(COUNTERS,I),": ",@($LI(COUNTERS,I))
```

If you run the above code from the Terminal, you should get the following output.

```
CNT1: 54
CNT2: 65
CNT3: 71
```

In Example 19-20, a *For Loop* command and the *List* system-supplied functions is used to display a list of counters. *$ListBuild* is used to build the list. Then *$ListLength* is used with *$List* to display the counters. Notice that *$ListLength* is used as the list limit, similar to *$Length* with two parameters.

## Display pieces in a List

**Example 19-21 Display pieces in a List**

```
Set PETS="Rover^Tiger^Lamont^Idiot"
For I=1:1:$L(PETS,"^") Write !,$P(PETS,"^",I)
```

If you run the above code from the Terminal, you should get the following output.

```
Rover
Tiger
Lamont
Idiot
```

In Example 19-21, a *For Loop* command, *$Length* and *$Piece* are used to display the pieces in a list of Pets. Notice the two parameter format for *$Length* which returns the number of pieces in the string and how *$Piece* is used within the *For Loop* command.

## De-piece a record

**Example 19-22 De-piece a record**

```
Set REC="Doe, John^Doe, Jane^Doe, Peter^Doe, Bambi"
Set LN="NAME1^NAME2^NAME3^NAME4"
For I=1:1:$L(LN,"^") Set @$P(LN,"^",I)=$P(REC,"^",I)
Write
```

If you run the above code from the Terminal, you should get the following output.

```
I=4
LN="NAME1^NAME2^NAME3^NAME4"
NAME1="Doe, John"
NAME2="Doe, Jane"
NAME3="Doe, Peter"
NAME4="Doe, Bambi"
REC="Doe, John^Doe, Jane^Doe, Peter^Doe, Bambi"
```

Example 19-22 demonstrates an elegant way of de-piecing a record. The variable REC contains a list of names delimited by the up-Caret (^). Variable LN contains a list of variable names to be assigned to the pieces in REC, respectively. The *For Loop* command then bounces through LN and, in turn, using indirection assigns each name to their respective variable.

## Example of returning a month's name

**Example 19-23 Example of returning a month's name**

```
Set
M=$LB("Jan","Feb","Mar","Apr","May","Jun","Jul","Aug","Sep","Oct","Nov","Dec"
)
Write !,$LI(M,5)
May
Write !,$LI(M,9)
```

Example 19-23 builds a list of month's abbreviations. Then, by just using the month's number, the abbreviations are returned.

## *Chapter 19 Summary*

In this chapter, we covered a number of miscellaneous examples. 1) Replace multiple spaces with a single space, 2) Fill a line with words, 3) Count the number of words or characters, 4) Scan and replace text, 5) Find a value in a List multiple times, 6) Create a line of characters, 7) Find a variable string with spaces, 8) Find the last piece in a string or list, 9) Search a Global, 10) Set a List of variables to null, 11) Set a number of variables or counters to zero, 12) Set a List of variables to zero, 13) Display a number of variables, 14) Display a number of counters, 15) Display a List of Counters, 16) Display a pieces in a list, 17) De-piece a record and 18) Example of returning a month's name.

*"Every man is a volumne, if you know how to read him."*
*– William Ellery Channing*

# Chapter 20 Date and Time System Supplied Functions

## Date and Time Functions and Variables

The primary Date and Time Functions and Variables are:

- ➤ $HOROLOG special variable
- ➤ $ZDATETIME and $ZDATETIMEH Functions
- ➤ $ZTIMESTAMP Function
- ➤ $ZDATE and $ZDATEH Functions
- ➤ $ZTIME and $ZTIMEH Functions

## $HOROLOG

**$HOROLOG** is a special variable that returns two numbers separated by a comma. These two numbers represent the date and time. The first number is the number of days since Dec 31, 1840. The second number is the number of seconds since midnight of the current day. *$HOROLOG* or *$H* plays a role in all System-Supplied Functions used with Date and Time.

---

Note: Many of the examples in this chapter like the one below displays the code you would type in on the Terminal with the results displayed immediately below.

---

**Example 20-1 $HOROLOG or $H**

```
Write !,$H
61305,66339
```

Example 20-1 displays the contents of *$H* for the current date time. The first number is the number of days since Dec 31, 1840. The second number is the number of seconds since midnight of the current day.

# $ZDATETIME

**$ZDATETIME** converts the date and time based on the input date (in *$HOROLOG* format) to a readable format. It accepts a number of input parameters.

## Parameters for $ZDATETIME

Table 20-1 Input Parameters for $ZDATETIME

|  | Parameter | Required/ Optional | Description | |
|---|---|---|---|---|
| 1 | Date and Time | Required | Input date and time, in $HOROLOG format. | |
| 2 | Date format | Optional | Format of the date to be returned. | See Table 20-2 for all possible Date formats. |
| 3 | Time format | Optional | Format of the time to be returned. | See Table 20-3 for possible Time formats. |
| 4 | Time Precision | Optional | Number of decimal places in time to be returned. | |
| 5 | Month List | Optional | List of the month names. | See Table 20-4 for Date formats that can be used with Month List. |
| 6 | Year Option | Optional | Window to display the year in two-digits. | See Table 20-5 for Date formats that can be used with Year Option<br>See Table 20-6 for Year Option formats. |
| 7 | 2 Digit Year Start | Optional | The start of the sliding window to display a two-digit year. | |
| 8 | 2 Digit Year End | Optional | The end of the sliding window to display a two-digit year. | |
| 9 | Minimum valid date | Optional | Lower limit of the range of valid dates. | |
| 10 | Maximum valid date | Optional | The upper limit of the range of valid dates. | |
| 11 | Error Option | Optional | This parameter suppresses error messages associated with invalid or out of range values. | |

## $ZDATETIME with One parameter

> ➤ Parameter one is the input date and time, in $HOROLOG format

**Example 20-2 $ZDATETIME with One parameter**

```
Write $ZDATETIME($H)                ;display current date and time
11/12/2008 11:47:45

Write $ZDATETIME($H+5)              ;display date 5 days from now
11/17/2008

Write $ZDATETIME($H-5)             ;display date 5 days before now
11/07/2008

Write $ZDATETIME("61312,42310")    ;display date and time from literal input
11/12/2008 11:45:10

Write $ZDATETIME("61312")          ;display date from literal input, time
11/12/2008                          ;is blank

Write $ZDATETIME(",42310")         ;display time from literal input. Date of
12/31/1840 11:45:10                 ;blank is assumed zero, thus 12/31/1840
```

Example 20-2 demonstrates several uses of *$ZDATETIME* with one parameter.

## $ZDATETIME with Two parameters

> ➤ Parameter one is the input date and time, in *$HOROLOG* format

> ➤ Parameter two is the format of the date to be returned

## Date Formats

**Table 20-2 Date Formats**

| Date Format | Description |
|-------------|-------------|
| 1 | MM/DD/[YY]YY |
| 2 | DD Mmm [YY]YY |
| 3 | YYYY-MM-DD |
| 4 | DD/MM/[YY]YY |
| 5 | Mmm DD, YYYY |
| 6 | Mmm DD YYYY |
| 7 | Mmm DD [YY]YY |
| 8 | YYYYMMDD |
| 9 | Mmmmm D, YYYY |
| 10 | Day number for the week – 01=Sun, 02=Mon, 03=Tues, etc. |
| 11 | Abbreviated day name – Sun, Mon, Tues, etc. |
| 12 | Full day name – Sunday, Monday, Tuesday, etc. |

Table 20-2 specifies the 12 of the most commonly used Date Formats used with the *$ZDATETIME* second parameter. For more detail, refer to the Caché documentation from InterSystems Inc., *www.intersystems.com*.

**Example 20-3 $ZDATETIME with Two parameters**

```
This code cannot be run from the Terminal, it needs to be put in a Routine and
then run the Routine.

For DateFormat=1:1:12 {
    Write !,"Date Format: ",DateFormat," - ",$ZDATETIME($H,DateFormat)
}
Date Format: 1 - 11/12/2008 12:02:24
Date Format: 2 - 12 Nov 2008 12:02:24
Date Format: 3 - 2008-11-12 12:02:24
Date Format: 4 - 12/11/2008 12:02:24
Date Format: 5 - Nov 12, 2008 12:02:24
Date Format: 6 - Nov 12 2008 12:02:24
Date Format: 7 - Nov 12 2008 12:02:24
Date Format: 8 - 20081112 12:02:24
Date Format: 9 - November 12, 2008 12:02:24
Date Format: 10 - 3 12:02:24
Date Format: 11 - Wed 12:02:24
Date Format: 12 - Wednesday 12:02:24
```

Example 20-3 demonstrates the 12 Date Formats and their outputs.

## $ZDATETIME with Three parameters

➤ Parameter one is the input date and time, in *$HOROLOG* format

➤ Parameter two is the format of the date to be returned

➤ Parameter three is the format of the time to be returned

### Time Formats

**Table 20-3 Time Formats**

| Time Format | Description |
|---|---|
| 1 | hh:mm:ss (24-hour clock) format |
| 2 | hh:mm (24-hour clock) format |
| 3 | hh:mm:ss[AM/PM] (12-hour clock) format |
| 4 | hh:mm[AM/PM] (12-hour clock) format |

Table 20-3 specifies commonly used Time Formats used in the *$ZDATETIME* third parameter. Not all available Time Formats are shown. For more detail, refer to the Caché documentation from InterSystems Inc., *www.intersystems.com*.

**Example 20-4 $ZDATETIME with Three parameters**

```
This code cannot be run from the Terminal, it needs to be put in a Routine and
then run the Routine.
```

```
Set DateFormat=1
For TimeFormat=1:1:4 {
  Write !,"Time Format: ",TimeFormat," - "
  Write $ZDATETIME($H,DateFormat,TimeFormat)
}

Time Format: 1 - 11/13/2008 12:12:40
Time Format: 2 - 11/13/2008 12:13
Time Format: 3 - 11/13/2008 12:12:40PM
Time Format: 4 - 11/13/2008 12:13PM
```

Example 20-4 demonstrates the four time formats and their outputs.

## *$ZDATETIME with Four parameters – Time Precision*

➢ Parameter one is the input date and time, in *$HOROLOG* format

➢ Parameter two is the format of the date to be returned

➢ Parameter three is the format of the time to be returned

➢ Parameter four is the number of decimal places in the time to be returned

**Example 20-5 $ZDATETIME with Four parameters – Time Precision**

```
This code cannot be run from the Terminal, it needs to be put in a Routine and
then run the Routine.
```

```
For Format=1:1:4 {
   Write !,"Time Format: ",Format," - ",$ZDATETIME($H,,Format,2)   ;2 decimal
}
Time Format: 1 - 11/13/2008 12:22:22.00        ;2 decimal precision
Time Format: 2 - 11/13/2008 12:22
Time Format: 3 - 11/13/2008 12:22:22.00PM      ;2 decimal precision
Time Format: 4 - 11/13/2008 12:22PM

For Format=1:1:4 {
   Write !,"Time Format: ",Format," - ",$ZDATETIME($H,,Format,4)   ;4 decimals
}
Time Format: 1 - 11/13/2008 12:22:30.0000      ;4 decimal precision
Time Format: 2 - 11/13/2008 12:22
Time Format: 3 - 11/13/2008 12:22:30.0000PM    ;4 decimal precision
Time Format: 4 - 11/13/2008 12:22PM
```

Example 20-5 demonstrates the Time Precision parameter.

## $ZDATETIME with Five parameters - MonthList

> Parameter one is the input date and time, in $HOROLOG format

> Parameter two is the format of the date to be returned

> Parameter three is the format of the time to be returned

> Parameter four is the number of decimals in time to be returned

> Parameter five is the list of month names

The *MonthList* parameter is valid for Date Formats 2, 5, 6, 7 and 9 only.

## Date Formats that can be used with MonthList

Table 20-4 Date Formats that can be used with MonthList

| Date Format | Description |
|---|---|
| 2 | DD Mmm [YY]YY |
| 5 | Mmm DD, YYYY |
| 6 | Mmm DD YYYY |
| 7 | Mmm DD [YY]YY |
| 9 | Mmmmm D, YYYY |

The first character of the *MonthList* is the delimiter that separates the name of the months.

## MonthList Delimiter

Example 20-6 MonthList Delimiter

```
; Delimiter is a space
Set MonthList=" Jan Feb Mar Apr May Jun Jul Aug Sep Oct Nov Dec"

; Delimiter is ^
Set MonthList="^Jan^Feb^Mar^Apr^May^Jun^Jul^Aug^Sep^Oct^Nov^Dec"

; Delimiter is ~
Set MonthList="~Jan~Feb~Mar~Apr~May~Jun~Jul~Aug~Sep~Oct~Nov~Dec"
```

Example 20-6 demonstrates how to specify and use the delimiter in the MonthList. The delimiter is the first character in the MonthList.

Example 20-7 $ZDATETIME with Five parameters - MonthList

```
;note: 1st character of the variable Months is the delimiter
Set Months=" Mon1 Mon2 Mon3 Mon4 Mon5 Mon6"
Set Months=Months_" Mon7 Mon8 Mon9 Mon10 Mon11 Mon12"  ;string of month names

Set StartDate=$ZDH("1/1/2005")          ;$ZDH, which will be covered later
                                        ;converts a date into $H format

For Date=StartDate:30:StartDate+365 Write !,$ZDT(Date,2,,,Months)
01 Mon1 2005
```

```
31 Mon1 2005
02 Mon3 2005
01 Mon4 2005
01 Mon5 2005
31 Mon5 2005
30 Mon6 2005
30 Mon7 2005
29 Mon8 2005
28 Mon9 2005
28 Mon10 2005
27 Mon11 2005
27 Mon12 2005
```

Example 20-7 demonstrates using a Month string (variable Months) to change the name of the individual months. Note that $ZDH, which will be covered later, converts a date into $H format.

**Example 20-8 $ZDATETIME with Five parameters - MonthList**

```
Set Months=" January Febuary March April May June July"
Set Months=Months_" August September October November December"

Set StartDate=$ZDH("1/1/2005")          ;$ZDH, which will be covered later
                                        ;converts a date into $H format

 For Date=StartDate:30:StartDate+365 Write !,$ZDT(Date,6,,,Months)
January 1 2005
January 31 2005
March 2 2005
April 1 2005
May 1 2005
May 31 2005
June 30 2005
July 30 2005
August 29 2005
September 28 2005
October 28 2005
November 27 2005
December 27 2005
```

Example 20-8 is another demonstration of using a Month string (variable Months) to change the name of the individual months. Note that $ZDH, which will be covered later, converts a date into $H format.

## *$ZDATETIME with Six parameters -Year Option*

➢ Parameter one is the input date and time, in *$HOROLOG* format

➢ Parameter two is the format of the date to be returned

➢ Parameter three is the format of the time to be returned

➢ Parameter four is the number of decimals in time to be returned

➢ Parameter five is the list of month names

➢ Parameter six is the *Year Option*

The *Year Option* may only be used for date formats 1, 2, 4, and 7.

## Date Formats that can be used with Year Options

Table 20-5 Date Formats that can be used with Year Options

| Date Format | Description |
|---|---|
| 1 | MM/DD/[YY]YY |
| 2 | DD Mmm [YY]YY |
| 4 | DD/MM/[YY]YY |
| 7 | Mmm DD [YY]YY |

## Year Option Formats

Table 20-6 Year Option Formats

| Year Option | Description |
|---|---|
| 0 | Years 1900 through 1999 displayed with two-digit years, otherwise use 4 digit years. |
| 1 | 20th century dates displayed with two-digit years. |
| 2 | All years are two-digit years. |
| 3 | *Year Option* of 3 works with Parameters 6 and 7, start and end of two-digit year display. With this option, the start and end date are absolute years. |
| 4 | All years are four-digit years. |
| 5 | *Year Option* of 5 works with Parameters 6 and 7, start and end of two-digit year display. With this option, the start and end date are relative years. |
| 6 | All dates in the current century are two-digit years and all others are four-digit years. |

## $ZDATETIME with Six parameters - Year Option of Zero

Example 20-9 $ZDATETIME with Six parameters - Year Option of Zero

```
Set YearOpt=0     ; Years 1900 through 1999 are displayed with two-digit years,
                  ; otherwise use 4 digit years.

Set Year(1)=$ZDH("1/1/1850")        ;$ZDH, which will be covered later
Set Year(2)=$ZDH("1/1/1950")        ;converts a date into $H format
Set Year(3)=$ZDH("1/1/2050")

For I=1:1:3 Set Date=Year(I) Write !,"Year ",I," - ",$ZDATETIME(Date,1,,,,YearOpt)
Year 1 - 01/01/1850              ;not years 1900 through 1999, four digit year
Year 2 - 01/01/50                ;years 1900 through 1999, two-digit year
Year 3 - 01/01/2050              ;not years 1900 through 1999, four digit year
```

Example 20-9 sets the YearOpt to Zero which displays years 1900 through 1999 with two-digit years, otherwise 4 digit years. Note that *$ZDH*, which will be covered later, converts a date into *$H* format.

## $ZDATETIME with Six parameters -Year Option of One

Example 20-10 $ZDATETIME with Six parameters - Year Option of One

```
Set YearOpt=1      ; 20th century dates are displayed with two-digit years,
                   ; otherwise use 4 digit years.

Set Year(1)=$ZDH("1/1/1850")    ;$ZDH, which will be covered later
Set Year(2)=$ZDH("1/1/1950")    ;converts a date into $H format
Set Year(3)=$ZDH("1/1/2050")

For I=1:1:3 Set Date=Year(I) Write !,"Year ",I," - ",$ZDATETIME(Date,1,,,,YearOpt)
Year 1 - 01/01/1850             ;not the 20th century, four-digit year
Year 2 - 01/01/50               ;20th century, two-digit year
Year 3 - 01/01/2050             ;not the 20th century, four-digit year
```

Example 20-10 sets the YearOpt to One, which displays all 20<sup>th</sup> century years with two-digit years, otherwise four digit years. Note that *$ZDH*, which will be covered later, converts a date into *$H* format.

## $ZDATETIME with Six parameters - Year Option of Two

Example 20-11 $ZDATETIME with Six parameters - Year Option of Two

```
Set YearOpt=2                          ; All years are two-digit years.

Set Year(1)=$ZDH("1/1/1850")           ;$ZDH, which will be covered later
Set Year(2)=$ZDH("1/1/1950")           ;converts a date into $H format
Set Year(3)=$ZDH("1/1/2050")

For I=1:1:3 Set Date=Year(I) Write !,"Year ",I," - ",$ZDATETIME(Date,1,,,,YearOpt)
Year 1 - 01/01/50
Year 2 - 01/01/50
Year 3 - 01/01/50
```

Example 20-11 sets the YearOpt to Two, which displays all years as two-digit years. Note that *$ZDH*, which will be covered later, converts a date into *$H* format.

## $ZDATETIME with Six parameters - Year Option of Four

Example 20-12 $ZDATETIME with Six parameters - Year Option of Four

```
Set YearOpt=4                          ;All years are four-digit years.

Set Year(1)=$ZDH("1/1/1850")           ;$ZDH, which will be covered later
Set Year(2)=$ZDH("1/1/1950")           ;converts a date into $H format
Set Year(3)=$ZDH("1/1/2050")

For I=1:1:3 Set Date=Year(I) Write !,"Year ",I," - ",$ZDATETIME(Date,1,,,,YearOpt)
Year 1 - 01/01/1850
Year 2 - 01/01/1950
Year 3 - 01/01/2050
```

Example 20-12 sets the YearOpt to Four, which displays all years as four-digit years. Note that *$ZDH*, which will be covered later, converts a date into *$H* format.

## $ZDATETIME with Six parameters - Year Option of Six

Example 20-13 $ZDATETIME with Six parameters - Year Option of Six

```
Set YearOpt=6      ; All dates in the current century are two-digit years
                   ; and all others are four-digit years.

Set Year(1)=$ZDH("1/1/1850")     ;$ZDH, which will be covered later
Set Year(2)=$ZDH("1/1/1950")     ;converts a date into $H format
Set Year(3)=$ZDH("1/1/2050")

For I=1:1:3 Set Date=Year(I) Write !,"Year ",I," - ",$ZDATETIME(Date,1,,,,YearOpt)
Year 1 - 01/01/1850               ;Not the current century, four-digit year
Year 2 - 01/01/1950               ;Not the current century, four-digit year
Year 3 - 01/01/50                 ;Current century, two digit-year
```

Example 20-13 sets the YearOpt to Six, which displays all years in the current century as two-digit years, otherwise four-digit years. Note that *$ZDH*, which will be covered later, converts a date into *$H* format.

## $ZDATETIME with Eight parameters - Two Digit Start and End Year

> ➤ Parameter one is the input date and time, in *$HOROLOG* format

> ➤ Parameter two is the format of the date to be returned

> ➤ Parameter three is the format of the time to be returned

> ➤ Parameter four is the number of decimals in time to be returned

> ➤ Parameter five is the list of month names

> ➤ Parameter six is the Year Option

> ➤ Parameter seven specifies start of the sliding window to display a two-digit year

> ➤ Parameter eight specifies end of the sliding window to display a two-digit year

## $ZDATETIME with Eight parameters - Two Digit Year Start and End

Example 20-14 $ZDATETIME with Eight parameters -Two Digit Year Start and End

```
Set YearOpt=3                ;YearOpt of 3, used with Start and End Date

Set Start=$ZDH("1/1/2002")   ;Start Date of two-digit year
Set End=$ZDH("12/31/2005")   ;End Date of two-digit year
                             ;$ZDH, which will be covered later
                             ;converts a date into $H format


For Date=($H-(10*365)):365:+$H Write !,$ZDATETIME(Date,1,,,,YearOpt,Start,End)
12/30/1998
12/30/1999
12/29/2000
12/29/2001
12/29/02                     ;year 2002
```

```
12/29/03                    ;year 2003
12/28/04                    ;year 2004
12/28/05                    ;year 2005
12/28/2006
12/28/2007
12/27/2008
```

Example 20-14 demonstrates using parameters 6, 7 and 8. Parameter 6, the YearOpt is set to three. Parameter 7, the Start Year to display a two-digit year is set to 1/1/2002 and parameter 8, the End Year is set to 1/1/2006. Ten consecutive years are displayed. As you can see, Years 2002 thru 2005 only display a two-digit year.

Parameters 6, 7 and 8 have more functionality, which is beyond the scope of this book. For more detail, refer to the Caché documentation from InterSystems Inc., *www.intersystems.com*

## $ZDATETIME with Ten parameters – Minimum and Maximum Valid Date

➢ Parameter one is the input date and time, in $HOROLOG format

➢ Parameter two is the format of the date to be returned

➢ Parameter three is the format of the time to be returned

➢ Parameter four is the number of decimals in time to be returned

➢ Parameter five is the list of month names

➢ Parameter six is the Year Option

➢ Parameter seven specifies start of the sliding window to display a two-digit year

➢ Parameter eight specifies end of the sliding window to display a two-digit year

➢ Parameter nine specifies the minimum valid date

➢ Parameter ten  specifies the maximum valid date

➢

**Example 20-15 $ZDATETIME with Ten parameters – Minimum and Maximum Valid Date**

```
Write $ZDATETIME($H-5,,,,,,,,$H-3)      ; Minimum Valid Date of $H-3 is greater
^                                       ; than $H-5
<VALUE OUT OF RANGE>


Set Date1=$ZDH("6/1/2008")              ; Minimum Valid Date
Set Date2=$ZDH("5/31/2008")             ; Date to be passed
                                        ; $ZDH, which will be covered later
                                        ; converts a date into $H format


Write $ZDATETIME(Date2,,,,,,,,Date1)    ; Minimum Valid Date of 6/1/2008 is
^                                       ; greater than 5/31/2008
<VALUE OUT OF RANGE>


Write $ZDATETIME($H+4,,,,,,,,,$H)       ; Maximum Valid Date of $H is less
```

```
 ^                                            ; than $H+4
<VALUE OUT OF RANGE>


 Set Date1=$ZDH("6/1/2008")                   ; Maximum Valid Date
 Set Date2=$ZDH("6/5/2008")                   ; Date to be passed
                                              ; $ZDH, which will be covered later
                                              ; converts a date into $H format


 Write $ZDATETIME(Date2,,,,,,,,,Date1)        ; Maximum Valid Date of 6/1/2008 is
 ^                                            ; less than 6/5/2008
<VALUE OUT OF RANGE>
```

> ➤

Example 20-15 demonstrates using the Minimum Valid Date and Maximum Valid Date to verify the correctness of the date being passed.

## $ZDATETIME with Eleven parameters - Error Option

The last or 11th parameter is the **Error Option**. Normally when $ZDATETIME is passed a bad value in one of the first 10 options it will produce an error message. You can override this behavior with the Error Option.

### Error Option to suppress error messages demonstrated

**Example 20-16 Error Option demonstrated**

```
 Set ReturnValue=$ZDATETIME("61312,42310")              ;Call with valid values
 Write ReturnValue
 "11/12/2008 11:45:10"

 Set ReturnValue=$ZDATETIME("-61312,42310")             ;Call with invalid values
 Set ReturnValue=$ZDATETIME("-61312,42310")
 ^
<ILLEGAL VALUE>

 Set ReturnValue=$ZDATETIME("-61312,42310",,,,,,,,,,1)  ;Call supressing error
 Write ReturnValue
 1
```

Example 20-16 demonstrates the error option. Setting the Error Option parameter to one will suppress errors caused by invalid values. A Return Value of one indicates an error; otherwise, the Return Value would be the date.

# $ZDATETIMEH

Whereas *$ZDATETIME* converts the date and time based on the input date which is in *$HOROLOG* format, **$ZDATETIMEH** validates the date and time and converts it to *$HOROLOG* format.

**Table 20-7 Input Parameters for $ZDATETIMEH**

| Parameter | Required/ Optional | Description |
|---|---|---|
| Date and Time String | Required | Input date and time string |
| Date format | Optional | Input date format. |
| Time format | Optional | Input time format. |
| Time Precision | Optional | Number of decimals in the time. |

## $ZDATETIMEH with One parameter

➤ Parameter one is the input date and time as a string

**Example 20-17 $ZDATETIMEH with One parameter**

```
Write $ZDATETIMEH("11/12/2008 11:47:45")      ;validate and convert to $H format
61312,42465

Write $ZDATETIMEH("11/12/2008")               ;Time excluded, assume 0 (midnight)
61312,0

Write $ZDATETIMEH("13/12/2008 11:47:45")      ;invalid month
^
<ILLEGAL VALUE>

Write $ZDATETIMEH("11/12/2008 11:61:45")      ;invalid minutes
^
<ILLEGAL VALUE>
```

Example 20-17 demonstrates several uses of *$ZDATETIMEH* with one parameter.

## Date Formats

| Date Format | Description |
|---|---|
| 1 | MM/DD/[YY]YY |
| 2 | DD Mmm [YY]YY |
| 3 | YYYY-MM-DD |
| 4 | DD/MM/[YY]YY |
| 5 | Mmm D, YYYY |
| 6 | Mmm D YYYY |
| 7 | Mmm DD [YY]YY |
| 8 | YYYYMMDD |
| 9 | Mmmmm D, YYYY |

Table 20-8 specifies the Date Formats used in the *$ZDATETIMEH* second parameter.

## $ZDATETIMEH with Two parameters

> ➢ Parameter one is the input date and time as a string

> ➢ Parameter two is the input date format

## $ZDATETIMEH with Two parameters, date format 1

Example 20-18 $ZDATETIMEH with Two parameters, date format 1

```
                Date Format 1, MM/DD/YY[YY]

Set Date=$ZDATETIMEH("11/12/2008",1)         ;Date Format 1, MM/DD/YYYY
Write Date
61312,0
Write $ZDATETIME(Date)
11/12/2008 00:00:00

Set Date=$ZDATETIMEH("11/12/08",1)           ;Date Format 1, MM/DD/YY
Write Date
24787,0

Write $ZDATETIME(Date)
11/12/2008 00:00:00
```

Example 20-18 demonstrates date format 1. As shown in the second example, when using the MM/DD/YY format a different *$H* value is passed back. The *$H* value passed back (24787) is actually for year 1908. You should always use a four-digit year when possible to avoid this confusion.

## $ZDATETIMEH with Two parameters, date format 2

**Example 20-19 $ZDATETIMEH with Two parameters, date format 2**

```
   Date Format 2, DD Mmm YY[YY]

Set Date=$ZDATETIMEH("12 Nov 2008",2)        ;Date Format 2, DD Mmm YYYY
Write Date
61312,0
Write $ZDATETIME(Date)
11/12/2008 00:00:00

Set Date=$ZDATETIMEH("12 Nov 08",2)          ;Date Format 2, DD Mmm YY
Write Date
24787,0
Write $ZDATETIME(Date)
11/12/2008 00:00:00
```

Example 20-19 demonstrates date format 2. As shown in the second example, when using the DD Mmm YY format a different *$H* value is passed back. The *$H* value passed back (24787) is actually for year 1908. You should always use a four-digit year when possible to avoid this confusion.

## $ZDATETIMEH with Two parameters, date format 3

**Example 20-20 $ZDATETIMEH with Two parameters, date format 3**

```
   Date Format 3, YYYY-MM-DD

Set Date=$ZDATETIMEH("2008-11-12",3)         ;Date Format 3, YYYY-MM-DD
Write Date
61312,0
Write $ZDATETIME(Date)
11/12/2008 00:00:00
```

Example 20-20 demonstrates date format 3 of *$ZDATETIMEH*.

## $ZDATETIMEH with Two parameters, date format 4

**Example 20-21 $ZDATETIMEH with Two parameters, date format 4**

```
   Date Format 4, DD/MM/YY[YY]

Set Date=$ZDATETIMEH("05/12/2008",4)         ;Date Format 4, DD/MM/YYYY
Write Date
61335,0
Write $ZDATETIME(Date)
12/05/2008 00:00:00

Set Date=$ZDATETIMEH("05/12/08",4)           ;Date Format 4, DD/MM/YY
Write Date
24810,0
Write $ZDATETIME(Date)
12/05/08 00:00:00
```

Example 20-21 demonstrates date format 4. As shown in the second example, when using the DD/MM/YY format a different *$H* value is passed back. The *$H* value passed back (24810) is actually for year 1908. You should always use a four-digit year when possible to avoid this confusion.

## *$ZDATETIMEH with Two parameters, date format 5*

Example 20-22 $ZDATETIMEH with Two parameters, date format 5

```
Date Format 5, Mmm D, YYYY

Set Date=$ZDATETIMEH("Dec 5, 2008",5)        ;Date Format 5, Mmm D, YYYY
Write Date
61335,0

Write $ZDATETIME(Date)
12/05/2008 00:00:00
```

Example 20-22 demonstrates date format 5 of *$ZDATETIMEH*.

## *$ZDATETIMEH with Two parameters, date format 6*

Example 20-23 $ZDATETIMEH with Two parameters, date format 6

```
Date Format 6, Mmm D YYYY

Set Date=$ZDATETIMEH("Dec 5 2008",6)         ;Date Format 6, Mmm D YYYY
Write Date
61335,0

Write $ZDATETIME(Date)
12/05/2008 00:00:00
```

Example 20-23 demonstrates date format 6 of *$ZDATETIMEH*.

## *$ZDATETIMEH with Two parameters, date format 7*

Example 20-24 $ZDATETIMEH with Two parameters, date format 7

```
Date Format 7, Mmm DD YY[YY]

Set Date=$ZDATETIMEH("Nov 12 2008",7)        ;Date Format 7, Mmm DD YY[YY]
Write Date
61312,0
Write $ZDATETIME(Date)
11/12/2008 00:00:00

Set Date=$ZDATETIMEH("Nov 12 08",7)          ;Date Format 7, Mmm DD YY
Write Date
24787,0

Write $ZDATETIME(Date)
11/12/08 00:00:00
```

Example 20-24 demonstrates date format 7. As shown in the second example, when using the Mmm DD YY format a different *$H* value is passed back. The *$H* value passed back (24787) is actually for year 1908. You should always use a four-digit year when possible to avoid this confusion.

## *$ZDATETIMEH with Two parameters, date format 8*

**Example 20-25 $ZDATETIMEH with Two parameters, date format 8**

```
   Date Format 8, YYYYMMDD

Set Date=$ZDATETIMEH("20081112",8)          ;Date Format 8, YYYYMMDD
Write Date
61312,0

Write $ZDATETIME(Date)
11/12/2008 00:00:00
```

Example 20-25 demonstrates date format 8 of *$ZDATETIMEH*.

## *$ZDATETIMEH with Two parameters, date format 9*

**Example 20-26 $ZDATETIMEH with Two parameters, date format 9**

```
   Date Format 9, Mmmmm DD, YYYY

Set Date=$ZDATETIMEH("November 12, 2008",9)   ;Date Format 9, Mmmmm DD, YYYY
Write Date
61312,0

Write $ZDATETIME(Date)
11/12/2008 00:00:00
```

Example 20-26 demonstrates date format 9 of *$ZDATETIMEH*.

*$ZDATETIMEH* automatically recognizes several date formats. In addition, *$ZDATETIMEH* recognizes the suffixes "AM, PM, NOON, and MIDNIGHT."

## *$ZDATETIMEH with Three parameters*

> ➤ Parameter one is the input date and time as a string

> ➤ Parameter two is the input date format

> ➤ Parameter three is the input time format

## Time Formats

**Table 20-9 Time Formats**

| Time Format | Description |
|---|---|
| 1 | hh:mm:ss (24-hour clock) format |
| 2 | hh:mm (24-hour clock) format |
| 3 | hh:mm:ss[AM/PM] (12-hour clock) format |
| 4 | hh:mm[AM/PM] (12-hour clock) format |

Table 20-9 specifies some Time Formats used in the *$ZDATETIMEH* third parameter. Not all available Time Formats are shown. For more detail, refer to the Caché documentation from InterSystems Inc., *www.intersystems.com.*

## $ZDATETIMEH with Three parameters, time format 1

**Example 20-27 $ZDATETIMEH with Three parameters, time format 1**

```
Time Format 1, hh:mm:ss (24-hour clock)

Set Date=$ZDATETIMEH("11/12/2008 10:22:30",1,1)      ;hh:mm:ss (24-hour clock)
Write Date
61312,37350
Write $ZDATETIME(Date)
11/12/2008 10:22:30

Set Date=$ZDATETIMEH("11/12/2008 23:22:30",1,1)      ;hh:mm:ss (24-hour clock)
Write Date
61312,84150
Write $ZDATETIME(Date)
11/12/2008 23:22:30
```

Example 20-27 demonstrates calling *$ZDATETIMEH* with a date (11/12/2008), times of 10:22:30 and 23:22:30 and two parameters. The first parameter is for the input date format (MM/DD/YY) and the second parameter is for the input time format (hh:mm:ss - 24-hour clock)).

## $ZDATETIMEH with Three parameters, time format 2

**Example 20-28 $ZDATETIMEH with Three parameters, time format 2**

```
Time Format 2, hh:mm (24-hour clock)

Set Date=$ZDATETIMEH("11/12/2008 10:22",1,2) ; hh:mm:ss (24-hour clock)
Write Date
61312,37320
Write $ZDATETIME(Date)
11/12/2008 10:22:00

Set Date=$ZDATETIMEH("11/12/2008 23:22",1,2) ;hh:mm:ss (24-hour clock)
Write Date
61312,84120
Write $ZDATETIME(Date)
```

*11/12/2008 23:22:00*

Example 20-28 demonstrates calling *$ZDATETIMEH* with a date (11/12/2008), times of 10:22:30 and 23:22:30 and two parameters. The first parameter is for the input date format (MM/DD/YY) and the second parameter is for the input time format (hh:mm - 24-hour clock))

## *$ZDATETIMEH with Three parameters, time format 3*

**Example 20-29 $ZDATETIMEH with Three parameters, time format 3**

```
   Time Format 3, hh:mm:ss (12-hour clock)

Set Date=$ZDATETIMEH("11/12/2008 10:22:30",1,3)      ;hh:mm:ss (12-hour clock)
Write Date
61312,37350
Write $ZDATETIME(Date)
11/12/2008 10:22:30

Set Date=$ZDATETIMEH("11/12/2008 10:22:30AM",1,3)    ;hh:mm:ss (12-hour clock)
Write Date
61312,37350
Write $ZDATETIME(Date)
11/12/2008 10:22:30

Set Date=$ZDATETIMEH("11/12/2008 10:22:30PM",1,3)    ;hh:mm:ss (12-hour clock)
Write Date
61312,80550
Write $ZDATETIME(Date)
11/12/2008 22:22:30
```

Example 20-29 demonstrates calling *$ZDATETIMEH* with a date (11/12/2008), time (10:22:30) and two parameters. The first parameter is for the input date format (MM/DD/YY) and the second parameter is for the input time format (hh:mm:ss - 12-hour clock). Note the adding AM and PM in the second and third example respectively.

## *$ZDATETIMEH with Three parameters, time format 4*

**Example 20-30 $ZDATETIMEH with Three parameters, time format 4**

```
   Time Format 4, hh:mm (12-hour clock)

Set Date=$ZDATETIMEH("11/12/2008 10:22",1,4)    ;hh:mm (12-hour clock)
Write Date
61312,37320
Write $ZDATETIME(Date)
11/12/2008 10:22:00

Set Date=$ZDATETIMEH("11/12/2008 10:22AM",1,4) ;hh:mm (12-hour clock)
Write Date
61312,37320
Write $ZDATETIME(Date)
11/12/2008 10:22:00

Set Date=$ZDATETIMEH("11/12/2008 10:22PM",1,4) ;hh:mm (12-hour clock)
Write Date
```

```
61312,80520
Write $ZDATETIME(Date)
11/12/2008 22:22:00
```

Example 20-30 demonstrates calling *$ZDATETIMEH* with a date (11/12/2008), time (10:22) and two parameters. The first parameter is for the input date format (MM/DD/YY) and the second parameter is for the input time format (hh:mm - 12-hour clock)). Note the adding AM and PM in the second and third example respectively.

## *$ZDATETIMEH with Four parameters*

> Parameter one is the input date and time as a string

> Parameter two is the input date format

> Parameter three is the input time format

> Parameter four is the Time Precision

**Example 20-31 $ZDATETIMEH with Four parameters**

```
Time Format 1, hh:mm:ss.dddd
with Time Precision

Set Date=$ZDATETIMEH("11/12/2008 10:22:30.1234",1,1,4);hh:mm:ss.dddd
Write Date
61312,37350.1234
Write $ZDATETIME(Date,1,1,4)
11/12/2008 10:22:30.1234
```

Example 20-31 demonstrates calling *$ZDATETIMEH* with a decimal time precision of four decimals.

## *$ZTIMESTAMP*

*$ZTIMESTAMP* returns the current date and time with *Coordinated Universal Time* values. The *Coordinated Universal Time* is a standard based *International Atomic Time* based with leap seconds added at random intervals to compensate for the Earth's slowing rotation.

**Example 20-32 $ZTIMESTAMP**

```
Write $ZTIMESTAMP
61306,14437.019298
ddddd,ttttt.ffffff
```

Example 20-32 demonstrates $ZTIMESTAMP.

Where:

> ddddd is an integer for the number of days since December 31, 1840

> ttttt is an integer for the number of seconds since midnight, and

> fff is a varying number of digits specifying fractional seconds

This format is similar to *$HOROLOG*, except for the fractional seconds.

A complete discussion of *$ZTIMESTAMP* is beyond the scope of this book. For more detail, refer to the Caché documentation from InterSystems Inc., *www.intersystems.com*

## *$ZDATE and $ZDATEH*

*$ZDATE* uses the contents of *$H* to display the current date. *$ZDATEH* uses the current date and convert it back to $H format.

**Example 20-33 $ZDATE and $ZDATEH**

```
Write $ZDATE($H)
11/05/2008

Write $ZDATE($H-2)
11/03/2008

Write $ZDATE($H+5)
11/10/2008

Write $ZDATEH("11/05/2008")
61305
```

Example 20-33 demonstrates $ZDATE and $ZDATEH.

## *$ZTIME and $ZTIMEH*

*$ZTIME* uses the contents of *$H* to display the current time. *$ZTIMEH* uses the current time and converts it back to $H format.

**Example 20-34 $ZTIME and $ZTIMEH**

```
Write $ZTIME($P($H,",",2))
13:57:28

Write $ZTIMEH("13:57:28")
50284                          ;number of seconds since midnight
```

Example 20-34 demonstrates $ZTIME and $ZTIMEH.

## Examples using Date and Time

### Elapsed Time

**Example 20-35 Elapsed Time**

```
This code cannot be run from the Terminal, it needs to be put in a Routine and
then run the Routine.
```

```
Set Start=$P($H,",",2)-200
Set Now=$P($H,",",2)
Set Delta=Now-Start
If Delta<10 Set Delta="0"_Delta
If Delta<60 Set Elapsed="00:00:"_Delta
If Delta>59 {
    Set Min=Delta\60,Sec=Delta#60
    If Sec<10 Set Sec="0"_Sec
    If Min<10 Set Min="0"_Min
    If Min<60 Set Elapsed="00:"_$E(Min,1,2)_":"_Sec
    If Min>59 {
        Set Hour=Min\60,Min=Min#60
        If Sec<10 Set Sec="0"_Sec
        If Min<10 Set Min="0"_Min
        If Hour<10 Set Hour="0"_Hour
        Set Elapsed=Hour_":"_$E(Min,1,2)_":"_Sec
    }
}

Write Elapsed
00:03:20
```

Example 20-35 is an example of computing elapsed time. Note, it does not consider if the time crosses midnight.

### DeltaDate Routine

Following is a routine that accepts two date and time parameters and returns the difference or delta in hours, minutes, and seconds.

**Example 20-36 DeltaDate Routine**

```
DeltaDate(HDATE1,HDATE2)
    ;------------------------------------------------------------------
    ;  Examples of calling this routine:
    ;    Write $$^DeltaDate(HDATE1,HDATE2)
    ;    Set DIFF=$$^DeltaDate(HDATE1,HDATE2)
    ;  The HDATE1 and HDATE2 parameters are in $H date and time format.
    ;------------------------------------------------------------------
    New (HDATE1,HDATE2)
    Set HDATE1=$G(HDATE1)
    Set HDATE2=$G(HDATE2)
    Set Day1=$P(HDATE1,",",1)
    Set Day2=$P(HDATE2,",",1)
    Set Time1=$P(HDATE1,",",2)
    Set Time2=$P(HDATE2,",",2)
```

```
Set DeltaSec=(Day2-Day1)*24*60*60+(Time2-Time1)
If DeltaSec<0 Set DeltaSec=DeltaSec*-1
Set DeltaDay=0 If DeltaSec>86399 {          ;86400 seconds in a day
  Set DeltaDay=DeltaSec\86400
  Set DeltaSec=DeltaSec-(DeltaDay*86400)
}
Set DeltaHour=0 If DeltaSec>3600 {
  Set DeltaHour=DeltaSec\3600
  Set DeltaSec=DeltaSec-(DeltaHour*3600)
}
Set DeltaMin=0 If DeltaSec>60 {
  Set DeltaMin=DeltaSec\60
  Set DeltaSec=DeltaSec-(DeltaMin*60)
}
If $L(DeltaSec)=1 Set DeltaSec="0"_DeltaSec
If $L(DeltaMin)=1 Set DeltaMin="0"_DeltaMin
If $L(DeltaHour)=1 Set DeltaHour="0"_DeltaHour
Q DeltaDay_" - "_DeltaHour_":"_DeltaMin_"."_DeltaSec
```

## Calling DeltaDate Routine

The following example calls the *DeltaDate* routine with different date and time formats and displays the return value.

**Example 20-37 Calling DeltaDate Routine**

```
Set HDATE1=$ZDATEH("12/30/1995",5)        ;MM/DD/YYYY format
Set HDATE2=$ZDATEH("12/31/1995",5)
Write !,$$^DeltaDate(HDATE1,HDATE2)
1 - 00:00                                 ;1 day difference

Set HDATE1=$ZDATEH("12/30/95",5)          ;MM/DD/YY format
Set HDATE2=$ZDATEH("12/31/95",5)
Write !,$$^DeltaDate(HDATE1,HDATE2)
1 - 00:00                                 ;1 day difference

Set HDATE1=$ZDATEH("30 Dec 1995",5)       ;DD Mmm YYYY format
Set HDATE2=$ZDATEH("31 Dec 1995",5)
Write !,$$^DeltaDate(HDATE1,HDATE2)
1 - 00:00                                 ;1 day difference

Set HDATE1=$ZDATEH("1995-12-30",5)        ;YYYY-MM-DD format
Set HDATE2=$ZDATEH("1995-12-31",5)
Write !,$$^DeltaDate(HDATE1,HDATE2)
1 - 00:00                                 ;1 day difference

Set HDATE1=$ZDATEH("31/12/95",4);DD/MM/YY format
Set HDATE2=$ZDATEH("30/12/95",4)
Write !,$$^DeltaDate(HDATE1,HDATE2)
1 - 00:00                                 ;1 day difference

Set HDATE1=$ZDATEH("31/12/1995",4)        ;DD/MM/YYYY format
Set HDATE2=$ZDATEH("30/12/1995",4)
Write !,$$^DeltaDate(HDATE1,HDATE2)
1 - 00:00                                 ;1 day difference

Set HDATE1=$ZDATEH("Dec 30 1995",5)       ;Mmm DD YYYY format
Set HDATE2=$ZDATEH("Dec 31 1995",5)
Write !,$$^DeltaDate(HDATE1,HDATE2)
```

```
1 - 00:00                              ;1 day difference

Set HDATE1=$ZDATEH("19951230",5);YYYYMMDD format
Set HDATE2=$ZDATEH("19951231",5)
Write !,$$^DeltaDate(HDATE1,HDATE2)
1 - 00:00                              ;1 day difference

Set HDATE1=$ZDATEH("951230",5)         ;YYMMDD format
Set HDATE2=$ZDATEH("951231",5)
Write !,$$^DeltaDate(HDATE1,HDATE2)
1 - 00:00                                   ;1 day difference

Set HDATE1=$ZDATEH("December 31, 1995",5)    ;Mmmmmm DD, YYYY format
Set HDATE2=$ZDATEH("December 30, 1995",5)
Write !,$$^DeltaDate(HDATE1,HDATE2)
1 - 00:00                                   ;1 day difference

Set HDATE1=$H
Set HDATE2=$H
Set $P(HDATE1,",",2)=$ZTIMEH("14:05",2) ;HH:MM format
Set $P(HDATE2,",",2)=$ZTIMEH("14:10",2)
Write !,$$^DeltaDate(HDATE1,HDATE2)
0 - 00:05                                   ;five minute difference

Set HDATE1=$H
Set HDATE2=$H
Set $P(HDATE1,",",2)=$ZTIMEH("04:05AM",4)    ;HH:MMAM/PM format
Set $P(HDATE2,",",2)=$ZTIMEH("04:05PM",4)
Write !,$$^DeltaDate(HDATE1,HDATE2)
0 - 12:00                                   ;12 hours difference

Set HDATE1=$H
Set HDATE2=$H
Set $P(HDATE1,",",2)=$ZTIMEH("04:05 AM",4)   ;HH:MM AM/PM format
Set $P(HDATE2,",",2)=$ZTIMEH("04:05 PM",4)
Write !,$$^DeltaDate(HDATE1,HDATE2)
0 - 12:00                                   ;12 hour difference

Set HDATE1=$H
Set HDATE2=$H
Set $P(HDATE1,",",2)=$ZTIMEH("04:05:35 AM",4)  ;HH:MM:SS AM/PM format
Set $P(HDATE2,",",2)=$ZTIMEH("04:05:40 PM",4)
Write !,$$^DeltaDate(HDATE1,HDATE2)
0 - 12:00.05                                ;12 hour and 5 sec difference
```

Example 20-37 contains multiple calls to the *DeltaDate* routine passing it different formats of date and time.

## *Chapter 20 Summary*

Chapter 20 on Date and Time explains the $HOROLOG Special Variable upon which Caché basis it Date and Time calculations. It then goes one to explain how to use: 1) $ZDATETIME, 2) $ZDATETIMEH, 3) $ZTIMESTAMP, 4) $ZDATE and 5) $ZDATEH with all it various parameters and formats. It also includes a DeltaDate routine to compare two date/times.

# Chapter 21 Object Technology

# *Introduction*

Chapter 21 covers **Object Technology** as used in InterSystem's Caché. *Object Technology* is a complicated and still emerging field in programming. This book does not purport to teach the entire range of *Object Technology,* it is beyond its scope. The reader is encouraged to obtain several good books on *Object Technology*.

Using *Object Technology* to design a system is a paradigm shift in thinking from traditional system design. With traditional system design the data is separated from its processing. Data and processing are normally related since processing modifies the data. *Object Technology* is an attempt to marry the processing with the data. This "marriage" of processing and data is defined as self-contained entities referred to as "**objects**."

For example, suppose we have procedures for changing a car's tires; in object oriented programming the procedures would already know the car's specifications. Data (tires) and processing (how to change the tire) are married together in the *object*.

Three features of *Object Technology* or object-oriented programming are:

➢ Encapsulation

➢ Inheritance and

➢ Polymorphism

## *Encapsulation*

Encapsulation may be thought of as the creation of self-contained modules that marry processing to data. These are called **Classes** and one instance of a class is an **Object**. An *Object* is roughly analogous to a record in a file that has a number of fields. Encapsulation enforces code modularity through **Methods** (more on Methods later).

## *Inheritance*

*Classes* are created in hierarchies. *Methods* in one *Class* can be passed down to other *Classes*. This means that a function in one *Class* can be passed down to another *Class* eliminating redundancy. Then the *Class* that the *Method* is passed down to can modify it to suit its own purposes, this is what is known as *Polymorphism*.

## *Polymorphism*

Poly – many, morphism – change. This allows *Classes* to inherit a *Method* from another *Class*, changing it for its own purposes. Let's go back to the changing a car's tire example. A *Class* further up in the hierarchy can have the general steps to changing a tire, a *Method* can inherit the steps and modify them for its own purpose.

"There are persons who constantly clamor. They complain of oppression, speculation, and pernicious influence of wealth. They cry out loudly against all banks and corporations, and a means by which small capitalists become united in order to produce important and beneficial results. They carry on mad hostility against all established institutions. They would choke the fountain of human civilization."

\- Daniel Webster

Illustration 21-1 Class Hierarchy, Inheritance and Polymorphism

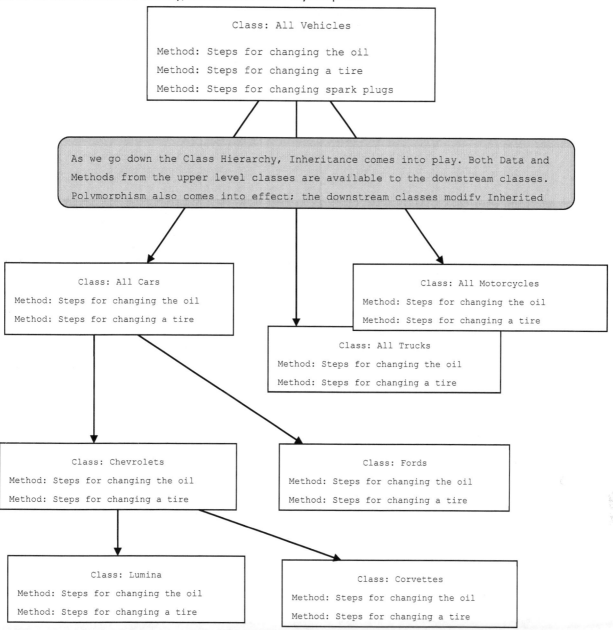

Illustration 21-1 attempts to show graphically how Class *Hierarchy*, *Inheritance*, and *Polymorphism* work. As previously stated, these classes are in a *Hierarchy* with information flowing from the top classes to the lower classes. Both data and methods (code) from the upper classes are available to the lower classes. As the lower classes have access to this data, they are said to inherit from the upper classes, hence the name Class *Hierarchy*. *Methods* from the upper classes are also available to the lower classes, but the lower classes may alter the methods for their own purposes, this is what is known as *Polymorphism*.

One of the differences between *Methods* and Legacy MUMPS routines, is that all variables created inside a *Method* are by default private and do not exist outside the *Method*. It is said that the *Method* Encapsulates data, hence the term previously stated; *Encapsulation*.

This book does not cover *Object Technology* thoroughly or in detail. What it attempts to do is give examples as to how InterSystems has implemented Objects through Caché.

As has been our style, we will attempt to illustrate concepts by use of examples. We will consider the very basics of *Object Technology* as it applies specifically to Caché. We will start with a Caché Object Class or just a Caché Class.

## *Object Class or Class*

An **Object Class OR Class** is a template or blueprint from which **Objects** are created. A *Class* also contains Metadata that controls how objects behave.

Metadata is loosely defined as data about data. It controls how data is defined, structured and updated.

A *Class* contains two major components:

> ➤ One or more *Object Properties* (data)

> ➤ One or more *Methods* (code)

One of the main aims of *Object Technology* is to tie together data and the code that modifies it.

A *Class* also contains a number of other components:

> ➤ Tables – one way a *Class* is projected or represented

> ➤ Parameters – modify the behavior of a *Class*

> ➤ Queries – a special type of *Method*

> ➤ Indexes – or data indices

> ➤ Triggers - precursor of some action

> ➤ Foreign Keys – a type of Index

> ➤ Storage Specifications – how the *Objects* are stored

> ➤ SQL – Structured Query Language - used with *Tables*

## *Object(s)*

An **OBJECT** represents data, a person's name is data, and a car's speed is also considered data. Data is something tangible that can be quantified with words.

## *Method(s)*

**Methods** represent the software necessary to change the *Object* or data. A procedure for modifying a person's name would be one example of a *Method*.

## Table(s)

A TABLE in Caché is another way of representing or *Projecting* Objects or data.

## A simple table of rows and columns

Table 21-1 simple table with rows and columns

| | | | |
|---|---|---|---|
| | | | |
| | | | |
| | | | |

Table 21-1, has a simple table with rows and columns. For the sake of simplicity:

- ➢ think of the whole table as a *projection* of a *Class*
- ➢ think of a Row as an *Object*
- ➢ think of the Columns as *Object Properties*
- ➢ think of a cell as an individual instantiation of an Object Property which contains real data

Now let's take this simple table a step further.

## A Class (Table) of People

Table 21-2 A Class (Table) of People

| Person Name | Person's Date of Birth | Person's Sex | Person's Address |
|---|---|---|---|
| Ben Dover | 5/5/1970 | M | 123 Main St. Somewhere |
| Ilene Dover | 10/2/1972 | F | 456 Simple Rd Anywhere |
| Jack Snow | 3/3/1956 | M | 789 First St. Sometown |

Table 21-2 we have:

- ➢ A *Class* or Table of People
- ➢ In this class we have three *Objects*: the rows containing Ben Dover, Ilene Dover and Jack Snow
- ➢ Each of the three objects has the same *Object Properties*, Name, Date of Birth, Sex and Address. And each of the *Object Properties* contains real substantial data

Note that each object or row has the same list of *Object Properties*. The Class acts as a template and contains the same *Object Properties* for each of its Objects, whereas the actual data for each of the *Object Properties* is specific to the Object or Person.

## Methods (ways of changing the value of Object Properties)

An *Object Class* also contains *Methods*, or ways of changing the value of the *Object Properties*. The *Method* is applied to all properties in the same way. The same method we apply to changing Ben's address we must also apply to changing Jack's address. We would have a separate method for each of the *Properties*; a *Method* for changing a Name, another *Method* for changing the address. But whatever *Method* is developed for changing an address must be applied to all addresses in the class.

## Instance Methods

So *Methods* are tied to *Object Properties*. This is a key concept in *Object Technology*. And the *Methods* that are tied to *Object Properties* are referred to as **Instance Methods**, because they are tied to the instantiation of an Object Property. Now the word "instantiate" is thrown around by the heavies in the Object world with different variations of meanings. The meaning of instantiate is to represent by an instance, this is not much help however. Think of an Object instantiation as roughly analogous to having a file open and having just read a specific record, the fields are ready for processing.

However, there is another type of *Method*.

## Class Methods

**Class Methods**, unlike *Instance Methods* are not restricted to *Object Properties*, but have greater latitude in what they can modify.

## Terminology

Here are some terms you will need in the chapters that follow.

## Object Id

An **Object ID** is a unique data item used to identify an *Object* in a *Class*. It also may be referred to as a *Key*.

Table 21-3 A Class (Table) of People with Object Ids

| Object ID | Person Name | Person's Date of Birth | Person's Sex | Person's Address |
|-----------|-------------|------------------------|--------------|------------------|
| 1 | Ben Dover | 5/5/1970 | M | 123 Main St. Somewhere |
| 2 | Ilene Dover | 10/2/1972 | F | 456 Simple Rd Anywhere |
| 3 | Jack Snow | 3/3/1956 | M | 789 First St. Sometown |

In Table 21-3, we have added an *Object Id* to each of the Objects. Once assigned, an *Object Id* never changes.

In Caché Object Technology, *Object Ids* are represented in several ways:

> **Oref** (Object Reference) – represents a specific, in-memory Class and Object. It also provides access to *Object Properties* and *Methods* through *Instance Methods*

> **Oid** (Object Id) – uniquely identifies an object stored on disk. Once an object has received an *Oid*, it does not change

> **Id** – (Object Identifier) - uniquely identifies an object. It does not include any class information. The *Id* cannot be changed. If it helps, you can think of an *Id* as the Global subscript

> **Key** – a more generic way of referring to *Ids*

## *Direct Global Manipulation*

There are some legacy MUMPS programmers, who, when they come to Caché Objects, continue to write programs the way they use to by directly accessing Globals. This is not necessary, and in fact, can cause problems. While programming in Caché Objects, direct Global manipulation is not necessary, even reading a Global directly is not required. Begin using Dynamic SQL (Chapter 23) to read your Globals and either SQL or setting Object properties to save your data. Caché Objects does its own Global access and manipulation and if you are also doing it, it can cause serious problems.

## *Chapter 21 Summary*

In this chapter, we briefly introduce *Object Technology*. *Object Technology* is a complicated and still emerging field in programming, it is a paradigm shift in thinking for most programmers. The concepts of *Encapsulation*, *Inheritance* and *Polymorphism* are introduced. *Object Technology* is an attempt to marry the processing with the data. This "marriage" of processing and data is defined as self-contained entities referred to as "Objects."

The Object Class contains Properties and Methods; Properties being the data and Methods being the code that modified the data. Methods can be of two types: Instance Methods and Class Methods. Objects are accessed in one of three ways: Oref, Oid and Id.

A warning is given against direct Global manipulation.

*"A proud man is always looking down on things and people; and, of course, as long as you are looking down, you cannot see something that is above you."*
— C.S. Lewis, Mere Christianity

# Chapter 22 Object Class & Properties

Chapter 22 expands upon chapter 21 on **Object Technology** as used in Caché ObjectScript (COS) to process Caché Classes and Object Properties.

## Object Class

An **Object Class** is a template or blueprint from which *Objects* are created. It also contains metadata that controls how objects behave.

## Objects

An **Object** is a data item created based on the specifications of the *Object Class* to which it belongs.

## Object Properties

An **Object Property** is one Attribute of an Object. An Object may have many Attributes.

If you are new to *Object Oriented Programming,* these definitions may seem unsatisfactory, but using Objects is an acquired taste, so to speak. Classes and Objects will become more understandable as you work with them. Let us start with Caché by defining a Class of "Actors" with an Object Property of "Name" (Name of the Actors). This Class of "Actors" will be used in a number of chapters that follow.

## Defining a Class of Actors

The easiest way to create a class is by using the *Caché Studio* application from the *Caché Cube* software. If you do not have the Caché Cube on your PC or computer, you can download a free copy of Caché for personal evaluation from www.intersytems.com.

After starting up Caché, click on Studio from the Caché Cube (a small blue cube in your system tray). In Caché Studio click on **File -> New,** then select **Caché Class Definition,** and follow the prompts. Caché Studio includes helpful wizards in creating Classes, Objects Properties and Methods, etc.

A *Package* name is a way of grouping common classes together. Specify a *Package* name of *MyPackage* and a Class name of *Actor*. Select a Class Type of **Persistent** (Persistent means it will be stored on disk) and take the defaults for the rest of the wizard.

From the top row in Studio, click on **Class -> Add -> Property.** Call your new property "Name" with a type of "%String." Your new class should look like the one in Example 22-1.

## Class and Object Definition for MyPackage.Actor

**Example 22-1 Class and Object Definition for MyPackage.Actor**

```
Class MyPackage.Actor Extends %Persistent
{

Property Name As %String;

}
```

Example 22-1 defines the class *MyPackage.Actor* with an Object Property called *Name*. From the top row in Studio, click on **Build** -> **Compile** to compile the class.

---

# *Types of Classes*

Classes are of several basic types, they are:

Data Type Classes – strings, integers, dates, etc.

Object Classes:

Persistent Object Class – data stored on disk

Serial Object Class – data embedded with other objects

Transient Object Class – exist only in memory

---

## Object Properties

**Object Properties** are of several basic types, they include:

> Data Type - strings, integers, dates, etc. or other classes

> References to Persistent Objects – these Properties point to or reference other Persistent Objects in another class

> References to Embedded Objects – these Properties point to or reference Embedded Objects that reside (or are embedded) in the current class

We will cover each of the *Object Properties* types in turn.

## Data Type Classes

Our first example in this chapter used the *Name property* in the *Actor Class*. *Name* uses a *Data Type* of *%String*. More data types are available such as: *%Binary, %Boolean, %Currency, %Date, %Float (a floating point value), %Integer, %List, %Name, %Numeric, %Status (an error status), %String, %Time and %TimeStamp*. Chapter 24 expands upon *Data Type Classes*.

So far, we have created a *Name Property*; this is our *Object Property* of *Data Type %String*, or Literal Value.

**Table 22-1 Object Properties**

| Object Property | Data Type | Name we chose |
|---|---|---|
| Data Type | %String | Name |

## Populating the "Name" Object Property

Populating the *Name* Property requires several steps:

➢ Create a new blank **Object Reference**, or **Oref** as it is called when in memory

➢ Add a value to the *Object Property*, an actual name

➢ Save the *Oref* to disk

➢ Write out the system assigned **Id**, or **Object Id**

We are using names of famous actors as our name values. We build on the MyPackage.Actor Class throughout the next few chapters.

**Example 22-2 Populating the "Name" Object Property**

```
The "Name" Property is defined as a Data Type Class

To run this code you must put the code in a routine, save the routine, and then
run the routine from the terminal.

 For Name="John Wayne","Jodie Foster" D CreateObject(Name)
 For Name="Clint Eastwood","Julie Andrews" D CreateObject(Name)
 For Name="Johnny Depp","Carol Burnett" D CreateObject(Name)
 For Name="Will Smith","Ann Margaret" D CreateObject(Name)
 For Name="Dean Martin","Ally Sheedy" D CreateObject(Name)
 For Name="Humphrey Bogart","Katharine Hepburn" D CreateObject(Name)
 Quit

CreateObject(Name) [] Public {
   Set ActorOref=##class(MyPackage.Actor).%New()    ;create a new object
   Set ActorOref.Name=Name                 ;populate the object property with a name
   Do ActorOref.%Save()                    ;save the object
   Set NewId=ActorOref.%Id()               ;obtain the newly assigned Id
   Write !,"Id: ",NewId                    ;write the Id of new Object
   Write " - ",ActorOref.Name              ;write the name of the new Object Property
 }
```

```
Id: 1 - John Wayne
Id: 2 - Jodie Foster
Id: 3 - Clint Eastwood
Id: 4 - Julie Andrews
Id: 5 - Johnny Depp
Id: 6 - Carol Burnett
Id: 7 - Will Smith
Id: 8 - Ann Margaret
Id: 9 - Dean Martin
Id: 10 - Ally Sheedy
Id: 11 - Humphrey Bogart
Id: 12 - Katharine Hepburn
```

In Example 22-2, we have added 12 actors to our *Name* Property. First, we create a new blank *Oref* (Object Reference). Next, we assign a specific Name to the *Oref* and use the *%Save() Method* to write the Object to disk. Finally, we obtain and display the *Object Id* of our new Name. This *Object Id* will never change and will always be associated with the specific object.

## System Dump command for Orefs

Sometimes it is nice to see what is actually in an Oref, we can do this will a system Dump command.

**Example 22-3 System Dump command for Orefs**

```
Set ActorOref=##class(MyPackage.Actor).%OpenId(1)

Do $system.OBJ.Dump(ActorOref)
+----------------- general information ---------------
|      oref value: 1
|      class name: MyPackage.Actor
| reference count: 1
+----------------- attribute values -----------------
|      %Concurrency = 1   <Set>
|              Name = "John Wayne"
```

In Example 22-3 we use the system Dump command to see what is inside an Oref. This is very useful.

## Test whether an Oref is valid

Every time you create a new Oref, it is a good ideal to test whether it is valid or not.

**Example 22-4 Test whether an Oref is valid**

```
Set ActorOref=##class(MyPackage.Actor).%OpenId(1)          ;valid

If $IsObject(ActorOref) Write "Object is valid."
Object is valid.
If '$IsObject(ActorOref) Write "Object is not valid."

Set ActorOref=##class(MyPackage.Actor).%OpenId(1000)       ;invalid

If $IsObject(ActorOref) Write "Object is valid."
```

```
 If '$IsObject(ActorOref) Write "Object is not valid."
Object is not valid.
```

In Example 22-4 we test whether an Oref is valid.

Now let's see what the data looks like in a Global generated by the system.

## Global generated from Class MyPackage.Actor

**Example 22-5 Global generated from Class MyPackage.Actor**

```
ZW ^MyPackage.ActorD
^MyPackage.ActorD=12
^MyPackage.ActorD(1)=$lb("","John Wayne")
^MyPackage.ActorD(2)=$lb("","Jodie Foster")
^MyPackage.ActorD(3)=$lb("","Clint Eastwood")
^MyPackage.ActorD(4)=$lb("","Julie Andrews")
^MyPackage.ActorD(5)=$lb("","Johnny Depp")
^MyPackage.ActorD(6)=$lb("","Carol Burnett")
^MyPackage.ActorD(7)=$lb("","Will Smith")
^MyPackage.ActorD(8)=$lb("","Ann Margaret")
^MyPackage.ActorD(9)=$lb("","Dean Martin")
^MyPackage.ActorD(10)=$lb("","Ally Sheedy")
^MyPackage.ActorD(11)=$lb("","Humphrey Bogart")
^MyPackage.ActorD(12)=$lb("","Katharine Hepburn")
```

Example 22-5 shows the Global generated from the Class *MyPackage.Actor*. As you can see, the Global has the same name as the Package and Class but with a "D" appended to the end. The *Object Property Id* is stored as subscripts with the data stored to the right side of the equals sign. This gives you an idea of how Caché stores the data.

Our next step is to redefine the MyPackage.Actor class to create an **Index** for the *Name* Property. An Index is a means to quickly look up a property.

## Actor Class Redefinition – Index the "Name" Property

**Example 22-6 Actor Class Redefinition - Index the "Name" Property**

```
Class MyPackage.Actor Extends %Persistent
{
Property Name As %String [ Required ];

Index NameIndex On Name;
}
```

After starting up Caché Studio from the Caché Cube (a small blue cube in your system tray), click on **File** -> **Open,** then select the package MyPackage and Class Actor. Add the *Required* parameter to the *Name* Property and the "Index NameIndex On Name" line as shown in Example 22-6. From the top row in Studio, click on **Build** -> **Compile** to recompile the class.

## Index the Name Property in the MyPackage.Actor Class

```
Write ##class(MyPackage.Actor).%BuildIndices()
1
```

Example 22-7 shows the *%BuildIndices() Method* of building or rebuilding all indices in the MyPackage.Actor Class. After starting up *Terminal* from the Caché Cube (a small blue cube in your system tray), you can execute the %BuildIndices Method.

## Studio Inspector

One nice way to modify a class and its components is to use the **Inspector**. If the *Inspector pane* (normally on the right side of Studio) is not visible in Caché Studio, click on **View -> Inspector.** The *Inspector* is very useful but requires a bit of practice.

Now we need to make the Index effective for the Name Property in the MyPackage.Actor Class. This only needs to be done once because we added our names without the Index option being effective. New Names added later will automatically be indexed. This is a nice feature about Caché Objects; it takes care of keeping indexes up to date.

## Global generated from Indexing the Name Property in the MyPackage.Actor Class

Example 22-8 Example of the Index Global after indexing

```
ZW ^MyPackage.ActorI
^MyPackage.ActorI("NameIndex"," ALLY SHEEDY",10)=""
^MyPackage.ActorI("NameIndex"," ANN MARGARET",8)=""
^MyPackage.ActorI("NameIndex"," CAROL BURNETT",6)=""
^MyPackage.ActorI("NameIndex"," CLINT EASTWOOD",3)=""
^MyPackage.ActorI("NameIndex"," DEAN MARTIN",9)=""
^MyPackage.ActorI("NameIndex"," HUMPHREY BOGART",11)=""
^MyPackage.ActorI("NameIndex"," JODIE FOSTER",2)=""
^MyPackage.ActorI("NameIndex"," JOHN WAYNE",1)=""
^MyPackage.ActorI("NameIndex"," JOHNNY DEPP",5)=""
^MyPackage.ActorI("NameIndex"," JULIE ANDREWS",4)=""
^MyPackage.ActorI("NameIndex"," KATHARINE HEPBURN",12)=""
^MyPackage.ActorI("NameIndex"," WILL SMITH",7)=""
```

Example 22-8 shows the "Index Global" after the indexes have been built. As you can see, the index Global has the same name as the Package Class but with an "I" appended to the end. Notice the added space at the start of every name. This is to ensure correct collating of the data.

## %ExistsId Method – see if an Object Id Exists

Example 22-9 %ExistsId Method – see if an Object Id Exists

```
The "Name" Property is defined as a Data Type Class

Write ##class(MyPackage.Actor).%ExistsId(1)     ;see if an Object Id Exists
1
```

```
Write ##class(MyPackage.Actor).%ExistsId(101)   ;see if an Object Id Exists
0
```

In Example 22-9, we call the *%ExistsId* Method to see if a specific Object Id exists. If the Method returns a 1 then the Id exist, if the Method returns a zero then the Id does not exist.

## Add another Actor to the MyPackage.Actor Class

**Example 22-10 Add another Actor to the MyPackage.Actor Class**

The "Name" Property is defined as a Data Type Class

```
Set ActorOref=##class(MyPackage.Actor).%New()   ;create a new object
Set ActorOref.Name="Jack Nicholson"             ;populate with Jack Nicholson
Do ActorOref.%Save()                            ;save the object
Set NewId=ActorOref.%Id()                       ;obtain the newly assigned Id
Write !,"Id: ",NewId                            ;write ID of new Object
Write " - ",ActorOref.Name                      ;write the name of the new Object
```

If you run the above code from the Terminal, you should get the following output.

```
Id: 13 - Jack Nicholson
```

In Example 22-10, we added the actor Jack Nicholson to the *Name* Property.

## Embedded SQL

Later we discover we added Jack Nicholson by mistake and need to remove him. Further, his *Id* is unknown and we need to write the code to find his *Id*. The simplest way to do this lookup is through *Embedded SQL (Structured Query Language)*. We cover *SQL* in Chapter 23 but give a brief introduction here to complete our task of looking up and removing Jack Nicholson.

## Delete an Actor from the MyPackage.Actor Class

**Example 22-11 Delete an Actor from the MyPackage.Actor Class**

The "Name" Property is defined as a Data Type Class

To run this code you must put the code in a routine, save the routine, and then run the routine from the terminal.

```
New SearchName,id,name

Set SearchName="Jack Nicholson"          ;Name to search for

&sql(SELECT %Id,Name INTO :id, :name
    FROM MyPackage.Actor
    WHERE name = :SearchName)

If '$Data(id) {
    Write "Object Not Found"
}
Else {
    Set ReturnCode = ##class(MyPackage.Actor).%DeleteId(id)    ;Delete Id
```

```
    If ReturnCode=1 {
        Write "Object Deleted."
    }
    Else {
        Write "Object Not Deleted."
    }
}
```

*Object Deleted.*

In Example 22-11:

> ➤ First we *New* the variables *SearchName*, *id*, and *name*

> ➤ Next we set the variable *SearchName* to Jack Nicholson

> ➤ Using *Embedded SQL,* we search for the *Id* of the Object corresponding to the name Jack Nicholson. Note that while in *Embedded SQL* variables need to be preceded by a colon, ":"

> ➤ If the *Id* is found we use the *%DeleteID Method* to delete the object

> ➤ If you run this example twice, the second time it will say "Object Not Deleted", this is because you already deleted it on your first run

So far, we have seen how to add an Object Property of *%String* to our class, how to populate this Object Property, how to add an additional name, and how to delete the name.

## *References to Persistent Objects*

We just looked at a *Data Type Class* of %String, now we will consider an Object Property that references another Persistent Class and Object. We will use *MyPackage.Accountants* as the referenced Persistent Class and Object.

**Table 22-2 Object Properties**

| Object Property | Data Type | Reference Object Class and Name | Name we chose |
|---|---|---|---|
| Name of Data Type Class | %String | | Name (Name of Actor) |
| Reference to Persistent Objects | | Persistent Object MyPackage.Accountants | MyAccountant (Accountants used by Actor) |

## Reference Property

When an Object Property of one class is a Persistent Object of another class, it is referred to as a **Reference Property**. *Reference Properties* are created separately from the object referring to it. A link establishes connectivity between the *Reference Property* and the object referring to it.

## Primary Object Property Links to a Referenced Object Property

**Table 22-3 Primary Object Property Links to a Referenced Object Property**

| Primary Object Property | | >> Link>> | Reference Object Property | |
|---|---|---|---|---|
| Class: MyPackage.Actor | | | Class: MyPackage.Accountants | |
| Object Properties | | | | |
| Name | Literal | | Object Properties | |
| MyAccountant | Reference Property | >>Link>> | AccountantName | Literal |

Table 22-3 shows our MyPackage.Actor Class with its Object Property of *Name* and a new object property, *MyAccountant*. The Object Property *Name* is a literal, but the Object Property *MyAccountant* is a *Reference Property* that points to the MyPackage.Accountants Class and the Object Property *AccountantName*.

Before we can establish a Reference Property, we need to create the Reference Property Class.

## Establish a New Class and Object to be used as a Reference Property

Say we define our **Reference Property** as **MyAccountant**.

## Class Definition – Creating the Accountants Class

**Example 22-12 Class Definition – Creating the Accountants Class**

```
Class MyPackage.Accountants Extends %Persistent
{
Property AccountantName As %String [ Required ];

Index AccountantNameIndex On AccountantName;

}
```

After starting up Caché Studio from the Caché Cube (a small blue cube in your system tray), click on **File -> New,** then select **Caché Class Definition,** next select the package MyPackage and add a new Class *Accountants*. Add the *AccountantName* Property (click on **Class -> Add -> Property)** to the Accountants Class. Also create the *Index* line either by copying the above *Index* line and pasting it into your class or adding the *Index* line (click on **Class -> Add -> Index**). Your class should look like Example 22-12. Recompile the class.

### *Populate the AccountantName Property in the MyPackage.Accountants Class*

Example 22-13 Populate the AccountantName Property in the MyPackage.Accountants Class

```
The "AccountantName" Property is defined as a Data Type Class

To run this code you must put the code in a routine, save the routine, and then
run the routine from the terminal.

  Do CreateObject("Fine Accountant")
  Do CreateObject("Fair Accountant")
  Do CreateObject("Really Bad Accountant")
  Do CreateObject("Down Right #%&$ Accountant")
 Quit

 CreateObject(Name) [] Public {
   Set AccountantOref=##class(MyPackage.Accountants).%New() ;create new object
   Set AccountantOref.AccountantName=Name       ;populate the object with a name
   Do AccountantOref.%Save()                    ;save the object
   Set NewId=AccountantOref.%Id()               ;obtain the newly assigned Id
   Write !,"Id: ",NewId                         ;write the ID of new Object
   Write " - ",AccountantOref.AccountantName    ;write the name of the new Object
 }

If you save the above code in a routine and then run the it from the Terminal,
you should get the following output.

Id: 1 - Fine Accountant
Id: 2 - Fair Accountant
Id: 3 - Really Bad Accountant
Id: 4 - Down Right #%&$ Accountant
```

In Example 22-13, we have created four Accountant Names. First, we create a new blank *Oref*. Next, we assign a specific *Name* to *Oref*. Finally we use the *%Save()* Method to write the Object to disk, and then display the *Id* of our new Accountant Name.

### *Actor Class Redefinition – add Reference Property that points to Accountants Class*

Example 22-14, Actor Class Redefinition – add Reference Property that points to the Accountants Class

```
Class MyPackage.Actor Extends %Persistent
{

Property Name As %String [ Required ];

Index NameIndex On Name;

Property MyAccountant As Accountants;
}
```

After starting up Caché Studio from the Caché Cube (a small blue cube in your system tray), click on **File -> Open,** then select the package MyPackage and Class Actor. Add the "Property MyAccountant

As Accountants" line (click on **Class** -> **Add** -> **Property)** to the Actor Class. Your class should look like Example 22-14. Recompile the class.

We shall use MyPackage.Actor Object Id of 3 (Clint Eastwood) as the object we will be manipulating. If we did not know the Id of Clint Eastwood, we could use *Embedded SQL* demonstrated in Example 22-11. *Embedded SQL* is covered in Chapter 23.

## *Modify Reference Property – associate Object Name MyAccountant with Class Accountants*

Example 22-15 Modify Reference Property – associate Object Name MyAccountant with Class Accountants

```
The MyAccountant Property is defined as a Reference to a Persistent Object

Set ActorOref=##class(MyPackage.Actor).%OpenId(3)      ;bring object Clint
                                                       ;Eastwood into memory

Set AccountantOref=##class(MyPackage.Accountants).%OpenId(2)  ;bring object
                                                       ;Fair Accountant into memory

Set ActorOref.MyAccountant = AccountantOref   ;associate MyAccountant
                                              ;(Fair Accountant) with Clint Eastwood

Do ActorOref.%Save()                          ;save the data

Write ActorOref.Name
Clint Eastwood

Write ActorOref.MyAccountant.AccountantName   ;association made
Fair Accountant
```

In Example 22-15, we associated the MyPackage.Actor object property *MyAccountant* with MyPackage.Accountants *AccountantName*. Specifically we associated Clint Eastwood with the Fair Accountant.

## *Globals generated from Classes MyPackage.Actor and MyPackage.Accountants*

Example 22-16 Globals generated from Classes MyPackage.Actor and MyPackage.Accountants

```
ZW ^MyPackage.ActorD
^MyPackage.ActorD=13
^MyPackage.ActorD(1)=$lb("","John Wayne")
^MyPackage.ActorD(2)=$lb("","Jodie Foster")
^MyPackage.ActorD(3)=$lb("","Clint Eastwood","2")
^MyPackage.ActorD(4)=$lb("","Julie Andrews")
^MyPackage.ActorD(5)=$lb("","Johnny Depp")
^MyPackage.ActorD(6)=$lb("","Carol Burnett")
^MyPackage.ActorD(7)=$lb("","Will Smith")
^MyPackage.ActorD(8)=$lb("","Ann Margaret")
^MyPackage.ActorD(9)=$lb("","Dean Martin")
^MyPackage.ActorD(10)=$lb("","Ally Sheedy")
^MyPackage.ActorD(11)=$lb("","Humphrey Bogart")
^MyPackage.ActorD(12)=$lb("","Katharine Hepburn")
```

```
ZW ^MyPackage.AccountantsD
^MyPackage.AccountantsD(1)=$lb("","Fine Accountant")
^MyPackage.AccountantsD(2)=$lb("","Fair Accountant")
^MyPackage.AccountantsD(3)=$lb("","Really Bad Accountant")
^MyPackage.AccountantsD(4)=$lb("","Down Right #%&$ Accountant")
```

Example 22-16 shows the Globals generated from the Classes MyPackage.Actor and MyPackage.Accountants. The reference to the Accountants Class is the quoted "2" at the end of the Clint Eastwood node. This is obviously a reference to Id 2, in the MyPackage.Accountants Class.

One nice thing about Referenced Properties, they can be associated to more than one Actor. Now suppose that Clint Eastwood thought the Fair Accountant does great work and suggested the Fair Accountant to Ally Sheedy (Id 10) and Katharine Hepburn (Id 12). We can now associate the Fair Accountant to these two friends of Clint Eastwood.

### *Modify Reference Property, associate the Fair Accountant with two more Actors*

Example 22-17 Modify Reference Property – associate the Fair Accountant with two more Actors

```
The MyAccountant Property is defined as a Reference to a Persistent Object

Set ActorOref1=##class(MyPackage.Actor).%OpenId(10)     ;bring object Ally
                                                        ;Sheedy into memory

Set AccountantOref=##class(MyPackage.Accountants).%OpenId(2)  ;bring object the
                                                        ;Fair Accountant into memory

Set ActorOref1.MyAccountant = AccountantOref   ;associate MyAccountant (Fair
                                               ;Accountant) with Ally Sheedy

Do ActorOref1.%Save()                          ;save the data

Write ActorOref1.Name
Ally Sheedy

Write ActorOref1.MyAccountant.AccountantName   ;association made
Fair Accountant

-  -  -  -  -  -  -  -  -  -  -  -  -  -  -  -  -  -  -  -

Set ActorOref2=##class(MyPackage.Actor).%OpenId(12)     ;bring object Katharine
                                                        ;Hepburn into memory

Set AccountantOref=##class(MyPackage.Accountants).%OpenId(2)  ;bring object
                                                        ;Fair Accountant into memory

Set ActorOref2.MyAccountant = AccountantOref   ;associate MyAccountant (Fair
                                               ;Accountant) with Katharine Hepburn

Do ActorOref2.%Save()                          ;save the data

Write ActorOref2.Name
Katharine Hepburn

Write ActorOref2.MyAccountant.AccountantName   ;association made
Fair Accountant
```

In Example 22-17, we associate the MyPackage.Actor Property *MyAccountant* with the MyPackage.Accountants Property *AccountantName.* Specifically we associate Ally Sheedy and Katharine Hepburn with the Fair Accountant.

Now let's suppose that Ally Sheedy does not get along with the Fair Accountant and asks to be disassociated with the Fair Accountant.

### *Modify Reference Property – Disassociate MyAccountant with Accountants*

**Example 22-18 Modify Reference Property – Disassociate MyAccountant with Accountants**

```
The MyAccountant Property is defined as a Reference to a Persistent Object

Set ActorOref=##class(MyPackage.Actor).%OpenId(10)     ;bring object Ally
                                                       ;Sheedy into memory

Set ActorOref.MyAccountant = ""  ;disassociate MyAccountant from Accountants

Do ActorOref.%Save()

Write ActorOref.Name
Ally Sheedy

Write ActorOref.MyAccountant.AccountantName     ;association broken
<>
```

In Example 22-18, disassociating MyAccountant from Accountants is a simple matter of setting MyAccountant to null. So the Actor Ally Sheedy no longer is associated with the Fair Accountant.

We have been looking at References to Persistent Objects; next we will consider References to *Embedded Objects*.

## *References to Embedded Objects*

**References TO Embedded Objects** are similar to *References to Persistent Objects*, except that the Object being referenced is an *Embedded Object,* or an Object stored within a *Persistent Class. Embedded Objects* are of the *%SerialObject Class*. They are also known as *Serial Objects*. These objects can only be stored within a persistent class and not stored by themselves.

Up to now we have seen:

> ➤ Data Type Classes, of which we have used the %String Data Type

> ➤ Persistent Object Classes, which exist on their own

And now we are considering *Serial Object Classes*, which exist inside or are *Embedded* with *Persistent Object Classes.*

We will use *MyPackage.Address* Class as the referred to Embedded Class and Object.

Table 22-4 Object Properties

| Object Property | Data Type | Reference Object Class and Name | Name we chose |
|---|---|---|---|
| Name of Data Type Class | %String | | Name (Name of Actor) |
| Reference to Persistent Objects | | Persistent Object MyPackage.Accountants | MyAccountant (Accountant used by the Actor) |
| Reference to Embedded Objects | | Embedded or Serial Object MyPackage.Address | MyHome (Address of the Actor) |

Our first step is to create an Address Class based on the *%Serial Object* to be embedded in the MyPackage.Actor Class.

## *Class Definition – Creating an Address Class of type %Serial*

Example 22-19 Class Definition – Creating an Address Class of type %Serial

```
Class MyPackage.Address Extends %SerialObject
{

Property Street As %String(MAXLEN = 80);

Property City As %String(MAXLEN = 30);

Property State As %String(MINLEN = 2);

Property Zip As %String(MAXLEN = 10);

}
```

After starting up Caché Studio from the Caché Cube (a small blue cube in your system tray), click on **File -> New,** then select **Caché Class Definition,** next select the package MyPackage and add a new class called *Address* of the *%SerialObject* class with the properties of Street, City, State and Zip, (click on **Class -> Add -> Property)** as shown in Example 22-19. Recompile the class.

Once the Address Class is defined, it can be used as an embedded object for the MyPackage.Actor Class.

Now we need to redefine the Actor Class to add a property that points to our newly created Address Class.

## Actor Class Redefinition – add Embedded Object Property MyHome that points to the Address Class

**Example 22-20 Actor Class Redefinition – add Embedded Object Property "MyHome" that points to the Address Class**

```
Class MyPackage.Actor Extends %Persistent
{
Property Name As %String [ Required ];

Index NameIndex On Name;

Property MyAccountant As Accountants;

Property MyHome As Address;

}
```

After starting up Caché Studio from the Caché Cube (a small blue cube in your system tray), click on **File** -> **Open,** then select the package MyPackage and Class Actor. Add the *"Property MyHome As Address"* line (click on **Class** -> **Add** -> **Property)** to the Address Class. Your class should look like Example 22-20. Recompile the class.

We shall use the MyPackage.Actor Object Id of 4 (Julie Andrews) as the object we will be manipulating. If we did not know the Id of Julie Andrews, we could use *Embedded SQL* demonstrated in Example 22-11.

## Modify or add Data to MyHome Object Property

**Example 22-21 Modify or add Data to the MyHome Object Property**

```
The MyHome Property is defined as a Reference to an Embedded Class

Set ActorOref=##class(MyPackage.Actor).%OpenId(4)    ;bring object Julie Andrews
                                                     ;into memory

Set ActorOref.MyHome.City = "Marlboro"

Set ActorOref.MyHome.State = "MA"

Set ActorOref.MyHome.Street = "123 Main St."

Set ActorOref.MyHome.Zip="01752"

Do ActorOref.%Save()
```

In Example 22-21, we see that the MyHome Object Property is mapped to the MyPackage.Address Class. This makes available City, State, Street and Zip to MyHome. Or a more proper way to put it is MyPackage.Address is *embedded* in MyPackage.Actor. MyPackage.Address is not saved by itself but only as a subset of MyPackage.Actor.

## Global generated from Class MyPackage.Actor with Embedded Class MyPackage.Address

**Example 22-22 Global generated from Class MyPackage.Actor with Embedded Class MyPackage.Address**

```
 ZW ^MyPackage.ActorD
^MyPackage.ActorD=13
^MyPackage.ActorD(1)=$lb("","John Wayne")
^MyPackage.ActorD(2)=$lb("","Jodie Foster")
^MyPackage.ActorD(3)=$lb("","Clint Eastwood","2")
^MyPackage.ActorD(4)=$lb("","Julie Andrews","",$lb("123 Main St.","Marlboro","MA","01752"))
^MyPackage.ActorD(5)=$lb("","Johnny Depp")
^MyPackage.ActorD(6)=$lb("","Carol Burnett")
^MyPackage.ActorD(7)=$lb("","Will Smith")
^MyPackage.ActorD(8)=$lb("","Ann Margaret")
^MyPackage.ActorD(9)=$lb("","Dean Martin")
^MyPackage.ActorD(10)=$lb("","Ally Sheedy","")
^MyPackage.ActorD(11)=$lb("","Humphrey Bogart")
^MyPackage.ActorD(12)=$lb("","Katharine Hepburn","2")
```

Example 22-22 shows the Global generated from the Class MyPackage.Actor. Under the Julie Andrews node you can see the Embedded Object Address Class data.

## Chapter 22 Summary

In Chapter 22 we learned about three types of Object Classes: 1) Data Type Classes, 2) References to Persistent Classes, and 3) References to Embedded Classes. We created and populated as an example to be used in this chapter and future chapters a Class of Actors. Embedded SQL was demonstrated in obtaining the ID of an actor. Next we created References to Persistent Objects and References to Embedded Objects and saw how these could be attached to the Class of Actors.

This chapter introduces several new concepts and is foundational to the future chapters. If you do not thoroughly understand this chapter I suggest you review it again.

# Chapter 23 Embedded and Dynamic SQL

Chapter 23 covers the basic concepts of Caché ObjectScript (COS) **SQL**, *Structured Query Language*. **Caché SQL** is an essential part of Caché. With the use of *Caché SQL* and *Caché Objects*, the programmer no longer needs to access Globals directly. *Caché SQL* provides high performance access to the Multi-Dimensional database (Global Structure) and *Caché SQL* is far more maintainable. In fact, direct Global access is discouraged because Global data may be inadvertently changed in ways that will make it inaccessible by *Caché SQL*.

This book does not purport to teach SQL. If you are new to this subject it is suggested that you do some research on it, there are a lot of good resources online.

## Caché SQL Basics

*Caché SQL* (pronounced *Sequel*) is based on Caché *Classes* and *Objects*. The *Caché SQL* tables are **Projections** of Caché *Classes* and *Objects*. **SQL** is industry standard software for modifying, accessing and reporting data; *Caché SQL* is based on *SQL*. Caché uses what it calls the **Unified Data Dictionary,** which is a repository of all Caché Class Definition meta-data. Caché automatically creates relational access (Caché SQL tables) for every persistent class stored within the *Unified Data Dictionary*.

*SQL* data is represented by Tables, Columns, Rows and Cells.

## Tables, Columns, Rows and Cells

Table 23-1 Tables, Columns, Rows and Cells.

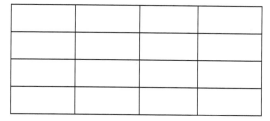

In Table 23-1, *SQL* data is represented by a Table, Columns, Rows and Cells. *Columns* are the vertical columns, *Rows* are the horizontal rows and *Cells* are where the *Columns* and *Rows* intersect.

## Table of Actors

In Table 23-2, we see the Actor Class created in Chapter 22 represented as a *SQL Table*. Column one is the ID number and Column two is the name. Each Row represents a different actor.

**Table 23-2 Table of Actors**

| ID | Name |
|----|------|
| 1 | John Wayne |
| 2 | Jodie Foster |
| 3 | Client Eastwood |
| 4 | Julie Andrews |
| 5 | Johnny Depp |
| 6 | Carol Burnett |
| 7 | Will Smith |
| 8 | Ann Margaret |
| 9 | Dean Martin |
| 10 | Ally Sheedy |
| 11 | Humphrey Bogart |
| 12 | Katharine Hepburn |

We will use the table of Actors in the following examples.

## Embedded SQL and Dynamic SQL

There are two methods of including *SQL* within a COS Routine or Method (Chapter 32 and 33 will cover more advanced techniques of including *SQL* in a Caché Method):

➢ Embedded SQL

➢ Dynamic SQL

In the following chapters we explore different types of Caché Object Persistent Structures and the *SQL* code to access them.

## Embedded SQL

**Embedded SQL** is implanted within *Methods* or *COS Routines*. The *Embedded SQL* code is compiled at *compilation time* as opposed to *Dynamic SQL* which is compiled at *execute time*. One reason this is important is that the tables or data items you wish to query must exist at compile time.

## Embedded SQL Routine to Display the Actors Class

**Example 23-1 Embedded SQL Routine to Display the Actors Class**

```
To run this code you must put the code in a routine (SQLROUTINE), save the
routine, and then run the routine from the terminal.

SQLROUTINE                          ;Start of routine to hold Embedded SQL

  New Id, Name                      ;Host variables, pass variables into Embedded SQL

                                    ;"&sql" - the SQL directive, start of Embedded SQL
  &sql(
        Declare MyCursor CURSOR FOR
        SELECT ID, Name
        INTO :Id, :Name
        FROM MyPackage.Actor
        ORDER BY Name)

  &sql(OPEN MyCursor)               ;Open Cursor to start at top of data
  &sql(FETCH MyCursor)              ;Does initial Fetch of data

  While (SQLCODE = 0) {             ;loop as long as we have a good SQLCODE
        Write !,?5,"Id: ",Id        ;good return code, display data
        Write ?15,"Name: ",Name
        &sql(FETCH MyCursor)        ;do subsequent fetches
  }

  &sql(CLOSE MyCursor)              ;need to close cursor
```

In Example 23-1, we use *Embedded SQL* to select all actors from the class MyPackage.Actor established in Chapter 22.

Please note the following about this example

> The "&sql" string is the SQL directive and signifies the start of Embedded SQL inside a Routine or Method, the closing parenthesis ends Embedded SQL

> A "Cursor" (MyCursor) points to the data as Embedded *SQL* traverses it. You must first declare an *SQL* Cursor, giving it a unique name. It is used in the Open, Fetch and Close

> The SELECT statement is selecting properties from the MyPackage.Actor Class created in Chapter 22

> The INTO statement is depositing data items selected into Host Variables

> The FROM statement is referring back to the Chapter 22 Class: MyPackage.Actor

> The ORDER statement is specifying the SORT Order

> The &sql(OPEN MyCursor) opens the Cursor to start at the top of the data

> The &sql(FETCH MyCursor) Fetches the data

> The While Construct iterates through the data

> SQLCODE contains the Status Code and %msg contains the return message

**Example 23-2 Run Embedded SQL Routine to access the Actors Class**

```
Do ^SQLROUTINE

    Id: 10      Name: Ally Sheedy
    Id: 8       Name: Ann Margaret
    Id: 6       Name: Carol Burnett
    Id: 3       Name: Clint Eastwood
    Id: 9       Name: Dean Martin
    Id: 11      Name: Humphrey Bogart
    Id: 2       Name: Jodie Foster
    Id: 1       Name: John Wayne
    Id: 5       Name: Johnny Depp
    Id: 4       Name: Julie Andrews
    Id: 12      Name: Katharine Hepburn
    Id: 7       Name: Will Smith
```

In Example 23-2, we run the routine SQLROUTINE and see the output.

## *Embedded SQL Routine to Display the Actors Class with a Where clause*

**Example 23-3 Embedded SQL Routine to Display the Actors Class with a Where clause**

To run this code you must put the code in a routine (SQLROUTINE), save the routine, and then run the routine from the terminal.

```
SQLROUTINE                              ;Start of routine to hold Embedded SQL

    New Id, Name                        ;Host variables, pass variables into Embedded SQL

    &sql(
            Declare MyCursor CURSOR FOR
            SELECT ID, Name
            INTO :Id, :Name
            FROM MyPackage.Actor
            WHERE Name = 'John Wayne'
            ORDER BY Name)

    &sql(OPEN MyCursor)                 ;Open Cursor to start at top of data
    &sql(FETCH MyCursor)                ;Does initial Fetch of data

    While (SQLCODE = 0) {               ;loop as long as we have a good SQLCODE
            Write !,?5,"Id: ",Id        ;good return code, display data
            Write ?15,"Name: ",Name
            &sql(FETCH MyCursor)        ;do subsequent fetches
    }

    &sql(CLOSE MyCursor)                ;need to close cursor
```

If you save the above code in a routine and then run the it from the Terminal, you should get the following output.

```
Do ^SQLROUTINE

    Id: 1       Name: John Wayne
```

In Example 23-3, we run the routine SQLROUTINE and see the output. Note that we are only selecting Actor "John Wayne" with the Where Clause.

Now let us use *Caché SQL* to add new data to our Actor Class, we shall add Favorite Color as a new column. First, we need to redefine our Class Definition of MyPackage.Actor to include FavoriteColor.

## Actor Class Redefinition

**Example 23-4 Actor Class Redefinition**

```
Class MyPackage.Actor Extends %Persistent
{

Property Name As %String [ Required ];

Index NameIndex On Name;

Property MyAccountant As Accountants;

Property MyHome As Address;

Property FavoriteColor As %String;

}
```

Example 23-4, redefines the class *MyPackage.Actor* we created in Chapter 22. After starting up Caché Studio from the Caché Cube(a small blue cube in your system tray), click on **File -> Open,** then select the package MyPackage and Class Actor and create a new Property, FavoriteColor (click on **Class -> Add -> Property)**. From the top row in Studio, click on **Build -> Compile** to compile the class.

## Embedded SQL Routine to Populate the Actor Class with Favorite Color

**Example 23-5 Embedded SQL Routine to Populate the Actor Class with Favorite Color**

```
To run this code you must put the code in a routine (SQLROUTINE), save the
routine, and then run the routine from the terminal.

SQLROUTINE                          ;Start of routine to hold Embedded SQL

   Do AddFavoriteColor("John Wayne","Blue")
   Do AddFavoriteColor("Jodie Foster","Green")
   Do AddFavoriteColor("Clint Eastwood","Cyan")
   Do AddFavoriteColor("Julie Andrews","Brown")
   Do AddFavoriteColor("Johnny Depp","Tan")
   Do AddFavoriteColor("Carol Burnett","Red")
   Do AddFavoriteColor("Will Smith","Navy")
   Do AddFavoriteColor("Ann Margaret","Yellow")
   Do AddFavoriteColor("Dean Martin","Green")
   Do AddFavoriteColor("Ally Sheedy","Black")
   Do AddFavoriteColor("Humphrey Bogart","Brown")
   Do AddFavoriteColor("Katharine Hepburn","Blue")
Quit
;
AddFavoriteColor(Actor,Color)
   Write !,"Inserting Color: ",Color, " for Actor: ",Actor
```

```
&sql(UPDATE MyPackage.Actor (FavoriteColor)
   VALUES (:Color)
   WHERE Name=:Actor)

If SQLCODE'=0 {
   Write !,"Error inserting Color into Actors"
   Write "SQLCODE=",SQLCODE," : ",%msg
}
```

If you save the above code in a routine and then run the it from the Terminal, you should get the following output.

```
Do ^SQLROUTINE

Inserting Color: Blue for Actor: John Wayne Inserting Color: Green for Actor:
Jodie Foster
Inserting Color: Cyan for Actor: Clint Eastwood
Inserting Color: Brown for Actor: Julie Andrews
Inserting Color: Tan for Actor: Johnny Depp
Inserting Color: Red for Actor: Carol Burnett
Inserting Color: Navy for Actor: Will Smith
Inserting Color: Yellow for Actor: Ann Margaret
Inserting Color: Green for Actor: Dean Martin
Inserting Color: Black for Actor: Ally Sheedy
Inserting Color: Brown for Actor: Humphrey Bogart
Inserting Color: Blue for Actor: Katharine Hepburn
```

In Example 23-5, we have created a subroutine (AddFavoriteColor) that uses *Embedded SQL* to add a Favorite Color to each of the Actors and Actresses.

## Global generated from Class MyPackage.Actor

**Example 23-6 Global generated from Class MyPackage.Actor**

```
ZW ^MyPackage.ActorD
^MyPackage.ActorD=13
^MyPackage.ActorD(1)=$lb("","John Wayne","",$lb("","","",""), "Blue")
^MyPackage.ActorD(2)=$lb("","Jodie Foster","",$lb("","","",""), "Green")
^MyPackage.ActorD(3)=$lb("","Clint Eastwood","2",$lb("","","",""), "Cyan")
^MyPackage.ActorD(4)=$lb("","Julie Andrews","",$lb("123 Main St.","Marlboro","MA",
"01752"), "Brown")
^MyPackage.ActorD(5)=$lb("","Johnny Depp","",$lb("","","",""), "Tan")
^MyPackage.ActorD(6)=$lb("","Carol Burnett","",$lb("","","",""), "Red")
^MyPackage.ActorD(7)=$lb("","Will Smith","",$lb("","","",""), "Navy")
^MyPackage.ActorD(8)=$lb("","Ann Margaret","",$lb("","","",""), "Yellow")
^MyPackage.ActorD(9)=$lb("","Dean Martin","",$lb("","","",""), "Green")
^MyPackage.ActorD(10)=$lb("","Ally Sheedy","",$lb("","","",""), "Black")
^MyPackage.ActorD(11)=$lb("","Humphrey Bogart","",$lb("","","",""), "Brown")
^MyPackage.ActorD(12)=$lb("","Katharine Hepburn","2",$lb("","","",""), "Blue")
```

Example 23-6 shows the Global generated from the *Class MyPackage.Actor*. You can see how the *FavoriteColor* is stored. Your Global may not look exactly like this one if you have not worked through all the examples in the previous Chapters.

## Embedded SQL Routine to Display the Actors Class "Reference to Persistent Object" Property, MyAccountant – MyPackage.Accountants Class

In Chapter 22, Example 22-14, we added a *Reference Property* of *MyAccountant* that points to the MyPackage.Accountants Class. This is what is known as a *Reference Property* or a *Reference to a Persistent Property*. When an Object Property of one class is a Persistent Object of another class, it is referred to as a **Reference Property**. *Reference Properties* are created separately from the object referring to it. A link establishes connectivity between the *Reference Property* and the object referring to it. In Chapter 22 we associated or linked Accountant "Fair Accountant" to Clint Eastwood and Katharine Hepburn.

**Example 23-7 Embedded SQL Routine to Display the Actors Class "Reference to Persistent Object" Property**

```
To run this code you must put the code in a routine (SQLROUTINE), save the
routine, and then run the routine from the terminal.

SQLROUTINE                          ;Start of routine to hold Embedded SQL

   New Id, Name, MyAccountantName ;Host variables, pass variables into Embedded SQL

   &sql(
        Declare MyCursor CURSOR FOR
        SELECT ID, Name, MyAccountant->AccountantName
        INTO :Id, :Name, :MyAccountantName
        FROM MyPackage.Actor
        ORDER BY MyPackage.Actor.Name)

   &sql(OPEN MyCursor)                ;Open Cursor to start at top of data
   &sql(FETCH MyCursor)               ;Does initial Fetch of data

   While (SQLCODE = 0) {              ;loop as long as we have a good SQLCODE
        Write !,?5,"Id: ",Id ;good return code, display data
        Write ?15,"Name: ",Name
        If MyAccountantName'="" {
             Write ?40,"Accountant Name : ",MyAccountantName
        }
        &sql(FETCH MyCursor)          ;do subsequent fetches
   }

   &sql(CLOSE MyCursor)               ;need to close cursor
```

```
If you save the above code in a routine and then run the it from the Terminal,
you should get the following output.
```

```
Do ^SQLROUTINE

    Id: 10    Name: Ally Sheedy
    Id: 8     Name: Ann Margaret
    Id: 6     Name: Carol Burnett
    Id: 3     Name: Clint Eastwood      Accountant Name : Fair Accountant
    Id: 9     Name: Dean Martin
    Id: 11    Name: Humphrey Bogart
    Id: 2     Name: Jodie Foster
    Id: 1     Name: John Wayne
    Id: 5     Name: Johnny Depp
    Id: 4     Name: Julie Andrews
    Id: 12    Name: Katharine Hepburn   Accountant Name : Fair Accountant
```

```
     Id: 7      Name: Will Smith
```

In Example 23-7, we use *Embedded SQL* to select all actors from the class MyPackage.Actor and at the same time reach out to the Referenced Class MyPackage.Accountants. Please note the special syntax whereby we reach out to the Referenced Class, "->", as in MyAccountants -> AccountantName

## *Embedded SQL Routine to Display the Actors Class "Reference to Embedded Class" Property, MyHome – MyPackage.Address Class*

In Chapter 22, Example 22-20, we added a Reference Property of *MyHome* that points to the MyPackage.Address Class. This is what is known as a *Reference to an Embedded Class*. **References to Embedded Classes** are similar to *References to Persistent Objects*, except that the Object being referenced is an *Embedded Class,* or a Class stored within the *Persistent Object. Embedded Classes* are %SerialObject Classes. These classes can only be stored within a persistent object and are not stored by themselves. In Chapter 22 we associated or linked as *MyHome* to Julie Andrews.

Example 23-8 Embedded SQL Routine to Display the Actors Class "Reference to Embedded Class" Property, MyHome – MyPackage.Address Class

```
To run this code you must put the code in a routine (SQLROUTINE), save the
routine, and then run the routine from the terminal.

SQLROUTINE                              ;Start of routine to hold Embedded SQL

   New Id, Name, Street, City, State, Zip ;Host variables, passed to Embedded SQL

   &sql(
        Declare MyCursor CURSOR FOR
        SELECT ID, Name, MyHome_Street, MyHome_City, MyHome_State, MyHome_Zip
        INTO :Id, :Name, :Street, :City, :State, :Zip
        FROM MyPackage.Actor
        ORDER BY MyPackage.Actor.Name)

   &sql(OPEN MyCursor)                  ;Open Cursor to start at top of data
   &sql(FETCH MyCursor)                 ;Does initial Fetch of data

   While (SQLCODE = 0) {                 ;loop as long as we have a good SQLCODE
        Write !,?5,"Id: ",Id            ;good return code, display data
        Write ?15,"Name: ",Name
        If Street'="" Write ?40,"Street : ",Street
        If City'=""   Write !,?40,"City   : ",City
        If State'=""  Write !,?40,"State  : ",State
        If Zip'=""    Write !,?40,"Zip    : ",Zip
        &sql(FETCH MyCursor)            ;do subsequent fetches
   }

   &sql(CLOSE MyCursor)                 ;need to close cursor

If you save the above code in a routine and then run the it from the Terminal,
you should get the following output.

Do ^SQLROUTINE

     Id: 10     Name: Ally Sheedy
     Id: 8      Name: Ann Margaret
```

```
Id: 6        Name: Carol Burnett
Id: 3        Name: Clint Eastwood
Id: 9        Name: Dean Martin
Id: 11       Name: Humphrey Bogart
Id: 2        Name: Jodie Foster
Id: 1        Name: John Wayne
Id: 5        Name: Johnny Depp
Id: 4        Name: Julie Andrews     Street : 123 Main St.
                                     City   : Marlboro
                                     State  : MA
                                     Zip    : 01752

Id: 12       Name: Katharine Hepburn
Id: 7        Name: Will Smith
```

Example 23-8 allows us to display the Actors Class and the Reference to Embedded Class Property, MyHome.

# Dynamic SQL

**Dynamic SQL** is when *SQL* is implanted within *Methods* or *COS Routines*. The *Dynamic SQL* code is compiled at *execute time* as opposed to *Embedded SQL* which is compiled at *compilation time*.

*The steps to Dynamic SQL are:*

➢ Define your Query

➢ Create a new Instance of %SQL.Statement

➢ Prepare the Query

➢ Execute the Query

➢ Process the Query Results

## Dynamic SQL Routine to Display the Actors Class

**Example 23-9 Dynamic SQL Routine to Display the Actors Class**

```
To run this code you must put the code in a routine (SQLROUTINE), save the
routine, and then run the routine from the terminal.

SQLROUTINE                         ;Start of routine to hold Dynamic SQL

  Set MyQuery="SELECT * FROM MyPackage.Actor"  ;Define the Query

  Set ActorOref = ##class(%SQL.Statement).%New() ;New Instance of %SQL.Statement

  Set Status = ActorOref.%Prepare(MyQuery) ;Prepare the Query

  Set ResultSet = ActorOref.%Execute() ;Execute the Query

  While ResultSet.%Next() {                   ;Return each row of the Query
     Write !,?5,"Id: ",ResultSet.Id           ;good return code, display data
     Write ?15,ResultSet.Name
     Write ?40,ResultSet.FavoriteColor
  }
```

```
Do ^SQLROUTINE

        Id: 1       John Wayne          Blue
        Id: 2       Jodie Foster        Green
        Id: 3       Clint Eastwood      Cyan
        Id: 4       Julie Andrews       Brown
        Id: 5       Johnny Depp         Tan
        Id: 6       Carol Burnett       Red
        Id: 7       Will Smith          Navy
        Id: 8       Ann Margaret        Yellow
        Id: 9       Dean Martin         Green
        Id: 10      Ally Sheedy         Black
        Id: 11      Humphrey Bogart     Brown
        Id: 12      Katharine Hepburn   Blue
```

Example 23-9 demonstrates a simple query using *Dynamic SQL to display the name and favorite color.*

In Example 23-9 we have not checked the status code after executing the "Prepare" call. As with all programming, it is a good idea to always check a "Status" returned by a call. In the next example we are going to modify the MyQuery variables to be invalid to demonstrate how the "Prepare" call picks up the problem."

**Example 23-10 Dynamic SQL Routine to Display the Actors Class**

```
SQLROUTINE                          ;Start of routine to hold Dynamic SQL

  Set MyQuery="SELECT * FROM MyPackage.Actors" ;Define the Query

  Set ActorOref = ##class(%SQL.Statement).%New() ;New Instance of %SQL.Statement

  Set Status = ActorOref.%Prepare(MyQuery)      ;Prepare the Query
  If +Status'=1 {
      Write !,"Invalid Status returned from the %Prepare Call."
      Write !,"Status: ",Status
      Quit 0
  }

  Set ResultSet = ActorOref.%Execute()  ;Execute the Query

  While ResultSet.%Next() {                      ;Return each row of the Query
    Write !,?5,"Id: ",ResultSet.Id              ;good return code, display data
    Write ?15,ResultSet.Name
    Write ?40,ResultSet.FavoriteColor
  }
```

```
Do ^SQLROUTINE
```

```
Invalid Status returned from the %Prepare Call.
Status: 0
n—————————————————â% Table 'MYPACKAGE.Actor' not found
```

Example 23-10 demonstrates a simple query using *Dynamic SQL* where the *MyQuery is invalid and the Status returned from the Prepare call catches the problem.*

*Caché provides Dynamic SQL with a nice print method for simple table, %Display.*

## Dynamic SQL Routine to Display the Actors Class using %Display

**Example 23-11 Dynamic SQL Routine to Display the Actors Class using %Display**

To run this code you must put the code in a routine (SQLROUTINE), save the routine, and then run the routine from the terminal.

```
SQLROUTINE                          ;Start of routine to hold Dynamic SQL

   Set MyQuery="SELECT * FROM MyPackage.Actor" ;Define the Query

   Set ActorOref = ##class(%SQL.Statement).%New() ;New Instance of %SQL.Statement

   Set Status = ActorOref.%Prepare(MyQuery)     ;Prepare the Query

   Set ResultSet = ActorOref.%Execute()         ;Execute the Query

   Do ResultSet.%Display()                      ;Display
```

If you save the above code in a routine and then run the it from the Terminal, you should get the following output.

```
Do ^SQLROUTINE

ID       FavoriteColor   MyAccountant    Name      MyHome_City
MyHome_StateMyHome_Street        MyHome_Zip
1        Blue            John Wayne
2        Green           Jodie Foster
3        Cyan      2     Clint Eastwood
4        Brown           Julie Andrews   Marlboro         MA  123 Main St.01752
5        Tan             Johnny Depp
6        Red             Carol Burnett
7        Navy            Will Smith
8        Yellow          Ann Margaret
9        Green           Dean Martin
10       Black           Ally Sheedy
11       Brown           Humphrey Bogart
12       Blue      2     Katharine Hepburn

12 Rows(s) Affected
```

Example 23-11 demonstrates the use of *%Display* method for simple table. Unfortunately, MyPackage.Actor is not a simple table and you can see the results.

## Dynamic SQL Routine to Display the Actors Class "Reference to a Persistent Object" Property

In Chapter 22, Example 22-14, we added a *Reference Property* of *MyAccountant* that points to the MyPackage.Accountants Class. This is what is known as a *Reference Property* or a *Reference to a Persistent Property*. When an Object Property of one class is a Persistent Object of another class, it is referred to as a **Reference Property**. *Reference Properties* are created separately from the object referring to it. A link establishes connectivity between the *Reference Property* and the object referring to it. In Chapter 22 we associated or linked Clint Eastwood and Katharine Hepburn from MyPackage.Actor to Accountant "Fair Accountant" from MyPackage.Accountants.

**Example 23-12 Dynamic SQL Routine to Display the Actors Class "Reference to Persistent Object" Property**

To run this code you must put the code in a routine (SQLROUTINE), save the routine, and then run the routine from the terminal.

```
SQLROUTINE                          ;Start of routine to hold Dynamic SQL

    Set MyQuery="SELECT Id, Name, FavoriteColor, MyAccountant->AccountantName "
    Set MyQuery=MyQuery_" FROM MyPackage.Actor"        ;Define the Query

    Set ActorOref = ##class(%SQL.Statemenew Instance of %SQL.Statement

    Set Status = ActorOref.%Prepare(MyQuery)           ;Prepare the Query

    If Status=1 {
        Set ResultSet = ActorOref.%Execute()           ;Execute the Query
        While ResultSet.%Next() {                       ;Return each row of the Query
            Write !,?5,"Id: ",ResultSet.Id
            Write ?15,ResultSet.Name
            Write ?35,ResultSet.FavoriteColor
            If ResultSet.AccountantName'="" {
                Write ?45,"Accountant Name : ",ResultSet.AccountantName
            }
        }
    }
```

If you save the above code in a routine and then run the it from the Terminal, you should get the following output.

```
Do ^SQLROUTINE

    Id: 1      John Wayne         Blue
    Id: 2      Jodie Foster       Green
    Id: 3      Clint Eastwood     Cyan      Accountant Name : Fair Accountant
    Id: 4      Julie Andrews      Brown
    Id: 5      Johnny Depp        Tan
    Id: 6      Carol Burnett      Red
    Id: 7      Will Smith         Navy
    Id: 8      Ann Margaret       Yellow
    Id: 9      Dean Martin        Green
    Id: 10     Ally Sheedy        Black
    Id: 11     Humphrey Bogart    Brown
    Id: 12     Katharine Hepburn  Blue      Accountant Name : Fair Accountant
```

In Example 23-12, we use *Dynamic SQL* to select all actors from the class MyPackage.Actor and at the same time reach out to the Referenced Class MyPackage.Accountants. Please note the special syntax whereby we reach out to the Referenced Class, "->", as in MyAccountants -> AccountantName

## Dynamic SQL Routine to Display the Actors Class "Reference to Embedded Class" Property

In Chapter 22, Example 22-20, we added a Reference Property of *MyHome* that points to the MyPackage.Address Class. This is what is known as a *Reference to an Embedded Class*. **References to Embedded Classes** are similar to *References to Persistent Objects*, except that the Object being referenced is an *Embedded Class,* or a Class stored within the *Persistent Object. Embedded Classes* are *%SerialObject Class*. These classes can only be stored within a persistent object and are not stored by themselves. In Chapter 22, Example 22-21 we associated or linked Julie Andrews from MyPackage.Actor to an address in MyPackage.Address.

**Example 23-13 Dynamic SQL Routine to Display the Actors Class "Reference to Embedded Class" Property**

```
To run this code you must put the code in a routine (SQLROUTINE), save the
routine, and then run the routine from the terminal.

  SQLROUTINE                      ;Start of routine to hold Dynamic SQL

    Set MyQuery="SELECT ID, Name, MyHome_Street, MyHome_City, MyHome_State, MyHome_Zip"
    Set MyQuery=MyQuery_" FROM MyPackage.Actor"  ;Define the Query

    Set ActorOref = ##class(%SQL.Statement).%New() ;New Instance of %SQL.Statement

    Set Status = ActorOref.%Prepare(MyQuery) ;Prepare the Query

    Set ResultSet = ActorOref.%Execute() ;Execute the Query

    While ResultSet.%Next() {                    ;Return each row of the Query
        Write !,?5,"Id: ",ResultSet.Id
        Write ?15,"Name: ",ResultSet.Name
        If ResultSet.MyHomeStreet'="" Write ?35,"Street : ",ResultSet.MyHomeStreet
        If ResultSet.MyHomeCity'=""   Write !,?35,"City : ",ResultSet.MyHomeCity
        If ResultSet.MyHomeState'=""  Write !,?35,"State : ",ResultSet.MyHomeState
        If ResultSet.MyHomeZip'=""    Write !,?35,"Zip : ",ResultSet.MyHomeZip
    }
```

```
If you save the above code in a routine and then run the it from the Terminal,
you should get the following output.

Do ^SQLROUTINE

    Id: 1      Name: John Wayne
    Id: 2      Name: Jodie Foster
    Id: 3      Name: Clint Eastwood
    Id: 4      Name: Julie Andrews Street : 123 Main St.
                             City : Marlboro
                             State : MA
                             Zip : 01752
    Id: 5      Name: Johnny Depp
    Id: 6      Name: Carol Burnett
    Id: 7      Name: Will Smith
```

```
Id: 8      Name: Ann Margaret
Id: 9      Name: Dean Martin
Id: 10     Name: Ally Sheedy
Id: 11     Name: Humphrey Bogart
Id: 12     Name: Katharine Hepburn
```

Example 23-13 demonstrates a simple query using *Dynamic SQL*. We used *Dynamic SQL* to select all actors from the class MyPackage.Actor and at the same time reach out to the Referenced Class MyPackage.Address. Please note how the MyPackage.Address objects are referenced, in the Select Statement an underscore is used to separate "MyHome" from the individual entries. But in the Write Statement, the underscore is not necessary.

## *Chapter 23 Summary*

In this chapter, we briefly looked at *Embedded* and *Dynamic SQL Queries*, two ways of including Caché *SQL Queries* in a COS Routine or Method. First we covered some basic ideas of Caché *SQL*. Then we accessed the Actor Class (created in Chapter 22) from *SQL*. We used *SQL* to insert data into the Actor Class. Next *SQL* is used to select data and then display data from the Actor Class. Finally we showed how to connect to References to Persistent Objects (MyPackage.Accountants) and References to Embedded Classes (MyPackage.Address) from the Actor Class. In the chapters that follow we will expand upon the information presented here.

# Chapter 24 Object Property Datatypes

Chapter 24 covers the basic concepts of Caché ObjectScript (COS), Object Property Datatypes. *Datatypes* define, describe or restrict the value an *Object Property may contain*. For example, a *Datatype* may tell you that an Object Property is numeric, or a string, or a formatted string. A *Datatype* may determine the behavior or validation of an *Object Property*. The Application Programmer may create customized *Datatypes* for their own purposes. Most computer programming languages employ Datatypes.

## Common Datatypes

Table 24-1 Common Datatypes

| Datatypes | Source | Description |
|---|---|---|
| %String | %Library.String | The %String *Datatype* class represents a string of characters. |
| %Name | %Library.Name | The %Name *Datatype* class represents a string containing a name in the format:"lastname,firstname". |
| %Numeric | %Library.Numeric | The %Numeric *Datatype* class represents a real number. |
| %Integer | %Library.Integer | The %Integer *Datatype* class represents an integer value. |
| %Date | %Library.Date | The %Date *Datatype* class represents a date. The value of the %Date is in $H format. |
| %Time | %Library.Time | The %Time *Datatype* is the number of seconds past midnight. |
| %Status | %Library.Status | The %Status *Datatype* represents a status code. |

The above is only a partial list of *DataTypes*. For a full list of *Datatypes* see the system Class %Library.DataType.

## Create a Datatypes1 Class

For this Chapter you will need to create a "Datatypes1" Class and several properties.

The easiest way to create a class is by using the *Caché Studio* application from the *Caché Cube* software. If you do not have the Caché Cube on your PC or computer, you can download a free copy of Caché for personal evaluation from www.intersytems.com.

After starting up Caché, click on Caché Studio from the Caché Cube (a small blue cube in your system tray). In Caché Studio click on **File** -> **New,** then select **Caché Class Definition,** and follow the prompts. Caché Studio includes helpful wizards in creating Classes, Objects Properties and Methods, etc.

You will be asked for a **Package** name, A *Package* name is a way of grouping common classes. Specify a *Package* name of *User* and a Class name of *Datatypes1*. Select a Class Type of **Persistent** (Persistent means it will be stored on disk) and take the defaults for the rest of the wizard.

From the top row in Studio, click on **Class** -> **Add -> Property.**  Create the DataItem1 Property as specified by Example 24-1.

## Define the User.Datatypes1 Class with DataItem1 Property

**Example 24-1 Define User.Datatypes1 Class with DataItem1 Property**

```
Class User.Datatypes1 Extends %Persistent
{

Property DataItem1 As %String [ Required ];

}
```

Example 24-1 creates the class *User.Datatypes1* with an Object Property called *DataItem1* that is of *Datatype* %String and is required.  From the top row in Studio, click on **Build** -> **Compile** to compile the class.

## Property Data Validation with Datatypes, Required

**Example 24-2 Property Data Validation – Required - Demonstration**

```
Set oref=##class(User.Datatypes1).%New()  ;create a new oref or Object Reference

Set oref.DataItem1=""                      ;DataItem1 set to null

Set status=oref.%Save()                     ;attempt to save

If status'=1 Do $system.OBJ.DisplayError(status)      ;save not successful
ERROR #5659: Property 'User.Datatypes1::DataItem1(1@User.Datatypes1,ID=)'
Required

  = = = = = = = = = = = = = = = = = = = = = = = = = = = = = = = =

Set oref.DataItem1="somevalue"             ;DataItem1 set to somevalue

Set status=oref.%Save()                     ;attempt to save
```

```
If status'=1 Do $system.OBJ.DisplayError(status)
<>                                              ;save successful

Write status
1                                               ;save successful
```

In Example 24-2, we first create a new Object Reference or *Oref* for our User.Datatypes1 Class. Next we set the DataItem1 Property to null, when we attempt to save the object we receive an error because DataItem1 is Required. The next step is to set DataItem1 to "somevalue" and attempt the save again, which is successful.

## Define Properties with Datatypes, Min and Max Length

**Example 24-3 Define Properties with Data Types, Min and Max Length**

```
Class User.Datatypes1 Extends %Persistent
{

Property DataItem1 As %String [ Required ];

Property DataItem2 As %String(MAXLEN = 10, MINLEN = 5);

}
```

In Example 24-3, we add a second Property, DataItem2 with a Maximum and Minimum Length. From the top row in Studio, click on **Class -> Add -> Property,** create the DataItem2 Property. From the top row in Studio, click on Build -> Compile to compile the class.

## Property Data Validation – Min and Max Length - Demonstration

**Example 24-4 Property Data Validation – Min and Max Length - Demonstration**

```
Set oref=##class(User.Datatypes1).%New() ;create a new oref or Object Reference

Set oref.DataItem1="SomeValue"             ;DataItem1 is required

Set oref.DataItem2="abc"                   ;DataItem2 set to less than min length

Set status=oref.%Save()                    ;attempt to save

If status'=1 Do $system.OBJ.DisplayError(status)       ;save not successful

ERROR #7202: Datatype value 'abc' length less than MINLEN allowed of 5
 > ERROR #5802: Datatype validation failed on property
'User.Datatypes1:DataItem2'
, with value equal to "abc"

   = = = = = = = = = = = = = = = = = = = = = = = = = = = = = = =

Set oref.DataItem2="abcde"       ;DataItem2 set to the specified minimum length

Set status=oref.%Save()          ;attempt to save

If status'=1 Do $system.OBJ.DisplayError(status)
<>                                      ;save successful
```

```
Write status
1                                              ;save successful
```

In Example 24-4, we first create a new Object Reference or *Oref* for our User.Datatypes1 Class. Next we set the DataItem2 Property to "abc" which is less than the specified minimum length. When we attempt to save the object we receive the error. The next step is to set DataItem2 to "abcde" which satisfies the minimum length and attempt the save again, which is successful.

The next few examples will demonstrate certain data validation specifications, specifically:

> MINLEN – minimum length

> MAXLEN – maximum length

> VALUELIST – list of acceptable values

> PATTERN – pattern matching

We can verify the data before attempting to save it. This is done with the "IsValid" function. This function is demonstrated in the next few examples.

## *Property Data Validation – Min and Max Length - IsValid*

**Example 24-5 Property Data Validation – Min and Max Length - IsValid**

```
Set oref=##class(User.Datatypes1).%New()   ;create a new oref or Object Reference

Set oref.DataItem1="SomeValue"          ;DataItem1 is required

Set oref.DataItem2="abc"                ;DataItem2 set to less than min length

Set status=##class(User.Datatypes1).DataItem2IsValid(oref.DataItem2)

If status'=1 Do $system.OBJ.DisplayError(status)     ;validation not successful

ERROR #7202: Datatype value 'abc' length less than MINLEN allowed of 5
```

Example 24-5 is the same as Example 24-4 except we use the *IsValid* function to verify DataItem2 Property. Notice that "IsValid" is concatenated onto the Property name and the value of the Property is passed in the parentheses.

## *Define Properties with Datatypes, Pattern*

**Example 24-6 Define Properties with Data Types, Pattern**

```
Class User.Datatypes1 Extends %Persistent
{

Property DataItem1 As %String [ Required ];

Property DataItem2 As %String(MAXLEN = 10, MINLEN = 5);

Property SSN As %String(PATTERN = "3N""-""2N""-""4N");

}
```

In Example 24-6, we add a Social Security Number (SSN) Property with a Pattern. See Chapter 10 for a review of Pattern Matching. From the top row in Studio, click on **Class** -> **Add** -> **Property;** create the SSN Property with the Pattern as shown. From the top row in Studio, click on Build -> Compile to compile the class.

## Property Data Validation – Pattern - Demonstration

**Example 24-7 Property Data Validation – Pattern - Demonstration**

```
Set oref=##class(User.Datatypes1).%New()    ;create a new oref or Object Reference

Set oref.DataItem1="SomeValue"              ;DataItem1 is required

Set oref.DataItem2="abcde"                  ;DataItem2 set to the  min length

Set oref.SSN="123-45-66"                    ;SSN set to wrong pattern

Set status=##class(User.Datatypes1).SSNIsValid(oref.SSN)

If status'=1 Do $system.OBJ.DisplayError(status)        ;validation not successful

ERROR #7209: Datatype value '123-45-66' does not match PATTERN '3N1"-"2N1"-
"4N'

   = = = = = = = = = = = = = = = = = = = = = = = = = = = = = = =

Set oref.SSN="123-45-6677"                             ;SSN set to correct pattern

Set status=##class(User.Datatypes1).SSNIsValid(oref.SSN)

If status'=1 Do $system.OBJ.DisplayError(status)        ;validation successful
<>

Write status
1
```

In Example 24-7, we first create a new Object Reference or *Oref* for our User.Datatypes1 Class. Next we set the SSN Property to '123-45-66' which does not match our required pattern. When we verify our SSN Property with a call to SSNIsValid we receive an error. We next change SSN to be in accordance to the Pattern and then call SSNIsValid and save our object.

## Define Properties with Datatypes, Valuelist

**Example 24-8 Define Properties with Data Types, Valuelist**

```
Class User.Datatypes1 Extends %Persistent
{

Property DataItem1 As %String [ Required ];

Property DataItem2 As %String(MAXLEN = 10, MINLEN = 5);

Property SSN As %String(PATTERN = "3N1""-""2N1""-""4N");
```

```
Property StatusCode As %String(VALUELIST = "-Success-Fail-Pend");

}
```

In Example 24-8, we add a *StatusCode* Property with a *Valuelist*. A *Valuelist* specifies what values this property can hold. The first character of the *Valuelist* specifies the delimiter. So this *StatusCode* property can contain one of three values, "Success", "Fail" or "Pend".

## *Property Data Validation – Valuelist - Demonstration*

**Example 24-9 Property Data Validation – Value - Demonstration**

```
Set oref=##class(User.Datatypes1).%New()    ;create a new oref or Object Reference

Set oref.DataItem1="SomeValue"                ;DataItem1 is required

Set oref.DataItem2="abcde"                    ;DataItem2 set to the  min length

Set oref.SSN="123-45-6677"                    ;SSN set to correct pattern

Set oref.StatusCode="WrongValue"              ;Set StatusCode to a wrong value

Set status=##class(User.Datatypes1).StatusCodeIsValid(oref.StatusCode)

If status'=1 Do $system.OBJ.DisplayError(status)      ;validation not successful

ERROR #7205: Datatype value 'WrongValue' not in VALUELIST '-Success-Fail-
Pend'

   = = = = = = = = = = = = = = = = = = = = = = = = = = = = = =

Set oref.StatusCode="Success"                 ;Set StatusCode to a correct value

Set status=##class(User.Datatypes1).StatusCodeIsValid(oref.StatusCode)

If status'=1 Do $system.OBJ.DisplayError(status)      ;validation successful
<>

Write status
1
```

In Example 24-9, we first create a new Object Reference or *Oref* for our User.Datatypes1 Class. Next we set the StatusCode Property to "WrongValue" which does not match our *Valuelist*. When we verify our StatusCode Property with a call to *StatusCodeIsValid* we receive an error. We next change StatusCode to be according to the Valuelist and then call *StatusCodeIsValid* and save our object.

## Custom Datatypes

In addition to using the system defined *Datatypes*, you can create your own *Datatype* classes. The next few examples show some of the possibilities of using *Custom Datatype* classes.

This next example demonstrates how to use a custom *Datatype* class to define a Name property. First we will create a custom Datatype Class called *User.NameDatatype*.

## Define a Custom Datatype Class for Name

**Example 24-10 Define a Custom Datatype Class for Name**

```
Class User.NameDatatype Extends %Persistent
{

Property FirstName As %String;

Property MiddleInitial As %String;

Property LastName As %String;

}
```

In Example 24-10, we define a new custom *Datatype* class for Name. The class has 3 properties, FirstName, MiddleInitial and LastName. Next we will use the class as a *Datatype* to define our Name property.

## Add Name Property to User.Datatypes1

**Example 24-11 Add Name Property to User.Datatypes1**

```
Class User.Datatypes1 Extends %Persistent
{

Property DataItem1 As %String [ Required ];

Property DataItem2 As %String(MAXLEN = 10, MINLEN = 5);

Property SSN As %String(PATTERN = "3N1""-""2N1""-""4N");

Property StatusCode As %String(VALUELIST = "-Success-Fail-Pend");

Property Name As User.NameDatatype;

}
```

In Example 24-11, we add a Name Property to our User.Datatypes1 Class. The Name Property points to the NameDatatype Class for name we created in Example 24-10. Now we shall see how this works.

## Property Data Validation – Custom Datatype - Demonstration

**Example 24-12 Property Data Validation – Custom Datatype - Demonstration**

```
Set oref=##class(User.Datatypes1).%New()      ;create a new Object Reference

Set oref.DataItem1="SomeValue"                 ;DataItem1 is required

Set oref.DataItem2="abcde"                     ;DataItem2 set to the  min length

Set oref.SSN="123-45-6677"                     ;SSN set to correct pattern

Set oref.StatusCode="Success"                  ;Set StatusCode to a correct value

Set NameOref=##class(User.NameDatatype).%New() ;create a new oref for
                                               ;the NameDatatype Class

Set NameOref.FirstName="Ben"                   ;Populate the Name Class
Set NameOref.MiddleInitial="T"
Set NameOref.LastName="Dover"

Set oref.Name=NameOref                         ;Point the Name Property to
                                               ;the Customer Name Datatype

Write oref.%Save()
1

Write oref.Name.FirstName                      ;Reference the Name
Ben
Write oref.Name.MiddleInitial
T
Write oref.Name.LastName
Dover
```

Example 24-12 we first create a new Object Reference or *Oref* for our User.Datatypes1 Class. Next we create a new Object for our User.NameDatatype Class. Then we populate the User.NameDatatype Class with FirstName, MiddleInitial and LastName. The next step is to point the Name Property of the User.Datatypes1 Class to the NameOref of the User.NameDatatype Class. Finally we save the data and display the Name.

## Chapter 24 Summary

In chapter 24 we covered *Datatypes* of Object Properties. *Datatypes* define, describe or restrict Object Properties. Common system datatypes include %String, %Name, %Numeric, %Integer, %Date, %Time and %Status. Datatypes can also be used to Validate Object Properties through Length, Value or Pattern restrictions among others. The programmer may also create Custom Datatypes to further define or restrict Object Properties.

# *Chapter 25 Class & Object Properties - Collection List of Data Types*

Chapters 25 through 30 cover the basic concepts of Caché ObjectScript (COS) to process Caché Class and Objects Properties - **Collections**. In Chapter 22 we looked at:

> ➤ Data Types
>
> ➤ References to Persistent Objects – these Properties point to or reference other Persistent Objects in another class
>
> ➤ References to Embedded Objects – these Properties point to or reference an Embedded Object that reside (or are embedded) in the current class

Now we are going to apply the concept of *Collections* or *Multiple Entries* to each of the above three.

## *Introduction to Collections*

A **Collection** is an ordered list of information, or multiple entries.

*Collections* in Caché fall into these categories:

> ➤ List Collection of Data Types - Chapter 25
>
> ➤ Array Collection of Data Types - Chapter 26
>
> ➤ List Collection of References to Persistent Objects – Chapter 27
>
> ➤ Array Collection of References to Persistent Objects – Chapter 28
>
> ➤ List Collection of References to Embedded Objects – Chapter 29
>
> ➤ Array Collection of References to Embedded Objects - Chapter 30

As a base Class we will use *MyPackage.Actor* created in Chapter 22 and modified in subsequent chapters.

We have already seen *Data Types*, *References to Persistent Objects* and *References to Embedded Objects*. Now by using *Collections* we will expand their capability.

## Collection Lists and Collection Arrays

Each element in a *Collection List* has a *Slot Number* and associated *Value*.

### A Collection List of Shirts

**Table 25-1 A Collection List of Shirts**

| Slot Number | Value |
|---|---|
| 1 | RedShirt |
| 2 | WhiteShirt |
| 3 | BlueShirt |

In Table 25-1 we have three Slots and three Shirts, this is a *List Collection*.

Each element in a *Collection Array* has a *Key* and associated *Value*.

### A Collection Array of Hats

**Table 25-2 A Collection Array of Hats**

| Key | Value |
|---|---|
| 1 | Bowler |
| 2 | Straw |
| Mesh | FruitMesh |
| Top | TopHat |

In Table 25-2, we have a *Collection Array*. As you can see we use a *Key* instead of a *Slot*, and the Key can be either numeric or alphanumeric.

## Table of Collection Methods

*Collections* may refer to *Data Types*, *References to Persistent Objects*, and *References to Embedded Objects*. A number of *Methods* manipulate these three types of *Collections*. Not all *Methods* apply to every type of *Collection*. In Table 25-3, we see the various *Methods* demonstrated. This table is a guide for the *Methods* in Chapters 25 through 30.

**Table 25-3 Table Collection Methods**

| | Chapter 25 | Chapter 26 | Chapter 27 | Chapter 28 | Chapter 29 | Chapter 30 | |
|---|---|---|---|---|---|---|---|
| Actor used | John Wayne | Jodi Foster | Johnny Depp | Carol Burnett | Dean Martin | Ann Margaret | |
| Associated data | MyShirts | MyHats | MyContacts | MyClients | MyRentals | MyPets | |
| | Data Types | | References to Persistent Objects | | References to Embedded Objects | | |
| Methods | Collection Lists of Data Types | Collection Arrays of Data Types | Collection Lists of References To Persistent Objects | Collection Arrays of References To Persistent Objects | Collection Lists of References To Embedded Objects | Collection Arrays of References To Embedded Objects | Description |
| Clear() | Example 25 – 2 | Example 26 – 2 | Example 27 – 4 | Example 28 – 4 | Example 29 – 3 | Example 30 – 3 | Clears or Deletes the Collection of Elements |
| Count() | Example 25 – 2 | Example 26 – 2 | Example 27 – 4 | Example 28 – 4 | Example 29– 3 | Example 30 – 3 | Returns the Number of Elements in the Collection |
| GetAt(Slot) | Example 25 – 5 | | | | | | Returns the Element associated with a Slot |
| GetAt(Key) | | Example 26 – 6 | Example 27 – 7 | Example 28 – 8 | Example 29 – 6 | Example 30 – 7 | Returns the Element associated with a Key |
| Find(Element, Slot) | Example 25 – 6 | | | | | | Finds the Element starting at the Slot |
| Find(Element, Key) | | Example 26 – 7 | | | | | Finds the Element starting at the Key |
| Find(String) | | | Example 27 – 8 | Example 28 – 9 | Example 29 – 7 | Example 30 – 8 | Code to emulate a Find. Finds the associated Key for a String |
| IsDefined(Key) | | Example 26 – 5 | | Example 28 – 7 | | Example 30 – 6 | Returns a 1 if the Key is defined otherwise 0 |
| Next(Slot) | Example 25 – 7 | | | | | | Returns the next Slot position |
| Next(Key) | | Example 26 – 9 | Example 27 – 9 | Example 28 – 10 | Example 29 –8 | Example 30 –9 | Returns the Element for the next Key |
| Previous(Slot) | Example 25 – 8 | | | | | | Returns the previous Slot position |
| Previous(Key) | | Example 26 – 10 | Example 27 – 10 | Example 28 – 11 | Example 29 – 9 | Example 30 –10 | Returns the Element for the |

| | | | | | | |
|---|---|---|---|---|---|---|
| | | | | | | previous Key |
| GetNext(.Slot) (slot passed by reference) | Example 25 – 9 | | | | | | Returns the Element for the next Slot |
| GetNext(.Key) (key passed by reference) | | Example 26 – 11 | Example 27 – 11 | Example 28 – 12 | Example 29 – 10 | Example 30 –11 | Returns the Element for the next Key |
| GetPrevious(.Slot) (slot passed by reference) | Example 25 – 10 | | | | | | Returns the Element for the previous Slot |
| GetPrevious(.Key) (Key passed by reference) | | Example 26 – 12 | Example 27 – 12 | Example 28 – 13 | Example 29 – 11 | Example 30 –12 | Returns the Element for the previous Key |
| | | | | | | | |
| Insert(Element) | Example 25 – 3 | | | | | | Inserts an Element at the end of the collection |
| Insert(Oref) | | | Example 27 – 5 | | Example 29 – 4 | | Inserts an Oref at the end of the collection |
| InsertAt(Element,Slot) | Example 25 – 11 | | | | | | Inserts an Element into a Collection at a specified Slot |
| InsertAt(Oref,Key) | | | Example 27 – 13 | | Example 29 – 12 | | Insert an Oref into a Collection at a specific Key |
| | | | | | | | |
| InsertOrdered(Value) | Example 25 – 13 | | | | | | Inserts an Element into a collection |
| | | | | | | | |
| SetAt(Element, Slot) | Example 25 – 12 | | | | | | Sets an Element at the specified Slot |
| SetAt(Element, Key) | | Example 26 – 3 Example 26 – 8 | Example 27 – 14 | | | | Set or Replace an Element at a specific Key |
| SetAt(Oref,Key) | | | | Example 28 – 5 Example 28 – 14 | Example 29 – 4 | Example 30 – 4 Example 30 – 13 | Set an Oref at the specific Key |
| RemoveAt(Slot) | Example 25 – 14 | | | | | | Remove the Element at the specified Slot position |
| RemoveAt(Key) | | Example 26 – 13 | Example 27 – 15 | Example 28 – 15 | Example 29 – 14 | Example 30 – 14 | Remove the Element associated with a Key |
| | | | | | | | |
| Select data with Embedded SQL | Example 25 – 15 | Example 26 – 14 | Example 27 - 16 | Example 28 – 16 | Example 29 – 15 | Example 30 - 15 | |
| Display data with Embedded SQL | Example 25 – 15 | Example 26 – 14 | Example 27 - 16 | Example 28 – 16 | Example 29 – 15 | Example 30 - 15 | |
| Select data with Dynamic SQL | Example 25 – 16 | Example 26 - 15 | Example 27 - 17 | Example 28 - 17 | Example 29 - 16 | Example 30 - 16 | |
| Display data with Dynamic SQL | Example 25 – 16 | Example 26 - 15 | Example 27 - 17 | Example 28 - 17 | Example 29 - 16 | Example 30 - 16 | |

In Table 25-3, the various Methods are listed for Collections, including those in Chapters 25 through 30. The most common and useful Methods are listed, to see all available Method available reference the *documentation at* www.InterSystems.com.

## Collection List of Data Types

The first Object Property we will consider is *Data Types*. For the sake of clarity we will only use one *Data Type*, that of *%String*. Please refer to the InterSystems documentation at *www.intersystems.com* for the other Data Types, such as: *%Binary, %Boolean, %Currency, %Date, %Float (a floating point value), %Integer, %List, %Name, %Numeric, %Status, %Time and %TimeStamp*.

We now turn our attention to a *Collection List of Data Types* with a size limit 32k.

**Table 25-4 Object Properties**

| Object Property | Data Type | Name we chose | Special Considerations |
|---|---|---|---|
| Data Types | %String | Name (Name of Actor) | |
| Collection List of Data Types | %String | MyShirts (Shirts belonging to an Actor) | Total length cannot exceed 32k |
| Collection Array of Data Types | %String | MyHats (Hats belonging to an Actor) | No length limit In SQL must be handled as a Child table Must specify a Key when accessing |

We need to redefine our *MyPackage.Actor* (first defined in Chapter 22) class to include a *Collection List of Data Types*. We shall use MyShirts as our Property name. Be aware that *Collection Lists* have a maximum string length of all strings of 32k. If our list of shirts consists of four shirts with short names, we are in no danger of exceeding 32k. However, if we have 5,000 shirts, each with long elaborate names, perhaps a *Collection List* is not what we should use.

## Actor Class Redefinition – Include the Collection List Property: MyShirts

**Example 25-1 Actor Class Redefinition - Include the Collection List Property: MyShirts**

```
Class MyPackage.Actor Extends %Persistent
{

Property Name As %String [ Required ];

Index NameIndex On Name;

Property MyAccountant As Accountants;

Property MyHome As Address;

Property FavoriteColor As %String;

Property MyShirts As list Of %String;

}
```

After starting up Caché Studio from the Caché Cube (a small blue cube in your system tray), click on **File -> Open**, then select the package MyPackage and Class Actor. Add the "Property MyShirts As list Of

%String" line (click on **Class -> Add -> Property)** to the Actor Class. Your class should look like Example 25-1. Recompile the class.

The following are a number of methods whereby we manipulate the *Collection List Property: MyShirts*. We shall use *MyPackage.Actor Object Id 1*, John Wayne. If we did not know the *Object Id* of John Wayne, we could use *Embedded SQL* to find his Id as demonstrated in Chapter 22 Example 11 and in Chapter 23.

## Clear and Count Methods – Delete all elements and show the count

Example 25-2 Clear and Count Methods - Deletes all elements and show the count

```
The MyShirts Property is defined as a Collection List of Data Types

Clear Method - Clears or Deletes the Collection of Elements

Count Method - Returns the Number of Elements in the Collection

 Set ActorOref=##class(MyPackage.Actor).%OpenId(1)      ;bring object John
                                                        ;Wayne into memory

 Do ActorOref.MyShirts.Clear()                          ;clear list of shirts
 Write !,"Count: ",ActorOref.MyShirts.Count()           ;count of elements
 Write !,ActorOref.%Save()                              ;Save the object

If you run the above code from the Terminal, you should get the following
output.

Count: 0
1
```

In Example 25-2, we start by bringing into memory an Actor Object with an Id of 1, (John Wayne). Next we ensure there is no data in our *Collection List Property: MyShirts* so we use the *Clear()* and *Count() Methods*. Lastly, we use the *%Save() Method* to save all changes to disk.

## Insert Method – Insert three shirts into the Collection

Example 25-3 Insert Method – Insert three shirts into the Collection

```
The MyShirts Property is defined as a Collection List of Data Types

Insert Method - Inserts an Element at the end of the collection

 Set ActorOref=##class(MyPackage.Actor).%OpenId(1)      ;bring object John Wayne
                                                        ;into memory

 Do ActorOref.MyShirts.Insert("BlueShirt")             ;insert RedShirt
 Do ActorOref.MyShirts.Insert("RedShirt")              ;insert WhiteShirt
 Do ActorOref.MyShirts.Insert("WhiteShirt")            ;insert BlueShirt

 Write !,"Count: ",ActorOref.MyShirts.Count()          ;count of elements
 Write !,ActorOref.%Save()                             ;Save the object
```

```
If you run the above code from the Terminal, you should get the following
output.
```

```
Count: 3
1
```

In Example 25-3, we use the *Insert() Method* to add three shirts to the *Collection List Property: MyShirts*.

## Global generated from Class MyPackage.Actor

**Example 25-4 Global generated from Class MyPackage.Actor**

```
zw ^MyPackage.ActorD
^MyPackage.ActorD=13
^MyPackage.ActorD(1)=$lb("","John
Wayne","",$lb("","","",""),"Blue",$lb("BlueShirt","RedShirt","WhiteShirt"))
^MyPackage.ActorD(2)=$lb("","Jodie Foster","",$lb("","","",""),"Green")
^MyPackage.ActorD(3)=$lb("","Clint Eastwood","2",$lb("","","",""),"Cyan")
^MyPackage.ActorD(4)=$lb("","Julie Andrews","",$lb("123 Main St.","Marlboro",
"MA","01752"),"Brown")
^MyPackage.ActorD(5)=$lb("","Johnny Depp","",$lb("","","",""),"Tan")
^MyPackage.ActorD(6)=$lb("","Carol Burnett","",$lb("","","",""),"Red")
^MyPackage.ActorD(7)=$lb("","Will Smith","",$lb("","","",""),"Navy")
^MyPackage.ActorD(8)=$lb("","Ann Margaret","",$lb("","","",""),"Yellow")
^MyPackage.ActorD(9)=$lb("","Dean Martin","",$lb("","","",""),"Green")
^MyPackage.ActorD(10)=$lb("","Ally Sheedy","",$lb("","","",""),"Black")
^MyPackage.ActorD(11)=$lb("","Humphrey Bogart","",$lb("","","",""),"Brown")
^MyPackage.ActorD(12)=$lb("","Katharine Hepburn","2",$lb("","","",""),"Blue")
```

Example 25-4 shows a listing of the Global generated from the Class MyPackage.Actor. You can see how the three shirts are stored for John Wayne. Your Global may not look exactly like this one if you have not worked through all the examples in the previous Chapters.

## GetAt Method – Display the Collection List

**Example 25-5 GetAt Method – Display the Collection List**

```
The MyShirts Property is defined as a Collection List of Data Types

GetAt Method - Returns the Element associated with a Slot

To run this code you must put the code in a routine, save the routine, and then
run the routine from the terminal.
```

```
 Set ActorOref=##class(MyPackage.Actor).%OpenId(1)      ;bring object John
Wayne
                                                        ;into memory

 Write !,"Count: ",ActorOref.MyShirts.Count()           ;count of elements

 For Slot=1:1:ActorOref.MyShirts.Count() {              ;Display each element
   Write !,"Slot: ",Slot                                ;of the Collection
List
   Write " - ",ActorOref.MyShirts.GetAt(Slot)           ;Property: MyShirts
 }
```

```
If you save the above code in a routine and then run the it from the Terminal,
you should get the following output.
```

```
Count: 3
Slot: 1 - BlueShirt
Slot: 2 - RedShirt
Slot: 3 - WhiteShirt
```

Example 25-5 demonstrates the *GetAt() Method* which displays each element of the *Collection List Property: MyShirts*.


## Find Method – Find a shirt in the Collection List starting at a Slot number

**Example 25-6 Find a shirt in the Collection List starting at a Slot number**

```
The MyShirts Property is defined as a Collection List of Data Types

Find Method - Finds the Element starting at the Slot

  Set ActorOref=##class(MyPackage.Actor).%OpenId(1)      ;bring object John Wayne
                                                         ;into memory

  Set Slot=ActorOref.MyShirts.Find("RedShirt",0) ;find RedShirt starting
                                                         ;at Slot 0 or the
                                                         ;beginning of the collection

  Write !,"Slot: ",Slot," - ",ActorOref.MyShirts.GetAt(Slot)      ;display RedShirt
Slot: 2 - RedShirt

  Set Slot=ActorOref.MyShirts.Find("WhiteShirt",0)       ;find WhiteShirt starting
                                                         ;at Slot 0 or the
                                                         ;beginning of the collection

  Write !,"Slot: ",Slot," - ",ActorOref.MyShirts.GetAt(Slot)      ;display WhiteShirt
Slot: 3 - WhiteShirt

  Set Slot=ActorOref.MyShirts.Find("BlueShirt",2)        ;find BlueShirt starting at
                                                         ;Slot 2, since BlueShirt is in
                                                         ;Slot 1, nothing is found.
  Write !,"Slot: ",Slot
Slot:
```

In Example 25-6, we use the *Find Method* to locate the Slot number that corresponds to the shirt value. In the first two examples, we use 0 as the second parameters telling *Find* to start searching at Slot 0. In the last example, we use 2 as the second parameter telling *Find* to start searching at Slot 2. Since BlueShirt exists at Slot 1, the *Find* cannot locate it, which is expected.

# Traversing Methods

The *Next, Previous, GetNext* and *GetPrevious Methods* all provide the capability of traversing Object data, similar to the *$Order* command. *Next* and *GetNext* traverse through the data forward and *Previous* and *GetPrevious* traverse through the data backwards. *Next* and *Previous* accepts the Key/Slot parameter passed by value whereas *GetNext* and *GetPrevious* accept the Key/Slot parameter passed by reference.

**Table 25-5 Traversing Methods**

| Method | | How Key or Slot is passed |
|---|---|---|
| Next | Traversing Forward | Key or Slot passed by Value |
| Previous | Traversing Backward | Key or Slot Passed by Value |
| GetNext | Traversing Forward | Key or Slot Passed by Reference |
| GetPrevious | Traversing Backward | Key or Slot Passed by Reference |

## Next Method – Returns the Element for the next Slot

**Example 25-7 Next Method – Returns the Element for the next Slot**

```
The MyShirts Property is defined as a Collection List of Data Types

Next Method - Returns the next Slot position

To run this code you must put the code in a routine, save the routine, and then
run the routine from the terminal.
```

```
Set ActorOref=##class(MyPackage.Actor).%OpenId(1)    ;bring object John Wayne
                                                      ;into memory

Write !,"Count: ",ActorOref.MyShirts.Count()          ;count of elements

Set Slot = "" Do {                                    ;start with slot null
    Set Slot=ActorOref.MyShirts.Next(Slot)            ;get the next slot
    If Slot'="" {
        Write !,"Slot: ",Slot                         ;display the slot number
        Write " - ",ActorOref.MyShirts.GetAt(Slot)    ;display the shirt
    }
} While (Slot '= "")
```

```
If you save the above code in a routine and then run the it from the Terminal,
you should get the following output.
```

```
Count: 3
Slot: 1 - BlueShirt
Slot: 2 - RedShirt
Slot: 3 - WhiteShirt
```

In Example 25-7, we use the *Next() Method* to obtain the next *Slot*. Initially we set the *Slot* to null then we use *Next()* to cycle through the *Slots*, finally when the *Slot* equals null again we stop.

## Previous Method – Returns the Element for the previous Slot

Example 25-8 Previous Method – Returns the Element for the previous Slot

```
The MyShirts Property is defined as a Collection List of Data Types

Previous Method - Returns the previous Slot position

To run this code you must put the code in a routine, save the routine, and then
run the routine from the terminal.
```

```
Set ActorOref=##class(MyPackage.Actor).%OpenId(1)      ;bring object John Wayne
                                                       ;into memory

Write !,"Count: ",ActorOref.MyShirts.Count()           ;count of elements

Set Slot = "" Do {                                     ;start with slot null
    Set Slot=ActorOref.MyShirts.Previous(Slot)         ;get the previous slot
    If Slot'="" {
        Write !,"Slot: ",Slot                          ;display the slot number
        Write " - ",ActorOref.MyShirts.GetAt(Slot)     ;display the shirt
    }
} While (Slot '= "")
```

```
If you save the above code in a routine and then run the it from the Terminal,
you should get the following output.
```

```
Count: 3
Slot: 3 - WhiteShirt
Slot: 2 - RedShirt
Slot: 1 - BlueShirt
```

In Example 25-8, we use the *Previous() Method* to obtain the previous *Slot* number. Initially we set the *Slot* to null, and then we use the *Previous() Method* to cycle through the *Slots* backwards, finally when the *Slot* equals null we stop.

## GetNext Method – Returns the Element for the next Slot

Example 25-9 GetNext Method – Returns the Element for the next Slot

```
The MyShirts Property is defined as a Collection List of Data Types

GetNext Method - Returns the Element for the next Slot

To run this code you must put the code in a routine, save the routine, and then
run the routine from the terminal.
```

```
Set ActorOref=##class(MyPackage.Actor).%OpenId(1)      ;bring object John Wayne
                                                       ;into memory

Write !,"Count: ",ActorOref.MyShirts.Count()           ;count of elements
```

```
    Set Slot = "" Do {                                    ;start with beginning slot
        Set Shirt=ActorOref.MyShirts.GetNext(.Slot)           ;get next slot
        If Slot'="" {
            Write !,"Slot: ",Slot                         ;display the slot
            Write " ",Shirt                               ;display the shirt
        }
    } While (Slot '= "")
```

If you save the above code in a routine and then run the it from the Terminal, you should get the following output.

```
Count: 3
Slot: 1 - BlueShirt
Slot: 2 - RedShirt
Slot: 3 - WhiteShirt
```

In Example 25-9, we see the *GetNext() Method*. This *Method* is similar to the *Next Method* except that the Slot is passed by reference. Initially we set the Slot number to null then we use *GetNext()* to cycle through the Slots, finally when the Slot equals null we stop.

## GetPrevious Method– Returns the Element for the Previous Slot

Example 25-10 GetPrevious Method – Returns the Element for the Previous Slot

The MyShirts Property is defined as a Collection List of Data Types

GetPrevious Method - Returns the Element for the previous Slot

To run this code you must put the code in a routine, save the routine, and then run the routine from the terminal.

```
    Set ActorOref=##class(MyPackage.Actor).%OpenId(1)     ;bring object John Wayne
                                                          ;into memory

    Write !,"Count: ",ActorOref.MyShirts.Count()          ;count of elements

    Set Slot = "" Do {                                    ;start with beginning slot
        Set Shirt=ActorOref.MyShirts.GetPrevious(.Slot)       ;get previous slot
        If Slot'="" {
            Write !,"Slot: ",Slot                         ;display the slot
            Write " ",Shirt                               ;display the shirt
        }
    } While (Slot '= "")
```

If you save the above code in a routine and then run the it from the Terminal, you should get the following output.

```
Count: 3
Slot: 3 - WhiteShirt
Slot: 2 - RedShirt
Slot: 1 - BlueShirt
```

In Example 25-10, we see the *GetPrevious() Method*. This *Method* is similar to the *Previous Method* except that the Slot is passed by reference. Initially we set the Slot number to null then we use *GetPrevious()* to cycle through the Slots backwards. Finally when the Slot equals null we stop.

## InsertAt Method – Insert a shirt between the 1st and 2nd shirts

```
The MyShirts Property is defined as a Collection List of Data Types

InsertAt Method - Inserts an Element into a Collection at a specified Slot

To run this code you must put the code in a routine, save the routine, and then
run the routine from the terminal.
```

```
Set ActorOref=##class(MyPackage.Actor).%OpenId(1)      ;bring object John Wayne
                                                       ;into memory

Do ActorOref.MyShirts.InsertAt("PurpleShirt",2)        ;Insert PurpleShirt into the
                                                       ; 2rd Slot pushing the other
                                                       ;shirts out

Write !,"Count: ",ActorOref.MyShirts.Count()           ;count of elements

For Slot=1:1:ActorOref.MyShirts.Count() {              ;Display each element
    Write !,"Slot: ",Slot                              ;of Collection List
    Write " - ",ActorOref.MyShirts.GetAt(Slot)         ;Property: MyShirts
}
Write !,ActorOref.%Save()                              ;Save the Object
```

```
If you save the above code in a routine and then run the it from the Terminal,
you should get the following output.
```

```
Count: 4
Slot: 1 - BlueShirt
Slot: 2 - PurpleShirt
Slot: 3 - RedShirt
Slot: 4 - WhiteShirt
1
```

Example 25-11 demonstrates the *InsertAt() Method* to insert a PurpleShirt between the 1st and 2nd shirts.

Now suppose we made a mistake and the 2nd shirt should be CyanShirt and not PurpleShirt.

## SetAt Method – Replace a specific shirt

Example 25-12 SetAt Method – Replace a specific shirt

```
The MyShirts Property is defined as a Collection List of Data Types

SetAt Method - Sets an Element at the specified Slot

To run this code you must put the code in a routine, save the routine, and then
run the routine from the terminal.
```

```
Set ActorOref=##class(MyPackage.Actor).%OpenId(1)      ;bring object John Wayne
                                                       ;into memory

Do ActorOref.MyShirts.SetAt("CyanShirt",2)             ;Change the value in Slot 2
                                                       ;to CyanShirt
```

```
Write !,"Count: ",ActorOref.MyShirts.Count()          ;count of elements

For Slot=1:1:ActorOref.MyShirts.Count() {             ;Display each element
    Write !,"Slot: ",Slot                             ;of Collection List
    Write " - ",ActorOref.MyShirts.GetAt(Slot)        ;Property: MyShirts
}
Write !,ActorOref.%Save()                             ;Save the Object
```

If you save the above code in a routine and then run the it from the Terminal, you should get the following output.

```
Count: 4
Slot: 1 - BlueShirt
Slot: 2 - CyanShirt
Slot: 3 - RedShirt
Slot: 4 - WhiteShirt
1
```

In Example 25-12, we use the *SetAt() Method* to change the value of the shirt in Slot number 2 from PurpleShirt to CyanShirt.

## InsertOrdered Method – Add a shirt to the collection

**Example 25-13 InsertOrdered Method – Add a shirt to the collection**

The MyShirts Property is defined as a Collection List of Data Types

InsertOrdered Method - Inserts an Element into the collection

To run this code you must put the code in a routine, save the routine, and then run the routine from the terminal.

```
Set ActorOref=##class(MyPackage.Actor).%OpenId(1)     ;bring object John Wayne
                                                      ;into memory

Do ActorOref.MyShirts.InsertOrdered("PinkShirt")      ;Insert PinkShirt into
                                                      ;the Collections

Write !,"Count: ",ActorOref.MyShirts.Count()          ;count of elements

For Slot=1:1:ActorOref.MyShirts.Count() {             ;Display each element
    Write !,"Slot: ",Slot                             ;of Collection List
    Write " - ",ActorOref.MyShirts.GetAt(Slot)        ;Property: MyShirts
}
Write !,ActorOref.%Save()                             ;Save the Object
```

If you save the above code in a routine and then run the it from the Terminal, you should get the following output.

```
Count: 5
Slot: 1 - BlueShirt
Slot: 2 - CyanShirt
Slot: 3 - PinkShirt
Slot: 4 - RedShirt
Slot: 5 - WhiteShirt
1
```

In Example 25-13, we use the *InsertOrdered() Method* to add a PinkShirt to the Collection.

## RemoveAt Method – Remove an Element at a Slot

**Example 25-14 RemoveAt Method – Remove an Element at a Slot**

```
The MyShirts Property is defined as a Collection List of Data Types

RemoveAt Method - Remove the Element at the specified Slot position

To run this code you must put the code in a routine, save the routine, and then
run the routine from the terminal.
```

```
Set ActorOref=##class(MyPackage.Actor).%OpenId(1)     ;bring object John Wayne
                                                      ;into memory

Do ActorOref.MyShirts.RemoveAt(3)                     ;Remove Shirt at Slot 3

Write !,"Count: ",ActorOref.MyShirts.Count()          ;count of elements

For I=1:1:ActorOref.MyShirts.Count() {
    Write !,"Slot: ",I
    Write " - ",ActorOref.MyShirts.GetAt(I)
}
Write !,ActorOref.%Save()                              ;Save the Object
```

```
If you save the above code in a routine and then run the it from the Terminal,
you should get the following output.
```

```
Count: 4
Slot: 1 - BlueShirt
Slot: 2 - CyanShirt
Slot: 3 - RedShirt
Slot: 4 - WhiteShirt
1
```

In Example 25-14 we remove the Element at Slot 3 and notice what happens, all the Slots following Slot 3 move up one Slot.

## Select MyShirts Data using Embedded SQL

**Example 25-15 Select MyShirts Data using Embedded SQL**

```
The MyShirts Property is defined as a Collection List of Data Types

To run this code you must put the code in a routine, save the routine, and then
run the routine from the terminal.
```

```
New name, myshirts
&sql(Declare MyCursor CURSOR FOR
    SELECT Name, MyShirts
    INTO :name, :myshirts
    FROM MyPackage.Actor
    WHERE FOR SOME %ELEMENT(MyShirts) (%Value='BlueShirt')
    ORDER BY Name)
 &sql(OPEN MyCursor)
```

```
    &sql(FETCH MyCursor)
While (SQLCODE = 0) {
    Write !,"Name: ",name
    If myshirts'="" {
        For I=1:1:$LL(myshirts) {
            Write !,?20,$LI(myshirts,I)
        }
    }
    &sql(FETCH MyCursor)
}
&sql(CLOSE MyCursor)
```

If you save the above code in a routine and then run the it from the Terminal, you should get the following output.

```
Name: John Wayne
                    BlueShirt
                    CyanShirt
                    RedShirt
                    WhiteShirt
```

In Example 25-14 we demonstrate how to select MyShirts data using *Embedded SQL*. Using the "FOR SOME %ELEMENT" SQL Statement we select any actor who has in their List of Shirts a value of "BlueShirt," which of course is John Wayne. Note how MyShirts needs to be broken out with the *$List* command.

## Display MyShirts Data using Embedded SQL

**Example 25-16 Display MyShirts Data using Embedded SQL**

The MyShirts Property is defined as a Collection List of Data Types

To run this code you must put the code in a routine, save the routine, and then run the routine from the terminal.

```
New name,myshirts
&sql(Declare MyCursor CURSOR FOR
    SELECT Name, MyShirts
    INTO :name, :myshirts
    FROM MyPackage.Actor
    ORDER BY Name)
&sql(OPEN MyCursor)
&sql(FETCH MyCursor)
While (SQLCODE = 0) {
    Write !,"Name: ",name
    If myshirts'="" {
        For I=1:1:$LL(myshirts) {
            Write !,?20,$LI(myshirts,I)
        }
    }
    &sql(FETCH MyCursor)
}
&sql(CLOSE MyCursor)
```

If you save the above code in a routine and then run the it from the Terminal, you should get the following output.

```
Name: Ally Sheedy
Name: Ann Margaret
Name: Carol Burnett
Name: Clint Eastwood
Name: Dean Martin
Name: Humphrey Bogart
Name: Jodie Foster
Name: John Wayne
                    BlueShirt
                    CyanShirt
                    RedShirt
                    WhiteShirt
Name: Johnny Depp
Name: Julie Andrews
Name: Katharine Hepburn
Name: Will Smith
```

Example 25-16 demonstrates *Embedded SQL* to display MyShirts for John Wayne. Note how MyShirts needs to be broken out with the *$List* command.

## *Select MyShirts Data using Dynamic SQL*

**Example 25-17 Select MyShirts Data using Dynamic SQL**

The MyShirts Property is defined as a Collection List of Data Types

To run this code you must put the code in a routine, save the routine, and then run the routine from the terminal.

```
 Set MyQuery="SELECT Name,MyShirts FROM MyPackage.Actor"      ;Define the Query
 Set MyQuery=MyQuery_" WHERE FOR SOME %ELEMENT(MyShirts) (%Value='BlueShirt')"

 Set ResultSet=##class(%ResultSet).%New("%DynamicQuery:SQL")
                                            ;Create a new Instance of %ResultSet

 Set Status=ResultSet.Prepare(MyQuery)        ;Prepare the Query
 If Status'=1 Write "Status'=1, return from Prepare Statement" Quit

 Set Status=ResultSet.Execute()               ;Execute the Query
 If Status'=1 Write "Status'=1, return from Execute Statement" Quit

 While ResultSet.Next() {                      ;Process the Query results
     Write !,ResultSet.Data("Name")
     Set myshirts=ResultSet.Data("MyShirts")
     If myshirts'="" {
         For I=1:1:$LL(myshirts) {
             Write !,?15,$LI(myshirts,I)
         }
     }
 }
 Set SC=ResultSet.Close()                      ;Close the Query
```

If you save the above code in a routine and then run the it from the Terminal, you should get the following output.

```
John Wayne
            BlueShirt
            CyanShirt
            RedShirt
```

```
                WhiteShirt
```

Example 25-17 we demonstrate how to select *MyShirts* data using *Embedded SQL*. Using the "FOR SOME %ELEMENT" SQL Statement we select any actor who has in their List of Shirts a value of "BlueShirt," which of course is John Wayne. Note how MyShirts needs to be broken out with the *$List* command.

## Display MyShirts Data using Dynamic SQL

**Example 25-18 Display MyShirts Data using Dynamic SQL**

```
The MyShirts Property is defined as a Collection List of Data Types

To run this code you must put the code in a routine, save the routine, and then
run the routine from the terminal.
```

```
 Set MyQuery="SELECT Name,MyShirts FROM MyPackage.Actor"        ;Define the Query

 Set ResultSet=##class(%ResultSet).%New("%DynamicQuery:SQL")
                                             ;Create a new Instance of %ResultSet

 Set Status=ResultSet.Prepare(MyQuery)           ;Prepare the Query
 If Status'=1 Write "Status'=1, return from Prepare Statement" Quit

 Set Status=ResultSet.Execute()                  ;Execute the Query
 If Status'=1 Write "Status'=1, return from Execute Statement" Quit

 While ResultSet.Next() {                        ;Process the Query results
     Write !,ResultSet.Data("Name")
     Set myshirts=ResultSet.Data("MyShirts")
     If myshirts'="" {
         For I=1:1:$LL(myshirts) {
             Write !,?15,$LI(myshirts,I)
         }
     }
 }
 Set SC=ResultSet.Close()                        ;Close the Query
```

```
If you save the above code in a routine and then run the it from the Terminal,
you should get the following output.
```

```
John Wayne
              BlueShirt
              CyanShirt
              RedShirt
              WhiteShirt
Jodie Foster
Clint Eastwood
Julie Andrews
Johnny Depp
Carol Burnett
Will Smith
Ann Margaret
Dean Martin
Ally Sheedy
Humphrey Bogart
Katharine Hepburn
```

Example 25-17 demonstrates *Dynamic SQL* to display MyShirts for John Wayne.  Note how the MyShirts needs to be broken out with the *$List* command.

## *Chapter 25 Summary*

In Chapter 25, we looked at a Collection Lists of datatypes (Strings) and a number of various Methods to update and access the data "MyShirts". These Methods included: Clear and Count Methods, Insert, GetAt, Find, Next, Previous, GetNext, GetPrevious, InsertAt, SetAt, InsertOrdered and RemoveAt Methods. In addition we also demonstrated Embedded SQL and Dynamic SQL to select and display "MyShirts" data.

# Chapter 26 Class & Object Properties - Collection Array of Data Types

Chapters 25 through 30 cover the basic concepts of Caché ObjectScript (COS) to process Caché Class and Objects Properties - **Collections**. In Chapter 22 we looked at:

➢ Data Types

➢ References to Persistent Objects – these Properties point to or reference other Persistent Objects in another class

➢ References to Embedded Objects – these Properties point to or reference an Embedded Object that reside (or are embedded) in the current class

Now we are going to apply the concept of *Collections* or *Multiple Entries* to each of the above three.

## Introduction to Collections

A **Collection** is an ordered list of information, or multiple entries.

*Collections* in Caché fall into these categories:

➢ List Collection of Data Types - Chapter 25

➢ Array Collection of Data Types - Chapter 26

➢ List Collection of References to Persistent Objects  – Chapter 27

➢ Array Collection of References to Persistent Objects – Chapter 28

➢ List Collection of References to Embedded Objects – Chapter 29

➢ Array Collection of References to Embedded Objects - Chapter 30

As a base Class we will use *MyPackage.Actor* created in Chapter 22 and modified in subsequent chapters.

We have already seen *Data Types*, *References to Persistent Objects* and *References to Embedded Objects.* Now by using *Collections* we will expand their capability.

## Collection Lists and Collection Arrays

Each element in a *Collection List* has a *Slot Number* and associated *Value*.

### A Collection List of Shirts

Table 26-1 A Collection List of Shirts

| Slot Number | Value |
|:-----------:|:-----:|
| 1 | RedShirt |
| 2 | WhiteShirt |
| 3 | BlueShirt |

In Table 26-1 we have three Slots and three Shirts, this is a *List Collection*.

Each element in a *Collection Array* has a *Key* and associated *Value*.

### A Collection Array of Hats

Table 26-2 A Collection Array of Hats

| Key | Value |
|:---:|:-----:|
| 1 | Bowler |
| 2 | Straw |
| Mesh | FruitMesh |
| Top | TopHat |

In Table 26-2 we have a *Collection Array*. As you can see we use a *Key* instead of a *Slot*, and the Key can be either numeric or alphanumeric.

## Collection Array of Data Types

In this chapter, we will consider how to handle a *Collection Array of Data Types*. As we said before the *Collection List of Data Types* has a string length limit of 32k, but a *Collection Array of Data Types* has no limit and can include as many entries as necessary.

When dealing with a *Collection Array of Data Types* you need to specify an *Array Key* as opposed to a *Collection List of Data Types*, which uses a *Slot*.

**Table 26-3 Object Properties**

| Object Property | Data Type | Name we chose | Special Considerations |
|---|---|---|---|
| Data Types | %String | Name<br>(Name of Actor) | |
| Collection List of Data Types | %String | MyShirts<br>(Shirts belonging to an<br>Actor) | Total length cannot exceed 32k |
| Collection Array of Data Types | %String | MyHats<br>(Hats belonging to an<br>Actor) | No length limit<br>In SQL must be handled as a Child table<br>Must specify a Key when accessing |

Our first step is to redefine the MyPackage.Actor class to create a *Collection Array of Data Types* for an array of MyHats.

## Actor Class Redefinition – Include the Collection Array Property: MyHats

**Example 26-1 Actor Class Redefinition - Include the Collection Array Property: MyHats**

```
Class MyPackage.Actor Extends %Persistent
{

Property Name As %String [ Required ];

Index NameIndex On Name;

Property MyAccountant As Accountants;

Property MyHome As Address;

Property FavoriteColor As %String;

Property MyShirts As list Of %String;

Property MyHats As array Of %String;

}
```

After starting up Caché Studio from the Caché Cube, click on File -> Open, then select the package MyPackage and Class Actor. Add the *"Property: MyHats As array Of %String"* line (click on Class -> Add -> Property) to the Actor Class. Your class should look like in Example 26-1. Recompile the class.

The following are a number of methods whereby we manipulate the *Collection Array Property: MyHats*. We shall use *MyPackage.Actor Object Id of 2*, Jodi Foster. If we did not know the *Object Id* of Jodi Foster, we could use *Embedded SQL* to find her Id as demonstrated in Chapter 22 Example 11 and in Chapter 23.

## Clear and Count Methods – Delete all elements and show the count

**Example 26-2 Clear and Count Methods - Deletes all elements and show the count**

```
The MyHats Property is defined as a Collection Array of Data Types

Clear Method - Clears or Deletes the Collection of Elements

Count Method - Returns the Number of Elements in the Collection
```

```
 Set ActorOref=##class(MyPackage.Actor).%OpenId(2)      ;bring object Jodi
Foster
                                                        ;into memory

 Do ActorOref.MyHats.Clear()                            ;clear list of hats
 Write !,"Count: ",ActorOref.MyHats.Count()            ;count of elements

 Write !,ActorOref.%Save()                              ;Save the object
```

```
If you run the above code from the Terminal, you should get the following
output.
```

```
Count: 0
1
```

In Example 26-2, we start by bringing into memory an Actor Object with an Id of 2, (Jodi Foster). Next we ensure there is no data in out *Collection Array Property: MyHats* so we use the *Clear()* and *Count() Methods*. Lastly we use the *%Save() Method* to save all changes to disk.

## SetAt Method – Add Four Hats to the Collection

When using the *SetAt() Method* with a *Collection Array Property* you need to specify the *Array Key*. The *Array Key* can be either numeric or alpha.

**Example 26-3 SetAt Method – Add Four Hats to the Collection**

```
The MyHats Property is defined as a Collection Array of Data Types

SetAt Method - Set or Replace an Element at the specific Key
```

```
 Set ActorOref=##class(MyPackage.Actor).%OpenId(2)      ;bring object Jodi Foster
                                                        ;into memory

 Do ActorOref.MyHats.SetAt("Bowler",1)                 ;keyed by numeric 1
 Do ActorOref.MyHats.SetAt("Straw",2)                  ;keyed by numeric 2
 Do ActorOref.MyHats.SetAt("FruitMesh","Mesh")         ;keyed by alpha "Mesh"
 Do ActorOref.MyHats.SetAt("TopHat","Top")             ;keyed by alpha "Top"

 Write !,"Count: ",ActorOref.MyHats.Count()            ;count of elements

 Write !,ActorOref.%Save()                              ;Save the object
```

```
If you run the above code from the Terminal, you should get the following
output.
```

```
Count: 4
```

In Example 26-3, we use the *SetAt() Method* to add four Hats to the *Collection Array Property: MyHats.* Note that the first parameter is the Hat string and the second is the *Array Key.* A numeric key is used for the Bowler and Straw hats and an alphanumeric key is used for the FruitMesh and Top Hats.

## Global generated from Class MyPackage.Actor

**Example 26-4 Global generated from Class MyPackage.Actor**

```
zw ^MyPackage.ActorD
^MyPackage.ActorD=13
^MyPackage.ActorD(1)=$lb("","John
Wayne","",$lb("","","",""),"Blue",$lb("BlueShirt","CyanShirt","RedShirt",""WhiteShirt""))
^MyPackage.ActorD(2)=$lb("","Jodie Foster","",$lb("","","",""),"Green","")
^MyPackage.ActorD(2,"MyHats",1)="Bowler"
^MyPackage.ActorD(2,"MyHats",2)="Straw"
^MyPackage.ActorD(2,"MyHats","Mesh")="FruitMesh"
^MyPackage.ActorD(2,"MyHats","Top")="TopHat"
^MyPackage.ActorD(3)=$lb("","Clint Eastwood","2",$lb("","","",""),"Cyan")
^MyPackage.ActorD(4)=$lb("","Julie Andrews","",$lb("123 Main St.","Marlboro",
"MA","01752"),"Brown")
^MyPackage.ActorD(5)=$lb("","Johnny Depp","",$lb("","","",""),"Tan")
^MyPackage.ActorD(6)=$lb("","Carol Burnett","",$lb("","","",""),"Red")
^MyPackage.ActorD(7)=$lb("","Will Smith","",$lb("","","",""),"Navy")
^MyPackage.ActorD(8)=$lb("","Ann Margaret","",$lb("","","",""),"Yellow")
^MyPackage.ActorD(9)=$lb("","Dean Martin","",$lb("","","",""),"Green")
^MyPackage.ActorD(10)=$lb("","Ally Sheedy","",$lb("","","",""),"Black")
^MyPackage.ActorD(11)=$lb("","Humphrey Bogart","",$lb("","","",""),"Brown")
^MyPackage.ActorD(12)=$lb("","Katharine Hepburn","2",$lb("","","",""),"Blue")
```

Example 26-4 shows a listing of the Global generated from the Class MyPackage.Actor. You can see how the array of four hats is stored for Jodi Foster. Your Global may not look exactly like this one if you have not worked through all the examples in the previous Chapters.

## IsDefined Method – See if a Key is defined

**Example 26-5 IsDefined Method – See if a Key is defined**

```
The MyHats Property is defined as a Collection Array of Data Types

IsDefined Method - Returns a 1 if the Key is defined otherwise 0

 Set ActorOref=##class(MyPackage.Actor).%OpenId(2)       ;bring object Jodi Foster
                                                         ;into memory

 Write ActorOref.MyHats.IsDefined("Mesh")       ;Is key "Mesh" defined? - Yes
1

 Write ActorOref.MyHats.IsDefined("Top")       ;Is key "Top" defined? - Yes
1

 Write ActorOref.MyHats.IsDefined(1)       ;Is key 1 defined? - Yes
1
```

```
Write ActorOref.MyHats.IsDefined(3)          ;Is key 3 defined? - No
0
```

In Example 26-5 we see a demonstration of the *IsDefined() Method* which determines if a Key exists.

## GetAt Method – Returns the Element for a Key

**Example 26-6 GetAt Method – Returns the Element for a Key**

```
The MyHats Property is defined as a Collection Array of Data Types

GetAt Method - Returns the Element associated with a Key

 Set ActorOref=##class(MyPackage.Actor).%OpenId(2)      ;bring object Jodi Foster
                                                        ;into memory

 Write ActorOref.MyHats.GetAt(2)                        ;Get Hat at Key 2
Straw

 Set Key="Mesh"
 Write ActorOref.MyHats.GetAt(Key)                      ;Get Hat at Key "Mesh"
FruitMesh
```

Example 26-6 demonstrates the *GetAt() Method*. By passing the appropriate *Key* to the *GetAt() Method* the Element can be retrieved.

## Find Method – Find a hat in the collection starting at Key

The *Find() Method* returns the *Array Key* based on the Element passed to it.

**Example 26-7 Find a hat in the collection starting at Key**

```
The MyHats Property is defined as a Collection Array of Data Types

Find Method - Finds the Element starting at the Key

 Set ActorOref=##class(MyPackage.Actor).%OpenId(2)      ;bring object Jodi Foster
                                                        ;into memory

 Write ActorOref.MyHats.Find("TopHat")     ;find the Element TopHat and display
Top                                        ;the key

 Write ActorOref.MyHats.Find("Bowler")     ;find the Element Bowler and display
1                                          ;the key

 Write ActorOref.MyHats.Find("Bowler",2)  ;find the Element Bowler starting at
<>                                         ;key 2, since Bowler is at key 1,
                                           ;nothing is found
```

In Example 26-7 we use the *Find() Method* to search for the Key that corresponds to the Hat Element. *Find()* takes two parameters, Element and Key, the Key being optional. If only the first parameter is specified, *Find()* searches the whole array for the Element. If a second parameter (Key) is used, *Find()* will start searching from that parameter or key.

# SetAt Method– Set or Replace an Element at a specific Key

**Example 26-8 SetAt Method – Set or Replace an Element at a specific Key**

```
The MyHats Property is defined as a Collection Array of Data Types

SetAt Method - Set or Replace an Element at the specific Key

To run this code you must put the code in a routine, save the routine, and then
run the routine from the terminal.

Set ActorOref=##class(MyPackage.Actor).%OpenId(2)        ;bring object Jodi Foster
                                                         ;into memory

Do ActorOref.MyHats.SetAt("BigBirdHat",2)                ;replace Hat at Key 2

Write !,"Count: ",ActorOref.MyHats.Count()               ;count of elements

Set Key = "" Do {                                        ;cycle through hats
    Set Hat=ActorOref.MyHats.GetNext(.Key)               ;get hat at specified key
    If Key'="" {
        Write !,"Key and hat: "
        Write Key," - ",Hat                              ;display key and hat
    }
} While (Key '= "")

Write !,ActorOref.%Save()                                ;Save the object
```

```
If you save the above code in a routine and then run the it from the Terminal,
you should get the following output.

Count: 4
Key and hat: 1 - Bowler
Key and hat: 2 - BigBirdHat
Key and hat: Mesh - FruitMesh
Key and hat: Top - TopHat
1
```

In Example 26-8, we use the *SetAt() Method* to replace or set the hat at *Array Key* 2 from Straw to "BigBirdHat."

## Traversing Methods

The *Next, Previous, GetNext* and *GetPrevious Methods* all provide the capability of traversing Object data, similar to the *$Order* command. *Next* and *GetNext* traverse through the data forward and *Previous* and *GetPrevious* traverse through the data backwards. *Next* and *Previous* accepts the Key/Slot parameter passed by value whereas *GetNext* and *GetPrevious* accept the Key/Slot parameter passed by reference.

Table 26-4 Traversing Methods

| Method | | How Key or Slot is passed |
|---|---|---|
| Next | Traversing Forward | Key or Slot passed by Value |
| Previous | Traversing Backward | Key or Slot Passed by Value |
| GetNext | Traversing Forward | Key or Slot Passed by Reference |
| GetPrevious | Traversing Backward | Key or Slot Passed by Reference |

## Next Method – Returns the Element for the next Key

**Example 26-9 Next Method – Returns the Element for the next Key**

```
The MyHats Property is defined as a Collection Array of Data Types

Next Method - Returns the Element for the next Key

To run this code you must put the code in a routine, save the routine, and then
run the routine from the terminal.
```

```
Set ActorOref=##class(MyPackage.Actor).%OpenId(2)      ;bring object Jodi Foster
                                                       ;into memory


Write !,"Count: ",ActorOref.MyHats.Count()            ;count of elements

Set Key = "" Do {                                     ;start with Key null
    Set Key=ActorOref.MyHats.Next(Key)               ;get the next Key
    If Key'="" {
        Write !,"Key: ",Key                          ;display the Key number
        Write " - ",ActorOref.MyHats.GetAt(Key)      ;display the hat
    }
} While (Key '= "")
```

```
If you save the above code in a routine and then run the it from the Terminal,
you should get the following output.
```

```
Count: 4
Key: 1 - Bowler
Key: 2 - BigBirdHat
Key: Mesh - FruitMesh
Key: Top - TopHat
```

In Example 26-9 we use the *Next() Method* to obtain the next *Key*. Initially we set the *Key* to null then we use *Next()* to cycle through the *Keys*, finally when the *Key* equals null again we stop.

## Previous Method – Returns the Element for the previous Key

Example 26-10 Previous Method – Returns the Element for the previous Key

```
The MyHats Property is defined as a Collection Array of Data Types

Previous Method - Returns the Element for the previous Key

To run this code you must put the code in a routine, save the routine, and then
run the routine from the terminal.
```

```
Set ActorOref=##class(MyPackage.Actor).%OpenId(2)      ;bring object Jodi Foster
                                                       ;into memory

Write !,"Count: ",ActorOref.MyHats.Count()            ;count of elements

Set Key = "" Do {                                     ;start with Key ""
    Set Key=ActorOref.MyHats.Previous(Key)            ;get the previous Key
    If Key'="" {
        Write !,"Key: ",Key                          ;display the Key number
        Write " - ",ActorOref.MyHats.GetAt(Key)      ;display the hat
    }
} While (Key '= "")
```

```
If you save the above code in a routine and then run the it from the Terminal,
you should get the following output.
```

```
Count: 4
Key: Top - TopHat
Key: Mesh - FruitMesh
Key: 2 - BigBirdHat
Key: 1 - Bowler
```

In Example 26-10, we use the *Previous() Method* to obtain the previous *Key*. Initially we set the *Key* to null then we use the *Previous() Method* to cycle through the *Keys* backwards, finally when the *Key* equals null we stop.

## GetNext Method – Returns the Element for the next Key

Example 26-11 GetNext Method – Returns the Element for the next Key

```
The MyHats Property is defined as a Collection Array of Data Types

GetNext Method - Returns the Element for the next Key

To run this code you must put the code in a routine, save the routine, and then
run the routine from the terminal.
```

```
Set ActorOref=##class(MyPackage.Actor).%OpenId(2)      ;bring object Jodi Foster
                                                       ;into memory

Write !,"Count: ",ActorOref.MyHats.Count()            ;count of elements

Set Key = "" Do {                                     ;start with beginning key
    Set Hat=ActorOref.MyHats.GetNext(.Key)            ;get next key (passed by reference)
    If Key'="" {
        Write !,"Key and hat: "
```

```
        Write Key," - ",Hat                              ;display key and hat
    }
} While (Key '= "")
```

```
Count: 4
Key and hat: 1 - Bowler
Key and hat: 2 - BigBirdHat
Key and hat: Mesh - FruitMesh
Key and hat: Top - TopHat
```

In Example 26-11, we see the *GetNext() Method*. This *Method* is similar to the *Next Method* except that the *Key* is passed by reference. Initially we set the *Key* to null then we use *GetNext()* to cycle through the *Keys*, finally when the *Key* equals null we stop.

## GetPrevious Method– Returns the Element for the Previous Key

**Example 26-12** *GetPrevious Method – Returns the Element for the Previous Key*

The MyHats Property is defined as a Collection Array of Data Types

GetPrevious Method - Returns the Element  for the previous Key

To run this code you must put the code in a routine, save the routine, and then
run the routine from the terminal.

```
Set ActorOref=##class(MyPackage.Actor).%OpenId(2)      ;bring object Jodi Foster
                                                       ;into memory

Write !,"Count: ",ActorOref.MyHats.Count()             ;count of elements

Set Key = "" Do {                                      ;start with beginning key
    Set Hat=ActorOref.MyHats.GetPrevious(.Key)         ;get previous key
    If Key'="" {                                        ; (passed by reference)
        Write !,"Key and hat: "
        Write Key," - ",Hat                            ;display key with hat
    }
} While (Key '= "")
```

```
Count: 4
Key and hat: Top - TopHat
Key and hat: Mesh - FruitMesh
Key and hat: 2 - BigBirdHat
Key and hat: 1 - Bowler
```

Example 26-12 we see the *GetPrevious() Method*. This *Method* is similar to the *Previous Method* except that the *Key* is passed by reference. Initially we set the *Key* to null then we use *GetPrevious()* to cycle through the *Keys* backwards. Finally when the *Key* equals null we stop.

# RemoveAt Method – Remove the Element associated with a Key

**Example 26-13 RemoveAt Method – Remove the Element associated with a Key**

```
The MyHats Property is defined as a Collection Array of Data Types

RemoveAt Method - Remove the Element associated with the Key

To run this code you must put the code in a routine, save the routine, and then
run the routine from the terminal.
```

```
Set ActorOref=##class(MyPackage.Actor).%OpenId(2)        ;bring object Jodi Foster
                                                         ;into memory

Do ActorOref.MyHats.RemoveAt("Mesh")                     ;remove Element associated
                                                         ;with key Mesh

Write !,"Count: ",ActorOref.MyHats.Count()               ;count of elements

Set Key = "" Do {
    Set Hat=ActorOref.MyHats.GetNext(.Key)
    If Key'="" {
        Write !,"Key and hat: "
        Write Key," - ",Hat                              ;display key and hat
    }
} While (Key '= "")

Write !,ActorOref.%Save()                                ;Save the object
```

```
If you save the above code in a routine and then run the it from the Terminal,
you should get the following output.
```

```
Count: 3
Key and hat: 1 - Bowler
Key and hat: 2 - BigBirdHat
Key and hat: Top - TopHat
1
```

In Example 26-13, we use the *RemoveAt() Method* to remove the Element associated with the Key "Mesh."

## Display MyHats Data using Embedded SQL

When Caché *Projects* a Table with a Collection Array of Data Types Property, it does so in two linked tables:

- ➢ MyPackage.Actor table

- ➢ MyPackage.Actor_MyHats table

In the example that follows we use the MyPackage.Actor_MyHats table in the SQL Select statement and point back up to the MyPackage.Actor table to obtain the actor's name.

**Example 26-14 Display MyHats Data using Embedded SQL**

> To run this code you must put the code in a routine, save the routine, and then run the routine from the terminal.

```
New actorname,myhats
&sql(Declare MyCursor CURSOR FOR
    SELECT Actor->Name, MyHats
    INTO :actorname, :myhats
    FROM MyPackage.Actor_MyHats
    ORDER BY Name)
&sql(OPEN MyCursor)
&sql(FETCH MyCursor)
While (SQLCODE = 0) {
    Write !,"Name: ",actorname
    Write ?25,"MyHats: ",myhats
    &sql(FETCH MyCursor)
}
&sql(CLOSE MyCursor)
```

> If you save the above code in a routine and then run the it from the Terminal, you should get the following output.

```
Name: Jodie Foster      MyHats: Bowler
Name: Jodie Foster      MyHats: BigBirdHat
Name: Jodie Foster      MyHats: TopHat
```

Example 26-14 demonstrates *Embedded SQL* to display MyHats data. Note the reference to the sub-table: Actor_MyHats and how the Actor's name must be referenced.

## Display MyHats Data using Dynamic SQL

**Example 26-15 MyHats Data using Dynamic SQL**

> To run this code you must put the code in a routine, save the routine, and then run the routine from the terminal.

```
Set MyQuery="SELECT Actor->Name,MyHats FROM MyPackage.Actor_MyHats"

Set ResultSet=##class(%ResultSet).%New("%DynamicQuery:SQL")
                                            ;Create a new Instance of %ResultSet

Set SC=ResultSet.Prepare(MyQuery)           ;Prepare the Query

Set SC=ResultSet.Execute()                  ;Execute the Query

While ResultSet.Next() {                     ;Process the Query results
    Write !,ResultSet.Data("Name")," - "
    Write ResultSet.Data("MyHats")
}

Set SC=ResultSet.Close()                    ;Close the Query
```

> If you save the above code in a routine and then run the it from the Terminal, you should get the following output.

```
Jodie Foster - Bowler
```

```
Jodie Foster - BigBirdHat
Jodie Foster - TopHat
```

Example 26-15 demonstrates *Dynamic SQL* to display MyHats data. Note the reference to the sub-table: Actor_MyHats and how the Actor's name must be referenced.

## *Chapter 26 Summary*

In this chapter, we looked at Collection Arrays of datatypes (Strings) and a number of various Methods to update and access the data "MyHats." These Methods included: Clear and Count Methods, SetAt, IsDefined, GetAt, Find, Next, Previous, GetNext, GetPrevious and RemoveAt Methods. In addition we also demonstrated Embedded SQL and Dynamic SQL to display "MyHats" data.

*"I am right 97% of the time, and don't care about the other 4%."*

# Chapter 27 Class & Object Properties - Collection List of References to Persistent Objects

Chapters 25 through 30 cover the basic concepts of Caché ObjectScript (COS) to process Caché Class and Objects Properties - **Collections**. In Chapter 22 we looked at:

> ➢ Data Types
>
> ➢ References to Persistent Objects – these Properties point to or reference other Persistent Objects in another class
>
> ➢ References to Embedded Objects – these Properties point to or reference an Embedded Object that reside (or are embedded) in the current class

Now we are going to apply the concept of *Collections* or *Multiple Entries* to each of the above three.

## Introduction to Collections

A **Collection** is an ordered list of information, or multiple entries.

*Collections* in Caché fall into these categories:

> ➢ List Collection of Data Types - Chapter 25
>
> ➢ Array Collection of Data Types - Chapter 26
>
> ➢ List Collection of References to Persistent Objects – Chapter 27
>
> ➢ Array Collection of References to Persistent Objects – Chapter 28
>
> ➢ List Collection of References to Embedded Objects – Chapter 29
>
> ➢ Array Collection of References to Embedded Objects - Chapter 30

As a base Class we will use *MyPackage.Actor* created in Chapter 22 and modified in subsequent chapters.

We have already seen *Data Types*, *References to Persistent Objects* and *References to Embedded Objects*. Now by using *Collections* we will expand their capability.

## Collection List of References to Persistent Objects

A *Collection List of References to Persistent Objects* combines a *Collection List* and *References to Persistent Objects*.

**Table 27 -1 Object Properties**

| Object Property | Data Type | Reference Object Class and Name | Name we chose | Special Considerations |
|---|---|---|---|---|
| Data Types | %String | | Name (Name of Actor) | |
| Collection List of Data Types | %String | | MyShirts (Shirts belonging to an Actor) | Total length cannot exceed 32k |
| Collection Array of Data Types | %String | | MyHats (Hats belonging to an Actor) | No length limit In SQL must be handled as a Child table Must specify a Key when accessing |
| Collection List of References to Persistent Objects | | Persistent Objects | MyContacts (Contacts of the Actor) | |
| Collection Array of References to Persistent Objects | | Persistent Objects | MyClients (Clients of the Actor) | |

## Base Class and Referenced Class

Our base class is *MyPackage.Actors* as we established in Chapter 22. Our referenced Class shall be *MyPackage.Contacts* or contacts of the Actors.

Our first step is to create a *Contacts* class; *MyPackage.Contacts* based on the *%Persistent Class*.

## Class Definition – Creating the Contacts Class

**Example 27-1 Class Definition – Creating the Contacts Class**

```
Class MyPackage.Contacts Extends %Persistent
{

Property ContactName As %String [ Required ];

Index ContactNameIndex On ContactName;

}
```

After starting up Caché Studio from the Caché Cube, click on **File -> New,** then select **Caché Class Definition,** next select the package MyPackage and add a new Class called Contacts. Add the Contact Name property (click on **Class -> Add -> Property)** to the Contacts Class. Also add the index *ContactNameIndex* (click on **Class -> Add -> Index)** to the Contacts Class. Your class should look like in Example 27-1. Recompile the class.

## *Populate the Contacts Class*

**Example 27-2 Populate the Contacts Class**

To run this code you must put the code in a routine, save the routine, and then run the routine from the terminal.

```
For Name="Contact1","Contact2","Contact3" Do CreateObject(Name)
For Name="Contact4","Contact5","Contact6" Do CreateObject(Name)
Quit

CreateObject(Name) [] Public {
  Set ContactsOref=##class(MyPackage.Contacts).%New() ;create a new object reference
  Set ContactsOref.ContactName=Name          ;populate the object with a name
  Do ContactsOref.%Save()                     ;save the object
  Set NewId=ContactsOref.%Id()                ;get the newly assigned ID
  Write !,"Id: ",NewId                        ;write ID of new Object
  Write " - ",ContactsOref.ContactName        ;write the name of the new Object
}
```

If you save the above code in a routine and then run the it from the Terminal, you should get the following output.

```
Id: 1 - Contact1
Id: 2 - Contact2
Id: 3 - Contact3
Id: 4 - Contact4
Id: 5 - Contact5
Id: 6 - Contact6
```

In Example 27-2 we populate the *Contacts Class* with names of contacts, specifically Contact1 through Contact 6.

## *Actor Class Redefinition – add a Reference Property that will point to the Contacts Class*

**Example 27-3 Actor Class Redefinition – add Reference Property that will point to the Contacts Class**

```
Class MyPackage.Actor Extends %Persistent
{

Property Name As %String [ Required ];

Index NameIndex On Name;

Property MyAccountant As Accountants;

Property MyHome As Address;
```

```
Property MyShirts As list Of %String;

Property MyHats As array Of %String;

Property MyContacts As list Of Contacts;

}
```

After starting up Caché Studio from the Caché Cube, click on **File -> Open,** then select the package MyPackage and Class Actor. Add the *Property MyContacts As list of Contacts* line (click on **Class -> Add -> Property)** to the Actor Class. Your class should look like in Example 27-3. Recompile the class.

The following are a number of methods whereby we manipulate the *Collection List of Reference of Persistent Objects: MyContacts*. We shall use *MyPackage.Actor Object Id 5*, Johnny Depp. If we did not know the *Object Id* of Johnny Depp we could use *Embedded SQL* to find his Id as demonstrated in Chapter 22 Example 11 and in Chapter 23.

## Clear and Count Methods – Delete all elements and show the count

**Example 27-4 Clear and Count Methods - Deletes all elements and show the count**

```
The MyContacts Property is defined as a
Collection List of References to Persistent Objects

Clear Method - Clears or Deletes the Collection of Elements

Count Method - Returns the Number of Elements in the Collection

 Set ActorOref=##class(MyPackage.Actor).%OpenId(5)      ;bring object Johnny Depp
                                                        ;into memory
 ;
 Do ActorOref.MyContacts.Clear()                  ;clear list of contacts
 Write !,"Count: ",ActorOref.MyContacts.Count() ;count of elements

 Write !,ActorOref.%Save()                        ;Save the object

If you run the above code from the Terminal, you should get the following
output.

Count: 0
1
```

In Example 27-4 we start by bringing into memory an Actor Object with an Id of 5, (Johnny Depp). Next we ensure there is no data in our *Collection List of References to Persistent Objects Property: MyContacts* so we use the *Clear()* and *Count() Methods*. Lastly we use the *%Save() Method* to save all changes to disk.

## Insert Method – Insert four Contacts into the Collection

Example 27-5 Insert Method – Insert four Contacts into the Collection

```
The MyContacts Property is defined as a
Collection List of References to Persistent Objects

Insert Method - Inserts an Oref at the end of the collection

Set ActorOref=##class(MyPackage.Actor).%OpenId(5)        ;bring object Johnny Depp
                                                          ;into memory

Set Contact1Oref=##class(MyPackage.Contacts).%OpenId(1)  ;bring object Contact1
                                                          ;into memory

Set Contact2Oref=##class(MyPackage.Contacts).%OpenId(2)  ;bring object Contact2
                                                          ;into memory

Set Contact3Oref=##class(MyPackage.Contacts).%OpenId(3)  ;bring object Contact3
                                                          ;into memory

Set Contact4Oref=##class(MyPackage.Contacts).%OpenId(4)  ;bring object Contact4
                                                          ;into memory

Do ActorOref.MyContacts.Insert(Contact1Oref)    ;associate Contact1 with
                                                 ;Actor Johnny Depp
Do ActorOref.MyContacts.Insert(Contact2Oref)    ;associate Contact2 with
                                                 ;Actor Johnny Depp
Do ActorOref.MyContacts.Insert(Contact3Oref)    ;associate Contact3 with
                                                 ;Actor Johnny Depp
Do ActorOref.MyContacts.Insert(Contact4Oref)    ;associate Contact4 woith
                                                 ;Actor Johnny Depp

Write !,"Count: ",ActorOref.MyContacts.Count()
Write !,ActorOref.%Save()                        ;Save the object

If you run the above code from the Terminal, you should get the following
output.
```

```
Count: 4
1
```

In Example 27-5 first we bring our actor (Johnny Depp) into memory using ActorOref. Next we bring 4 Contacts into memory using Contact1Oref thru Contact4Oref. Then we associate the ActorOref with the 4 Contacts using the *Insert() Method*.

## Global generated from Class MyPackage.Actor

Example 27-6 Global generated from Class MyPackage.Actor

```
zw ^MyPackage.ActorD
^MyPackage.ActorD=13
^MyPackage.ActorD(1)=$lb("","John
Wayne","",$lb("","","",""),"Blue",$lb("BlueShirt","CyanShirt","RedShirt","WhiteShirt"))
^MyPackage.ActorD(2)=$lb("","Jodie Foster","",$lb("","","",""),"Green","")
^MyPackage.ActorD(2,"MyHats",1)="Bowler"
^MyPackage.ActorD(2,"MyHats",2)="BigBirdHat"
```

```
^MyPackage.ActorD(2,"MyHats","Top")="TopHat"
^MyPackage.ActorD(3)=$lb("","Clint Eastwood","2",$lb("","","",""),"Cyan")
^MyPackage.ActorD(4)=$lb("","Julie Andrews","",$lb("123 Main St.",
"Marlboro","MA","01752"),"Brown")
^MyPackage.ActorD(5)=$lb("","Johnny
Depp","",$lb("","","",""),"Tan","",$lb($lb("1"),$lb("2"),$lb("3"),$lb("4")))
^MyPackage.ActorD(6)=$lb("","Carol Burnett","",$lb("","","",""),"Red")
^MyPackage.ActorD(7)=$lb("","Will Smith","",$lb("","","",""),"Navy")
^MyPackage.ActorD(8)=$lb("","Ann Margaret","",$lb("","","",""),"Yellow")
^MyPackage.ActorD(9)=$lb("","Dean Martin","",$lb("","","",""),"Green")
^MyPackage.ActorD(10)=$lb("","Ally Sheedy","",$lb("","","",""),"Black")
^MyPackage.ActorD(11)=$lb("","Humphrey Bogart","",$lb("","","",""),"Brown")
^MyPackage.ActorD(12)=$lb("","Katharine Hepburn","2",$lb("","","",""),"Blue")

ZW ^MyPackage.ContactsD
^MyPackage.ContactsD=6
^MyPackage.ContactsD(1)=$lb("","Contact1")
^MyPackage.ContactsD(2)=$lb("","Contact2")
^MyPackage.ContactsD(3)=$lb("","Contact3")
^MyPackage.ContactsD(4)=$lb("","Contact4")
^MyPackage.ContactsD(5)=$lb("","Contact5")
^MyPackage.ContactsD(6)=$lb("","Contact6")
```

Example 27-6 shows the Global generated from the Class MyPackage.Actor as well as the Class MyPackage.Contacts. You can see how the pointers to the four contacts are stored for Johnny Depp, as well as how the Contacts are stored. Your Global may not look exactly like this one if you have not worked through all the examples in the previous Chapters.

## GetAt Method – Returns the Element associated with a Key List

**Example 27-7 GetAt Method – Returns the Element associated with a Key**

```
The MyContacts Property is defined as a
Collection List of References to Persistent Objects

GetAt Method - Returns the Element associated with a Key

To run this code you must put the code in a routine, save the routine, and then
run the routine from the terminal.
```

```
 Set ActorOref=##class(MyPackage.Actor).%OpenId(5)      ;bring object Johnny Depp
                                                        ;into memory

 Write !,"Count: ",ActorOref.MyContacts.Count()         ;count of elements
 For Key=1:1:ActorOref.MyContacts.Count() {             ;Display each element
   Write !,"Key: ",Key                                  ;of Collection List
   Write " Name ",ActorOref.MyContacts.GetAt(Key).ContactName  ;Property: MyContacts
 }
```

```
If you save the above code in a routine and then run the it from the Terminal,
you should get the following output.
```

```
Count: 4
Key: 1 - Contact1
Key: 2 - Contact2
Key: 3 - Contact3
Key: 4 - Contact4
```

Example 27-7 demonstrates the *GetAt() Method* which returns the Element associated with a Key. In this example it is used to display each Element of the *Collection List of References to Persistent Objects Property: MyContacts* that is associated with the Actor Johnny Depp.

## Find Method – Finds the associated Key for a String

Currently Caché does not support a *Find Method* for a *Collection List of References to Persistent Object* that allows you to search for a string. However, the following code will do this.

**Example 27-8 Find Method – Finds the associated Key for a String**

```
The MyContacts Property is defined as a
Collection List of References to Persistent Objects

Find Code - Finds the associated Key for a String

To run this code you must put the code in a routine, save the routine, and then
run the routine from the terminal.
```

```
Set ActorOref=##class(MyPackage.Actor).%OpenId(5)        ;bring object Johnny Depp
                                                         ;into memory

Set NameToFind="Contact3"                                ;Name to Find
Set FoundKey=""                                          ;initialized FoundKey

For Key=1:1:ActorOref.MyContacts.Count() {
   If NameToFind=ActorOref.MyContacts.GetAt(Key).ContactName Set FoundKey=Key Quit
}

If FoundKey'="" {
   Write !, "Found: ", NameToFind," at Key: ",FoundKey
   }
Else {
   Write !, "Could not find: ", NameToFind
   }
```

```
If you save the above code in a routine and then run the it from the Terminal,
you should get the following output.
```

```
Found: Contact3 at Key: 3

   = = = = = = = = = = = = = = = = = = = = = = = = = = = = = = =

Set ActorOref=##class(MyPackage.Actor).%OpenId(5)        ;bring object Johnny Depp
                                                         ;into memory

Set NameToFind="Contact5"                                ;Name to Find
Set FoundKey=""                                          ;initialized FoundKey

For Key=1:1:ActorOref.MyContacts.Count() {
   If NameToFind=ActorOref.MyContacts.GetAt(Key).ContactName Set FoundKey=Key Quit
}

If FoundKey'="" {
   Write !, "Found: ", NameToFind," at Key: ",FoundKey
   }
Else {
   Write !, "Could not find: ", NameToFind
```

```
        }
```

*Could not find: Contact5*

The code in Example 27-8 will find the associated Key for Contact3 and Contact5. The Key for Contact3 is 3 but since Contact5 does not exist for Johnny Depp no Key is returned.

## *Traversing Methods*

The *Next, Previous, GetNext* and *GetPrevious Methods* all provide the capability of traversing Object data, similar to the **$Order** command. *Next* and *GetNext* traverse through the data forward and *Previous* and *GetPrevious* traverse through the data backwards. *Next* and *Previous* accepts the Key/Slot parameter passed by value whereas *GetNext* and *GetPrevious* accept the Key/Slot parameter passed by reference.

**Table 27-1 Traversing Methods**

| Method | | How Key or Slot is passed |
|---|---|---|
| Next | Traversing Forward | Key or Slot passed by Value |
| Previous | Traversing Backward | Key or Slot Passed by Value |
| GetNext | Traversing Forward | Key or Slot Passed by Reference |
| GetPrevious | Traversing Backward | Key or Slot Passed by Reference |

## *Next Method – Returns the Element for the next Key*

**Example 27-9 Next Method – Returns the Element for the next Key**

```
The MyContacts Property is defined as a
Collection List of References to Persistent Objects

Next Method - Returns the Element for the next Key

To run this code you must put the code in a routine, save the routine, and then
run the routine from the terminal.
```

```
 Set ActorOref=##class(MyPackage.Actor).%OpenId(5)      ;bring object Johnny Depp
                                                        ;into memory

 Write !,"Count: ",ActorOref.MyContacts.Count()         ;count of elements
 Set Key = "" Do {                                      ;start with Key null
     Set Key=ActorOref.MyContacts.Next(Key)             ;get the next Key
     If Key'="" {
         Write !,"Key: ",Key                            ;display the Key number
         Write " - ",ActorOref.MyContacts.GetAt(Key).ContactName ;display the contact
     }
 } While (Key '= "")
```

```
Count: 4
Key: 1 - Contact1
Key: 2 - Contact2
Key: 3 - Contact3
Key: 4 - Contact4
```

In Example 27-9 we use the *Next() Method* to obtain the next *Key*. Initially we set the *Key* to null then we use *Next()* to cycle through the *Keys*, finally when the *Key* equals null again we stop.

## Previous Method – Returns the Element for the previous Key

**Example 27-10 Previous Method – Returns the Element for the previous Key**

The MyContacts Property is defined as a
Collection List of References to Persistent Objects

Previous Method - Returns the Element for the previous Key

To run this code you must put the code in a routine, save the routine, and then
run the routine from the terminal.

```
Set ActorOref=##class(MyPackage.Actor).%OpenId(5)      ;bring object Johnny Depp
                                                       ;into memory

Write !,"Count: ",ActorOref.MyContacts.Count()         ;count of elements
Set Key = "" Do {                                      ;start with Key null
    Set Key=ActorOref.MyContacts.Previous(Key)         ;get the previous Key
    If Key'="" {
        Write !,"Key: ",Key                            ;display the Key number
        Write " - ",ActorOref.MyContacts.GetAt(Key).ContactName ;display the contact
    }
} While (Key '= "")
```

```
Count: 4
Key: 4 - Contact4
Key: 3 - Contact3
Key: 2 - Contact2
Key: 1 - Contact1
```

In Example 27-10 we use the *Previous() Method* to obtain the previous *Key*. Initially we set the *Key* to null, and then we use the *Previous() Method* to cycle through the *Keys* backwards, finally when the *Key* equals null we stop.

### GetNext Method – Returns the Element for the next Key

```
The MyContacts Property is defined as a
Collection List of References to Persistent Objects

GetNext Method - Returns the Element for the next Key

To run this code you must put the code in a routine, save the routine, and then
run the routine from the terminal.
```

```
Set ActorOref=##class(MyPackage.Actor).%OpenId(5)      ;bring object Johnny Depp
                                                       ;into memory

Write !,"Count: ",ActorOref.MyContacts.Count()         ;count of elements
Set Key = "" Do {                                      ;start with beginning Key
    Set Contact=ActorOref.MyContacts.GetNext(.Key)     ;get next Key
    If Key'="" Write !,"Key: ",Key," ",Contact.ContactName    ;display Key with Contact
} While (Key '= "")
```

```
If you save the above code in a routine and then run the it from the Terminal,
you should get the following output.
```

```
Count: 4
Key: 1 - Contact1
Key: 2 - Contact2
Key: 3 - Contact3
Key: 4 - Contact4
```

In Example 27-11 we see the *GetNext() Method. This Method* is similar to the *Next Method* except that the *Key* is passed by reference. Initially we set the *Key* to null then we use *GetNext()* to cycle through the *Keys,* finally when the *Key* equals null we stop.

### GetPrevious Method– Returns the Element for the Previous Key

```
The MyContacts Property is defined as a
Collection List of References to Persistent Objects

GetPrevious Method - Returns the Element  for the previous Key

To run this code you must put the code in a routine, save the routine, and then
run the routine from the terminal.
```

```
Set ActorOref=##class(MyPackage.Actor).%OpenId(5)      ;bring object Johnny Depp
                                                       ;into memory

Write !,"Count: ",ActorOref.MyContacts.Count()         ;count of elements
Set Key = "" Do {                                      ;start with beginning Key
    Set Contact=ActorOref.MyContacts.GetPrevious(.Key)      ;get previous Key
    If Key'="" Write !,"Key: ",Key," ",Contact.ContactName    ;display Key with Contact
} While (Key '= "")
```

```
If you save the above code in a routine and then run the it from the Terminal,
you should get the following output.
```

```
Count: 4
Key: 4 - Contact4
Key: 3 - Contact3
Key: 2 - Contact2
Key: 1 - Contact1
```

In Example 27-12 we see the *GetPrevious() Method*. This *Method* is similar to the *Previous Method* except that the *Key* is passed by reference. Initially we set the *Key* to null then we use *GetPrevious()* to cycle through the *Keys* backwards. Finally when the *Key* equals null we stop.

## InsertAt Method – Insert a new Contact between the 1st and 2nd Contact

**Example 27-13 InsertAt Method – Insert a new Contact between the 1st and 2nd Contact**

```
The MyContacts Property is defined as a
Collection List of References to Persistent Objects

InsertAt Method - Insert an Oref into a Collection at a specific key

To run this code you must put the code in a routine, save the routine, and then
run the routine from the terminal.
```

```
Set ActorOref=##class(MyPackage.Actor).%OpenId(5)      ;bring object Johnny Depp
                                                       ;into memory

Set Contact5Oref=##class(MyPackage.Contacts).%OpenId(5)  ;bring object
                                                         ;Contact 5 into memory

Do ActorOref.MyContacts.InsertAt(Contact5Oref,2)       ;Insert Contact5 into the
                                                       ;2nd Key pushing the other
                                                       ;contacts out

Write !,"Count: ",ActorOref.MyContacts.Count()         ;count of elements
For Key=1:1:ActorOref.MyContacts.Count() {             ;display each element
    Write !,"Key: ",Key                                ;of collection List
    Write " - ",ActorOref.MyContacts.GetAt(Key).ContactName   ;Property: MyContacts
}

Write !,ActorOref.%Save()                              ;Save the object
```

```
If you save the above code in a routine and then run the it from the Terminal,
you should get the following output.
```

```
Count: 5
Key: 1 - Contact1
Key: 2 - Contact5
Key: 3 - Contact2
Key: 4 - Contact3
Key: 5 - Contact4
1
```

Example 27-13 demonstrates the *InsertAt() Method* to insert Contact5 between the 1st and 2nd contacts pushing the other keys out.

Now suppose we made a mistake and the 2nd contact should be Contact6 and not Contact5.

## SetAt Method – Set or Replace a specific Contact

**Example 27-14 SetAt Method – Set or Replace a specific Contact**

```
The MyContacts Property is defined
as a Collection List of References to Persistent Objects

SetAt Method - Set or Replace an Element at a specific Key

To run this code you must put the code in a routine, save the routine, and then
run the routine from the terminal.
```

```
Set ActorOref=##class(MyPackage.Actor).%OpenId(5)      ;bring object Johnny Depp
                                                       ;into memory

Set Contact6Oref=##class(MyPackage.Contacts).%OpenId(6)  ;bring object into
                                                       ;memory - Contact6

Do ActorOref.MyContacts.SetAt(Contact6Oref,2)          ;Replace contact with
                                                       ;Contact6 at the 2nd
                                                       ;position

Write !,"Count: ",ActorOref.MyContacts.Count()         ;count of elements
For Key=1:1:ActorOref.MyContacts.Count() {             ;display each element
    Write !,"Key: ",Key                                ;of Collection List
    Write " - ",ActorOref.MyContacts.GetAt(Key).ContactName   ;Property: MyContacts
}
Write !,ActorOref.%Save()                              ;Save the object
```

```
If you save the above code in a routine and then run the it from the Terminal,
you should get the following output.
```

```
Count: 5
Key: 1 - Contact1
Key: 2 - Contact6
Key: 3 - Contact2
Key: 4 - Contact3
Key: 5 - Contact4
1
```

In Example 27-14 the contact in Key 2 from Contact5 to Contact6.

## RemoveAt Method – Remove a specific Contact

**Example 27-15 RemoveAt Method – Remove a specific Contact**

```
The MyContacts Property is defined as a
Collection List of References to Persistent Objects

RemoveAt Method - Remove the Element associated with a Key

To run this code you must put the code in a routine, save the routine, and then
run the routine from the terminal.
```

```
Set ActorOref=##class(MyPackage.Actor).%OpenId(5)        ;bring object Johnny Depp
                                                         ;into memory

Do ActorOref.MyContacts.RemoveAt(3)                      ;remove contact at
                                                         ;Key 3, Contact2

Write !,"Count: ",ActorOref.MyContacts.Count()           ;count of elements
For Id=1:1:ActorOref.MyContacts.Count() {                ;display each element
    Write !,"Id: ",Id                                    ;of Collection List
    Write " - ",ActorOref.MyContacts.GetAt(Id).ContactName   ;Property: MyContacts
}
Write !,ActorOref.%Save()                                ;Save the object
```

If you save the above code in a routine and then run the it from the Terminal, you should get the following output.

```
Count: 4
Id: 1 - Contact1
Id: 2 - Contact6
Id: 3 - Contact3
Id: 4 - Contact4
1
```

In Example 27-15 we remove the Contact at Key 3 that is Contact2.

## Display MyContacts Data using Embedded SQL

We cannot display a *Collection List of References to Persistent Objects* with SQL alone. SQL will gather the MyPackage.Actors together and the *Next Method* will be used to display the MyPackage.Contacts data.

**Example 27-16 Display MyContacts Data using Embedded SQL**

The MyContacts Property is defined as a
Collection List of References to Persistent Objects

To run this code you must put the code in a routine, save the routine, and then run the routine from the terminal.

```
New id, actorname, mycontacts
&sql(Declare MyCursor CURSOR FOR
    SELECT Id, Name, MyContacts
    INTO :id, :actorname, :mycontacts
    FROM MyPackage.Actor
    ORDER BY Id)
&sql(OPEN MyCursor)
&sql(FETCH MyCursor)
While (SQLCODE = 0) {
    Write !, "Id: ",id
    Write " Name: ",actorname
    Set ActorOref=##class(MyPackage.Actor).%OpenId(id)
    Set Key = "" Do {
        Set Key=ActorOref.MyContacts.Next(Key) ;get the next Key
        If Key'="" {
            Write !,?12,"Key: ",Key
            Write " - ",ActorOref.MyContacts.GetAt(Key).ContactName
        }
    } While (Key '= "")
```

```
    &sql(FETCH MyCursor)
}
&sql(CLOSE MyCursor)
```

```
Id: 1 Name: John Wayne
Id: 2 Name: Jodie Foster
Id: 3 Name: Clint Eastwood
Id: 4 Name: Julie Andrews
Id: 5 Name: Johnny Depp
                Key: 1 - Contact1
                Key: 2 - Contact6
                Key: 3 - Contact3
                Key: 4 - Contact4
Id: 6 Name: Carol Burnett
Id: 7 Name: Will Smith
Id: 8 Name: Ann Margaret
Id: 9 Name: Dean Martin
Id: 10 Name: Ally Sheedy
Id: 11 Name: Humphrey Bogart
Id: 12 Name: Katharine Hepburn
```

In Example 27-16 we use *Embedded SQL* to display MyPackage.Actor data and the *Next Method* to display MyPackage.MyContacts.

## Display MyContacts Data using Dynamic SQL

We cannot display a *Collection List of References to Persistent Objects* with SQL alone. SQL will gather the MyPackage.Actors together and the *Next Method* will be used to display the MyPackage.Contacts data.

**Example 27-17 Display MyContacts Data using Dynamic SQL**

```
Set MyQuery="SELECT Id, Name FROM MyPackage.Actor"

Set ResultSet=##class(%ResultSet).%New("%DynamicQuery:SQL")

Set SC=ResultSet.Prepare(MyQuery)

Set SC=ResultSet.Execute()

While ResultSet.Next() {
    Set Id=ResultSet.Data("ID")
    Write !, "Id:",Id
    Write "Name: ",ResultSet.Data("Name")
    Set ActorOref=##class(MyPackage.Actor).%OpenId(Id)
    Set Key = "" Do {
        Set Key=ActorOref.MyContacts.Next(Key) ;get the next Key
        If Key'="" {
```

```
            Write !,?7,"Key: ",Key ;display the Key number
            Write " Name ",ActorOref.MyContacts.GetAt(Key).ContactName
        }
    } While (Key '= "")
}
Set SC=ResultSet.Close()
```

```
Id: 1 Name John Wayne
Id: 2 Name Jodie Foster
Id: 3 Name Clint Eastwood
Id: 4 Name Julie Andrews
Id: 5 Name Johnny Depp
            Key: 1 - Contact1
            Key: 2 - Contact6
            Key: 3 - Contact3
            Key: 4 - Contact4
Id: 6 Name: Carol Burnett
Id: 7 Name: Will Smith
Id: 8 Name: Ann Margaret
Id: 9 Name: Dean Martin
Id: 10 Name: Ally Sheedy
Id: 11 Name: Humphrey Bogart
Id: 12 Name: Katharine Hepburn
```

In Example 27-17 we use *Dynamic SQL* to display MyPackage.Actor data and the *Next Method* to display MyPackage.Contacts.

## *Chapter 27 Summary*

In this chapter, we look at a *Collection Lists of Persistent Object* and a number of various Methods to update and access "MyContacts". These Methods included: Clear and Count Methods, Insert, GetAt, Find, Next, Previous, GetNext, GetPrevious, InsertAt, SetAt and RemoveAt Methods. In addition we also demonstrated *Embedded SQL* and *Dynamic SQL* to display "MyContacts".

*"It is not hard, when you don't know what you are talking about."*

# Chapter 28 Class & Object Properties - Collection Array of References to Persistent Objects

Chapters 25 through 30 cover the basic concepts of Caché ObjectScript (COS) to process Caché Class and Objects Properties - **Collections**. In Chapter 22 we looked at:

 ➢ Data Types

 ➢ References to Persistent Objects – these Properties point to or reference other Persistent Objects in another class

 ➢ References to Embedded Objects – these Properties point to or reference an Embedded Object that reside (or are embedded) in the current class

Now we are going to apply the concept of *Collections* or *Multiple Entries* to each of the above three.

## Introduction to Collections

A **Collection** is an ordered list of information, or multiple entries.

*Collections* in Caché fall into these categories:

 ➢ List Collection of Data Types - Chapter 25

 ➢ Array Collection of Data Types - Chapter 26

 ➢ List Collection of References to Persistent Objects  – Chapter 27

 ➢ Array Collection of References to Persistent Objects – Chapter 28

 ➢ List Collection of References to Embedded Objects – Chapter 29

 ➢ Array Collection of References to Embedded Objects - Chapter 30

As a base Class we will use *MyPackage.Actor* created in Chapter 22 and modified in subsequent chapters.

We have already seen *Data Types*, *References to Persistent Objects* and *References to Embedded Objects*. Now by using *Collections* we will expand their capability.

# Collection Array of References to Persistent Objects

A *Collection Array of References to Persistent Objects* combines a *Collection Array* and *References to Persistent Objects*.

**Table 28-1 Object Properties**

| Object Property | Data Type | Reference Object Class and Name | Name we chose | Special Considerations |
|---|---|---|---|---|
| Data Types | %String | | Name (Name of Actor) | |
| Collection List of Data Types | %String | | MyShirts (Shirts belonging to an Actor) | Total length cannot exceed 32k |
| Collection Array of Data Types | %String | | MyHats (Hats belonging to an Actor) | No length limit In SQL must be handled as a Child table Must specify a Key when accessing |
| Collection List of References to Persistent Objects | | Persistent Objects | MyContacts (Contacts of the Actor) | |
| Collection Array of References to Persistent Objects | | Persistent Objects | MyClients (Clients of the Actor) | |

# Base Class and Referenced Class

Our base class is MyPackage.Actors as we established in Chapter 22. Our referenced Class shall be MyPackage.Clients or clients of the Actors.

Our first step is to create a *Client* class; *MyPackage.Clients* based on the *%Persistent Class*.

# Class Definition – Creating the Clients Class

**Example 28-1 Class Definition – Creating the Clients Class**

```
Class MyPackage.Clients Extends %Persistent
{

Property ClientName As %String [ Required ];

Index ClientNameIndex On ClientName;

}
```

After starting up Caché Studio from the Caché Cube (a small blue cube in your system tray), click on **File -> New,** then select **Caché Class Definition,** next select the package MyPackage and add a new Class called *Clients*. Add the property *ClientName* (click on **Class -> Add -> Property)** to the Clients Class. Also add the index *ClientNameIndex* (click on **Class -> Add -> Index)** to the Clients Class. Your class should look like in Example 28-1. Recompile the class.

## *Populate the Clients Class*

**Example 28-2 Populate the Clients Class**

```
For Name="Client1","Client2","Client3" Do CreateObject(Name)
For Name="Client4","Client5","Client6" Do CreateObject(Name)
Quit

CreateObject(Name) [] Public {
    Set ActorOref=##class(MyPackage.Clients).%New()  ;create new object reference
    Set ActorOref.ClientName=Name                     ;populate object with a name
    Do ActorOref.%Save()                              ;save the object
    Set NewId=ActorOref.%Id() Write !,"Id: ",NewId    ;write ID of new Object
    Write " - ",ActorOref.ClientName                  ;write name of the new Object
}
```

If you save the above code in a routine and then run the it from the Terminal, you should get the following output.

```
Id: 1 - Client1
Id: 2 - Client2
Id: 3 - Client3
Id: 4 - Client4
Id: 5 - Client5
Id: 6 - Client6
```

In Example 28-2 we populate the *Clients Class* with names of Client1 through Client6.

## *Actor Class Redefinition – add Reference Property that will point to the Clients Class*

**Example 28-3 Actor Class Redefinition – add Reference Property that will point to the Clients Class**

```
Class MyPackage.Actor Extends %Persistent
{

Property Name As %String [ Required ];

Index NameIndex On Name;

Property MyAccountant As Accountants;

Property MyHome As Address;

Property MyShirts As list Of %String;

Property MyHats As array Of %String;
```

```
Property MyContacts As list Of Contacts;

Property MyClients As array Of Clients;

}
```

After starting up Caché Studio from the Caché Cube (a small blue cube in your system tray), click on **FILE -> OPEN,** then select the package MyPackage and Class Actor. Add the *Property MyClients As Array of Clients* line (click on **CLASS -> ADD -> PROPERTY)** to the Actor Class. Your class should look like in Example 28-3. Recompile the class.

The following are a number of methods whereby we manipulate the *Collection Array of Reference of Persistent Objects: MyClients*. We shall use *MyPackage.Actor Object Id 6*, Carol Burnett. If we did not know the *Object Id* of Carol Burnett, we could use *Embedded SQL* to find her Id as demonstrated in Chapter 22 Example 11 and in Chapter 23.

## Clear and Count Methods – Delete all elements and show the count

Example 28-4 Clear and Count Methods - Deletes all elements and show the count

```
The MyClients Property is defined as a
Collection Array of References to Persistent Objects

Clear Method - Clears or Deletes the Collection of Elements

Count Method - Returns the Number of Elements in the Collection

Set ActorOref=##class(MyPackage.Actor).%OpenId(6)      ;bring object Carol Burnett
                                                       ;into memory
;
Do ActorOref.MyClients.Clear()                         ;clear Array of Clients
Write !,"Count: ",ActorOref.MyClients.Count()          ;count of elements
Write !,ActorOref.%Save()                              ;Save the object

If you run the above code from the Terminal, you should get the following
output.

Count: 0
1
```

In Example 28-4 we start by bringing into memory an Actor Object with an Id of 6, (Carol Burnett). Next we ensure there is no data in our *Collection Array of References to Persistent Objects Property: MyClients* so we use the *Clear()* and *Count() Methods*. Lastly, we use the *%Save() Method* to save all changes to disk.

## SetAt Method – SetAt four Clients into the Collection

**Example 28-5 SetAt Method – SetAt four Clients into the Collection**

```
The MyClients Property is defined as a
Collection Array of References to Persistent Objects

SetAt Method - Set an Oref at the specific Key

Set ActorOref=##class(MyPackage.Actor).%OpenId(6)        ;bring object Carol Burnett
                                                         ;into memory

Set Client1Oref=##class(MyPackage.Clients).%OpenId(1)    ;bring object Client1
                                                         ;into memory

Set Client2Oref=##class(MyPackage.Clients).%OpenId(2)    ;bring object Client2
                                                         ;into memory

Set Client3Oref=##class(MyPackage.Clients).%OpenId(3)    ;bring object Client3
                                                         ;into memory

Set Client4Oref=##class(MyPackage.Clients).%OpenId(4)    ;bring object Client4
                                                         ;into memory

Do ActorOref.MyClients.SetAt(Client1Oref,1)       ;associate Client1 with
                                                   ;Actress Carol Burnett at key 1
Do ActorOref.MyClients.SetAt(Client2Oref,2)       ;associate Client2 with
                                                   ;Actress Carol Burnett at key 2
Do ActorOref.MyClients.SetAt(Client3Oref,3)       ;associate Client3 with
                                                   ;Actress Carol Burnett at key 3
Do ActorOref.MyClients.SetAt(Client4Oref,4)       ;associate Client4 with
                                                   ;Actress Carol Burnett at key 4

Write !,"Count: ",ActorOref.MyClients.Count()

Write !,ActorOref.%Save()                          ;Save the object

If you run the above code from the Terminal, you should get the following
output.

Count: 4
1
```

In Example 28-5 we use the *SetAt() Method* to add four clients to the *Collection Array of References to Persistent Objects*. First we bring our Actress (Carol Burnett) into memory. Next we bring four Clients into memory using Client1Oref thru Client4Oref. Then we associate the ActorOref with the four Clients using the *SetAt() Method*.

## Global generated from Class MyPackage.Actor

**Example 28-6 Global generated from Class MyPackage.Actor**

```
ZW ^MyPackage.ActorD
^MyPackage.ActorD=13
^MyPackage.ActorD(1)=$lb("","John
Wayne","",$lb("","","",""),"Blue",$lb("BlueShirt","CyanShirt","RedShirt",""WhiteShirt""))
^MyPackage.ActorD(2)=$lb("","Jodie Foster","",$lb("","","",""),"Green","")
```

```
 ^MyPackage.ActorD(2,"MyHats",1)="Bowler"
 ^MyPackage.ActorD(2,"MyHats",2)="BigBirdHat"
 ^MyPackage.ActorD(2,"MyHats","Top")="TopHat"
 ^MyPackage.ActorD(3)=$lb("","Clint Eastwood","2",$lb("","","",""),"Cyan")
 ^MyPackage.ActorD(4)=$lb("","Julie Andrews","",$lb("123 Main St.","Marlboro",
"MA","01752"),"Brown")
 ^MyPackage.ActorD(5)=$lb("","Johnny
Depp","",$lb("","","",""),"Tan","",$lb($lb("1"),$lb("6"),$lb("3"),$lb("4")))
 ^MyPackage.ActorD(6)=$lb("","Carol Burnett","",$lb("","","",""),"Red","","")
 ^MyPackage.ActorD(6,"MyClients",1)=1
 ^MyPackage.ActorD(6,"MyClients",2)=2
 ^MyPackage.ActorD(6,"MyClients",3)=3
 ^MyPackage.ActorD(6,"MyClients",4)=4
 ^MyPackage.ActorD(7)=$lb("","Will Smith","",$lb("","","",""),"Navy")
 ^MyPackage.ActorD(8)=$lb("","Ann Margaret","",$lb("","","",""),"Yellow")
 ^MyPackage.ActorD(9)=$lb("","Dean Martin","",$lb("","","",""),"Green")
 ^MyPackage.ActorD(10)=$lb("","Ally Sheedy","",$lb("","","",""),"Black")
 ^MyPackage.ActorD(11)=$lb("","Humphrey Bogart","",$lb("","","",""),"Brown")
 ^MyPackage.ActorD(12)=$lb("","Katharine Hepburn","2",$lb("","","",""),"Blue")

ZW ^MyPackage.ClientsD
^MyPackage.ClientsD=6
^MyPackage.ClientsD(1)=$lb("","Client1")
^MyPackage.ClientsD(2)=$lb("","Client2")
^MyPackage.ClientsD(3)=$lb("","Client3")
^MyPackage.ClientsD(4)=$lb("","Client4")
^MyPackage.ClientsD(5)=$lb("","Client5")
^MyPackage.ClientsD(6)=$lb("","Client6")
```

Example 28-6 shows the Global generated from the Class MyPackage.Actor as well as Class MyPackage.Clients. You can see how the pointers to the four Clients are stored for Carol Burnett as well as how the Clients are stored. Your Global may not look exactly like this one if you have not worked through all the examples in the previous Chapters.

## IsDefined Method – See if a Key is defined

**Example 28-7 IsDefined Method – See if a Key is defined**

```
The MyClients Property is defined as a
Collection Array of References to Persistent Objects

IsDefined Method - Returns a 1 if the Key is defined otherwise 0
```

```
Set ActorOref=##class(MyPackage.Actor).%OpenId(6)      ;bring object Carol Burnett
                                                       ;into memory

 Write ActorOref.MyClients.IsDefined(1)        ;Is key 1 defined? - Yes
1

 Write ActorOref.MyClients.IsDefined(3)        ;Is key 3 defined? - Yes
1

 Write ActorOref.MyClients.IsDefined(6)        ;Is key 6 defined? - No
0
```

In Example 28-7 we see a demonstration of the *IsDefined Method* that determines if a *key* exists.

## GetAt Method – Returns the Elements associated with the Key

**Example 28-8 GetAt Method – Returns the Elements associated with the Key**

```
  The MyClients Property is defined as a
Collection Array of References to Persistent Objects

GetAt Method - Returns the Element associated with a Key

  Set ActorOref=##class(MyPackage.Actor).%OpenId(6)    ;bring object Carol Burnett
                                                       ;into memory

  Write !,"Count: ",ActorOref.MyClients.Count()        ;count of elements
  For Id=1:1:ActorOref.MyClients.Count() {             ;Display each element
    Write !,"Id: ",Id                                  ;of Collection Array
      Write " - ",ActorOref.MyClients.GetAt(Id).ClientName ;Property: MyClients
  }

If you save the above code in a routine and then run the it from the Terminal,
you should get the following output.

Count: 4
Id: 1 - Client1
Id: 2 - Client2
Id: 3 - Client3
Id: 4 - Client4
```

Example 28-8 demonstrates the *GetAt() Method* which displays each Element of the *Collection Array of References to Persistent Objects Property: MyClients* that is associated with Actress Carol Burnett.

## Find Method – Finds the associated Id for a String

Currently Caché does not support a *Find Method* for a *Collection Array of References to Persistent Object* that allows you to search for a string. The following code will do this.

**Example 28-9 Find Method – Finds the associated ID for a String**

```
The MyClients Property is defined as a
Collection Array of References to Persistent Objects

Find Code - Finds the associated Id for a String

  Set ActorOref=##class(MyPackage.Actor).%OpenId(6)    ;bring object Carol Burnett
                                                       ;into memory

  Set NameToFind="Client3"                             ;Name to Find
  Set FoundId=""                                       ;initialized FoundId

  For Id=1:1:ActorOref.MyClients.Count() {
      If ActorOref.MyClients.IsDefined(Id) {           ;Does the Id exist?
          If NameToFind= ActorOref.MyClients.GetAt(Id).ClientName Set FoundId=Id Quit
    }
  }

  If FoundId'="" {
      Write !, "Found: ", NameToFind," at Id: ",FoundId
```

```
}
Else{
    Write !, "Could not find: ", NameToFind
}
```

*Found: Client3 at Id: 3*


    = = = = = = = = = = = = = = = = = = = = = = = = = = = = = = = = =

```
Set NameToFind="Client5"                    ;Name to Find
Set FoundId=""                              ;initialized FoundId

For Id=1:1:ActorOref.MyClients.Count() {
    If ActorOref.MyClients.IsDefined(Id) {          ;Does the Id exist?
        If NameToFind= ActorOref.MyClients.GetAt(Id).ClientName Set FoundId=Id Quit
    }
}

If FoundId'="" {
    Write !, "Found: ", NameToFind," at Id: ",FoundId
}
Else{
    Write !, "Could not find: ", NameToFind
}
```

*Could not find: Client5*

The code in Example 28-9 will find the associated Id for Client3 and Client5. The Id for Client3 is 3 but since Client5 does not exist no Id is returned.

## Traversing Methods

The *Next, Previous, GetNext* and *GetPrevious Methods* all provide the capability of traversing Object data, similar to the *$Order* command. *Next* and *GetNext* traverse through the data forward and *Previous* and *GetPrevious* traverse through the data backwards. *Next* and *Previous* accepts the Key/Slot parameter passed by value whereas *GetNext* and *GetPrevious* accept the Key/Slot parameter passed by reference.

Table 28-2 Traversing Methods

| Method | | How Key or Slot is passed |
|---|---|---|
| Next | Traversing Forward | Key or Slot passed by Value |
| Previous | Traversing Backward | Key or Slot Passed by Value |
| GetNext | Traversing Forward | Key or Slot Passed by Reference |
| GetPrevious | Traversing Backward | Key or Slot Passed by Reference |

## Next Method – Returns the Element for the next Key

**Example 28-10 Next Method – Returns the Element for the next Key**

```
The MyClients Property is defined as a
Collection Array of References to Persistent Objects

Next Method - Returns the Element for the next Key

  Set ActorOref=##class(MyPackage.Actor).%OpenId(6)        ;bring object Carol Burnett
                                                           ;into memory

  Write !,"Count: ",ActorOref.MyClients.Count()            ;count of elements
  Set Key = "" Do {                                        ;start with Key null
       Set Key=ActorOref.MyClients.Next(Key)                 ;get the next Key
       If Key'="" {
           Write !,"Key: ",Key                                 ;display the Key number
           Write " - ",ActorOref.MyClients.GetAt(Key).ClientName ;display the Client
       }
  } While (Key '= "")
```

```
If you save the above code in a routine and then run the it from the Terminal,
you should get the following output.
```

```
Count: 4
Key: 1 - Client1
Key: 2 - Client2
Key: 3 - Client3
Key: 4 - Client4
```

In Example 28-10 we use the *Next() Method* to obtain the next *Key*. Initially we set the *Key* to null then we use *Next()* to cycle through the *Keys*, finally when the *Key* equals null again we stop.

## Previous Method – Returns the Element for the previous Key

**Example 28-11 Previous Method – Returns the Element for the previous Key**

```
The MyClients Property is defined as a
Collection Array of References to Persistent Objects

Previous Method - Returns the Element  for the previous Key

  Set ActorOref=##class(MyPackage.Actor).%OpenId(6)        ;bring object Carol Burnett
                                                           ;into memory

  Write !,"Count: ",ActorOref.MyClients.Count()            ;count of elements
  Set Key = "" Do {                                        ;start with Key null
       Set Key=ActorOref.MyClients.Previous(Key)             ;get the previous Key
       If Key'="" {
           Write !,"Key: ",Key                                 ;display the Key number
           Write " - ",ActorOref.MyClients.GetAt(Key).ClientName ;display the Client
       }
  } While (Key '= "")
```

```
If you save the above code in a routine and then run the it from the Terminal,
you should get the following output.
```

```
Count: 4
Key: 4 - Client4
Key: 3 - Client3
Key: 2 - Client2
Key: 1 - Client1
```

In Example 28-11 we use the *Previous() Method* to obtain the previous *Key*. Initially we set the *Key* to null, and then we use the *Previous() Method* to cycle through the *Keys* backwards, finally when the *Key* equals null we stop.

## GetNext Method – Returns the Element for the next Key

Example 28-12 GetNext Method – Returns the Element for the next Key

```
The MyClients Property is defined as a
Collection Array of References to Persistent Objects

GetNext Method - Returns the Element for the next Key

  Set ActorOref=##class(MyPackage.Actor).%OpenId(6)      ;bring object Carol Burnett
                                                         ;into memory

  Write !,"Count: ",ActorOref.MyClients.Count()          ;count of elements
  Set Key = "" Do {                                      ;start with beginning Key
      Set Client=ActorOref.MyClients.GetNext(.Key)       ;get next Key
      If Key'="" Write !,"Key: ",Key," ",Client.ClientName   ;display Key with Client
  } While (Key '= "")

If you save the above code in a routine and then run the it from the Terminal,
you should get the following output.
```

```
Count: 4
Key: 1 - Client1
Key: 2 - Client2
Key: 3 - Client3
Key: 4 - Client4
```

In Example 28-12 we see the *GetNext() Method. This Method* is similar to the *Next Method* except that the *Key* is passed by reference. Initially we set the *Key* to null then we use *GetNext()* to cycle through the *Keys*, finally when the *Key* equals null we stop.

## GetPrevious Method– Returns the Element for the Previous Key

Example 28-13 GetPrevious Method – Returns the Element for the Previous Key

```
The MyClients Property is defined as a
Collection Array of References to Persistent Objects

GetPrevious Method – Returns the Element  for the previous Key

  Set ActorOref=##class(MyPackage.Actor).%OpenId(6)      ;bring object Carol Burnett
                                                         ;into memory

  Write !,"Count: ",ActorOref.MyContacts.Count()         ;count of elements
```

```
Set Key = "" Do {                                              ;start with beginning Key
    Set Client=ActorOref.MyClients.GetPrevious(.Key)   ;get previous Key
    If Key'="" Write !,"Key: ",Key," ",Client.ClientName ;display Key with Client
} While (Key '= "")
```

```
Count: 4
Key: 4 - Client4
Key: 3 - Client3
Key: 2 - Client2
Key: 1 - Client1
```

In Example 28-13 we see the *GetPrevious() Method*. This *Method* is similar to the *Previous Method* except that the *Key* is passed by reference. Initially we set the *Key* to null then we use *GetPrevious()* to cycle through the *Keys* backwards. Finally when the *Key* equals null we stop.

Now suppose we made a mistake and the 2nd Client should be Client6 and not Client2.

## SetAt Method – Replace a specific Client

**Example 28-14 SetAt Method – Replace a specific Client**

```
The MyClients Property is defined as a
Collection Array of References to Persistent Objects

SetAt Method - Set an Oref at the specific Key
```

```
Set ActorOref=##class(MyPackage.Actor).%OpenId(6)    ;bring object Carol Burnett
                                                      ;into memory

Set Client6Oref=##class(MyPackage.Clients).%OpenId(6) ;bring object into
                                                      ;memory - Client6

Do ActorOref.MyClients.SetAt(Client6Oref,2)          ;Replace Client with
                                                      ;Client6 at the 2nd
                                                      ;position

Write !,"Count: ",ActorOref.MyClients.Count()        ;count of elements
For Id=1:1:ActorOref.MyClients.Count() {             ;Display each element
    Write !,"Id: ",Id                                ;of Collection Array
    Write " - ",ActorOref.MyClients.GetAt(Id).ClientName  ;Property: MyClients
}

Write !,ActorOref.%Save()                             ;Save the Object
```

```
Count: 5
Id: 1 - Client1
Id: 2 - Client6
Id: 3 - Client3
Id: 4 - Client4
1
```

In Example 28-14 we use the *SetAt() Method* to change the Client in Key 2 from Client2 to Client6

## RemoveAt Method – Remove a specific Client

**Example 28-15 RemoveAt Method – Remove a specific Client**

```
The MyClients Property is defined as a
Collection Array of References to Persistent Objects

RemoveAt Method - Remove the Element associated with the Key

    Set ActorOref=##class(MyPackage.Actor).%OpenId(6)     ;bring object Carol Burnett
                                                          ;into memory

    Do ActorOref.MyClients.RemoveAt(3)                    ;Remove Client at
                                                          ;Key 3, Client3
    Write !,"Count: ",ActorOref.MyClients.Count()         ;count of elements
    Set Key = "" Do {                                     ;start with beginning Key
        Set Client=ActorOref.MyClients.GetNext(.Key)      ;get next Key
        If Key'="" Write !,"Key: ",Key," ",Client.ClientName ;display Key with Client
    } While (Key '= "")

    Write !,ActorOref.%Save()                             ;Save the object

If you save the above code in a routine and then run the it from the Terminal,
you should get the following output.

Count: 3
Id: 1 - Client1
Id: 2 - Client6
Id: 4 - Client4
1
```

In Example 28-15 we remove the Client at Key 3 that is Client3.

## Display MyClients Data using Embedded SQL

When Caché *Projects* a Table with a Collection Array of References to Persistent Objects Property, it does so in two linked tables:

> ➤ MyPackage.Actor table

> ➤ MyPackage. Actor_MyClients table

In the example that follows we use the MyPackage. Actor_MyClients table in the SQL Select statement and point back up to the MyPackage.Actor table to obtain the actor's name.

**Example 28-16 Display MyClients Data using Embedded SQL**

```
New actorname,myclients
&sql(Declare MyCursor CURSOR FOR
    SELECT Actor->Name, MyClients
    INTO :actorname, :myclients
    FROM MyPackage.Actor MyClients
    ORDER BY Name)
&sql(OPEN MyCursor)
&sql(FETCH MyCursor)
While (SQLCODE = 0) {
    Write !,"Name: ",actorname
```

```
    Write ?25,"MyClients: ",myclients
    &sql(FETCH MyCursor)
}
&sql(CLOSE MyCursor)
```

```
Name: Carol Burnett      MyClients: 1
Name: Carol Burnett      MyClients: 6
Name: Carol Burnett      MyClients: 4
```

Example 28-16 demonstrates *Embedded SQL* to display the Client data. Note the reference to the sub-table: Actor_MyClients and how the Actor's name must be referenced.

## Display MyClients Data using Dynamic SQL

When Caché *Projects* a Table with a Collection Array of References to Persistent Objects Property, it does so in two linked tables:

➢ MyPackage.Actor table

➢ MyPackage. Actor_MyClients table

In the example that follows we use the MyPackage. Actor_MyClients table in the SQL Select statement and point back up to the MyPackage.Actor table to obtain the actor's name.

### Example 28-17 Display MyClients Data using Dynamic SQL

```
Set MyQuery="SELECT Actor->Name,MyClients FROM MyPackage.Actor_MyClients"

Set ResultSet=##class(%ResultSet).%New("%DynamicQuery:SQL")
                                 ;Create a new Instance of %ResultSet

Set SC=ResultSet.Prepare(MyQuery)          ;Prepare the Query

Set SC=ResultSet.Execute()                 ;Execute the Query

While ResultSet.Next() {                    ;Process the Query results
    Write !,ResultSet.Data("Name")," - "
    Write "Client: ",ResultSet.Data("MyClients")
}

Set SC=ResultSet.Close()                    ;Close the Query
```

```
Carol Burnett - Client: 1
Carol Burnett - Client: 6
Carol Burnett - Client: 4
```

Example 28-17 demonstrates *Dynamic SQL* to MyClients Array data. Note how the Actor's name must be referenced.

## Chapter 28 Summary

In this chapter, we look at a *Collection Array of References to Persistent Objects* and a number of various Methods to update and access the data "MyClients". These Methods included: Clear and Count Methods, SetAt, IsDefined, GetAt, Find, Next, Previous, GetNext, GetPrevious, and RemoveAt Methods. In addition we also demonstrated Embedded SQL and Dynamic SQL to display "MyClients" data.

*"Let another praise you, and not your own mouth; a stranger, and not your own lips." - Proverbs 27:2*

# Chapter 29 Class & Object Properties - Collection List of References to Embedded Objects

Chapters 25 through 30 cover the basic concepts of Caché ObjectScript (COS) to process Caché Class and Objects Properties - **Collections**. In Chapter 22 we looked at:

> ➢ Data Types

> ➢ References to Persistent Objects – these Properties point to or reference other Persistent Objects in another class

> ➢ References to Embedded Objects – these Properties point to or reference an Embedded Object that reside (or are embedded) in the current class

Now we are going to apply the concept of *Collections* or *Multiple Entries* to each of the above three.

## Introduction to Collections

A **Collection** is an ordered list of information, or multiple entries.

*Collections* in Caché fall into these categories:

> ➢ List Collection of Data Types - Chapter 25

> ➢ Array Collection of Data Types - Chapter 26

> ➢ List Collection of References to Persistent Objects – Chapter 27

> ➢ Array Collection of References to Persistent Objects – Chapter 28

> ➢ List Collection of References to Embedded Objects – Chapter 29

> ➢ Array Collection of References to Embedded Objects - Chapter 30

As a base Class we will use *MyPackage.Actor* created in Chapter 22 and modified in subsequent chapters.

We have already seen *Data Types*, *References to Persistent Objects* and *References to Embedded Objects*. Now by using *Collections* we will expand their capability.

## Collection List of References to Embedded Objects

A *Collection List of References to Embedded Objects* combines a *Collection List* and *References to Embedded Objects*.

**Table 29-1 Object Properties**

| Object Property | Data Type | Reference Object Class and Name | Name we chose | Special Considerations |
|---|---|---|---|---|
| Data Types | %String | | Name (Name of Actor) | |
| Collection List of Data Types | %String | | MyShirts (Shirts belonging to an Actor) | Total length cannot exceed 32k |
| Collection Array of Data Types | %String | | MyHats (Hats belonging to an Actor) | No length limit In SQL must be handled as a Child table Must specify a Key when accessing |
| Collection List of References to Persistent Objects | | Persistent Objects | MyContacts (Contacts of the Actor) | |
| Collection Array of References to Persistent Objects | | Persistent Objects | MyClients (Clients of the Actor) | |
| Collection List of References to Embedded Objects | | Embedded Objects %Serial Class | MyRentals (Rental Property of the Actor) | |
| Collection Array of References to Embedded Objects | | Embedded Objects %Serial Class | MyPets (Pets of the Actor) | |

## Base Class and Referenced Class

Our base class is MyPackage.Actors as we established in Chapter 22. Our referenced Class shall be MyPackage.Rentals or rental property of the Actors.

Our first step is to create a Rentals class; *MyPackage.Rentals* based on the *%Serial Class*. The *%SerialObject* class is *embedded* within the Actor Class.

## Class Definition – Creating the Rentals Class

**Example 29-1 Class Definition – Creating the Rentals Class**

```
Class MyPackage.Rentals Extends %SerialObject
{

Property Street As %String(MAXLEN = 80);

Property City As %String(MAXLEN = 30);

Property State As %String(MAXLEN = 2);

Property Zip As %String(MAXLEN = 10);

}
```

After starting up Caché Studio from the Caché Cube, click on **File** -> **New,** then select **Caché Class Definition,** next select the package MyPackage and add a new Class called *Rentals*. Add the Properties Street, City, State, and Zip (click on **Class** -> **Add** -> **Property)** to the Rentals Class. Your class should look like in Example 29-1. Recompile the class.

## Actor Class Redefinition – add Reference Property that will point to the Rentals Class

**Example 29-2 Actor Class Redefinition – add Reference Property that will point to the Rentals Class**

```
Class MyPackage.Actor Extends %Persistent
{

Property Name As %String [ Required ];

Index NameIndex On Name;

Property MyAccountant As Accountants;

Property MyHome As Address;

Property MyShirts As list Of %String;

Property MyHats As array Of %String;

Property MyContacts As list Of Contacts;

Property MyClients As array Of Clients;

Property MyRentals As list Of Rentals;

}
```

After starting up Caché Studio from the Caché Cube, click on **File** -> **Open,** then select the package MyPackage and Class Actor. Add the *"Property MyRentals As list of Rentals"* line (click on **Class** -> **Add** -> **Property** TO the Actor Class. Your class should look like in Example 29-2. Recompile the class.

The following are a number of methods whereby we manipulate the *Collection List of Reference of Embedded Objects: MyRentals*. We shall use *MyPackage.Actor Object Id 9*, Dean Martin. If we did not know the *Object Id* of Dean Martin, we could use *Embedded SQL* to find his Id as demonstrated in Chapter 22 Example 11 and in Chapter 23.

## *Clear and Count Methods – Delete all elements and show the count*

Example 29-3 Clear and Count Methods - Deletes all elements and show the count

```
The MyRentals Property is defined as a
Collection List of References to Embedded Objects

Clear Method - Clears or Deletes the Collection of Elements

Count Method - Returns the Number of Elements in the Collection
```

```
Set ActorOref=##class(MyPackage.Actor).%OpenId(9)      ;bring object Dean Martin
                                                       ;into memory
;
Do ActorOref.MyRentals.Clear()                         ;clear list of Rentals
Write !,"Count: ",ActorOref.MyRentals.Count()          ;count of elements

Write !,ActorOref.%Save()                              ;Save the object
```

```
If you run the above code from the Terminal, you should get the following
output.
```

```
Count: 0
1
```

In Example 29-3 we start by bringing into memory an Actor Object with an Id of 9, (Dean Martin). Next we ensure there is no data in our *Collection List of References to Embedded Objects Property: MyRentals* so we use the *Clear()* and *Count() Methods*. Lastly we use the *%Save() Method* to save all changes to disk.

## *Insert Method – Insert three Rentals into the Collection*

Example 29-4 Insert Method – Insert three Rentals into the Collection

```
The MyRentals Property is defined as a
Collection List of References to Embedded Objects

Insert Method - Inserts an Oref at the end of the collection
```

```
Set ActorOref=##class(MyPackage.Actor).%OpenId(9)       ;bring object Dean Martin
                                                        ;into memory

Set AddressOref1=##class(MyPackage.Rentals).%New()      ;create new Address Oref1
Set AddressOref1.Street="123 Main St."                  ;Set the Street
Set AddressOref1.City="Pittsburgh"                      ;Set the City
Set AddressOref1.State="PA"                             ;Set the State
Set AddressOref1.Zip="01600"                            ;Set the Zip

Set AddressOref2=##class(MyPackage.Rentals).%New()      ;create new Address Oref2
```

```
Set AddressOref2.Street="53 Elm St."                    ;Set the Street
Set AddressOref2.City="L.A."                            ;Set the City
Set AddressOref2.State="CA"                             ;Set the State
Set AddressOref2.Zip="95602"                            ;Set the Zip

Set AddressOref3=##class(MyPackage.Rentals).%New()      ;create new Address Oref3
Set AddressOref3.Street="9 Pershing St."                ;Set the Street
Set AddressOref3.City="Worcester"                       ;Set the City
Set AddressOref3.State="MA"                             ;Set the State
Set AddressOref3.Zip="01752"                            ;Set the Zip

Do ActorOref.MyRentals.Insert(AddressOref1)   ;associate AddressOref1 with Actor
Do ActorOref.MyRentals.Insert(AddressOref2)   ;associate AddressOref2 with Actor
Do ActorOref.MyRentals.Insert(AddressOref3)   ;associate AddressOref3 with Actor

Write !,ActorOref.%Save()                               ;Save the object
```

In Example 29-4 first we bring our actor (Dean Martin) into memory using ActorOref. Next, we establish 3 Rental property addresses in memory. Then we associate the ActorOref with the 3 Rental property addresses using the *Insert() Method*.

## Global generated from Class MyPackage.Actor

**Example 29-5 Global generated from Class MyPackage.Actor**

```
 ZW ^MyPackage.ActorD
 ^MyPackage.ActorD=13
^MyPackage.ActorD(1)=$lb("","John
Wayne","",$lb("","","",""),"Blue",$lb("BlueShirt","CyanShirt","RedShirt","WhiteShirt"))
 ^MyPackage.ActorD(2)=$lb("","Jodie Foster","",$lb("","","",""),"Green","")
 ^MyPackage.ActorD(2,"MyHats",1)="Bowler"
 ^MyPackage.ActorD(2,"MyHats",2)="BigBirdHat"
 ^MyPackage.ActorD(2,"MyHats","Top")="TopHat"
 ^MyPackage.ActorD(3)=$lb("","Clint Eastwood","2",$lb("","","",""),"Cyan")
 ^MyPackage.ActorD(4)=$lb("","Julie Andrews","",$lb("123 Main St.","Marlboro",
"MA","01752"),"Brown")
 ^MyPackage.ActorD(5)=$lb("","Johnny
Depp","",$lb("","","",""),"Tan","",$lb($lb("1"),$lb("6"),$lb("3"),$lb("4")))
 ^MyPackage.ActorD(6)=$lb("","Carol Burnett","",$lb("","","",""),"Red","","")
 ^MyPackage.ActorD(6,"MyClients",1)=1
 ^MyPackage.ActorD(6,"MyClients",2)=6
 ^MyPackage.ActorD(6,"MyClients",4)=4
 ^MyPackage.ActorD(7)=$lb("","Will Smith","",$lb("","","",""),"Navy")
 ^MyPackage.ActorD(8)=$lb("","Ann Margaret","",$lb("","","",""),"Yellow")
 ^MyPackage.ActorD(9)=$lb("","Dean Martin","",$lb("","","",""),"Green","","",
$lb($lb($lb("123 Main St.","Pittsburgh","PA","01600")),$lb($lb("53 Elm
St.","L.A.","CA","95602")),$lb($lb("9 Pershing St.","Worcester","MA","01752"))))
 ^MyPackage.ActorD(10)=$lb("","Ally Sheedy","",$lb("","","",""),"Black")
 ^MyPackage.ActorD(11)=$lb("","Humphrey Bogart","",$lb("","","",""),"Brown")
 ^MyPackage.ActorD(12)=$lb("","Katharine Hepburn","2",$lb("","","",""),"Blue")
```

Example 29-5 shows the Global generated from the Class MyPackage.Actor including the 3 Rental properties for Dean Martin. Your Global may not look exactly like this one if you have not worked through all the examples in the previous Chapters.

## GetAt Method – Returns the Elements associated with the Key List

**Example 29-6 GetAt Method – Returns the Elements associated with the Key**

```
The MyRentals Property is defined as a
Collection List of References to Embedded Objects

GetAt Method - Returns the Element associated with a Key
```

```
Set ActorOref=##class(MyPackage.Actor).%OpenId(9)      ;bring object Dean Martin
                                                        ;into memory

Write !,"Count: ",ActorOref.MyRentals.Count()  ;count of elements
For Key=1:1:ActorOref.MyRentals.Count() {               ;Display each element
  Write !,"Key: ",Key                                   ;of Collection List
  Write " - ",ActorOref.MyRentals.GetAt(Key).Street     ;Property: MyRentals - Street
  Write ?30,ActorOref.MyRentals.GetAt(Key).City         ;Property: MyRentals - City
  Write ?50,ActorOref.MyRentals.GetAt(Key).State        ;Property: MyRentals - State
  Write ?60,ActorOref.MyRentals.GetAt(Key).Zip          ;Property: MyRentals - Zip
}
```

```
If you save the above code in a routine and then run the it from the Terminal,
you should get the following output.
```

```
Count: 3
Key: 1 - 123 Main St.        Pittsburgh        PA        01600
Key: 2 - 53 Elm St.          L.A.              CA        95602
Key: 3 - 9 Pershing St.      Worcester         MA        01752
```

Example 29-6 demonstrates the *GetAt() Method* which displays each Element of the *Collection List of References to Embedded Objects Property: MyRentals* that is associated with Actor Dean Martin.

## Find Method – Finds the associated Key for a String

Currently Caché does not support a *Find Method* for a *Collection List of References to Embedded Objects* that allows you to search for a string. The following code will do this.

**Example 29-7 Find Method – Finds the associated KEY for a String**

```
The MyRentals Property is defined as a
Collection List of References to Embedded Objects

Find Code - Finds the associated Key for a String
```

```
Set ActorOref=##class(MyPackage.Actor).%OpenId(9)      ;bring object Dean Martin
                                                        ;into memory

Set StreetToFind="53 Elm St."                           ;Street to Find
Set FoundKey=""                                         ;initialized FoundKey

For Key=1:1:ActorOref.MyRentals.Count() {
    If StreetToFind=ActorOref.MyRentals.GetAt(Key).Street Set FoundKey=Key
}

If FoundKey'="" {
    Write !, "Found: ", StreetToFind," at Key: ",FoundKey
}
```

```
Else{
    Write !, "Could not find: ", StreetToFind
}
```

*Found: 53 Elm St. at Key: 2*

= = = = = = = = = = = = = = = = = = = = = = = = = = = = = = =

```
Set CityToFind="Worcester"                          ;City to Find
Set FoundKey=""                                     ;initialized FoundKey

For Key=1:1:ActorOref.MyRentals.Count() {
  If CityToFind=ActorOref.MyRentals.GetAt(Key).City Set FoundKey=Key
}

If FoundKey'="" {
    Write !, "Found: ", CityToFind," at Key: ",FoundKey
    }
Else{
    Write !, "Could not find: ", CityToFind
    }
```

*Found: Worcester at Key: 3*

The code in Example 29-7 will find the associated Key for a Street and City.

## Traversing Methods

The *Next, Previous, GetNext* and *GetPrevious Methods* all provide the capability of traversing Object data, similar to the **$Order** command. *Next* and *GetNext* traverse through the data forward and *Previous* and *GetPrevious* traverse through the data backwards. *Next* and *Previous* accepts the Key/Slot parameter passed by value whereas *GetNext* and *GetPrevious* accept the Key/Slot parameter passed by reference.

**Table 29-2 Traversing Methods**

| Method | | How Key or Slot is passed |
|---|---|---|
| Next | Traversing Forward | Key or Slot passed by Value |
| Previous | Traversing Backward | Key or Slot Passed by Value |
| GetNext | Traversing Forward | Key or Slot Passed by Reference |
| GetPrevious | Traversing Backward | Key or Slot Passed by Reference |

### Next Method – Returns the Element for the next Key

**Example 29-8 Next Method – Returns the Element for the next Key**

```
The MyRentals Property is defined as a
Collection List of References to Embedded Objects

Next Method - Returns the Element for the next Key

  Set ActorOref=##class(MyPackage.Actor).%OpenId(9)      ;bring object Dean Martin
                                                          ;into memory

  Write !,"Count: ",ActorOref.MyRentals.Count()          ;count of elements
  Set Key = "" Do {                                      ;start with Key null
    Set Key=ActorOref.MyRentals.Next(Key)                ;get the next Key
    If Key'="" {
      Write !,"Key: ",Key                                ;display the Key number
      Write " - ",ActorOref.MyRentals.GetAt(Key).Street  ;Property: MyRentals - Street
      Write ?30,ActorOref.MyRentals.GetAt(Key).City      ;Property: MyRentals - City
      Write ?50,ActorOref.MyRentals.GetAt(Key).State     ;Property: MyRentals - State
      Write ?60,ActorOref.MyRentals.GetAt(Key).Zip       ;Property: MyRentals - Zip
    }
  } While (Key '= "")
```

```
If you save the above code in a routine and then run the it from the Terminal,
you should get the following output.
```

```
Count: 3
Key: 1 - 123 Main St.        Pittsburgh      PA      01600
Key: 2 - 53 Elm St.          L.A.            CA      95602
Key: 3 - 9 Pershing St.      Worcester       MA      01752
```

In Example 29-8 we use the *Next() Method* to obtain the next *Key*. Initially we set the *Key* to null then we use *Next()* to cycle through the *Keys*, finally when the *Key* equals null again we stop.

### Previous Method – Returns the Element for the previous Key

**Example 29-9 Previous Method – Returns the Element for the previous Key**

```
The MyRentals Property is defined as a
Collection List of References to Embedded Objects

Previous Method - Returns the Element  for the previous Key

  Set ActorOref=##class(MyPackage.Actor).%OpenId(9)      ;bring object Dean Martin
                                                          ;into memory

  Write !,"Count: ",ActorOref.MyRentals.Count()          ;count of elements
  Set Key = "" Do {                                      ;start with Key null
    Set Key=ActorOref.MyRentals.Previous(Key)            ;get the previous Key
    If Key'="" {
      Write !,"Key: ",Key                                ;display the Key number
      Write " - ",ActorOref.MyRentals.GetAt(Key).Street  ;Property: MyRentals - Street
      Write ?30,ActorOref.MyRentals.GetAt(Key).City      ;Property: MyRentals - City
      Write ?50,ActorOref.MyRentals.GetAt(Key).State     ;Property: MyRentals - State
      Write ?60,ActorOref.MyRentals.GetAt(Key).Zip       ;Property: MyRentals - Zip
```

```
      }
  } While (Key '= "")
```

```
Count: 3
Key: 3 - 9 Pershing St.        Worcester        MA        01752
Key: 2 - 53 Elm St.            L.A.             CA        95602
Key: 1 - 123 Main St.          Pittsburgh       PA        01600
```

In Example 29-9 we use the *Previous() Method* to obtain the previous *Key*. Initially we set the *Key* to null, then we use the *Previous() Method* to cycle through the *Keys* backwards, finally when the *Key* equals null we stop.

## GetNext Method – Returns the Element for the next Key

**Example 29-10 GetNext Method – Returns the Element for the next Key**

The MyRentals Property is defined as a
Collection List of References to Embedded Objects

GetNext Method - Returns the Element for the next Key

```
Set ActorOref=##class(MyPackage.Actor).%OpenId(9)      ;bring object Dean Martin
                                                       ;into memory

Write !,"Count: ",ActorOref.MyRentals.Count()          ;count of elements
Set Key = "" Do {                                      ;start with beginning Key
    Set Contact=ActorOref.MyRentals.GetNext(.Key)      ;get next Key
    If Key'="" {
      Write !,"Key: ",Key," "                           ;display Key
      Write " - ",ActorOref.MyRentals.GetAt(Key).Street ;Property: MyRentals - Street
      Write ?30,ActorOref.MyRentals.GetAt(Key).City     ;Property: MyRentals - City
      Write ?50,ActorOref.MyRentals.GetAt(Key).State    ;Property: MyRentals - State
      Write ?60,ActorOref.MyRentals.GetAt(Key).Zip      ;Property: MyRentals - Zip
    }
} While (Key '= "")
```

```
Count: 3
Key: 1  - 123 Main St.         Pittsburgh       PA        01600
Key: 2  - 53 Elm St.           L.A.             CA        95602
Key: 3  - 9 Pershing St.       Worcester        MA        01752
```

In Example 29-10 we see the *GetNext() Method. This Method* is similar to the *Next Method* except that the *Key* is passed by reference. Initially we set the *Key* to null then we use *GetNext()* to cycle through the *Keys*, finally when the *Key* equals null we stop.

## GetPrevious Method– Returns the Element for the Previous Key

Example 29-11 GetPrevious Method – Returns the Element for the Previous Key

```
The MyRentals Property is defined as a
Collection List of References to Embedded Objects

GetPrevious Method - Returns the Element  for the previous Key

  Set ActorOref=##class(MyPackage.Actor).%OpenId(9)      ;bring object Dean Martin
                                                         ;into memory

  Write !,"Count: ",ActorOref.MyRentals.Count()          ;count of elements
  Set Key = "" Do {
    Set Contact=ActorOref.MyRentals.GetPrevious(.Key)    ;get next Key
    If Key'="" {
      Write !,"Key: ",Key," "                            ;display Key
      Write " - ",ActorOref.MyRentals.GetAt(Key).Street  ;Property: MyRentals - Street
      Write ?30,ActorOref.MyRentals.GetAt(Key).City      ;Property: MyRentals - City
      Write ?50,ActorOref.MyRentals.GetAt(Key).State     ;Property: MyRentals - State
      Write ?60,ActorOref.MyRentals.GetAt(Key).Zip       ;Property: MyRentals - Zip
    }
} While (Key '= "")

If you save the above code in a routine and then run the it from the Terminal,
you should get the following output.

Count: 3
Key: 3 - 9 Pershing St.      Worcester      MA      01752
Key: 2 - 53 Elm St.          L.A.           CA      95602
Key: 1 - 123 Main St.        Pittsburgh     PA      01600
```

In Example 29-11 we see the *GetPrevious() Method*. This *Method* is similar to the *Previous Method* except that the *Key* is passed by reference. Initially we set the *Key* to null then we use *GetPrevious()* to cycle through the *Keys* backwards. Finally when the *Key* equals null we stop.

## InsertAt Method – Insert a new Address between the 1st and 2nd Address

Example 29-12 InsertAt Method – Insert a new Address between the 1st and 2nd Address

```
The MyRentals Property is defined as a
Collection List of References to Embedded Objects

InsetAt Method - Insert an Oref into a Collection at the specific key

  Set ActorOref=##class(MyPackage.Actor).%OpenId(9)       ;bring object Dean Martin
                                                          ;into memory

  Set AddressOref=##class(MyPackage.Rentals).%New()       ;create new Address ActorOref
  Set AddressOref.Street="39 Pinewold Ave"                ;Set the Street
  Set AddressOref.City="Burlington"                       ;Set the City
  Set AddressOref.State="MA"                              ;Set the State
  Set AddressOref.Zip="01803"                             ;Set the Zip

  Do ActorOref.MyRentals.InsertAt(AddressOref,2)          ;Insert AddressOref
                                                          ;at Key position 2
```

```
Do ActorOref.%Save()                                   ;save the object

Write !,"Count: ",ActorOref.MyRentals.Count()          ;count of elements
For Id=1:1:ActorOref.MyRentals.Count() {               ;Display each element
  Write !,"Id: ",Id                                    ;of Collection List
  Write " - ",ActorOref.MyRentals.GetAt(Id).Street     ;Property: MyRentals - Street
  Write ?30,ActorOref.MyRentals.GetAt(Id).City         ;Property: MyRentals - City
  Write ?50,ActorOref.MyRentals.GetAt(Id).State        ;Property: MyRentals - State
  Write ?60,ActorOref.MyRentals.GetAt(Id).Zip          ;Property: MyRentals - Zip
}
```

If you save the above code in a routine and then run the it from the Terminal,
you should get the following output.

```
Count: 4
Id: 1 - 123 Main St.      Pittsburgh      PA      01600
Id: 2 - 39 Pinewold Ave   Burlington      MA      01803
Id: 3 - 53 Elm St.        L.A.            CA      95602
Id: 4 - 9 Pershing St.    Worcester       MA      01752
```

Example 29-12 demonstrates the *InsertAt() Method* to insert a new address between the 1st and 2nd Rentals.

## SetAt Method – Replace a specific Address

**Example 29-13 SetAt Method – Replace a specific Address**

The MyRentals Property is defined as a
Collection List of References to Embedded Objects

SetAt Method - Set an Oref at the specified Key

```
Set ActorOref=##class(MyPackage.Actor).%OpenId(9) ;bring object Dean Martin
                                                  ;into memory

Set AddressOref=##class(MyPackage.Rentals).%New() ;create new ActorOref
Set AddressOref.Street="1040 Lincoln St."    ;Set the Street
Set AddressOref.City="Dallas"                ;Set the City
Set AddressOref.State="TX"                   ;Set the State
Set AddressOref.Zip="00000"                  ;Set the Zip


Do ActorOref.MyRentals.SetAt(AddressOref,2)  ;Replace AddressOref at Key 2

Do ActorOref.%Save()                         ;save the object

Write !,"Count: ",ActorOref.MyRentals.Count()          ;count of elements
For Id=1:1:ActorOref.MyRentals.Count() {               ;Display each element
  Write !,"Id: ",Id                                    ;of Collection List
  Write " - ",ActorOref.MyRentals.GetAt(Id).Street     ;Property: MyRentals - Street
  Write ?30,ActorOref.MyRentals.GetAt(Id).City         ;Property: MyRentals - City
  Write ?50,ActorOref.MyRentals.GetAt(Id).State        ;Property: MyRentals - State
  Write ?60,ActorOref.MyRentals.GetAt(Id).Zip          ;Property: MyRentals - Zip
}
```

If you save the above code in a routine and then run the it from the Terminal,
you should get the following output.

```
Count: 4
Id: 1 - 123 Main St.          Pittsburgh        PA        01600
Id: 2 - 1040 Lincoln St.      Dallas            TX        00000
Id: 3 - 53 Elm St.            L.A.              CA        95602
Id: 4 - 9 Pershing St.        Worcester         MA        01752
```

In Example 29-13 we use the *SetAt() Method* to replace the 2nd address.

## RemoveAt Method – Remove a specific Address Contact

**Example 29-14 RemoveAt Method – Remove a specific Address**

```
The MyRentals Property is defined as a
Collection List of References to Embedded Objects

RemoveAt Method - Remove the Element associated with the Key

Set ActorOref=##class(MyPackage.Actor).%OpenId(9)        ;bring object Dean Martin
                                                         ;into memory


Do ActorOref.MyRentals.RemoveAt(2)                       ;Remove contact at
                                                         ;Key 2


Do ActorOref.%Save()                                     ;save the object

Write !,"Count: ",ActorOref.MyRentals.Count()            ;count of elements
For Id=1:1:ActorOref.MyRentals.Count() {                 ;Display each element
   Write !,"Id: ",Id                                     ;of Collection List
   Write " - ",ActorOref.MyRentals.GetAt(Id).Street      ;Property: MyRentals - Street
   Write ?30,ActorOref.MyRentals.GetAt(Id).City          ;Property: MyRentals - City
   Write ?50,ActorOref.MyRentals.GetAt(Id).State         ;Property: MyRentals - State
   Write ?60,ActorOref.MyRentals.GetAt(Id).Zip           ;Property: MyRentals - Zip
}
```

```
If you save the above code in a routine and then run the it from the Terminal,
you should get the following output.
```

```
Count: 3
Id: 1 - 123 Main St.          Pittsburgh        PA        01600
Id: 2 - 53 Elm St.            L.A.              CA        95602
Id: 3 - 9 Pershing St.        Worcester         MA        01752
```

In Example 29-14 we remove the Rental Address at Key 2.

## Display MyRentals Data using Embedded SQL

We cannot display a *Collection List of References to Embedded Objects* with SQL alone. SQL will gather the MyPackage.Actors together and the *Next Method* will be used to display the MyPackage.Rentals data.

**Example 29-15 Display MyRentals Data using Embedded SQL**

```
New id, actorname, myrentals
&sql(Declare MyCursor CURSOR FOR
   SELECT Id, Name, MyRentals
   INTO :id, :actorname, :myrentals
   FROM MyPackage.Actor
   ORDER BY Id)
&sql(OPEN MyCursor)
&sql(FETCH MyCursor)
While (SQLCODE = 0) {
   Write !, "Id: ",id
   Write " Name: ",actorname
   Set ActorOref=##class(MyPackage.Actor).%OpenId(id)
   For Key=1:1:ActorOref.MyRentals.Count() {          ;Display each element
       Write !,"Key: ",Key                            ;of Collection List
       Write " - ",ActorOref.MyRentals.GetAt(Key).Street ;Property: MyRentals - Street
       Write ?30,ActorOref.MyRentals.GetAt(Key).City  ;Property: MyRentals - City
       Write ?50,ActorOref.MyRentals.GetAt(Key).State ;Property: MyRentals - State
       Write ?60,ActorOref.MyRentals.GetAt(Key).Zip   ;Property: MyRentals - Zip
   }
   &sql(FETCH MyCursor)
}
&sql(CLOSE MyCursor)
```

If you save the above code in a routine and then run the it from the Terminal, you should get the following output.

```
Id: 1 Name: John Wayne
Id: 2 Name: Jodie Foster
Id: 3 Name: Clint Eastwood
Id: 4 Name: Julie Andrews
Id: 5 Name: Johnny Depp
Id: 6 Name: Carol Burnett
Id: 7 Name: Will Smith
Id: 8 Name: Ann Margaret
Id: 9 Name: Dean Martin
Key: 1 - 123 Main St.       Pittsburgh      PA      01600
Key: 2 - 53 Elm St.         L.A.            CA      95602
Key: 3 - 9 Pershing St.     Worcester       MA      01752
Id: 10 Name: Ally Sheedy
Id: 11 Name: Humphrey Bogart
Id: 12 Name: Katharine Hepburn
```

In Example 29-15 we use Embedded SQL to display MyPackage.Actor data and the *Next Method* to display MyPackage.Rentals.

## Display MyRentals Data using Dynamic SQL

**Example 29-16 Display MyRentals Data using Dynamic SQL**

```
The MyRentals Property is defined as a
Collection List of References to Embedded Objects

  Set MyQuery="SELECT Id, Name FROM MyPackage.Actor"

  Set ResultSet=##class(%ResultSet).%New("%DynamicQuery:SQL")

  Set SC=ResultSet.Prepare(MyQuery)

  Set SC=ResultSet.Execute()

While ResultSet.Next() {
    Set Id=ResultSet.Data("ID")
    Write !, "Id:",Id
    Write " Name: ",ResultSet.Data("Name")
    Set ActorOref=##class(MyPackage.Actor).%OpenId(Id)
    Set Key = "" Do {
        Set Key=ActorOref.MyRentals.Next(Key) ;get the next Key
        If Key'="" {
            Write !,"Key: ",Key
            Write " - ",ActorOref.MyRentals.GetAt(Key).Street ;Prop: MyRentals - Street
            Write ?30,ActorOref.MyRentals.GetAt(Key).City    ;Prop: MyRentals - City
            Write ?50,ActorOref.MyRentals.GetAt(Key).State   ;Prop: MyRentals - State
            Write ?60,ActorOref.MyRentals.GetAt(Key).Zip     ;Prop: MyRentals - Zip
        }
    } While (Key '= "")
  }
  Set SC=ResultSet.Close()
```

```
If you save the above code in a routine and then run the it from the Terminal,
you should get the following output.

Id: 1 Name John Wayne
Id: 2 Name Jodie Foster
Id: 3 Name Clint Eastwood
Id: 4 Name Julie Andrews
Id: 5 Name Johnny Depp
Id: 6 Name: Carol Burnett
Id: 7 Name: Will Smith
Id: 8 Name: Ann Margaret
Id: 9 Name: Dean Martin
Key: 1 - 123 Main St.        Pittsburgh      PA      01600
Key: 2 - 53 Elm St.          L.A.            CA      95602
Key: 3 - 9 Pershing St.      Worcester       MA      01752
Id: 10 Name: Ally Sheedy
Id: 11 Name: Humphrey Bogart
Id: 12 Name: Katharine Hepburn
```

In Example 29-16 we use SQL to display MyPackage.Actor data and the *Next Method* to display MyPackage.Rentals.

## Chapter 29 Summary

In this chapter, we looked at a *Collection Lists of Embedded Object* and a number of various Methods to update and access "MyRentals". These Methods included: Clear and Count Methods, Insert, GetAt, Find, Next, Previous, GetNext, GetPrevious, InsertAt, SetAt and RemoveAt Methods. In addition we also demonstrated Embedded SQL and Dynamic SQL to display "MyRentals".

*"Whatever you think it's gonna take, double it. That applies to money, time, stress. It's gonna be harder that you think and take longer that you think."*

*– Richard A. Cortese*

# Chapter 30 Class & Object Properties - Collection Array of References to Embedded Objects

Chapters 25 through 30 cover the basic concepts of Caché ObjectScript (COS) to process Caché Class and Objects Properties - **Collections**. In Chapter 22 we looked at:

➢ Data Types

➢ References to Persistent Objects – these Properties point to or reference other Persistent Objects in another class

➢ References to Embedded Objects – these Properties point to or reference an Embedded Object that reside (or are embedded) in the current class

Now we are going to apply the concept of *Collections* or *Multiple Entries* to each of the above three.

## Introduction to Collections

A **Collection** is an ordered list of information, or multiple entries.

*Collections* in Caché fall into these categories:

➢ List Collection of Data Types - Chapter 25

➢ Array Collection of Data Types - Chapter 26

➢ List Collection of References to Persistent Objects – Chapter 27

➢ Array Collection of References to Persistent Objects – Chapter 28

➢ List Collection of References to Embedded Objects – Chapter 29

➢ Array Collection of References to Embedded Objects - Chapter 30

As a base Class we will use *MyPackage.Actor* created in Chapter 22 and modified in subsequent chapters.

We have already seen *Data Types*, *References to Persistent Objects* and *References to Embedded Objects*. Now by using *Collections* we will expand their capability.

## Collection Array of References to Embedded Objects

A *Collection Array of References to Embedded Objects* combines a *Collection Array* and *References to Embedded Objects*.

**Table 30-1 Object Properties**

| Object Property | Data Type | Reference Object Class and Name | Name we chose | Special Considerations |
|---|---|---|---|---|
| Data Types | %String | | Name (Name of Actor) | |
| Collection List of Data Types | %String | | MyShirts (Shirts belonging to an Actor) | Total length cannot exceed 32k |
| Collection Array of Data Types | %String | | MyHats (Hats belonging to an Actor) | No length limit In SQL must be handled as a Child table Must specify a Key when accessing |
| Collection List of References to Persistent Objects | | Persistent Objects | MyContacts (Contacts of the Actor) | |
| Collection Array of References to Persistent Objects | | Persistent Objects | MyClients (Clients of the Actor) | |
| Collection List of References to Embedded Objects | | Embedded Objects %Serial Class | MyRentals (Rental Property of the Actor) | |
| Collection Array of References to Embedded Objects | | Embedded Objects %Serial Class | MyPets (Pets of the Actor) | |

## Base Class and Referenced Class

Our base class is MyPackage.Actors as we established in Chapter 22. Our referenced Class shall be MyPackage.Pets or pets of the Actors.

Our first step is to create a *Pets* class; *MyPackage.Pets* based on the *%Serial Class*. The *%SerialObject* class will be embedded within the Actor Class.

## Class Definition – Creating the Pets Class

**Example 30-1 Class Definition – Creating the Pets Class**

```
Class MyPackage.Pets Extends %SerialObject
{

Property Name As %String;

Property Breed As %String;

Property Color As %String;

Property Weight As %String;

}
```

After starting up Caché Studio from the Caché Cube(a small blue cube in your system tray), click on **File -> New,** then select **Caché Class Definition,** next select the package MyPackage and add a new Class called *Pets*. Add the Properties Name, Color, and Breed and Weight (click on **Class -> Add -> Property)** to the Pets Class. Your class should look like in Example 30-1. Recompile the class.

## Actor Class Redefinition – add Reference Property that will point to the Pets Class

**Example 30-2 Actor Class Redefinition – add Reference Property that will point to the Pets Class**

```
Class MyPackage.Actor Extends %Persistent
{

Property Name As %String [ Required ];

Index NameIndex On Name;

Property MyAccountant As Accountants;

Property MyHome As Address;

Property MyShirts As list Of %String;

Property MyHats As array Of %String;

Property MyContacts As list Of Contacts;

Property MyClients As array Of Clients;

Property MyHomes As list Of Rentals;

Property MyPets As array Of Pets;

}
```

After starting up Caché Studio from the Caché Cube(a small blue cube in your system tray), click on **File -> Open,** then select the package MyPackage and Class Actor. Add the "*Property MyPets As Array of*

*Pets*" line (click on **Class -> Add -> Property)** to the Actor Class. Your class should look like in Example 30-2. Recompile the class.

The following are a number of methods whereby we manipulate the *Collection Array of References to Embedded Objects: MyPets*. We shall use *MyPackage.Actor Object Id of 8*, Ann Margaret. If we did not know the *Object Id* of Ann Margaret, we could use *Embedded SQL* to find her Id as demonstrated in Chapter 22 Example 11 and in Chapter 23.

## *Clear and Count Methods – Delete all elements and show the count*

**Example 30-3 Clear and Count Methods - Deletes all elements and show the count**

```
The MyPets Property is defined as a
Collection Array of References to Embedded Objects

Clear Method - Clears or Deletes the Collection of Elements

Count Method - Returns the Number of Elements in the Collection
```

```
Set ActorOref=##class(MyPackage.Actor).%OpenId(8)      ;bring object Ann Margaret
                                                       ;into memory

Do ActorOref.MyPets.Clear()                            ;clear Array of Pets
Write !,"Count: ",ActorOref.MyPets.Count()             ;count of elements

Write !,ActorOref.%Save()                              ;Save the object
```

```
If you save the above code in a routine and then run it from the Terminal, you
should get the following output.
```

```
Count: 0
1
```

In Example 30-3 we start by bringing into memory an Actor Object with an Id of 8, (Ann Margaret). Next we ensure there is no data in our *Collection Array of References to Embedded Objects Property: MyPets* so we use the *Clear()* and *Count() Methods*. Lastly, we use the *%Save() Method* to save all changes to disk.

## *SetAt Method – Insert three Pets into the Collection*

**Example 30-4 SetAt Method – Insert three Pets into the Collection**

```
The MyPets Property is defined as a
Collection Array of References to Embedded Objects

SetAt Method - Set an Oref at the specific Key
```

```
Set ActorOref=##class(MyPackage.Actor).%OpenId(8)      ;bring object Ann
                                                       ;Margaret into memory

Set PetsOref1=##class(MyPackage.Pets).%New()           ;create new Pet Oref1
Set PetsOref1.Name="Sandy"                             ;Set the Name
Set PetsOref1.Breed="Dog"                              ;Set the Breed
Set PetsOref1.Color="Brown"                            ;Set the Colr
```

```
    Set PetsOref1.Weight="35"                                ;Set the Weight

    Set PetsOref2=##class(MyPackage.Pets).%New()             ;create new Pet Oref2
    Set PetsOref2.Name="Tiger"                               ;Set the Name
    Set PetsOref2.Breed="Cat"                                ;Set the Breed
    Set PetsOref2.Color="Striped"                            ;Set the Color
    Set PetsOref2.Weight="10"                                ;Set the Weight

    Set PetsOref3=##class(MyPackage.Pets).%New()             ;create new Pet Oref3
    Set PetsOref3.Name="Lips"                                ;Set the Name
    Set PetsOref3.Breed="Pig"                                ;Set the Breed
    Set PetsOref3.Color="N/A"                                ;Set the Color
    Set PetsOref3.Weight="70"                                ;Set the Weight

    Do ActorOref.MyPets.SetAt(PetsOref1,1)   ;associate PetsOref1 with Actor at Key 1
    Do ActorOref.MyPets.SetAt(PetsOref2,2)   ;associate PetsOref2 with Actor at Key 2
    Do ActorOref.MyPets.SetAt(PetsOref3,3)   ;associate PetsOref3 with Actor at Key 3

    Write !,"Count: ",ActorOref.MyPets.Count()

    Write !,ActorOref.%Save()                                ;Save the object
```

If you save the above code in a routine and then run it from the Terminal, you should get the following output.

```
Count: 3
1
```

In Example 30-4 we use the *SetAt() Method* to add three Pets to the *Collection Array of References to Embedded Objects.* First we bring our Actress (Ann Margaret) into memory. Next we create 3 Pets using Pets1Oref thru Pets3Oref. Then we associate the ActorOref with the 3 Pets Oref using the *SetAt() Method.*

## Global generated from Class MyPackage.Actor

**Example 30-5 Global generated from Class MyPackage.Actor**

```
 zw ^MyPackage.ActorD
 ^MyPackage.ActorD=13
 ^MyPackage.ActorD(1)=$lb("","John Wayne","","",$lb("BlueShirt","CyanShirt",
"RedShirt","WhiteShirt"))
 ^MyPackage.ActorD(2)=$lb("","Jodie Foster","","","")
 ^MyPackage.ActorD(2,"MyHats",1)="Bowler"
 ^MyPackage.ActorD(2,"MyHats",2)="BigBirdHat"
 ^MyPackage.ActorD(2,"MyHats","Top")="TopHat"
 ^MyPackage.ActorD(3)=$lb("","Clint Eastwood","2",$lb("","","",""),"Cyan")
 ^MyPackage.ActorD(4)=$lb("","Julie Andrews","",$lb("123 Main St.","
Marlboro","MA","01752"),"Brown")
 ^MyPackage.ActorD(5)=$lb("","Johnny
Depp","",$lb("","","",""),"Tan","",$lb($lb("1"),$lb("6"),$lb("3"),$lb("4")))
 ^MyPackage.ActorD(6)=$lb("","Carol Burnett","",$lb("","","",""),"Red","","")
 ^MyPackage.ActorD(6,"MyClients",1)=1
 ^MyPackage.ActorD(6,"MyClients",2)=6
 ^MyPackage.ActorD(6,"MyClients",4)=4
 ^MyPackage.ActorD(7)=$lb("","Will Smith","",$lb("","","",""),"Navy")
 ^MyPackage.ActorD(8)=$lb("","Ann Margaret","",$lb("","","",""),"Yellow","","","")
 ^MyPackage.ActorD(8,"MyPets",1)=$lb("Sandy","Dog","Brown","35")
 ^MyPackage.ActorD(8,"MyPets",2)=$lb("Tiger","Cat","Striped","10")
```

```
^MyPackage.ActorD(8,"MyPets",3)=$lb("Lips","Pig","N/A","70")
 ^MyPackage.ActorD(9)=$lb("","Dean Martin","",$lb("","","",""),
"Green","","",$lb($lb($lb("123 Main  St.","Pittsburgh","PA","01600")),$lb($lb("53 Elm
St.","L.A.","CA","95602")),$lb($lb("9 Pershing St.","Worcester","MA","01752"))))
 ^MyPackage.ActorD(10)=$lb("","Ally Sheedy","",$lb("","","",""),"Black")
 ^MyPackage.ActorD(11)=$lb("","Humphrey Bogart","",$lb("","","",""),"Brown")
 ^MyPackage.ActorD(12)=$lb("","Katharine Hepburn","2",$lb("","","",""),"Blue")
```

Example 30-5 shows the Global generated from the Class MyPackage.Actor as well as the Embedded Class MyPackage.Pets. You can see how the three Pets are stored or embedded for Ann Margaret. Your Global may not look exactly like this one if you have not worked through all the examples in the previous Chapters.

## IsDefined Method – See if a Key is defined

**Example 30-6 IsDefined Method – See if a Key is defined**

```
The MyPets Property is defined as a
Collection Array of References to Embedded Objects

IsDefined Method - see if a Key is defined

Set ActorOref=##class(MyPackage.Actor).%OpenId(8)        ;bring object Ann
                                                         ;Margaret into memory

Write ActorOref.MyPets.IsDefined(1)            ;Is key 1 defined? - Yes
1

Write ActorOref.MyPets.IsDefined(2)            ;Is key 2 defined? - Yes
1

Write ActorOref.MyPets.IsDefined(4)            ;Is key 4 defined? - No
0
```

Example 30-6 we see a demonstration of the *IsDefined() Method* which determines if data represented by a *Key* exists.

## GetAt Method – Returns the Element associated with a Key

**Example 30-7 GetAt Method – Returns the Element associated with a Key**

```
The MyPets Property is defined as a
Collection Array of References to Embedded Objects

GetAt Method - Returns the Element associated with a Key

  Set ActorOref=##class(MyPackage.Actor).%OpenId(8)       ;bring object Ann
                                                          ;Margaret into memory

  Write !,"Count: ",ActorOref.MyPets.Count()              ;count of elements
  For Key=1:1:ActorOref.MyPets.Count() {                  ;Display each element
      Write !,"Key: ",Key                                 ;of Collection Array
      Write " - ",ActorOref.MyPets.GetAt(Key).Name        ;Property: MyPets - Name
      Write ?20,ActorOref.MyPets.GetAt(Key).Breed         ;Property: MyPets - Breed
      Write ?30,ActorOref.MyPets.GetAt(Key).Color         ;Property: MyPets - Color
```

```
      Write ?40,ActorOref.MyPets.GetAt(Key).Weight        ;Property: MyPets - Weight
   }
```

```
Count: 3
Key: 1 - Sandy       Dog       Brown      35
Key: 2 - Tiger       Cat       Striped    10
Key: 3 - Lips        Pig       N/A        70
```

Example 30-7 demonstrates the *GetAt() Method* which displays each Element of the *Collection Array of References to Embedded Objects Property: MyPets* that is associated with Actress Ann Margaret.

## Find Method – Finds the associated Id for a String

Currently Caché does not support a *Find Method* for a *Collection Array of References to Embedded Objects* that allows you to search for a string. The following custom code will do this

**Example 30-8 Find Method – Finds the associated Id for a String**

```
The MyPets Property is defined as a
Collection Array of References to Embedded Objects

Find Code - Finds the associated Id for a String

Set ActorOref=##class(MyPackage.Actor).%OpenId(8)    ;bring object Ann
                                                     ;Margaret into memory

Set NameToFind="Sandy"                               ;Pet Name to Find
Set FoundId=""                                       ;initialized FoundId

For Id=1:1:ActorOref.MyPets.Count() {
    If NameToFind=ActorOref.MyPets.GetAt(Id).Name Set FoundId=Id
}

If FoundId'="" {
    Write !, "Found: ", NameToFind," at Id: ",FoundId
  }
Else{
    Write !, "Could not find: ", NameToFind
  }
```

```
Found: Sandy at Id: 1


    = = = = = = = = = = = = = = = = = = = = = = = = = = = = = = = = =

Set ActorOref=##class(MyPackage.Actor).%OpenId(8)    ;bring object Ann
                                                     ;Margaret into memory
Set ColorToFind="Striped"                            ;Color to Find
Set FoundId=""                                       ;initialized FoundId

For Id=1:1:ActorOref.MyPets.Count() {
    If ColorToFind=ActorOref.MyPets.GetAt(Id).Color Set FoundId=Id
}
```

```
If FoundId'="" {
    Write !, "Found: ", ColorToFind," at Id: ",FoundId
    }
Else{
    Write !, "Could not find: ", ColorToFind
    }
```

If you save the above code in a routine and then run it from the Terminal, you should get the following output.

*Found: Striped at Id: 2*

The code in Example 30-8 will first find a Pet's name of Sandy in the Ann Margaret Object. Next it finds a Pet's Color of Striped.

## Traversing Methods

The *Next, Previous, GetNext* and *GetPrevious Methods* all provide the capability of traversing Object data, similar to the **$Order** command. *Next* and *GetNext* traverse through the data forward and *Previous* and *GetPrevious* traverse through the data backwards. *Next* and *Previous* accepts the Key/Slot parameter passed by value whereas *GetNext* and *GetPrevious* accept the Key/Slot parameter passed by reference.

**Table 30-2 Traversing Methods**

| Method | | How Key or Slot is passed |
|---|---|---|
| Next | Traversing Forward | Key or Slot passed by Value |
| Previous | Traversing Backward | Key or Slot Passed by Value |
| GetNext | Traversing Forward | Key or Slot Passed by Reference |
| GetPrevious | Traversing Backward | Key or Slot Passed by Reference |

## Next Method – Returns the Element for the next Key

**Example 30-9 Next Method – Returns the Element for the next Key**

The MyPets Property is defined as a
Collection Array of References to Embedded Objects.

Next Method - Returns the Element for the next Key

```
Set ActorOref=##class(MyPackage.Actor).%OpenId(8)      ;bring object Ann
                                                        ;Margaret into memory

Write !,"Count: ",ActorOref.MyPets.Count()             ;count of elements
Set Key = "" Do {                                       ;start with Key 0
  Set Key=ActorOref.MyPets.Next(Key)                    ;get the next Key
  If Key'="" {
      Write !,"Key: ",Key                                   ;display the Key
      Write " - ",ActorOref.MyPets.GetAt(Key).Name      ;Property: MyPets - Name
```

```
        Write ?20,ActorOref.MyPets.GetAt(Key).Breed      ;Property: MyPets - Breed
        Write ?30,ActorOref.MyPets.GetAt(Key).Color      ;Property: MyPets - Color
        Write ?40,ActorOref.MyPets.GetAt(Key).Weight     ;Property: MyPets - Weight
    }
} While (Key '= "")
```

If you save the above code in a routine and then run it from the Terminal, you should get the following output.

```
Count: 3
Key: 1 - Sandy      Dog       Brown      35
Key: 2 - Tiger      Cat       Striped    10
Key: 3 - Lips       Pig       N/A        70
```

In Example 30-9 we use the *Next() Method* to obtain the next *Key*. Initially we set the *Key* to null then we use *Next()* to cycle through the *Keys*, finally when the *Key* equals null again we stop.

## Previous Method – Returns the Element for the previous Key

Example 30-10 Previous Method – Returns the Element for the previous Key

The MyPets Property is defined as a
Collection Array of References to Embedded Objects

Previous Method - Returns the Element for the previous Key

```
Set ActorOref=##class(MyPackage.Actor).%OpenId(8)      ;bring object Ann
                                                        ;Margaret into memory

Write !,"Count: ",ActorOref.MyPets.Count()             ;count of elements
Set Key = "" Do {                                      ;start with Key null
    Set Key=ActorOref.MyPets.Previous(Key)             ;get the next Key
    If Key'="" {
        Write !,"Key: ",Key                            ;display the Key
        Write " - ",ActorOref.MyPets.GetAt(Key).Name   ;Property: MyPets - Name
        Write ?20,ActorOref.MyPets.GetAt(Key).Breed    ;Property: MyPets - Breed
        Write ?30,ActorOref.MyPets.GetAt(Key).Color    ;Property: MyPets - Color
        Write ?40,ActorOref.MyPets.GetAt(Key).Weight   ;Property: MyPets - Weight
    }
} While (Key '= "")
```

If you save the above code in a routine and then run it from the Terminal, you should get the following output.

```
Count: 3
Key: 3 - Lips       Pig       N/A        70
Key: 2 - Tiger      Cat       Striped    10
Key: 1 - Sandy      Dog       Brown      35
```

In Example 30-10 we use the *Previous() Method* to obtain the previous *Key*. Initially we set the *Key* to null then we use the *Previous() Method* to cycle through the *Keys* backwards, finally when the *Key* equals null we stop.

## GetNext Method – Returns the Element for the next Key

**Example 30-11 GetNext Method – Returns the Element for the next Key**

```
The MyPets Property is defined as a
Collection Array of References to Embedded Objects

GetNext Method - Returns the Element for the next Key

 Set ActorOref=##class(MyPackage.Actor).%OpenId(8)       ;bring object Ann
                                                         ;Margaret into memory
 Write !,"Count: ",ActorOref.MyPets.Count()             ;count of elements
 Set Key = "" Do {
     Set MyPetsOref=ActorOref.MyPets.GetNext(.Key)
     If Key'="" {
         Write !, "Key: ",Key
         Write " - ",MyPetsOref.Name                     ;Property: MyPets - Name
         Write ?20,MyPetsOref.Breed                      ;Property: MyPets - Breed
         Write ?30,MyPetsOref.Color                      ;Property: MyPets - Color
         Write ?40,MyPetsOref.Weight                     ;Property: MyPets - Weight
     }
 } While (Key '= "")
```

```
If you save the above code in a routine and then run it from the Terminal, you
should get the following output.
```

```
Count: 3
Key: 1 - Sandy      Dog      Brown      35
Key: 2 - Tiger      Cat      Striped    10
Key: 3 - Lips       Pig      N/A        70
```

In Example 30-11 we see the *GetNext() Method. This Method* is similar to the *Next Method* except that the *Key* is passed by reference. Initially we set the *Key* to null then we use *GetNext()* to cycle through the *Keys*, finally when the *Key* equals null we stop.

## GetPrevious Method– Returns the Element for the Previous Key

**Example 30-12 GetPrevious Method – Returns the Element for the Previous Key**

```
The MyPets Property is defined as a
Collection Array of References to Embedded Objects

GetPrevious Method - Returns the Element for the previous Key

 Set ActorOref=##class(MyPackage.Actor).%OpenId(8)       ;bring object Ann
                                                         ;Margaret into memory
 Write !,"Count: ",ActorOref.MyPets.Count()             ;count of elements
 Set Key = "" Do {
     Set MyPetsOref=ActorOref.MyPets.GetPrevious(.Key)
     If Key'="" {
         Write !, "Key: ",Key
         Write " - ",MyPetsOref.Name                     ;Property: MyPets - Name
         Write ?20,MyPetsOref.Breed                      ;Property: MyPets - Breed
         Write ?30,MyPetsOref.Color                      ;Property: MyPets - Color
         Write ?40,MyPetsOref.Weight                     ;Property: MyPets - Weight
     }
 } While (Key '= "")
```

If you save the above code in a routine and then run it from the Terminal, you should get the following output.

```
Count: 3
Key: 3 - Lips        Pig       N/A       70
Key: 2 - Tiger       Cat       Striped   10
Key: 1 - Sandy       Dog       Brown     35
```

In Example 30-12 we see the *GetPrevious() Method*. This *Method* is similar to the *Previous Method* except that the *Key* is passed by reference. Initially we set the *Key* to null then we use *GetPrevious()* to cycle through the *Keys* backwards. Finally when the *Key* equals null we stop.

## SetAt Method – Replace a specific Pet

**Example 30-13 SetAt Method – Replace a specific Pet**

The MyPets Property is defined as a Collection Array of References to Embedded Objects

SetAt Method - Set an Oref at the specific Key

```
Set ActorOref=##class(MyPackage.Actor).%OpenId(8)    ;bring object Ann
                                                     ;Margaret into memory

Set PetsOref=##class(MyPackage.Pets).%New()          ;create new Pet Oref
Set PetsOref.Name="Trixie"                           ;Set the Name
Set PetsOref.Breed="Dog"                             ;Set the Breed
Set PetsOref.Color="White"                           ;Set the Color
Set PetsOref.Weight="50"                             ;Set the Weight

Do ActorOref.MyPets.SetAt(PetsOref,2)          ;associate PetsOref with the Actress
                                               ;and replace the second pet

Write !,"Count: ",ActorOref.MyPets.Count()     ;count of elements
Set Key = "" Do {
    Set MyPetsOref=ActorOref.MyPets.GetNext(.Key)
    If Key'="" {
        Write !, "Key: ",Key
        Write " - ",MyPetsOref.Name             ;Property: MyPets - Name
        Write ?20,MyPetsOref.Breed              ;Property: MyPets - Breed
        Write ?30,MyPetsOref.Color              ;Property: MyPets - Color
        Write ?40,MyPetsOref.Weight             ;Property: MyPets - Weight
    }
} While (Key '= "")

Write !,ActorOref.%Save()                       ;Save the object
```

If you save the above code in a routine and then run it from the Terminal, you should get the following output.

```
Count: 3
Key: 1 - Sandy       Dog       Brown     35
Key: 2 - Trixie      Dog       White     50
Key: 3 - Lips        Pig       N/A       70
```

In Example 30-13 we use the *SetAt() Method* to change Tiger the cat to Trixie the dog as the second Pet.

## RemoveAt Method – Remove a specific Pet

**Example 30-14 RemoveAt Method – Remove a specific Pet**

```
The MyPets Property is defined as a Collection Array of References to Embedded
Objects

RemoveAt Method - Remove a specific Pet

    Set ActorOref=##class(MyPackage.Actor).%OpenId(8)      ;bring object Ann
                                                           ;Margaret into memory

    Do ActorOref.MyPets.RemoveAt(3)                        ;Remove Pet at Key 3

    Write !,"Count: ",ActorOref.MyPets.Count()      ;count of elements
    Set Key = "" Do {
        Set MyPetsOref=ActorOref.MyPets.GetNext(.Key)
        If Key'="" {
            Write !, "Key: ",Key
            Write " - ",MyPetsOref.Name              ;Property: MyPets - Name
            Write ?20,MyPetsOref.Breed               ;Property: MyPets - Breed
            Write ?30,MyPetsOref.Color               ;Property: MyPets - Color
            Write ?40,MyPetsOref.Weight              ;Property: MyPets - Weight
        }
    } While Key'=""

    Write !, ActorOref.%Save()                       ;Save the object

If you save the above code in a routine and then run it from the Terminal, you
should get the following output.

Count: 2
Key: 1 - Sandy        Dog        Brown      35
Key: 2 - Trixie       Dog        White      50
1
```

In Example 30-14 we remove the Pet at Key 3.

## Display Array of References to Embedded Objects using Embedded SQL

**Example 30-15 Display Array of References to Embedded Objects using Embedded SQL**

```
New actorname,mypets
&sql(Declare MyCursor CURSOR FOR
    SELECT Actor->Name, MyPets
    INTO :actorname, :mypets
    FROM MyPackage.Actor MyPets
    ORDER BY Name)
&sql(OPEN MyCursor)
&sql(FETCH MyCursor)
While (SQLCODE = 0) {
    Write !,"Name: ",actorname
    Write ?25,"MyPets: ",mypets
```

```
        &sql(FETCH MyCursor)
    }
    &sql(CLOSE MyCursor)
```

```
Name: Ann Margaret        MyPets: SandyDogBrown35
Name: Ann Margaret        MyPets:TrixieDogWhite50
```

Example 30-15 demonstrates *Embedded SQL* to display Array data. Note the reference to the sub-table: Actor_MyPets and how the Actor's name must be referenced. It is difficult to control the displaying of (Array of References to Embedded Objects) elements while using Embedded SQL.

## Display Array of References to Embedded Objects using Dynamic SQL

**Example 30-16 Display Array of References to Embedded Objects using Dynamic SQL**

```
Set MyQuery="SELECT Actor->Name,MyPets FROM MyPackage.Actor_MyPets"

Set ResultSet=##class(%ResultSet).%New("%DynamicQuery:SQL")
                                  ;Create a new Instance of %ResultSet

Set SC=ResultSet.Prepare(MyQuery) ;Prepare the Query

Set SC=ResultSet.Execute() ;Execute the Query

While ResultSet.Next() {                    ;Process the Query results
    Write !,ResultSet.Data("Name")," - "
    Write "Pet Name: ",$LI(ResultSet.Data("MyPets"),1)
    Write ?35," Breed: ",$LI(ResultSet.Data("MyPets"),2)
    Write ?50," Color: ",$LI(ResultSet.Data("MyPets"),3)
    Write ?65," Weight: ",$LI(ResultSet.Data("MyPets"),4)
  }

Set SC=ResultSet.Close()                    ;Close the Query
```

```
Ann Margaret - Pet Name: Sandy      Breed: Dog    Color: Brown   Weight: 35
Ann Margaret - Pet Name: Trixie     Breed: Dog    Color: White   Weight: 50
```

Example 30-16 demonstrates *Dynamic SQL* to display Array data. Note how the Actor's name must be referenced.

## *Chapter 30 Summary*

In this chapter, we looked at a *Collection Array of References to Embedded Objects* and a number of various Methods to update and access the data "MyPets". These Methods included: Clear and Count Methods, SetAt, IsDefined, GetAt, Find, Next, Previous, GetNext, GetPrevious, and RemoveAt Methods. In addition we also demonstrated Embedded SQL and Dynamic SQL to display "MyPets" data.

*"Everything is funny as long as it is happening to somebody else."*
*– Will Rogers*

# *Chapter 31 Object Relationships*

Chapter 31 covers the basic concepts of Caché ObjectScript (COS) **Object Relationships**. An *Object Relationship* is a connection between two Caché Objects. There is a one-to-many affiliation between the two Objects, which means there is a "One" side of the *Relationship*, and a "Many" side. Normally these two Caché Objects would exist in two separate Classes, that it is not a requirement. One Caché Class may have more than one *Object Relationship*. A *Relationship* is a special type of Object Property, and since a Class can contain more than one Property, it can contain more than one *Relationship*.

There are two types of *Object Relationships:*

➢ One-To-Many, where both sides of the *Relationship* exist independently of each other

➢ Parent-To-Child, where one side is dependent upon another

**Table 31-1 Table comparing One-to-Many and Parent-to-Child Relationships**

| Relationship | One-to-Many | Parent-to-Child | |
|---|---|---|---|
| Persons to Cars | Yes | No | Cars are not dependent upon persons and a person may own many cars |
| Books to Pages | No | Yes | Pages of a book cannot exist without a Book |
| Lawyer to Clients | Yes | No | Clients are not dependent upon Lawyers and Lawyers can have many clients |
| Parent to Children | No | Yes | Children cannot exist without Parents |

Table 31-1 demonstrates various related subjects and where they fall in regard to the *One-To-Many* or *Parent-To-Child* Relationship.

## *One-To-Many Object Relationships*

The links between *One-To-Many* are bi-directional in memory, the *One* has pointers to the *Many* and each of the *Many* has pointers to the *One*.

For Caché Object *Relationships* to work properly, the *Relationship* keywords must be defined correctly. These keywords are defined both on the *One* side and on the *Many* side. These keywords tie the relationship together, they are:

➢ Inverse —property name of the other side of the relationship

➢ Cardinality — "One" or "Many", defines the other side of the relationship

Let us consider a *One-To-Many* relationship of a Lawyer to his Clients.

**Table 31-2 One-to-many relationship of a Lawyer to his clients**

| | Classes | | |
|---|---|---|---|
| | MyPackage.Lawyer | | MyPackage.Client |
| **Name** | LawyerName | | ClientName |
| **Relationship Name** | MyClients | | MyLawyer |
| **Inverse** | MyLawyer | | MyClients |
| **Cardinality** | Many<br>(Many Clients) | | One<br>(One Lawyer) |

## *Define the Lawyer Class*

For this Chapter you will need to create a "Lawyer" and "Client" Class and several properties.

The easiest way to create a class is by using the *Caché Studio* application from the *Caché Cube* software. If you do not have the Caché Cube on your PC or computer, you can download a free copy of Caché for personal evaluation from www.intersytems.com.

After starting up Caché, click on Caché Studio from the Caché Cube (a small blue cube in your system tray). In Caché Studio click on **File -> New,** then select **Caché Class Definition,** and follow the prompts. The Caché Studio includes helpful wizards in creating Classes, Objects Properties and Methods, etc.

You will be asked for a **Package** name, A *Package* name is a way of grouping common classes. Specify a *Package* name of *MyPackage* and a Class name of *Lawyer*. Select a Class Type of **Persistent** (Persistent means it will be stored on disk) and take the defaults for the rest of the wizard.

From the top row in Studio, click on **Class -> Add -> New Property.** Create the *LawyerName* Property as specified by Example 31-1.

**Example 31-1 Define the Lawyer Class**

```
Class MyPackage.Lawyer Extends %Persistent
{

Property LawyerName As %String [ Required ];

}
```

Example 31-1 creates the class *MyPackage.Lawyer* with an Object Property called *LawyerName* that is of *Datatype* %String and is required. From the top row in Studio, click on **Build -> Compile** to compile the class.

## *Define the Client Class*

**Example 31-2 Define the Client Class**

```
Class MyPackage.Client Extends %Persistent
{

Property ClientName As %String [ Required ];

}
```

In the same manner as you created *MyPackage.Lawyer,* create *MyPackage.Client* as shown in Example 31-2. Recompile the class

## *Define the Relationship between Lawyer and Client*

Next, we need to define the relationship between Lawyer and Client. You can use the Studio wizard, Class->Add->Property->Relationship or just copy the underlined code below for both the Lawyer and Client Class.

**Example 31-3 Add a Relationship to the Lawyer Class**

```
Class MyPackage.Lawyer Extends %Persistent
{

Property LawyerName As %String [ Required ];

Relationship MyClients As MyPackage.Client [ Cardinality = many, Inverse = MyLawyer ];

}
```

**Example 31-4 The Relationship will automatically be added to the Client Class**

```
Class MyPackage.Client Extends %Persistent
{

Property ClientName As %String [ Required ];

Relationship MyLawyer As MyPackage.Lawyer [ Cardinality = one, Inverse = MyClients ];

Index MyLawyerIndex On MyLawyer;

}
```

The two classes should look like Example 31-3 and Example 31-4. Be sure and compile the two classes.

In the examples that follow, we will populate the Lawyer Class and Client Class and link the two.

## Populate the Lawyer and Client Classes

**Example 31-5 Populate the Lawyer and Client Classes**

```
Set LawyerOref=##class(MyPackage.Lawyer).%New()        ;create new lawyer
Set LawyerOref.LawyerName="HighPoweredLawyer"           ;lawyer name
Do LawyerOref.%Save()                                    ;save lawyer

Set ClientOref1=##class("MyPackage.Client").%New()      ;create new client
Set ClientOref1.ClientName="PoorClient1"                ;client name
Do ClientOref1.%Save()                                   ;save client

Set ClientOref2=##class("MyPackage.Client").%New()      ;create new client
Set ClientOref2.ClientName="PoorClient2"                ;client name
Do ClientOref2.%Save()                                   ;save client

Set ClientOref3=##class("MyPackage.Client").%New()      ;create new client
Set ClientOref3.ClientName="PoorClient3"                ;client name
Do ClientOref3.%Save()                                   ;save client
```

In Example 31-5, we populate one Lawyer and three Clients in their respective Classes.

## Link the Lawyer with the three Clients

**Example 31-6 Link the Lawyer with the three Clients**

```
Set LawyerOref=##class(MyPackage.Lawyer).%OpenId(1)
Set ClientOref1=##class(MyPackage.Client).%OpenId(1)
Set ClientOref2=##class(MyPackage.Client).%OpenId(2)
Set ClientOref3=##class(MyPackage.Client).%OpenId(3)

Set ClientOref1.MyLawyer=LawyerOref          ;link lawyer with Client1
Set ClientOref2.MyLawyer=LawyerOref          ;link lawyer with Client2
Set ClientOref3.MyLawyer=LawyerOref          ;link lawyer with Client3

Do LawyerOref.%Save()
Do ClientOref1.%Save()
Do ClientOref2.%Save()
Do ClientOref3.%Save()
```

In Example 31-6, we link the Clients with the Lawyer. The link only needs to be defined one way and Caché will establish it both ways.

## Access the Relationship Links

**Example 31-7 Access the relationship links**

```
; Find MyClients from the Lawyer Side
Set LawyerOref=##class(MyPackage.Lawyer).%OpenId(1)
Write LawyerOref.LawyerName                              ;lawyer name
HighPoweredLawyer

;Using the GetAt method, and going from the Lawyer side, we access Client1
Write LawyerOref.MyClients.GetAt(1).ClientName
PoorClient1
```

```
;Using the GetAt method, and going from the Lawyer side, we access Client2
Write LawyerOref.MyClients.GetAt(2).ClientName
PoorClient2

;Using the GetAt method, and going from the Lawyer side, we access Client3
Write LawyerOref.MyClients.GetAt(3).ClientName
PoorClient3

;Access the Lawyer from the Client Side
Set ClientOref=##class(MyPackage.Client).%OpenId(1)
Write ClientOref.MyLawyer.LawyerName
HighPoweredLawyer
```

In Example 31-7, we ensure the relationship links are both ways by accessing the Clients from the Lawyer side and accessing the Lawyer from the Clients side.

## Add another Client (Insert Method) and link it with the Lawyer

**Example 31-8 Add another Client (Insert Method) and link it with the Lawyer**

```
Set ClientOref4=##class(MyPackage.Client).%New()       ;define a new cliet
Set ClientOref4.ClientName="PoorClient4"               ;Client4
Do ClientOref4.%Save()                                 ;Save Client4

Set LawyerOref=##class(MyPackage.Lawyer).%OpenId(1)    ;bring our Lawyer into memory
Do LawyerOref.MyClients.Insert(ClientOref4)            ;link Client 4
                                                       ;with our Lawyer

Do LawyerOref.%Save()
Do ClientOref4.%Save()

Set ClientOref=##class(MyPackage.Client).%OpenId(4)
Write ClientOref.ClientName
PoorClient4
Write ClientOref.MyLawyer.LawyerName
HighPoweredLaywer
```

In Example 31-8, we add PoorClient4 using the Insert method and then link the Lawyer with the new Client.

So far, we have created our Lawyer and Clients and established the relationship between the two. Now, how do we display this information?

## Displaying our Relationship data between Lawyer and Clients

**Example 31-9 Displaying our Relationship data between Lawyer and Clients**

```
Set LawyerOref=##class(MyPackage.Lawyer).%OpenId(1)

Set Key="" Do {
   Set ClientOref=LawyerOref.MyClients.GetNext(.Key)
   If ClientOref'="" {
        Write "Key: ",Key," Name: ",ClientOref.ClientName,! }
} While Key'=""
```

```
Key: 1 Name: PoorClient1
Key: 2 Name: PoorClient2
Key: 3 Name: PoorClient3
Key: 4 Name: PoorClient4
```

Example 31-9, we first access the Lawyer and then display all the associated Clients using the *GetNext* Method.

We need to consider another aspect of the code in Example 31-9. If our Lawyer has many clients this code could easily fill up our memory capacity. For this reason, we should include an *UnSwizzle Method* to release the memory used for every entry when we are finished with it.

## Displaying our Relationship data between Lawyer and Clients, using UnSwizzle

**Example 31-10 Displaying our Relationship data between Lawyer and Clients, using UnSwizzle**

```
Set LawyerOref=##class(MyPackage.Lawyer).%OpenId(1)

Set Key="" Do {
   Set ClientOref=LawyerOref.MyClients.GetNext(.Key)
   If ClientOref'="" {
        Write "Key: ",Key," Name: ",ClientOref.ClientName,!
        Do LawyerOref.MyClients.%UnSwizzleAt(Key)
   }
} While Key'=""
```

```
Key: 1 Name: PoorClient1
Key: 2 Name: PoorClient2
Key: 3 Name: PoorClient3
Key: 4 Name: PoorClient4
```

Example 31-10 is the same as Example 31-9 except we are releasing memory with the *%UnSwizzleAt Method*.

## Embedded SQL to display the Relationship between Lawyer and Clients

**Example 31-11 Embedded SQL to display the Relationship between Lawyer and Clients**

```
New lawyerName,clientName
&sql(Declare MyCursor CURSOR FOR
   SELECT MyLawyer->LawyerName, ClientName
   INTO :lawyerName, :clientName
   FROM MyPackage.Client
   ORDER BY LawyerName)
&sql(OPEN MyCursor)
&sql(FETCH MyCursor)
While (SQLCODE = 0) {
   Write !,"Lawyer Name: ",lawyerName
   Write ?30," - Client Name: ",clientName
```

```
    &sql(FETCH MyCursor)
}
&sql(CLOSE MyCursor)
```

To run this code you must put the code in a routine, save the routine, and then run the routine from the terminal.

```
Lawyer Name: HighPoweredLawyer - Client Name: PoorClient1
Lawyer Name: HighPoweredLawyer - Client Name: PoorClient2
Lawyer Name: HighPoweredLawyer - Client Name: PoorClient3
Lawyer Name: HighPoweredLawyer - Client Name: PoorClient4
```

In Example 31-11, SQL displays the Lawyer and Client data. Note the "MyLawyer->LawyerName" syntax on line 3 that bridges the two classes.

Now let us look at the Globals generated from these classes and see how they represent the data.

## Global generated from Class MyPackage.Client

**Example 31-12 Global generated from Class MyPackage.Client**

```
ZW ^MyPackage.ClientD
^MyPackage.ClientD(1)=$lb("","PoorClient1","1")
^MyPackage.ClientD(2)=$lb("","PoorClient2","1")
^MyPackage.ClientD(3)=$lb("","PoorClient3","1")
^MyPackage.ClientD(4)=$lb("","PoorClient4","1")
```

In Example 31-12, we see the Global MyPackage.ClientD, which is generated from Class MyPackage.Client. As the third subscript we can clearly see the pointer back to our Lawyer which is ID = 1.

## Global generated from Class MyPackage.Lawyer

**Example 31-13 Global generated from Class MyPackage.Lawyer**

```
ZW ^MyPackage.LawyerD
^MyPackage.LawyerD(1)=$lb("","HighPoweredLawyer")
```

In Example 31-13, we see the Global MyPackage.LawyerD that is generated from Class MyPackage.Lawyer.

## Delete a Client

**Example 31-14  Delete a Client**

```
Set Key="" Do {
    Set LawyerOref=##class(MyPackage.Lawyer).%OpenId(1)
    Set ClientOref=LawyerOref.MyClients.GetNext(.Key)
    If ClientOref'="" {
            Write !,"Key: ",Key
            Write " Name: ",ClientOref.ClientName
            If ClientOref.ClientName="PoorClient2" {
                    Set status=##class(MyPackage.Client).%DeleteId(Key)
```

```
                    If status=1 Write " - deleted."
                    If status'=1 Write " - deleted failed."
            }
    }
} While Key'=""
```

```
Key: 1 Name: PoorClient1
Key: 2 Name: PoorClient2 - deleted.
Key: 3 Name: PoorClient3
Key: 4 Name: PoorClient4
```

In Example 31-14, we see how to delete Client PoorClient2.

## Delete the Lawyer

**Example 31-15 Delete the Lawyer**

```
Set Status=##class(MyPackage.Lawyer).%DeleteId(1)
If Status=1 Write "Lawyer Delete succeded."
If Status'=1 Write "Lawyer Delete failed."

Lawyer Delete failed.
```

In Example 31-15, we attempt to delete the Lawyer but because of the links to the Clients, we cannot. Before we delete the Lawyer, we must delete all the remaining Clients.

**Example 31-16 Delete a Lawyer after deleting all associated Clients**

```
Set LawyerOref=##class(MyPackage.Lawyer).%OpenId(1)

Set Key="" Do {
    Set ClientOref=LawyerOref.MyClients.GetNext(.Key)
    If Key'="" {
            Set Status=##class(MyPackage.Client).%DeleteId(Key)
            If Status=1 Write !,"Delete successful for key: ",Key
            If Status'=1 Write !,"Delete failed for key: ",Key
    }
} While Key'=""

Set Status=##class(MyPackage.Lawyer).%DeleteId(1)
If Status=1 Write !,"Lawyer Delete succeded."
If Status'=1 Write !,"Lawyer Delete failed."
```

```
Delete successful for key: 1
Delete successful for key: 2
Delete successful for key: 3
Lawyer Delete succeded.
```

In Example 31-16, we first delete all the remaining Clients and then we are able to delete the Lawyer.

## Parent-To-Child Relationship

In a *Parent-To-Child* relationship, one Class is dependent upon another. The relationship has the following attributes:

> ➢ If a Parent is deleted then all of its children are deleted
>
> ➢ A Child cannot be created and saved without an associated Parent
>
> ➢ A Parent can be created and saved without associated Children
>
> ➢ When a Child is associated with a Parent, it can never be associated with another Parent

Table 31-3 One-to-many relationship of a Parent to his children

| | Classes | | |
|---|---|---|---|
| **Class** | **MyPackage.Parent** | | **MyPackage.Child** |
| **Name** | ParentName | | ChildName |
| **Relationship Name** | MyChildren | | MyParent |
| **Inverse** | MyParent | | MyChildren |
| **Cardinality** | Children | | Parent |

## Define the Parent Class

For this Chapter you will need to create a "Parent" Class and several properties.

The easiest way to create a class is by using the *Caché Studio* application from the *Caché Cube* software. If you do not have the Caché Cube on your PC or computer, you can download a free copy of Caché for personal evaluation from www.intersytems.com.

After starting up Caché, click on Caché Studio from the Caché Cube (a small blue cube in your system tray). In Caché Studio click on **File -> New,** then select **Caché Class Definition,** and follow the prompts. Caché Studio includes helpful wizards in creating Classes, Objects Properties and Methods, etc.

You will be asked for a **Package** name, A *Package* name is a way of grouping common classes. Specify a *Package* name of *MyPackage* and a Class name of *Parent*. Select a Class Type of **Persistent** (Persistent means it will be stored on disk) and take the defaults for the rest of the wizard.

From the top row in Studio, click on **Class -> Add -> New Property.** Create the ParentName Property as specified by Example 31-17.

Example 31-17 Define the Parent Class

```
Class MyPackage.Parent Extends %Persistent
{

Property ParentName As %String;

}
```

Example 31-17 creates the class *MyPackage.Parent* with an Object Property called *ParentName* that is of *Datatype* %String and is required.  From the top row in Studio, click on **Build -> Compile** to compile the class.

## *Define the Child Class*

**Example 31-18 Define the Child Class**

```
Class MyPackage.Child Extends %Persistent
{

Property ChildName As %String;

}
```

In Example 31-18, we create a MyPackage.Child Class in the same manner as we created *MyPackage* as show in Example 31-17. Recompile the class

## *Define the Relationship between Parent and Child*

Next, we need to define the relationship between Parent and Child. Just define the Parent Class side and the Studio Wizard will automatically add the appropriate information to the Child Class.

**Example 31-19 Add a Relationship to the Parent Class**

```
Class MyPackage.Parent Extends %Persistent
{

Property ParentName As %String;

Relationship MyChildren As MyPackage.Child [ Cardinality = children, Inverse = MyParent ];

}
```

**Example 31-20 The Relationship will automatically be added to the Child Class**

```
Class MyPackage.Child Extends %Persistent
{

Property ChildName As %String;

Relationship MyParent As MyPackage.Parent [ Cardinality = parent, Inverse = MyChildren ];

}
```

The two classes should now look like Example 31-19 and Example 31-20. Be sure and compile the two classes.

In the following examples, we will populate the Parent and Child Classes and link the two.

## Populate the Parent and Child Classes and Link the two

Example 31-21 Populate the Parent and Child Classes and Link the two

```
Set ParentOref=##class(MyPackage.Parent).%New()       ;create new Parent
Set ParentOref.ParentName="Mr John Parent"            ;Parent name

Set ChildOref1=##class("MyPackage.Child").%New()      ;create new Child
Set ChildOref1.ChildName="Little Susie Child"         ;Child name

Set ChildOref2=##class("MyPackage.Child").%New()      ;create new Child
Set ChildOref2.ChildName="Little Judy Child"          ;Child name

Set ChildOref3=##class("MyPackage.Child").%New()      ;create new Child
Set ChildOref3.ChildName="Mean Cheryl Child"          ;Child name

Set ChildOref1.MyParent=ParentOref        ;link Parent with first Child
Set ChildOref2.MyParent=ParentOref        ;link Parent with second Child
Set ChildOref3.MyParent=ParentOref        ;link Parent with third Child

Do ParentOref.%Save()                     ;save Parent and Children
```

In Example 31-21, we populate one Parent and three Children and link the two classes. The Child Class cannot be saved without being linked with the Parent Class.

## Access the Relationship links

Example 31-22 Access the relationship links

```
Set ParentOref=##class(MyPackage.Parent).%OpenId(1)
Write ParentOref.ParentName                            ;Parent name
Mr John Parent

;Using the GetAt method, and going from the Parent side, we access Child1
Write ParentOref.MyChildren.GetAt(1).ChildName
Little Susie Child

;Using the GetAt method, and going from the Parent side, we access Child2
Write ParentOref.MyChildren.GetAt(2).ChildName
Little Judy Child

;Using the GetAt method, and going from the Parent side, we access Child3
Write ParentOref.MyChildren.GetAt(3).ChildName
Mean Cheryl Child
```

Example 31-1 we ensure the relationship links between Parent and Child are valid.

## Add another Child (Insert Method) and associate it with the Parent

Example 31-23 Add another Client (Insert Method) and associate it with the Parent

```
Set ChildOref=##class("MyPackage.Child").%New()       ;create new Child
Set ChildOref.ChildName="Little Chuck Child"          ;Child name

Set ParentOref=##class(MyPackage.Parent).%OpenId(1)   ;bring our Parent into
Do ParentOref.MyChildren.Insert(ChildOref)            ;memory assocate Child
```

```
Do ParentOref.%Save()                          ;with our Parent
                                               ;Save Parent and Child
```

In Example 31-23, we add Little Chuck Child using the Insert method and then associate the Parent with the new Child.

## Displaying our Relationship data between Parent and Children

Example 31-24 Displaying our Relationship data between Parent and Children

```
Set ParentOref=##class(MyPackage.Parent).%OpenId(1)

Set Key="" Do {
    Set ChildOref=ParentOref.MyChildren.GetNext(.Key)
    If ChildOref'="" {
        Write "Key: ",Key
        Write " Name: ",ChildOref.ChildName,!
    }
} While Key'=""
```

To run this code you must put the code in a routine, save the routine, and then
run the routine from the terminal.

```
Key: 1 Name: Little Susie Child
Key: 2 Name: Little Judy Child
Key: 3 Name: Mean Cheryl Child
Key: 4 Name: Little Chuck Child
```

In Example 31-24, we first access the Parent and then display all the associated Children using the *GetNext* Method.

We need to consider another aspect of the code in Example 31-24. If our Parent has many Children this code could easily fill up our memory capacity. For this reason, we should include an *UnSwizzle Method* to release the memory used for every entry when we are finished with it.

## Displaying our Relationship data between Parent and Children, using UnSwizzle

Example 31-25 Displaying our Relationship data between Parent and Children, using UnSwizzle

To run this code you must put the code in a routine, save the routine, and then
run the routine from the terminal.

```
Set ParentOref=##class(MyPackage.Parent).%OpenId(1)

Set Key="" Do {
    Set ChildOref=ParentOref.MyChildren.GetNext(.Key)
    If ChildOref'="" {
        Write "Key: ",Key
        Write " Name: ",ChildOref.ChildName,!
        Do ParentOref.MyChildren.%UnSwizzleAt(Key)
    }
} While Key'=""
```

Example 31-25 is the same as Example 31-24 except we are releasing memory with the *%UnSwizzleAt Method*.

So far, we have created our Parent and Children Classes and established the relationship between the two. Now, how do we display this information?

## Embedded SQL to display the Relationship between Parent and Children

**Example 31-26 Embedded SQL to display the Relationship between Parent and Children**

```
New ParentName,ChildName
&sql(Declare MyCursor CURSOR FOR
   SELECT MyParent->ParentName, ChildName
   INTO :ParentName, :ChildName
   FROM MyPackage.Child
   ORDER BY ParentName)
&sql(OPEN MyCursor)
&sql(FETCH MyCursor)
While (SQLCODE = 0) {
   Write !,"Parent Name: ",ParentName
   Write ?30," - Child Name: ",ChildName
   &sql(FETCH MyCursor)
}
&sql(CLOSE MyCursor)
```

To run this code you must put the code in a routine, save the routine, and then run the routine from the terminal.

```
Parent Name: Mr John Parent      - Child Name: Mean Cheryl Child
Parent Name: Mr John Parent      - Child Name: Little Susie Child
Parent Name: Mr John Parent      - Child Name: Little Judy Child
Parent Name: Mr John Parent      - Child Name: Little Chuck Child
```

In Example 31-26, Embedded SQL displays the Parent and Children data. Note the "MyParent->ParentName" syntax on line 3 that bridges the two classes.

Now let us look at the Globals generated from these classes and how the data is represented.

## Global generated from Class MyPackage.Child

**Example 31-27 Global generated from Class MyPackage.Child**

```
zw ^MyPackage.ChildD
^MyPackage.ChildD=4
^MyPackage.ChildD(1,1)=$lb("","Mean Cheryl Child")
^MyPackage.ChildD(1,2)=$lb("","Little Susie Child")
^MyPackage.ChildD(1,3)=$lb("","Little Judy Child")
^MyPackage.ChildD(1,4)=$lb("","Little Chuck Child")
```

In Example 31-27, we see the Global MyPackage.ChildD which is generated from Class MyPackage.Child. Note that the Child's key is a combination of the Parent Key and the individual Child's Key. We will use this fact when we attempt to delete a Child's node.

## Global generated from Class MyPackage.Parent

**Example 31-28 Global generated from Class MyPackage.Parent**

```
zw ^MyPackage.ParentD
^MyPackage.ParentD=1
^MyPackage.ParentD(1)=$lb("","Mr John Parent")
```

In Example 31-28 we see the Global MyPackage.ParentD which is generated from Class MyPackage.Parent.

## Delete a Child

**Example 31-29 Delete a Child**

To run this code you must put the code in a routine, save the routine, and then run the routine from the terminal.

```
Set ChildKey="" Do {
    Set ParentKey=1
    Set ParentOref=##class(MyPackage.Parent).%OpenId(ParentKey)
    Set ChildOref=ParentOref.MyChildren.GetNext(.ChildKey)
    If ChildOref'="" {
            Write !,"ChildKey: ",ChildKey
            Write " Name: ",ChildOref.ChildName
            If ChildOref.ChildName="Little Chuck Child" {
                    Set CombinedKey=ParentKey "||" ChildKey
                    Set status=##class(MyPackage.Child).%DeleteId(CombinedKey)
                    If status=1 Write " - deleted."
                    If status'=1 Write " - deleted failed."
            }
    }
} While ChildKey'=""
```

To run this code you must put the code in a routine, save the routine, and then run the routine from the terminal.

```
ChildKey: 1 Name: Mean Cheryl Child
ChildKey: 2 Name: Little Susie Child
ChildKey: 3 Name: Little Judy Child
ChildKey: 4 Name: Little Chuck Child - deleted.
```

In Example 31-29, we delete Little Chuck Child. Note that we must combine the Parent's Key with the Child's Key for the delete to be effective.

## Delete the Parent

**Example 31-30 Delete the Parent**

```
Set Status=##class(MyPackage.Parent).%DeleteId(1)
If Status=1 Write "Parent Delete succeeded."
If Status'=1 Write "Parent Delete failed."
```

The above code may be run from the Terminal.

```
Parent Delete succeeded.
```

In Example 31-30, we attempt to delete the Parent and succeeded, but upon closer look, we deleted all the Children as well because the Parent and Children are tied together.

## *Chapter 31 Summary*

In this chapter, we covered *Caché Object Relationships*. We saw how *Relationships* could be One-To-Many, where both sides of the relations can exist independently of each other and Parent-To-Child where the Child is dependent upon the Parent. We created both One-To-Many and Parent-To-Child *Relationships*, added data and displayed the results. Finally we deleted the data of these two types of *Relationships*.

*Customer: "I have a message on my screen that says: 'Disk Full'. What can that be?"*

*Tech Support: "Maybe your disk is full".*

*Customer: "Hmmm. OK."*

# Chapter 32 Methods

Chapter 32 covers the basic concepts of Caché ObjectScript (COS) **Methods**. *Methods* are procedural code that modifies *Object Properties*; they represent the software necessary to change an *Object Property* or data.

## Caché Class

A **Caché Class** is a template or blueprint for creating *Objects*. It also contains *Methods* that control *Object* behavior.

A *Class* contains two major components:

- ➢ Objects
- ➢ Methods

## Object(s)

An *Object* represents data, a person's name or Social Security Number is data.

## Method(s)

*Methods* represent the software necessary to change the *Object* or data. A procedure for modifying a person's name or Social Security Number would be an example of a *Method*.

Before we consider *Methods*, we need to create a small Class of Cars to use as our test data.

## Defining a Class of Cars

The easiest way to create a *Class* is by using the *Caché Studio* application from the *Caché Cube* software. If you do not have the Caché Cube on your PC or computer, you can download a free copy of Caché for personal evaluation from www.intersytems.com.

After starting up Caché, click on Caché Studio from the Caché Cube (a small blue cube in your system tray). In Caché Studio click on **File -> New,** then select **Caché Class Definition,** and follow the prompts. Caché Studio includes helpful wizards in creating Classes, Objects Properties and Methods, etc.

A *Package* name is a way of grouping common classes together. Specify a *Package* name of *MyPackage* and a Class name of *Cars*. Select a Class Type of **Persistent** (Persistent means it will be stored on disk) and take the defaults for the rest of the wizard.

## Class Definition for MyPackage.Cars

**Example 32-1: Class Definition for MyPackage.Cars**

```
Class MyPackage.Cars Extends %Persistent
{

}
```

Example 32-1 defines the class *MyPackage.Cars.* From the top row in studio, click on **Build -> Compile.**

## Object Property Definitions for MyPackage.Cars

From the top row in *Studio*, click on **Class** -> **Add** -> **New Property**. Add the following Properties to the MyPackackage.Cars (all of the following type as %String):

- ➢ MakeModel
- ➢ Year
- ➢ Color
- ➢ EnteredBy
- ➢ EnteredById

**Example 32-2 Class and Property Definitions for MyPackage.Cars**

```
Class MyPackage.Cars Extends %Persistent
{

Property MakeModel As %String;

Property Year As %String;

Property Color As %String;

Property EnteredBy As %String;

Property EnteredById As %String;

}
```

Example 32-2 defines the class *MyPackage.Cars* with five associated Properties. From the top row in studio, click on **Build -> Compile.**

## Methods

*Methods* live inside a *Class*. They accomplish some procedural task to change *Properties*, typically updating the database.

## Class Methods and Instance Methods

*Methods* are broken down into two main types:

➢ **Class Method** – does not need an instantiated object but may act on any objects

➢ **Instance Method** - acts on an instantiated object

# Class Method

## Class Method: AddNewCar

**Example 32-3 Class Method: AddNewCar**

```
Class MyPackage.Cars Extends %Persistent
{

Property MakeModel As %String;

Property Year As %String;

Property Color As %String;

Property EnteredBy As %String;

Property EnteredById As %String;

ClassMethod AddNewCar(UserName As %String, UserId As %String)
{
  Set CarOref=##class(MyPackage.Cars).%New()      ;create a new object

  Read !,"Enter New MakeModel: ",MakeModel    ;accept MakeModel from user
  Read !,"Enter New Year: ",Year              ;accept Year from user
  Read !,"Enter New Color: ",Color            ;accept Color from user

  Set CarOref.MakeModel=MakeModel             ;Set MakeModel into object
  Set CarOref.Year=Year                       ;Set Year into object
  Set CarOref.Color=Color                     ;Set Color into object
  Set CarOref.EnteredBy=UserName              ;Set EnteredBy
  Set CarOref.EnteredById=UserId              ;Set EnteredId

  Set Status=CarOref.%Save()
  If Status'=1 Write "Error from CarOref.%Save()" Quit Status
  Set Id=CarOref.%Id()
  Write !,"New Object with Id: ",Id," Saved",!
  Quit $$$OK

}
}
```

As shows in Example 32-3, the *Class* Method "AddNewCar", is part of the MyPackage.Cars Class. The Class Method adds a new object to the *MyPackage.Cars* database. First, we create a new object with the *%New Method*. We set our Properties to the input we accept from the user. We pass in two items by parameters, UserName and UserId; these two parameters are saved to EnteredBy and EnteredById respectively. Lastly, we save our newly created object with the *%Save Method*.

## Class Method: Run AddNewCar Method

Example 32-4 Run AddNewCar Method

```
Kill                                          ;Kill all local variables

Write ##class(MyPackage.Cars).AddNewCar("Jack Frost","12543")  ;you run this

Enter New MakeModel: Chevy
Enter New Year: 2001
Enter New Color: Yellow
New Object with ID: 1 Saved
1

Kill                                          ;Kill all local variables

Write ##class(MyPackage.Cars).AddNewCar("Amy Frost","43783")
Enter New MakeModel: Ford
Enter New Year: 2008
Enter New Color: Green
New Object with ID: 2 Saved
1

Kill                                          ;Kill all local variables

Write ##class(MyPackage.Cars).AddNewCar("Jill Frost","95602")
Enter New MakeModel: Dodge
Enter New Year: 2010
Enter New Color: Blue
New Object with ID: 3 Saved
1
```

In Example 32-4, we run our AddNewCar *Method* three times inputting our *Object Properties* and add three cars to our MyPackage.Cars database. When you run the AddNewCar Method just do the top two lines, and then enter all underlined items above.

# Instance Method

## Instance Method: DisplayCar

An *Instance Method* acts on an instantiated object. The object must already be instantiated before calling the *Instance Method*. The instantiated object's Oref (Object Reference) is used in the calling of the *Instance Method*.

Example 32-5 DisplayCar Instance Method

```
Class MyPackage.Cars Extends %Persistent
 {

 Property MakeModel As %String;

 Property Year As %String;

 Property Color As %String;
```

```
 Property EnteredBy As %String;

 Property EnteredById As %String;

ClassMethod AddNewCar(UserName As %String, UserId As %String)
{
  Set CarOref=##class(MyPackage.Cars).%New()     ;create a new object

  Read !,"Enter New MakeModel: ",MakeModel     ;accept MakeModel from user
  Read !,"Enter New Year: ",Year               ;accept Year from user
  Read !,"Enter New Color: ",Color             ;accept Color from user

  Set CarOref.MakeModel=MakeModel              ;Set MakeModel into object
  Set CarOref.Year=Year                        ;Set Year into object
  Set CarOref.Color=Color                      ;Set Color into object
  Set CarOref.EnteredBy=UserName               ;Set EnteredBy
  Set CarOref.EnteredById=UserId               ;Set EnteredId

  Set Status=CarOref.%Save()
  If Status'=1 Write "Error from CarOref.%Save()" Quit Status
  Set Id=CarOref.%Id()
  Write !,"New Object with Id: ",Id," Saved",!
  Quit $$$OK

}

Method DisplayCar() As %String
 {
  Write !,"MakeModel   : ",..MakeModel
  Write !,"Year        : ",..Year
  Write !,"Color       : ",..Color
  Write !,"EnteredBy   : ",..EnteredBy
  Write !,"EnteredById : ",..EnteredById
  Write !
  Quit $$$OK
 }
 }
```

In Example 32-5, we add an *Instance Method* to display our data. The DisplayCar Instance Method is part of the MyPackage.Cars Class. Note the ".." syntax; it refers to the object properties already present in the instantiated object.

## *Instance Method: Run DisplayCar Method*

**Example 32-6 Run DisplayCar Method**

```
Set oref=##class(MyPackage.Cars).%OpenId(1)          ;open ID 1
Write oref.DisplayCar()
                           ;DisplayCar passing oref
MakeModel   : Chevy
Year        : 2001
Color       : Yellow
EnteredBy   : Jack Frost
EnteredById : 125431
1

Set oref=##class(MyPackage.Cars).%OpenId(2)          ;open ID 2
Write oref.DisplayCar()                              ;DisplayCar passing oref
MakeModel    : Ford
```

```
 Year       : 2008
 Color      : Green
 EnteredBy  : Amy Frost
 EnteredById : 437831
1

 Set oref=##class(MyPackage.Cars).%OpenId(3)       ;open ID 3
 Write oref.DisplayCar()                            ;DisplayCar passing oref
 MakeModel  : Dodge
 Year       : 2010
 Color      : Blue
 EnteredBy  : Jill Frost
 EnteredById : 956021
1
```

In Example 32-6 we run our *DisplayCar (Instance) Method* passing the already instantiated *Oref (Object Reference)* for our three Cars. Instance Methods needs an instantiated *Oref* to work. Again, all you need to enter are the underlined lines.

## Elements of a Method

A *Method* is a block of Caché ObjectScript code inside a *Class* having a specific structure, control, scope, and syntax to accomplish an objective. It can be public or private and may or may not return a value. *Methods* are closely related to *Procedures*, covered in Chapter 15.

The elements of a *Method* are:

➢ Method Description

➢ Method declaration – either a *"Method"* or *"ClassMethod"* declaring a new Method is

    starting

➢ Method Name

➢ Method Access declaration (public or private)

➢ Parameters

➢ Public List

➢ Code

➢ Return Value

## Method Description

Typically, the *Method Description* comes before the *Method Declaration* and each line of the description is preceded by three ///. The three /// has the added advantages of being visible when viewing the Class Reference Documentation through either the System Management Portal or Documentation options within the Caché Cube."

Example 32-7 Class Method: AddNewCar - Description

```
/// Description for AddNewCar Class Method
ClassMethod AddNewCar(UserName As %String, UserId As %String) As %String
{
    .
    .
    .
}
```

## Method Declaration

The *Method Declaration* declares that a new Method or ClassMethod is starting, either:

> Method

> ClassMethod

## Method Name

We have defined two Methods so far, a Class Method and an Instance Method.

**Example 32-8 Class Method: AddNewCar**

```
ClassMethod AddNewCar(UserName As %String, UserId As %String) As %String
{
    .
    .
    .
}
```

**Example 32-9 Instance Method: DisplayCar**

```
Method DisplayCar() As %String
{
    .
    .
    .
}
```

## Method Access declaration

*Methods* may be **Public** or **Private**. A *Private Method* can only be called from within the Class in which it lives; a *Public Method* can be called from any Class. A *Method* declaration parameter defines whether it is public or private. The default is public if not specified.

**Example 32-10 Class Method: AddNewCar – demonstrate Private Method**

```
ClassMethod AddNewCar(UserName As %String, UserId As %String) As %String [Private ]
{
  .
  .
  .
}
```

Example 32-10 demonstrates the changes to the Method needed to specify a Private Method.

**Example 32-11 Class Method: AddNewCar – Attempting to access a Private Method**

```
Write ##Class(MyPackage.Cars).AddNewCar("Jack Frost","12543")
^
<PRIVATE METHOD>
```

In Example 32-11 we attempt to access a Private *Method* from outside the class, and receive a <PRIVATE METHOD> error.

## Method Parameters

*Methods* can have several input Parameters and one output parameter.

## Method with no Input nor Output Parameters

**Example 32-12 Class Method: AddNewCar – no input or output parameters**

```
ClassMethod AddNewCar()
{
  .
  .
  .
}
```

Example 32-12 shows a Method with no input and output parameters.

**Example 32-13 How to call a Method with no input or output parameters.**

```
Do ##CLASS(MyPackage.Cars).AddNewCar()
```

Example 32-13 shows how to call a Method with no input and output parameters.

## Method with Two Input and One Output Parameters

**Example 32-14 Class Method: AddNewCar – Method with 2 input parameters and one output parameter**

```
ClassMethod AddNewCar(UserName, UserId) As %Status
{
 .
 .
 .
 Quit 1
}
```

Example 32-14 shows a Method with two input parameters and one output parameter. The two input parameters (UserName and UserId) are contained inside the parentheses just after the Method name. There may be any number of input parameters or none at all. The output parameter is outside the right parenthesis just after the "As". This "As" specifies the *data type* of the output parameter as %Status. Another common output *data type* is %String. When an output parameter is specified, the Method must end with a *Quit* command and some value, typically a one or zero for a %Status or a may be a piece of data or text as a %String.

For more information about *data types* refer the the System Class %Library. In fact, the %String refers to %Library.String, and %Status refers to %Library.Status, as do all the *data types* that start with a "%".

**Example 32-15 How to call a Method with two input and one output parameter**

```
Write ##Class(MyPackage.Cars).AddNewCar("Jack Frost","12543")
1

Set Status=##Class(MyPackage.Cars).AddNewCar("Jack Frost","12543")
```

Example 32-15 shows two examples of calling a *Method* with two input parameters and one output parameter.

Input parameters may also contain a data type.

## Method with Two Input Parameters with data types and One Output Parameters

**Example 32-16 Class Method: AddNewCar – Method with 2 input parameters with data types and one output parameter**

```
ClassMethod AddNewCar(UserName As %String, UserId As %String) As %Status
{
 .
 .
 .
 Quit 1
}
```

Example 32-16 shows a *Method* with two input parameters and one output parameter. The two input parameters have a data type of %String.

Input parameters may also have a default value if no value is passed.

### Method with Two Input Parameters with data types and default values and One Output Parameters

Example 32-17 Class Method: AddNewCar – Method with 2 input parameters with data types and default values and one output parameter

```
ClassMethod AddNewCar(UserName As %String = "UserName Default", UserId As
%String = "UserId Default") As %Status
{
    .
    .
    .
    Quit 1
}
```

Example 32-17 shows a *Method* with two input parameters and one output parameter. The two input parameters (UserName and UserId) have a default value. So if no value is passed, the default value is used.

Example 32-18 Class Method: AddNewCar – demonstrate input parameters with default value

```
ClassMethod AddNewCar(UserName As %String = "UserName Default", UserId As
%String = "UserId Default") As %Status
{
    .
    .
    .
Write !,UserName
Write !,UserId
Write !
Quit 1
}

    = = = = = = = = = = = = = = = = = = = = = = = = = = = = = = =

Write ##Class(MyPackage.Cars).AddNewCar(,)

    = = = = = = = = = = = = = = = = = = = = = = = = = = = = = = =

UserName Default
UserId Default
1
```

Example 32-18 demonstrates calling a Class using null parameters forcing the class to use its default parameter specifications.

## Method Public List

A *Method* declaration line may also contain a *Public List*. A *Public List* is a list of variables accessible to all downstream Methods or Routines called from this Method. Normally variables created by a *Method* are *Private Variables* and not accessible to other *Methods* in the Class.

Each *Method* has its own *Public List*, and for a variable to be accessible to all *Methods* in the Class, it must be on each *Method's Public List*. For a variable to be accessible by other *Methods*, *Routines* or *Procedures* called within a *Method*, it too needs to be on the *Public List*, unless of course a variable is passed as a parameter.

## Method with a Public List

**Example 32-19 Class Method: AddNewCar – Method with a Public List**

```
ClassMethod AddNewCar(UserName, UserId) As %Status [PublicList = (Var1, Var2)]

{
}
```

Other parameters are available for the *Method* declaration line but we have covered the more useful ones here.

## Public List

Legacy programmers should pay close attention to the Public List. In Legacy MUMPS programs, all variables are available to all routines, this is not so when using Methods.Only those variables either passed as parameters or stored in the Public List are available.

After the *Method* declaration and *Method* Name, including any parameters on the declaration line, a *Method* must begin with an opening curly brace and end with a closing curly brace. By convention, these two curly braces are on their own line.

## Method Example, *putting it all together*

This example uses all the elements of a Method we have seen so far.

**Example 32-20 Class Method: AddNewCar**

```
/// This method adds a New Car Object to the database.
ClassMethod AddNewCar(UserName As %String = "UserName Default",
UserId As %String = "UserId Default") [ PublicList = (MakeModel, Year, Color) ]
{
  Set CarOref=##class(MyPackage.Cars).%New() ;create a new object

  If $G(MakeModel)="" {                            ;if MakeModel not already defined,
```

```
        Read !,"Enter MakeModel: ",MakeModel ;accept MakeModel from user
    }
    If $G(Year)="" {                              ;if Year not already defined,
        Read !,"Enter Year: ",Year ;accept Year from user
    }
    If $G(Color)="" {                             ;if Color not already defined,
        Read !,"Enter Color: ",Color ;accept Color from user
    }

    Set CarOref.MakeModel=MakeModel               ;Set MakeModel into object
    Set CarOref.Year=Year                         ;Set Year into object
    Set CarOref.Color=Color                       ;Set Color into object
    Set CarOref.EnteredBy=UserName                ;Set EnteredBy
    Set CarOref.EnteredById=UserId                ;Set EnteredId

    Do CarOref.%Save()
    Set Id=CarOref.%Id()
    Write !,"New Object with Id: ",Id," Saved",!
    Quit $$$OK
}
```

Example 32-20 is the same as Example 32-3 which the exception of:

> ➢ Note the use of description

> ➢ The input parameters have a default value associated with them

> ➢ This is a "private" Method

> ➢ Use of a "Public List" to pass data, specifically MakeModel, Year and Color

> ➢ The conditional acceptance of the Public List data of MakeModel, Year and Color

**Example 32-21 Run AddNewCar Method**

```
Kill                                    ;Kill all local variables
Set MakeModel="Chevy"
Set Year="2005"
Set Color="Green"
Write ##class(MyPackage.Cars).AddNewCar("Jack Frost","12543")
New Object with ID: 4 Saved
1

Kill                                    ;Kill all local variables
Set MakeModel="Ford"
Set Year="1"
Set Color="Cyan"
Write ##class(MyPackage.Cars).AddNewCar("","") ;Note the null parameters
New Object with ID: 5 Saved
1

Kill                                    ;Kill all local variables
Set MakeModel="Dodge"
Set Year="1999"
Set Color="Purple"
Write ##class(MyPackage.Cars).AddNewCar("Jill Frost","95602")

New Object with ID: 6 Saved
1
```

In Example 32-21, we run our AddNewCar *Method* 3 times inputting our *Object Properties*.

## Instance Method Example

For the sake of simplicity I created the AddNewCar *Method* as a *Class Method*. It can just as easily be created as an *Instance Method*. In *Object Technology* using an *Instance Method* is preferred because it ties a *Method* with an *Object*. Example 32-22 is a rewrite of Example 32-20 but using an *Instance Method* instead of a *Class Method*. I encourage you to use an *Instance Method* whenever possible; it will help you learn *Object Technology* concepts quicker.

### Example 32-22 Instance Method: AddNewCar

```
/// This method adds a New Car Object to the database.
Method AddNewCar(UserName As %String = "UserName Default",
UserId As %String = "UserId Default") [ PublicList = (MakeModel, Year, Color) ]
{

  If $G(MakeModel)="" {                          ;if MakeModel not already defined,
     Read !,"Enter New MakeModel: ",MakeModel ;accept MakeModel from user
  }
  If $G(Year)="" {                        ;if Year not already defined,
     Read !,"Enter New Year: ",Year ;accept Year from user
  }
  If $G(Color)="" {                            ;if Color not already defined,
     Read !,"Enter New Color: ",Color ;accept Color from user
  }

  Set ..MakeModel=MakeModel ;Set MakeModel into object
  Set ..Year=Year ;Set Year into object
  Set ..Color=Color ;Set Color into object
  Set ..EnteredBy=UserName                    ;Set EnteredBy
  Set ..EnteredById=UserId                    ;Set EnteredId
  Set sc=..%Save()
  Set Id=..%Id()
  Write !,"New Object with Id: ",Id," Saved"
  Quit $$$OK
}


  = = = = = = = = = = = = = = = = = = = = = = = = = = = = = = =

Set CarOref=##class(MyPackage.Cars).%New()    ;create a new object, this needs
                                              ;to be done before the
                                              ;Instance Method is invoked.

Write CarOref.AddNewCar("Snow Frost","54545") ;When you call the Instance
                                              ;Method, use the newly created
                                              ;Oref as the base of your call
```

Example 32-22 is the same as Example 32-20 but using an *Instance Method* instead of a *Class Method.* Note the differences:

➤ The *Object Reference* needs to be instantiated before the *Method* is invoked

➤ The *Object Reference* serves as a base for calling the *Method,* e.g. Write

CarOref.AddNewCar

> ➤ Inside the *Instance Method* the *Class Properties* are preceded by two dots, ".."

## *Chapter 32 Summary*

In this chapter, we looked at *Methods*, procedural code that modifies Object Properties. We saw that *Methods* are of two basic types: 1) Class *Methods* and 2) Instance *Method*, whereby the latter needs an instantiate object. We looked at the various parts of a *Method*; 1) *Method* Description, 2) *Method* declaration, 3) *Method* Name, 4) *Method* Access declaration, 5) Parameters, 6) Public List, Code, and Return Value.

# Chapter 33 SQL Queries and Class Queries

This chapter covers the basic concepts of Caché ObjectScript (COS) **SQL Queries** and **Class Queries.**

In Chapter 23 we covered *Embedded* and *Dynamic SQL Queries* and used these queries throughout the chapters on *Collections.* As you may recall, *Embedded* and *Dynamic Queries* are intended for use inside a Class or Routine.

*SQL Queries and Class Queries* are a special type of *Method* that resides in a Class.

> ➤ *SQL Query* – a canned approach to Queries. The easiest way to create a *SQL Query* is to use the *New Query Wizard* in Studio

> ➤ *Class Query* – this approach gives you more flexibility but requires more understanding of the *Class Query* Structure. As with the *SQL Query*, the easiest way to create a *Class Query* is to use the *New Query Wizard* in Studio

We will use the *MyPackage.Cars* Class we created in Chapter 32 as a basis for our Queries.

## SQL Query

**Example 33-1 Class MyPackage.Cars with SQL Query**

```
Class MyPackage.Cars Extends %Persistent
 {

 Property MakeModel As %String;

 Property Year As %Numeric;

 Property Color As %String;

 Property EnteredBy As %String;

 Property EnteredById As %String;

 Query DisplayAll() As %SQLQuery
  {
     Select * From MyPackage.Cars
  }

}
```

Example 33-1 shows the MyPackage.Cars class, the five properties of the Class and a *SQL Query* called DisplayAll. The *Class Query* selects all Objects and all columns (Properties) from the *MyPackage.Cars* Class.

To return the data from our DisplayAll SQL Query *MyPackage.Cars* class, we need to set up and use a *ResultSet*.

## Running SQL Query using a ResultSet

**Example 33-2 Running SQL Query ResultSet**

```
Set ResultSet=##class(%ResultSet).%New("MyPackage.Cars:DisplayAll")
Set Status=ResultSet.Execute()
If Status=1 {
   While ResultSet.Next() {
        Write !!,"MakeModel:      ",ResultSet.MakeModel
        Write !,"Year:           ",ResultSet.Year
        Write !,"Color:          ",ResultSet.Color
        Write !,"Entered by:     ",ResultSet.EnteredBy
        Write !,"Entered by id: ",ResultSet.EnteredById
   }
}
```

If you save the above code in a routine and then run it from the Terminal, you should get the following output.

```
MakeModel:      Chevy
Year:           2001
Color:          Yellow
Entered by:     Jack Frost
Entered by id: 12543

MakeModel:      Ford
Year:           2008
Color:          Green
Entered by:     Amy Frost
Entered by id: 43783

MakeModel:      Dodge
Year:           2010
Color:          Blue
Entered by:     Jill Frost
Entered by id: 95602

MakeModel:      Chevy
Year:           2005
Color:          Green
Entered by:     Jack Frost
Entered by id: 12543
```

Example 33-2 shows how to return data from an *SQL Query*.

Note that following points:

➢ The parameter to the %New Method (on the first line) is MyPackage.Cars:DisplayAll

➢ On the second line we invoke ResultSet.Execute() which passes back a status code

> ➤ Assuming the status code is 1, we issue the *While* construct which executes until all Objects have been processed

One of the problems with the above process is that there is no error checking as to whether the *SQL Query* is valid.

## Checking to ensure that the SQL Query is valid

**Example 33-3 Checking to ensure that the SQL Query is valid**

```
Set ResultSet=##class(%ResultSet).%New()
Set ResultSet.ClassName = "MyPackage.Cars"   ;Query Class and Method
Set ResultSet.QueryName = "DisplayAll"       ;passed to Resultset

Set QueryIsValid = ResultSet.QueryIsValid()    ;validate the Query
If 'QueryIsValid {
    ; - do error reporting
    Quit
}

Set Status=ResultSet.Execute()
If Status=1 {
    While ResultSet.Next() {
        Write !!,"MakeModel:     ",ResultSet.MakeModel
        Write !,"Year:          ",ResultSet.Year
        Write !,"Color:         ",ResultSet.Color
        Write !,"Entered by:     ",ResultSet.EnteredBy
        Write !,"Entered by id: ",ResultSet.EnteredById
    }
}
```

In Example 33-3, we add the code to validate the *SQL Query*. In this example we also passed the Query Class and Method to the ResultSet Oref in a different way than the last example.

Parameters may be passed into the *SQL Query* to modify the selection criteria.

## SQL Query with Input Parameters

**Example 33-4 SQL Query with Input Parameters.**

```
Class MyPackage.Cars Extends %Persistent
{

Property MakeModel As %String;

Property Year As %Numeric;

Property Color As %String;

Property EnteredBy As %String;

Property EnteredById As %String;

Query DisplayAll(InputMakeModel) As %SQLQuery
{
    Select * From MyPackage.Cars where MakeModel = :InputMakeModel
```

```
   }
}
```

Example 33-4 shows the MyPackage.Cars class, the five properties of the Class and a *SQL Query* called DisplayAll. The *SQL Query* accepts one parameter, "InputMakeModel" and selects all Objects with the MakeModel = InputMakeModel.

**Example 33-5 Running SQL Query with Input Parameters**

```
Set ResultSet=##class(%ResultSet).%New()
Set ResultSet.ClassName = "MyPackage.Cars"   ;Query Class and Method
Set ResultSet.QueryName = "DisplayAll"       ;passed to Resultset

Set Status=ResultSet.Execute("Ford")   ; parameter Ford is input here

If Status=1 {
   While ResultSet.Next() {
          Write !!,"MakeModel:      ",ResultSet.MakeModel
          Write !,"Year:          ",ResultSet.Year
          Write !,"Color:         ",ResultSet.Color
          Write !,"Entered by:    ",ResultSet.EnteredBy
          Write !,"Entered by id: ",ResultSet.EnteredById
   }
}

MakeModel:     Ford
Year:          2008
Color:         Green
Entered by:    Amy Frost
Entered by id: 43783
```

Example 33-5 shows how to return data from *a SQL Query*, specifying a value for MakeModel. Note that the input parameter is specified in the "Execute" line.

*SQL Queries* are fine for simple straightforward queries, but if more flexibility is needed, then we should consider *Class Queries*.

## Class Query

This approach is more accurately referred to as a *User Written Class Query*. It gives you more control and flexibility but requires more understanding of the pre-defined *Class Query* Structure. You should use the *New Query Wizard* in Studio to set up the basic structure.

When using the *New Query Wizard*, it will create one Query Statement and three Methods. Say your Query name is *DisplayData*, after running the *New Query Wizard* you will have a structure like:

**Example 33-6 Class Query structure**

```
Class MyPackage.Cars Extends %Persistent
 {

 Property MakeModel As %String;

 Property Year As %Numeric;

 Property Color As %String;
```

```
Property EnteredBy As %String;

Property EnteredById As %String;

Query DisplayData(Input) As %Query(ROWSPEC ="MakeModel:%String,Year:%String,Color:%String")
{
}

ClassMethod DisplayDataExecute(ByRef qHandle As %Binary) As %Status
{
    Quit $$$OK
}

ClassMethod DisplayDataClose(ByRef qHandle As %Binary) As %Status
[ PlaceAfter = DisplayDataExecute ]
{
    Quit $$$OK
}

ClassMethod DisplayDataFetch(ByRef qHandle As %Binary, ByRef Row As %List,
ByRef AtEnd As %Integer = 0)   As %Status [ PlaceAfter = DisplayDataExecute ]
{
    Quit $$$OK
}
```

Please take note of the following items from Example 33-6:

> The Query Statement at the top uses the "As %Query" statement

> The ROWSPEC defines the columns for the Query

> The three Methods, Execute, Close and Fetch all have the query name pre-pended to them, these Method names cannot be changed

> The three Methods all end with the Macro $$$OK

> Do not change the name of the Query or the Methods

> Do not modify any of the existing parameters

> Do not modify the "PlaceAfter" parameter

> Do not change the placement of the Query or Methods

Now, let's add some code to our Query and see how it works.

**Example 33-7 Class Query**

```
Query DisplayData() As %Query(ROWSPEC = "MakeModel:%String,Year:%String,Color:%String")
[ SqlName = MyCars, SqlProc ]
{
}

ClassMethod DisplayDataExecute(ByRef qHandle As %Binary) As %Status
{
    Set qHandle=0
    Quit $$$OK
}
```

```
ClassMethod DisplayDataAllClose(ByRef qHandle As %Binary) As %Status
[ PlaceAfter = DisplayDataExecute ]
{
    Quit $$$OK
}

ClassMethod DisplayDataFetch(ByRef qHandle As %Binary, ByRef Row As %List,
ByRef AtEnd As %Integer = 0) As %Status [ PlaceAfter = DisplayDataExecute ]
{
    Set Id=qHandle           ; qHandle is used to iterate through the objects
    Set Id=Id+1              ;increment qHandle to get the next object
    Set Oref=##class(MyPackage.Cars).%OpenId(Id)        ;get next object
    If '$IsObject(Oref) Set AtEnd=1,Row="" Quit $$$OK    ;end of objects is reached
    Set MakeModel=Oref.MakeModel
    Set Year=Oref.Year
    Set Color=Oref.Color
    Set Row=$LB(MakeModel,Year,Color)      ;Row must be $Listbuild
    Set qHandle=Id                         ;Reset qHandle to get next Object
    Quit $$$OK
}}
```

In Example 33-7 we set up to run through the cars in our Class.

Now, there are two ways we can run the Class Query, one is through the System Management Portal (keyword SQL). If we are going to run this through the System Management Portal we must include the keyword "SqlProc" in our Query line or the Query (also called Stored Procedure) will not display in our System Management Portal.

The second way to run this Query is from the Terminal using something called the ResultSet. In fact, we can run any Query from the Terminal using the ResultSet.

**Example 33-8 ResultSet to run the Query**

```
    Set ResultSet=##class(%ResultSet).%New()
    Set ResultSet.ClassName="MyPackage.Cars"
    Set ResultSet.QueryName="DisplayData"

    Set StatusCode=ResultSet.Execute()
    If StatusCode'=1 Write "Invalid Status Code Returned" Quit

    While ResultSet.%Next() {Do ResultSet.%Print() }

Chevy 2001 Yellow
Ford 2008 Green
Dodge 2010 Blue
Chevy 2005 Green
Ford 1 Cyan
Dodge 1999 Purple
```

In Example 33-8 we see the resutls of running the Resultset code feeding it our Class and Query MyPackage.Cars and DisplayData.

---

### qHandle

The variable qHandle is the means by which each iteration of the Fetch method passes the control from one iteration to the next.

---

## Chapter 33 Summary

In this chapter we considered two built in Queries:  1) The *SQL Query* and 2) The *Class Query*. The *SQL Query* is simple and easy to use but somewhat limited. The *Class Query* is more flexible and modifiable but you must understand its predefined structure. Also remember you have access to the *Embedded Query* and *Dynamic Query* as demonstrated in chapter 23.

*Customer: "Do I need a computer to use your software?"*
*Tech Support: "It helps"*

# Chapter 34 File Processing with Objects

This chapter is a rewrite of Chapter 12 on *File Processing* but uses Object Calls instead of Legacy MUMPS commands. *File Processing* allows the programmer to access external files.

Normally Caché ObjectScript (COS) saves and retrieves data from Globals, but there are times when it is necessary to access external files. External files are typically those used by the associated Operating System. External files can be any file type on any computer, but for the sake of simplicity, we will deal with "Text" files with a file extension of "TXT".

We will be creating directories and files based on the Windows PC format. If you use a flavour of Unix, MacOS or VMS, you may will need to modify some of the examples.

The code demonstrated in this chapter is not the only way to access external files. %Library.File is used as a base Class for the examples. InterSystems recommends using %Library.FileCharacterStream as a base Class, but %Library.File provides more control over accessing External files.

The first part of this chapter deals with accessing external files. The second part demonstrates miscellaneous file functions.

## Read and write an external files

### Write to an External file

**Example 34-1 Write an External File**

```
    ;Line1:
WriteFile ;
    ;Line2:
        Set Oref=##class(%File).%New("C:\FILE.TXT")  ;create new Oref
    ;Line3:
        Do Oref.%Close()                             ;close the file
    ;Line4:
        Do Oref.Open("WSN",10)                       ;open the file
    ;Line5:
        If 'Oref.IsOpen Quit "0 - File not open"     ;is the file open?
    ;Line6:
        Do Oref.WriteLine("First Record")
    ;Line7:
        Do Oref.WriteLine("Second Record")
    ;Line8:
        Do Oref.WriteLine("Third Record")
    ;Line9:
        Do Oref.WriteLine("Fourth Record")
    ;Line10:
        Do Oref.%Close()
    ;Line11;
        Quit 1
```

Example 34-1 demonstrates writing an external file. Consider the following observations:

- ➤ Line1 – Program Name
- ➤ Line2 – Open a new Oref (Object Reference). Note, this does not create a new file, but just an Oref that we will use to access the File
- ➤ Line3 – Close the file
- ➤ Line 4 - Open the file. The "WNS" says we want to write to the file (W), it is to be a new file (N) and of stream data type (S). The 10 is a Timeout, if we cannot open the file in 10 seconds then quit
- ➤ Line 5 – Ensure that the file is open
- ➤ Line 6,7,8,9 – Write four lines of data
- ➤ Line 10 - Close the file
- ➤ Line 11 – Quit, passing back a 1 for success

---

### *Closing a File before Opening it*

It is a good idea to close a file before opening it. More than once I have interrupted a process to debug it, and have forgotten that the file was still open. So I made it a habit to close a file before opening it, it makes debugging easier and less confusing.

---

### *Time Out*

When opening a file for reading or writing it is important to include a time out. Although you may expect the file to be there, or expect to be able to write to it, there are many circumstances when you cannot. The disk may be full or someone may have changed the device's protection so you no longer have access. In Chapter 14 on Testing and Debugging and Chapter 17 on Writing Robust Code I talk about assumptions. To assume you will always be able to access a file is poor programming.

---

Now we will read the file we just created.

## *Read a file and display its records*

**Example 34-2 Read a file and display its records**

```
To run this code you must put the code in a routine, save the routine, and
then run the routine from the terminal.

    ;Line1:
ReadFile ;
    ;Line2:
        Set Oref=##class(%File).%New("C:\FILE.TXT") ;create Oref for file
```

```
;Line3:
        Do Oref.%Close()                ;close file before opening it
;Line4:
        Do Oref.Open("R",10)            ;open file for read, timeout 10 sec
;Line5:
        If 'Oref.IsOpen Quit "0 - File not open"     ;file open?
;Line6:
        Set InCount=0                             ;init counter of records read
;Line7:
        While 'Oref.AtEnd {
;Line8:
                Set InRecord=Oref.ReadLine() ;read record from file
;Line9:
                Set X=$Increment(InCount)     ;increment counter
;Line10:
                Write !,InRecord               ;display record
;Line11:
        }
;Line12:
        Use 0 Write !,InCount," Records read"
;Line13:
        Use 0 Write !,"End of File reached"
;Line14:
        Quit 1
```

Example 34-2 demonstrates reading an external file and displaying each record read. Consider the following observations:

- ➢ Line1 – Program Name

- ➢ Line2 – Open a new Oref (Object Reference). Note, this does not create a new file, but just an Oref that we will use to access the File

- ➢ Line3 – Close the file first, always a good idea just in case it is open

- ➢ Line4 – Open the file for Reading, with a timeout of 10 seconds

- ➢ Line5 – Ensure that the file is open

- ➢ Line6 – Set the input record counter to zero

- ➢ Line7 – Set up the *While Loop* to read records until End of File

- ➢ Line8 - Read the next record

- ➢ Line9 – Increment the input record counter

- ➢ Line10 – Display the record just read

- ➢ Line11 – End of loop

- ➢ Line12 – Display records read

- ➢ Line 13 – Display records written

- ➢ Line14 – Quit

## Running Routine ^ReadFile

**Example 34-3 Running Routine ^ReadFile**

```
Do ^ReadFile
First Record
Second Record
Third Record
Forth Record
4 Records read
End of File reached
```

In Example 12-3 we run the Routine ^ReadFile created in Example 12-2.

## Read and Write an file

Now instead of just displaying each record read, we will read an input file and then write an output file.

**Example 34-4 Read and write a file**

```
To run this code you must put the code in a routine, save the routine, and then
run the routine from the terminal.

ReadAndWrite        ;

    Set InOref=##class(%File).%New("C:\FILE.TXT") ;create Oref for input file
    Do InOref.%Close()                      ;close file before opening it
    Do InOref.Open("R",10)                  ;open file for read
    If 'InOref.IsOpen Quit  Quit "0 - Input File cannot be opened."
    Set InCount=0                           ;init counter of records read

    Set OutOref=##class(%File).%New("C:\FILE2.TXT")  ;create Oref output file
    Do OutOref.%Close()                     ;close file before opening
    Do OutOref.Open("WSN",10)               ;open the file for writing
    If 'OutOref.IsOpen Quit  Quit "0 - Output File cannot be opened."
    Set OutCount=0                          ;counter of records written

    While 'InOref.AtEnd {
        Set InRecord=Oref.ReadLine()        ;read record from file
        Set X=$Increment(InCount)           ;increment counter
        Set X=$Increment(OutCount)          ;increment counter
        Do OutOref.WriteLine(InRecord)      ;write out record
    }
    Use 0 Write !,InCount," Records read"
    Use 0 Write !,OutCount," Records written"
    Use 0 Write !,"End of File reached"
    Quit
```

Example 12-4 demonstrates reading and writing a file.

## Running Routine ^ReadAndWrite

**Example 34-5 Running Routine ^ReadAndWrite**

```
Do ^ReadAndWrite
```

```
First Record
Second Record
Third Record
Fourth Record
4 Records read
4 Records written
End of File reached
```

In Example 12-5 we run the Routine ^ReadAndWrite created in Example 12-4.

## Use command

The **Use** command sets the specified device as the current device. There can only be one current device at a time.

> Use 0 – sets the specified device, or Zero as the current device, Zero normally being the terminal or default output device

> Use File – sets the specified device, the variable File as the current device

## Cycle through several Files

In the %Library.File Class contains a Query called "FileSet" that we can use to cycle through all the files in a directory.

**Example 34-6 Cycle through several files**

```
To run this code you must put the code in a routine, save the routine, and
then run the routine from the terminal.

CycleThruFiles    ;

    For File="C:\FILE1.TXT","C:\FILE2.TXT","C:\FILE3.TXT" {
        Set Oref=##class(%File).%New(File)      ;create Oref for the file
        Do Oref.Open("WSN",10)                  ;open file for read
        Do Oref.WriteLine("Data")               ;write data for the file
        Do Oref.%Close()                        ;close the file
    }

    Set ResultSet=##class(%ResultSet).%New("%Library.File:FileSet")

    Set sc=ResultSet.Execute("C:\","FILE*.TXT") ;execute the Query
    If $SYSTEM.Status.IsError(sc) {
        Quit "0 - Error on Execute Query"
    }

    While ResultSet.Next() {                     ;return the data
        Set FileName=ResultSet.Data("Name")
        Write !,FileName
    }
```

Example 12-6 first creates three files, FILE1.TXT, FILE2.TXT, and FILE3.TXT. Then it uses the %Library.File Query "FileSet" to traverse for these three files. In the "Execute" line the first parameter is the directory to search and the second is the file pattern to search for.

## Running Routine ^CycleThruFiles

**Example 34-7 Running Routine ^CycleThruFiles**

```
Do ^CycleThruFiles
C:\FILE.TXT
C:\FILE1.TXT
C:\FILE2.TXT
C:\FILE3.TXT
```

In Example 12-7 we run the Routine ^CycleThruFiles created in Example 12-6. Note that we picked up an unexpected file (FILE.TXT) that was created earlier.

# Search multiple files for a specific string

Now let us search through several files for a specific string.

**Example 34-8 Search multiple files for a specific string**

```
To run this code you must put the code in a routine, save the routine, and then
run the routine from the terminal.
```

```
SearchForString

    For File="C:\FILE1.TXT","C:\FILE3.TXT","C:\FILE5.TXT" { ;create files
        Set Oref=##class(%File).%New(File)       ;create Oref for the file
        Do Oref.Open("WSN",10)                   ;open file for read
        Do Oref.%Close()                         ;close the file
    }
    For File="C:\FILE2.TXT","C:\FILE4.TXT","C:\FILE6.TXT" { ;files - "fleas"
        Set Oref=##class(%File).%New(File)       ;create Oref for the file
      Do Oref.Open("WSN",10)                     ;open file for read
        Do Oref.WriteLine("My dog has fleas")    ;write data for the file
        Do Oref.%Close()                         ;close the file
    }

    Set ResultSet=##class(%ResultSet).%New("%Library.File:FileSet")

    Set sc=ResultSet.Execute("C:\","FILE*.TXT")          ;execute the Query
    If $SYSTEM.Status.IsError(sc) {
        Quit "0 - Error on Execute Query"
    }

    While ResultSet.Next() {                              ;return the data
        Set FileName=ResultSet.Data("Name") ;get filename
        Set Oref=##class(%File).%New(FileName) ;establish new Oref
        Do Oref.Open("R",10) ;open file
        If 'Oref.IsOpen Continue                 ;file not open?
        While 'Oref.AtEnd {
            Set InRecord=Oref.ReadLine()         ;read record
            If InRecord["fleas" {                ;file contains "fleas"
                Use 0 Write !,"File: "
                Write FileName," contains string 'fleas'."
            }
        }
    }
```

Example 12-8 first creates six files with three of them containing the string "fleas." Then it searches all files: "FILE*.TXT" and reads through all records looking for the string "fleas."

## *Running Routine ^SearchForString*

**Example 34-9 Running Routine ^SearchForString**

```
Do ^SearchForString

File: C:\FILE2.TXT contains string 'fleas'.
File: C:\FILE4.TXT contains string 'fleas'.
File: C:\FILE6.TXT contains string 'fleas'.
```

In Example 12-9 we run the Routine ^SearchForString created in Example 12-8.

Now suppose you want to "drill down" through several directory structures.

## *Search multiple files in multiple directories for a specific string*

**Example 34-10 Search multiple files in multiple directories for a specific string**

```
To run this code you must put the code in a routine, save the routine, and then
run the routine from the terminal.

SearchForString2

    ; Creating file for subdirectory C:\SUBDIR\
    Do ##class(%Library.File).CreateDirectory("C:\SUBDIR\")
    For File="FILE1.TXT","FILE3.TXT","FILE5.TXT" {
        Set Oref=##class(%File).%New("C:\SUBDIR\"_File) ;create Oref for file
        Do Oref.%Close()                     ;close file before opening it
        Do Oref.Open("WSN",10)               ;open file for write
        If 'Oref.IsOpen Continue
        Do Oref.WriteLine("Data")            ;write data for the file
        Do Oref.%Close()
    }
    For File="FILE2.TXT","FILE4.TXT","FILE6.TXT" {
        Set Oref=##class(%File).%New("C:\SUBDIR\"_File) ;create Oref for file
        Do Oref.%Close()                     ;close file before opening it
        Do Oref.Open("WSN",10)               ;open file for write
        If 'Oref.IsOpen Continue
        Do Oref.WriteLine("My dog has fleas")  ;write data for the file
        Do Oref.%Close()
    }

    ; Creating file for subdirectory C:\SUBDIR\SUB2DIR\
    Do ##class(%Library.File).CreateDirectory("C:\SUBDIR\SUB2DIR")
    For File="FILE1.TXT","FILE3.TXT","FILE5.TXT" {
        Set Oref=##class(%File).%New("C:\SUBDIR\SUB2DIR\"_File)
        Do Oref.%Close()                     ;close file before opening it
        Do Oref.Open("WSN",10)               ;open file for write
        If 'Oref.IsOpen Continue
        Do Oref.WriteLine("Data")            ;write data for the file
        Do Oref.%Close()
    }
    For File="FILE2.TXT","FILE4.TXT","FILE6.TXT" {
        Set Oref=##class(%File).%New("C:\SUBDIR\SUB2DIR\"_File)
```

```
            Do Oref.%Close()                            ;close file before opening it
            Do Oref.Open("WSN",10)                      ;open file for read
            If 'Oref.IsOpen Continue
            Do Oref.WriteLine("My dog has fleas")    ;write data for the file
            Do Oref.%Close()
      }

   Do MultiLevelSearch("C:\SUBDIR\")
   Quit

MultiLevelSearch(Dir)
      Set ResultSet=##class(%ResultSet).%New("%Library.File:FileSet")
      Set sc=ResultSet.Execute(Dir,"")                 ;execute the Query
      If $SYSTEM.Status.IsError(sc) {
            Quit "0 - Error on Execute Query"
      }

      While ResultSet.Next() {                          ;return the data
            Set FileName=ResultSet.Data("Name")          ;get filename
            Set FileType=ResultSet.Data("Type")
            If FileType="D" Do MultiLevelSearch(FileName)   ;"D" means directory
            Set Oref=##class(%File).%New(FileName)       ;establish new Oref
            Do Oref.Open("R",10)                         ;open file
            If 'Oref.IsOpen Continue                     ;file not open?
            While 'Oref.AtEnd {
                  Set InRecord=Oref.ReadLine()           ;read record
                  If InRecord["fleas" {                  ;file contains "fleas"
                        Use 0 Write !,"File: "
                        Write FileName," contains string 'fleas'."
                  }
            }
      }
```

Example 34-10 first creates twelve files in two different directories with six of them containing the string "fleas." Then it searches all files it finds looking for the string "fleas." Notice that if the FileType is "D", then it is a another directory and we "drill down" on it as well by recursively calling MultiLevelSearch.

## Running Routine ^SearchForString2

**Example 34-11 Running Routine ^SearchForString2**

```
Do ^SearchForString2

File: C:\SUBDIR\FILE2.TXT contains string 'fleas'.
File: C:\SUBDIR\FILE4.TXT contains string 'fleas'.
File: C:\SUBDIR\FILE6.TXT contains string 'fleas'.
File: C:\SUBDIR\SUB2DIR\FILE2.TXT contains string 'fleas'.
File: C:\SUBDIR\SUB2DIR\FILE4.TXT contains string 'fleas'.
File: C:\SUBDIR\SUB2DIR\FILE6.TXT contains string 'fleas'.
File: C:\SUBDIR\SUB2DIR\FILE6.TXT contains string 'fleas'.
```

In Example 34-11 we run the Routine ^SearchForString2 created in Example 34-10.

## Miscellaneous File Functions

Following are a number of miscellaneous and useful related file functions.

## Retrieve Date information about a file

**Example 34-12 Retrieve date information about a File**

```
Set Oref=##class(%File).%New("C:\FILE.TXT")

Do Oref.WriteLine("Rec1")
Do Oref.WriteLine("Rec2")
Do Oref.WriteLine("Rec3")
Do Oref.Close()

Set File="C:\FILE.TXT"
Set CreateDate=##Class(%File).GetFileDateCreated(File)
Write $Zdatetime(CreateDate)

Set ModifiedDate=##Class(%File).GetFileDateModified(File)
Write $Zdatetime(ModifiedDate)
```

Example 34-12 retrieves the created and modified date and time of a file.

## Check on the existence of a file

**Example 34-13 Check on the existence of a File**

```
Write ##class(%Library.File).Exists("C:\FILE.TXT")      ;Return 1, file exists
1

Write ##class(%Library.File).Exists("C:\FILExxx.TXT")  ;Returns 0, file does
not exist
0
```

Example 34-13 demonstrate how to check for the existence of a file.

## Is the File Writeable?

**Example 34-14 Is the File Writeable?**

```
Write ##Class(%Libarary.File).Writeable("C:\FILE.TXT") ;Return 1,file
writeable
1
```

Example 34-14 demonstrates how to check to see if a file is writeable or not.

## Copying a file

**Example 34-15 Copying a file**

```
Set File="C:\FILE.TXT"
Set NewFile="C:\NEWFILE.TXT"

Write ##Class(%Library.File).CopyFile(File,NewFile) ;Return 1, Copy
successful
1
```

Example 34-15 shows how to copy one filename to another.

## Renaming a file

**Example 34-16 Renaming a file**

```
Set File="C:\NEWFILE.TXT"
Set NewFile="C:\NEWFILE2.TXT"

Write ##Class(%Library.File).Rename(File,NewFile) ;Return 1, Rename
successful
1
```

Example 34-16 demonstrates how to rename a file.

## Delete a File

**Example 34-17 Delete a File**

```
Set NewFile="C:\NEWFILE2.TXT"

Write ##Class(%Library.File).Delete(NewFile) ;Return 1, Delete successful
1
```

Example 34-17 shows how to delete a file.

## Chapter 34 Summary

In this chapter, we considered *File Processing*. We saw how to:

- ➤ Write to an External file ,
- ➤ Read a file and display its records,
- ➤ Read from one file and write to another,
- ➤ Employ the *Use* command,
- ➤ Cycle through several Files,
- ➤ Search multiple files for a string,
- ➤ Search multiple files in multiple directories for a specific string
- ➤ Retrieve Date information about a file,
- ➤ Check on the existence of a file,
- ➤ Is the File Writeable?
- ➤ Copying a file,
- ➤ Renaming a file, and
- ➤ Delete a file

We also covered why it is a good idea to Close a file before Opening it and why a file access timeout is necessary.

*Tech Support: "I need you to boot the computer."*

*Customer: (THUMP! Pause.) "No, that didn't help."*

# Chapter 35 Caché ObjectScript – Object Commands Reference Table

This chapter lists some of the *Object Commands* for quick reference.

## General Help

| General Help on Object Calls | Do $system.OBJ.Help() |
|---|---|
| | Do $system.OBJ.Help(method) |
| General Help on Version Calls | Do $system.Version.Help() |
| | Do $system.Version.Help(method) |
| General Help on SQL Calls | Do $system.SQL.Help() |
| | Do $system.SQL.Help(method) |

## Calling a Class

| Calling a Class Method | Do ##class(package.class).method(params) |
|---|---|
| | Write ##class(package.class).method(params) |
| | Set Status=##class(package.class).method(params) |
| Create a new Oref (Object Reference) | Set Oref=##class(package.class).%New() |
| Opening an existing Object | Set Oref=##class(package.class).%OpenId(Id) |
| Calling an Instance Method | Do oref.method(params) |
| | Write oref.method(params) |
| | Set var=oref.method(params) |

## Save and Delete Calls

| Save an object | Set status=oref.%Save() |
|---|---|
| Delete an existing object | Set status=##class(package.class).%DeleteId(Id) |
| Delete all saved objects  (warning – this commands will kill the entire global, use with caution) | Set status=##class(package.class).%DeleteExtent() |

## Status Calls

| Return a good status | Quit $$$OK |
|---|---|
| Return an error status | Quit $$$ERROR($$$GeneralError,message) |
| Check if good status | If $$$ISOK(status) |
| Check if error status | If $$$ISERR(status) |
| Print the status (after an error) | Do $system.Status.DisplayError(status) |
| | Do $system.Status.DecomposeStatus(status) |

## Validate Calls

| Validate a string item | If ##class(%Library.String).IsValid(dataitem) |
|---|---|
| Validate an numeric item | If ##class(%Library.Numeric).IsValid(dataitem) |
| Validate an integer item | If ##class(%Library.Integer).IsValid(dataitem) |
| Validate a time item | If ##class(%Library.Time).IsValid(dataitem) |
| Validate a date item | If ##class(%Library.Date).IsValid(dataitem) |
| Ensure an Id exists | Write ##class(package.class).%ExistsId(Id) |
| | Write Oref.%ExistsId(Id) |
| Ensure an Oref exists | If $IsObject(Oref) |

## Link Objects Call

| Link two properties together | Set oref1.property=oref2 |
| --- | --- |
| | Set oref2.property=oref1 |

## Tests Calls

| Test whether a class exists | If ##class(%Dictionary.ClassDefinition). %Exists($LB("package.classname")) |
| --- | --- |
| Test whether an object is valid | If $IsObject(oref) |

## Obtain a Value Calls

| Obtain a property's value | Set value=oref.property |
| --- | --- |
| Obtain the Id of a saved object | Set Id=oref.%Id() |

## Set Calls

| Set a Property to a value | Set oref.property=value |
| --- | --- |

## Populate Call

| Populate a class | Set =##class(package.class).Populate(Num,{1,0}) |
| --- | --- |
| | Where |
| | -Num=number of items |
| | -1 for Verbose, 0 for not Verbose |
| | Note: the class needs to extend %Populate and the affected properties need POPSPEC parameters. |

## List/Display/Dump Calls

| List all objects in memory | Do $system.OBJ.ShowObjects() – pass "D" for details |
| --- | --- |
| Display an Oref | Do $system.OBJ.Dump(oref) |

## System/Product/Version Calls

| See what system you are on | Write $system.Version.GetBuildOS() |
|---|---|
| See what product version you are running | Write $system.Version.GetProduct() |
| Return the version number of the current object library | Write $system.OBJ.Version() |

## General Miscellaneous Calls

| View Class Name (must be inside a class) | Write $CLASSNAME |
|---|---|
| View Current Date/Time | Write $NOW() - 62416,35449.664935<br><br>Write $system.SYS.Horolog() - 62417,22848<br><br>Write $system.SYS.TimeStamp() - 62416,53709.534  (GMT) |
| View UserName | Write $USERNAME |
| View Platform | Write $system.Version.GetPlatform() |
| View Operating System | Write $system.Version.GetOS() |
| View Process Id | Write $system.SYS.ProcessID() |
| View Namespace | Write $system.SYS.NameSpace() |
| View Time Zone (delta time in minutes from GMT) | Write $system.SYS.TimeZone() |

## Chapter 35 Summary

This chapter lists some of the Object Commands for quick reference.

# Chapter 36 Caché ObjectScript - Good Programming Concepts

This chapter summarizes **Good Programming Concepts** while using Caché ObjectScript.

In many ways this chapter is just a review of some of the *Good Programming Concepts* already covered. They are reviewed and summarized here to add extra emphasis.

*Good Programming* encompasses many concepts, here are a few:

- ➢ Your code should be:
    - o Attractive and Easily Readable
    - o Thoroughly and Concisely  Documented
    - o Easily Maintainable
    - o Based on Modular Design Principles
    - o Well tested
- ➢ Your code should contain or include:
    - o Adequate Error handling
    - o Appropriate Displays
    - o Proper use of Dynamic Code
    - o Proper Report Design

## Attractive and Easily Readable

Code should invite the eye's attention. It should be pleasing to look at and well structured on the page. Adequate white spaces, documentation, appropriate indentation, clear crisp comments should all be part of your code.

## Thoroughly and Concisely Documented

There should be concise summary documentation at the top of every Routine or Method and at the top of every Procedure and tag. The documentation should be thorough, without droning on and on page after page. Brevity is the key, brief but at the same time complete. To be effective, documentation must be read!

Documentation should include:

> ➢ The purpose of the code as well as a summary and overview
>
> ➢ Inputs and outputs
>
> ➢ Significant Variables
>
> ➢ Significant Globals
>
> ➢ Control Variables

## Easily Maintainable

Ease of Maintainability depends upon several factors:

> ➢ Well documented
>
> ➢ Easy to read
>
> ➢ Organized in a logical fashion
>
> ➢ Modular Design

---

### Mark of a good system

The mark of a good system is how easily a new programmer can assume responsibility for it.

---

## Modular Design

Functions that are called multiple times should be segregated into their own module and called when needed, this eliminates redundant code. Higher level and more important functions should appear at the top or your code, whereas lower level functions should appear further down. And finally, code needs to be grouped together locally into separate modules.

## Well Tested

Testing measures the *Quality* of the software. See Chapter 14 on Testing and Debugging.

## Error handling

All anticipated errors should have code to deal with them. Getting a call in the middle of the night due to a system bug is not good *Error Handling*. Thought should be given to unanticipated errors and how to handle them as well. See Chapter 13 on Error Processing.

## Displays

When writing database update code it is a good idea to display status information along with date/time as the process is running.

## Dynamic Code

Just because you know how to use *Indirection* and *eXecute* statements does not mean you should. There are times when dynamic code is useful and well understood. There are times when it is not.

## Reports Design

Reports should have in their header the following information:

- ➢ Report Name
- ➢ Routine Name that produced the Report
- ➢ Date/Time of the report.
- ➢ Page Number
- ➢ Any Security or restrictive Information

Reports should be easy to read and the data well defined.

## Chapter 36 Summary

Good Programming includes code that is 1) Attractive and Easily Readable, 2) Thoroughly and Concisely Documented, 3) Easily Maintainable, 4) Based on Modular Design Principles and 6) Well tested. The code should contain or include: 7) Adequate Error handling, 8) Appropriate Displays, 9) Proper use of Dynamic Code and 10) Proper Report Design.

*Tech Support: "Type 'fix' with an 'f'."*
*Customer: "Is that 'f' as in 'fix'?"*

# Index

*"The man who smiles when things go wrong has thought of someone he can blame it on."*

Made in the USA
Lexington, KY
02 September 2012